ANTJIE KROG

COUNTRY
OF
MY SKULL

———

GUILT, SORROW,

AND THE LIMITS OF FORGIVENESS

IN THE NEW SOUTH AFRICA

THREE RIVERS PRESS • NEW YORK

For every victim who had an Afrikaner surname on her lips

Published by Three Rivers Press, New York, New York.
Member of the Crown Publishing Group.

Originally published in South Africa in 1998
by Random House South Africa (Pty) Ltd. First published in the
United States by Times Books, 1999.

Random House, Inc. New York, Toronto, London, Sydney, Auckland
www.randomhouse.com

THREE RIVERS PRESS is a registered trademark and the Three Rivers
Press colophon is a trademark of Random House, Inc.

Printed in the United States of America

Design by M. Kristen Bearse

Library of Congress Cataloging-in-Publication Data

Krog, Antjie.
Country of my skull : guilt, sorrow, and the limits of
forgiveness in the new South Africa / Antjie Krog. — 1st ed.
p.   cm.
Includes index.
1. South Africa.   Truth and Reconciliation Commission.
2. Apartheid—South Africa.   3. Political violence—
South Africa.   4. South Africa—Race relations.
5. South Africa—Ethnic relations.   I. Title.
DT1757.K76   1998
968.06'5—dc21   98-38121

ISBN 0-8129-3129-7

10   9   8   7

Contents

REACTIONS

UNWINDING

Introduction

When black South Africans by the millions turned out to vote for the first time in their lives in April 1994, the world saw them standing patiently from before dawn, in lines so long they often seemed endless. Even those who could not read, and that, arguably, was the vast majority, knew they were in the process of making their own miracle. The occasion was so awesome that when reporters like me asked the young, the old, the women and the men how they felt, one after another uttered the same response: "I'm so happy."

But beneath the patience and the pride lay the pain of indeterminate layers, the result of years of enduring a system so brutal that it has few parallels in modern history. The apartheid regime had kept the majority of its people—black and Indian and colored—separate, unequal. When they protested, they were often tortured. Death was frequently so gruesome as to defy even the most active imagination. And for a variety of reasons, those who suffered at the hands of the apartheid state usually suffered in silence.

The South Africans who negotiated the torturous route toward the 1994 elections knew that if the country was to sustain its peaceful transition to democracy, the victims' voices had to be heard. Some balm would be needed to dress, if not heal, their wounds. All South Africans would have to learn as much as possible about the causes, nature, and extent of the human-rights violations under apartheid. In order to forge a future, the nation would have to honestly and squarely confront its past. For these reasons, the final clauses of South Africa's interim constitution read as follows:

The adoption of this Constitution lays the secure foundation for the people of South Africa to transcend the divisions and strife of the past, which generated gross violations of human rights, the transgression of humanitarian principles in violent conflicts and a legacy of hatred, fear, guilt and revenge. These can now be addressed on the basis that there is a need for understanding but not for vengeance, a need for reparation but not for retaliation, a need for ubuntu [the African philosophy of humanism] but not for victimization.

In order to advance such reconciliation and reconstruction, amnesty shall be granted in respect of acts, omissions and offences associated with political objectives and committed in the course of the conflicts of the past. To this end, Parliament under this Constitution shall adopt a law determining a firm cut-off date which shall be a date after 8 October 1990 and before 6 December 1993 and providing for mechanisms, criteria and procedures, including tribunals, if any, through which such amnesty shall be dealt with at any time after the law has been passed.

Subsequently, the first independent body established in the post-apartheid era was the Truth and Reconciliation Commission. Created by an Act of Parliament known as the National Unity and Reconciliation Act, the TRC, as it came to be known, was designed to help facilitate a "truth recovery process." It was unique in the history of such commissions around the world in that it called for testimony before it to be held in public.

Controversy dogged the TRC from the start. There were those who believed that the perpetrators of gross human-rights violations should appear before a court of law, as Nazi war criminals were forced to do at Nuremberg; that, they insisted, was the only possible path to justice. But there were also those who pointed out that it was not a battlefield victory that had produced the end of apartheid, but a settlement negotiated by victims and perpetrators alike; amnesty, they argued, had been a necessary precondition for securing the cooperation of the previous government and its security forces. The deal was to hold out the promise of amnesty in exchange for the full truth about the past.

With strong support from President Nelson Mandela, the TRC began operating in December 1995, with Nobel Prize laureate Archbishop

Desmond Tutu as its chairman. Nongovernmental organizations compiled a list of possible members for President Mandela; the president, in turn, added some names and made the final selection. Archbishop Tutu's sixteen commissioners included ministers, doctors, lawyers and others from civil society. Their mission: to produce a report to Parliament and President Mandela that would paint the most complete picture of the abuses that occurred between March 1, 1960, and May 10, 1994.

The TRC was armed with subpoena powers and staffed with sixty investigators. It would hold hearings that would give victims an opportunity to tell the world their stories of pain, suffering and loss. And it would question victimizers about how and why they had caused that pain, suffering, and loss, with a particular emphasis on just how widespread the human-rights abuses had been and to what extent they had been sanctioned by the apartheid government. Gross violations of human rights were defined as murder, attempted murder, abduction, and torture or severe ill treatment.

The commission was organized into three committees: Human Rights Violations, Reparations and Rehabilitation and Amnesty. All told, commissioners took more than 20,000 statements from survivors and families of political violence. They held more than fifty public hearings, all around the country, over 244 days. The Amnesty Committee, by law independent of the others (its rulings could not be appealed or overruled, except by the country's highest court), received approximately 7,050 amnesty applications—fully 77 percent of them from prisoners. All three committees were plagued by a huge workload and inadequate resources. And even Archbishop Tutu's most eloquent pleas could not persuade whites to come forward to testify in significant numbers. Near the end of the process, one poll suggested that the Truth Commission had done more to hurt race relations than to promote reconciliation. Indeed, the commission itself had to confront internal allegations of racism.

But most agree that the reality is much more complex. Many Afrikaners who charge that the commission was biased against them from the start, for example, also acknowledge that they learned for the first time the full extent of state-sponsored crime from testimony before the Truth Commission. And while some victims and survivors of the apartheid government say their agony won't end so long as perpetrators get amnesty and victims get next to nothing (reparation, for those who qualify, comes to less than $200 per victim), others say that learning how and where their loved ones met their end has provided a certain closure, a measure of peace.

As of this writing, the Truth Commission's report is expected by the end of October; the TRC will then be suspended, to be reconvened once the amnesty process is completed in 1999. At that time, the commission likely will approve the Amnesty Committee's full report and determine whether it necessitates changing the final report in any way.

The commission hopes its report will provide the history lesson needed to ensure that South Africa's tragic past never repeats itself. The proof of the lesson may not be clear until future generations have had a chance to consider the findings with the grace of time and distance. But one of its certain legacies is the voices, so long unheard, that now speak for the record about a particularly brutal history. Those who testified, those who heard them and those, like Antjie Krog, who report on what they said, are all living South Africans who are struggling to make individual and collective sense of the past and to push ahead into a future that may or may not fulfill the promise felt by those first-time voters in 1994. The Truth Commission, no more perfect than the messy work-in-progress called democracy, allowed them to face together, for the first time, the profound task ahead.

—Charlayne Hunter-Gault
Johannesburg, South Africa
September, 1998

BEFORE THE
COMMISSION

CHAPTER ONE

They Never Wept,
the Men of My Race

Sunk low on their springs, three weathered white Sierras roar past the wrought-iron gates of Parliament. Heavy, hamlike forearms bulge through the open windows—honking, waving old Free State and Transvaal flags. Hairy fists in the air. I run across the cobblestone street—clutching notepad and recorder—to the old parliamentary venue where the Justice Portfolio Committee is hearing public submissions on what to include in the draft legislation establishing a Truth Commission.

The faces are grim in the hall with its dark paneling, old-fashioned microphones hanging from the ceiling, hard wooden gallery, and green-leather seats. "Bellington Mampe . . . Looksmart Ngudle . . . Suliman Salojee . . . Solomon Modipane . . . James Lenkoe . . ." A slow litany of names is read out into the quiet hall. The names of 120 people who died in police custody. "Imam Abdullah Haroon . . . Alpheus Maliba . . . Ahmed Timol . . . Steve Bantu Biko . . . Neil Aggett . . . Nicodemus Kgoathe . . ." The chairperson of the Black Sash, Mary Burton, concludes her submission in the same way the Sash's meetings have been concluded for years: name upon name upon name. They fall like chimes into the silence. Journalists stop taking notes, committee members put down their pens—stunned by this magnitude of death that is but a bare beginning.

The double doors snap open. The marching crunch of the black-clad *Ystergarde*—even on the carpet their boots make a noise. The Iron Guard, elite corps of the far-right Afrikaner Weerstandsbeweging (AWB). Black balaclavas worn like caps, ready to be rolled down over the faces. Three-armed swastikas on the sleeves. Then, dressed in ordinary khaki clothes, in walks Eugene Terre'Blanche as if taking a stroll on his farm. Suddenly another kind of noise fills the hall. Members of Parliament, secretaries, messengers, even a minister or two, shuffle into the already crowded gallery.

"We've asked for all the committee meetings to be adjourned," whispers a black senator. "We have to see this man with our own eyes—how real he is."

Expectation fills the air. Does Terre'Blanche's adjutant want to say anything? He jumps up. Salutes. "No, I say what my leader say!"

The chair of the Justice Portfolio Committee, Johnny de Lange, shows Terre'Blanche to his seat. "Mr. Terre'Blanche, what would you like to see in the Truth Commission legislation?"

It is so quiet you can hear an alliteration drop. Terre'Blanche stays seated. Barely audibly, he asks: *"Is hier waar ek vandag sit, hierdie sitplek, is dit die plek waar Sy Edele Dr. Verwoerd dertig jaar gelede vermoor is met 'n mes in sy hart?"* ("This seat I am sitting in, is it the same one where Dr. Verwoerd[1] was murdered with a knife in his heart thirty years ago?")

We look at one another. "Indeed," says the chairperson. Terre' Blanche stares at his hat until the changed context of blood and betrayal is dominating the silence.

He gets up. He moves out of the bench. Away from the microphones, the guards. He stands alone on the carpet. And the first word that enters the mind, despite the neatly trimmed gray beard, is "poor." The man is a poor Afrikaner. His khaki shirt is bleached, its collar threadbare. But poor as he is, he is a master of acoustics. He drenches us with sound—every tremor, boom, reverberating corner of that space, under his command.

"Laat. Die soldate . . . Huis toe gaan!" he shouts. Let the soldiers go home. Then in a normal voice: *"Agbare Meneer die Voorsitter, Agbare Lede van die Parlement . . . Laat AL . . . die soldate . . . HUIS toe gaan . . .* [whispering] *Laat. MY . . . soldate . . . huis toe gaan . . .* [in a crescendo] *sodat die weeklag van wagtende vroue en die wringende hande van kinders kan einde kry . . . my klere is nat van hulle trane . . ."*

Members of Parliament ransack desks for translation equipment. They don't want to miss a word.

"Amnesty is a gift! But for the political prisoner who has never

---

[1] Hendrik Frensch Verwoerd, prime minister of South Africa from 1958 to 1966, chief architect of apartheid.

known the coldness and the bleakness *[die koud-heid en die kil-heid]* of jail cells, whose life has always been woven into the wide waving veld of freedom, for him, Honorable Chair, for him amnesty is . . . a fire of joy."

Terre'Blanche asks for the cutoff date, now set at December 6, 1993, to be shifted forward, so that AWB members who committed violence right up to the first democratic election in April 1994 will qualify for amnesty. Then the AWB will cooperate with the government.

When Terre'Blanche is finished, committee member Jan van Eck praises his Afrikaans. Carl Niehaus, the Afrikaans-speaking member of Parliament for the African National Congress (ANC), is less enthusiastic. What does Terre'Blanche mean by the term "cooperation"?

"It seems Mr. Niehaus himself has mastered only Standard Two Afrikaans," Terre'Blanche sneers.

Someone starts to hiss. Dramatically Terre'Blanche throws two fingers in the air. "Two bomb-planters! The one drives a Mercedes-Benz, and the other one, like me, drives a Nissan bakkie [pickup truck]. The Nissan. Comes late. Five minutes *after* twelve his bomb goes off. But the Mercedes. Arrives on time. And that bomb explodes. Five minutes *to* twelve. Now *because* he drives a Mercedes, and not a Nissan, *he* . . . gets amnesty!"

Dene Smuts, another Afrikaner MP and a member of the Democratic Party, calls for a point of order. "No, Mr. Terre'Blanche, your Nissan did *not* come late. It burst with deafening noise through the glass windows of the World Trade Centre in Kempton Park. I was there. And your deeds were not aimed at the Big Stealer—as you insist on calling F. W. de Klerk—but at the negotiations for a democratic dispensation. Your people are in jail not because they drove Nissan bakkies, but because they refused to accept democracy."

Incensed, Terre'Blanche gasps for air. "That a woman—and my mother was also a woman," he shouts, "that a *woman* does not understand what I say!"

He ends his submission. "If the shifting of a date can bring peace, then you must shift the date . . . If justice rules . . . I will talk peace . . . because that is all that I am . . . a simple farmer from Westransvaal who has come to you to put my case."

The contrast between client and advocate is striking. General Johan van der Merwe, former commissioner of police, sits collapsed in the front row. Whether it is part of a calculated strategy or simply an effect of seeing him out of uniform for the first time, I cannot say. His color is yellowish, he blinks constantly, his mouth nibbles at times like a geriatric, and when he touch-touches the bandage on his finger, his hand trembles. But his case is taken up with a flourish by a rosy, confident, English-speaking lawyer from Natal. He is not taking up the general's case because he agrees with what happened in the past, the advocate assures the Justice Portfolio Committee, but because he believes the general has a point. And the point is politics. The mere fact that a deed must have a political motive to qualify the perpetrator for amnesty is proof enough that the politicians should be the essence of the Truth Commission's inquest. It is not the police who came up with apartheid, he says, but the politicians.

With an instinct for the dramatic, the advocate gestures in the direction of Van der Merwe. "Yesterday afternoon when we were flying to Cape Town, the general was staring out of the window of the plane. The sun was setting and he said to me . . . he said in this choked-up voice: 'The politicians have prostituted the police. Once I was a proud policeman, but here I am today—humiliated and despised. My career, to which I dedicated my entire life with such pride, is ending in this horrible shame and dishonor.' "

"We all know that the ultimate reconciliation should be between Afrikaner and African," Freedom Front leader General Constand Viljoen tells the committee, "and this could happen if the Truth Commission does not vilify the Afrikaner into being worse than we are . . ."

All of us have failed, Viljoen goes on. "We all used violence to get what we wanted. The terror of the tyrant invited the terror of the revolutionary."

Submissions from across the board. Orgies of alliteration. In the press, Afrikaner intellectuals point out that thanks to apartheid the new government inherited the most sophisticated infrastructure in Africa. Thanks to apartheid political prisoners all obtained quality degrees while on Robben Island—with the result that the ANC's senior leadership is better qualified than any other political party on the continent. Fewer people died under apartheid than were killed in Rwanda. So how bad could apartheid have been?

The oppressors are weary; the oppressed, foam-in-the-mouth angry.

This is the theme for a kind of overture—but at the time we could not hear it.

From the beginning of March 1995, the Justice Portfolio Committee, under the chairmanship of Johnny de Lange, meets daily to debate the submissions and draft the legislation. The civil servants, who physically write the law, sit somewhat apart. They work late into the night to have alternative formulations ready for the next day. "If I personally had to draft this legislation," one of them complains, "it would have been a lean, simple law—completed weeks ago. But because this has to be a *process*, it is developing into a hell of a unique but impossibly complex law."

As if back into a womb, I crawl—the heavy-light eiderdown, the hot-water bottle. Through the window, I see the sleeping farmyard washed away in moonlight. A plover calls far off. Overcome with the carefreeness of my youth, I doze—safe in this stinkwood bed, safe in this sandstone house, this part of the Free State. Everything so quiet.

Stars roar past the yard.

A sudden sound. Harsh. *"Hendrik, kom in! . . . Hendrik, kom in!"*

It must be around midnight.

My brother Andries, who lives on another part of the farm, is calling Hendrik, our younger brother, on the radio. The line crackles. *"Kom gou!* [Come quickly!] People are stealing cattle . . . don't switch on your lights—and bring your rifle."

The screen door of the rondavel slams as Hendrik leaves and drives away in the dark.

The radio crackles again: "How many?"

Andries: "Two and a dog. They have taken five cows and have just passed the *windpomp*. Do you have bullets?"

I put on my gown. In the dining room next to the radio, my parents are already sitting—in sheepskin slippers, each covered with a blanket—nervous and as if pinned down. I sit next to them. We do not talk. My mother brings a blanket for me. The night is suddenly filled with menace.

"What's going on?" I ask.

My mother explains. Andries's wife, Bettie, would now be standing on the roof of their house, from where she has a large part of the farm under surveillance with a night-vision scope. Bettie shouts the information down to nine-year-old Sumien at the radio, and she has to pass it on to her father in the bakkie.

It's nearly one o'clock. We wait.

Sumien: "Pa . . . ? Pa, come in . . . Ma says they have turned toward the road, but she can't see you . . . Where are you?"

Silence. My parents sit humped up—in the gray moonlight their faces seem carved to pieces.

Sumien: "Pa, where are you? Can you hear me?" Anxiety in her voice.

Only the silence zooms down the line . . . We wait in the dark.

After a quarter of an hour, the radio comes to life. It's Andries. Breathless: "We've found one, but the other got away. Tell Ma to get down from the roof and lock the doors."

We wait. Then we think we hear shots. The dogs bark. We wait. Who did the shooting? Who has been shot? And which is worse? What fierce scenes are being played out in the veld?

The family photo catches my eye. I look at my smiling, *borselkop* brothers. I remember how Hendrik clutched my mother's arm when she was paging to the bookmark in the children's Bible. "Please, please don't read the bit about that guy who wants to cut his child's throat in the veld."

What are my brothers experiencing tonight that I cannot even imagine?

We wait an eternity. At last, the line finds its voice: "Call an ambulance and tell them to come to the dam."

It is one of my brothers. But the voice sounds so tense that we cannot tell who's speaking. We three are sitting there—the moon has lost its abundance. We sit—each with our own disproportionate thoughts. My mother gets up with a tired heaviness. In the kitchen, she makes tea. My father and I sit without speaking. I take my tea to my icy bed. My eyes dry in the dark.

"The idea of a Truth Commission goes back to ANC decisions," Minister of Justice Dullah Omar says in an interview. "When the National Executive Committee of the ANC discussed what had happened in the country, and in particular what happened in ANC training camps like Quatro, there was a strong feeling that some mechanism must be found to deal with all violations in a way which would ensure that we put our country on a sound moral basis. And so a view developed that what South Africa needs is a mechanism which would open up the truth for public scrutiny. But to humanize our society we had to put across the idea of moral responsibility—that is why I suggested a combination of the amnesty process with the process of victims' stories."

Victims, and not perpetrators, should be the beginning, the focus, and the central point of the legislation, the ANC argues. Victims should have several points of entry into the process. Should losses be categorized? So many rand for an arm, so many for a leg, and so many for a life? Should compensation be available immediately or should the government wait for a coherent assessment?

Every discussion opens up new problem areas. Amnesty takes away the victim's right to a civil claim. Does compensation make amnesty constitutional? What about the state? Should the state ask for amnesty? Because victims who receive compensation could still decide to sue the state.

The Democratic Party also wants to shift a date: the starting date of the period the commission is mandated to consider. The workload is impossible, says Dene Smuts. This is the first Truth Commission required to investigate nearly four decades, and to look not only at disappearances, as in Chile, but at other gross violations such as murder, kidnapping, torture, and severe ill-treatment. Not only would a starting date of June 16, 1976, shorten the commission's area of research by sixteen years, but it would have symbolic resonance, because it ushered in the famous cycle of resistance and oppression.

But as possible scenarios are spelled out and the pressure mounts to finish the legislation, the parties start to work on one another's nerves. National Party member Sheila Camerer has the energetic chairperson collapsing onto his forearms, muttering next to the microphone: "*Ag, God help my,* the woman is driving me out of my mind!"

Between Johnny de Lange and the National Party's Jacko Maree there is nothing but total war. The solidly built chairperson with his working-class Afrikaner background and the skinny-looking Maree with his bow tie and delicate spectacles cannot stand each other. The moment Maree opens his mouth, the chair's facial color intensifies a shade.

One morning a note is sent to the media: "Don't leave too soon—promise to provide you with a row and an underhand ANC deal."

That someone has already shouted "Fire!" is clear the moment the room suddenly fills up with ANC faces never seen on the committee before. An unexpected extra National Party member also appears. The two parties are gearing up for a fight.

And it happens. Mr. De Lange says members should vote on the shifting of two other motions to the top of the agenda. Mr. Maree interrupts him. He would like three minutes to explain his request that the indemnity given to ANC members by the Currin Commission be discussed first. De Lange refuses. He is interrupted again. By NP member Danie Schutte, also asking for time to motivate Maree's request.

De Lange refuses again. Red in the face by now. He is the chair, he says, and this is his ruling. If Mr. Maree is not satisfied, he can go and complain to the highest authorities. As chairperson, he is not going to allow Mr. Maree to turn the Justice Portfolio Committee into a media spectacle. "You can make clowns of other people, but not of me, the chairperson."

"Please, Mr. Chairman," pleads Inkatha Freedom Party member Koos van der Merwe, "do not let the poison between you and Mr. Maree destroy the good relations the rest of us have built up over the year. Can't you resolve this in any other way?"

Maree thrashes around in his chair, his hand raised. In his other hand, he is waving a thick pile of documents, representing 100 ANC members who, he says, were stealthily granted indemnity just before Christmas by the Currin Commission.

De Lange is adamant. "We still have eight draft bills to discuss. We argued this agenda last week for more than an hour. We have accepted it. I will allow no discussion. I am putting it to the vote. Read my lips: I am putting it to the vote."

Whereupon the ANC outvotes the other parties by fifteen to seven.

As Maree storms out, Koos van der Merwe mutters: "The heavy hammer of democracy . . ."

But the rush to finish the bill has to take a backseat for a day or two.

"A blink and a wink—and it was all over, " I report on that afternoon's current affairs program. "After weeks of publicity—peaking this morning in a hysteria of upper-class British accents in the corridors of Parliament—the queen came, and saw, and left."

As always, the Cape knows when to behave herself. The southeaster meekly calms down, the sweepers sweep up the last bits of paper, the pupils line the streets, and the red carpet bleeds down the steps. Inside the Assembly Hall, the atmosphere is predominantly that of . . . how shall one put it? . . . dressing up for the queen. An opportunity to show off your traditional dress, your designer contacts, and your gravy-train menu.

Either shiny African-print dresses with puffed-up angel wings for sleeves, or shimmering Indian robes streaming over the shoulders, or a traditional beaded apron rounded off by the most massive flesh-colored Maidenform bra ever seen in the houses of Parliament. One of the visitors from the Free State seems to be hiding in some purple and gold shrubbery; another one from Stellenbosch wears a *potjie* like our own Johanna van Arkel. Two Hare Krishnas chant Queen Elizabeth II into the foyer with stained muslin pockets on their bare breasts.

The men, of course, are wearing traditional male dress: the expensive woolen suit, the loud tie, the gold-framed glasses, and the indispensable thick neck.

Then they enter.

In front walks the colored sergeant at arms carrying Parliament's golden traditional weapon in his white gloves. Then follows the black Black Rod—yes, for all these years, Parliament had a white Black Rod . . . but the times they are a-changin' . . .

The media have been fighting for weeks for the best seats in the press gallery. I stretch my neck. Blink my eyes.

Can it be true? She looks like anybody's auntie, complete with a clasp handbag and thick little shoes from an upmarket department store. Under any other circumstances, the brooch on her left shoulder could only be a fake, but we know, oh yes, we know, it is realer than real. She clips open her handbag, takes out her glasses, and puts her speech on the speaker's desk.

She speeches.

Can it be true? It sounds like something one would find at any small-town women's society meeting. Typed out on ordinary notepaper, one paragraph per page. With her gloves, she battles like other mortals to fold the pages into dog-ears to turn them more easily.

But don't be mistaken, the content may be ordinary, but it is delivered in the Accent that has intimidated half the earth for centuries. When last did Parliament hear the phrase "doughty champion"?

Then she folds up her speech, puts it in her handbag, and off she goes.

With bags flying, we ambush a taxi passing the gates of Parliament— "we" means the editor and myself.

"Go!" shouts the editor. "To the waterfront, to the *Britannia*!" We turn our bags inside out, pull down zips, rip open blouses—the taxi driver looks panicky.

"Go!" I yell. "We meet the queen in seven minutes."

"*Watter queen?*" He sounds skeptical.

"Princess Di's *skoonma*, but you must fly."

He turns right round in his seat: "We are talking about the queen, the one with"—he touches his head—"*our* diamond in her crown? The one who wears lead in her seams?"

"Yes, yes, yes," I yell in a strangled voice.

But nothing escapes my *op-en-wakker* editor: "Why lead?"

"So that the wind cannot blow her dress above her knees," says the taxi driver smartly.

He grabs the steering wheel as if possessed. He has a mission. He has a skill. He wants us to be on time. We scour bends; we cut corners. The man drives like a demon.

He asks sternly, "Why are you late?"

"Because," the editor shouts while dialing on her cell phone with one hand and fastening an earring with the other, "we had to report on the queen's speech in Parliament, to two hundred news bulletins and in eleven languages, and now she has invited some journalists for cocktails on her yacht . . ."

"And what did she say in Parliament?" he asks.

"Nothing . . ."

Our legs shoot past him in new charcoal pantyhose.

"So what did you report?"

In the heap of rubble on the backseat, we dig up prehistoric lipsticks, rouge that needs quarrying with fingernails, mascara brushes clogged with gravel, empty perfume bottles, buckled bangles—and apply them all, to the tune of howling tires and a racing engine.

"We asked how such mediocrity could stay so luxuriously swaddled. We said to live like her you need to plunder your own people for centuries and thereafter suck half the world dry."

The taxi driver races down the jetty and skids to an impressive stop just behind a group of Solemn Male Political Analysts in Deep Conversation, fondling their old school ties.

We tumble out. We have made it.

On the deck of the *Britannia*, our names are called out with the proverbial imaginary roll of a drum; our ordinary names are treated with the Accent: "Rrrina Smithhh: Afrrikaans Stereo!" And one walks up and puts one's hand in the white glove. ("And how did it feel?" my friends ask afterward. I can't remember; my eyes were nailed to the seam of the queen's chirpy yellow dress.)

A man walks up to us. He is the spokesperson for the palace. He says the queen will move from group to group. He says we will speak only when addressed. He says no one will ask her any questions. He says we will not report on this friendly royal gesture.

The gin and tonic is deadly accurate. Next to the railings, I become drunker and drunker. A sailor with a lot of golden rope on his shoulders tells me the problems of sailing the *Britannia* so that the Queen could arrive in South Africa *twice*. Unofficially by plane, the first time; then helicoptered to the *Britannia* for the official arrival—the second coming—sailing under a rousing twenty-one-gun salute into the harbor. During all this, his mustache never moves. Not once.

General Constand Viljoen of the Freedom Front asks the queen to visit the Women's Memorial in Bloemfontein and to apologize to Afrikaners for what was done to them in the name of the British. But her schedule is already full.

The Justice Portfolio Committee spent 6½ hours on the Truth Commission Bill before any public submission was made. It listened for more than 20 hours to submissions, and it discussed, compiled, and drafted the various clauses of the bill in 100 hours and 53 minutes. Many a time, the civil servants turned up at the meeting with red eyes and wrinkled clothes, having worked through the night to prepare a new discussion document. All told, the committee spent 127 hours and 30 minutes on the Truth Commission Bill.

Eventually the legislation to establish the Truth Commission is introduced in the National Assembly. Over time it has earned different descriptions. It is regarded as the most sensitive, technically complex, controversial, and important legislation ever to be passed by Parliament. It is also called the Mother of All Laws. For the occasion, the visitors' gallery is packed with schoolchildren and—so the speculation goes—possible candidates for the commission.

Just as it did in the committee, the discussion of the bill quickly turns into an emotional spectacle. After a sedate plea by President Nelson Mandela not to use the Truth Commission to score political points, the theme of injustice incites speakers to oratorical heights.

Everybody has a story to tell—from members of Parliament whose houses were firebombed, to friends' children whose fingers were put in a coffee grinder, to criminals already walking the streets while right-wingers languish in jail. Most of the speeches are in Afrikaans. It is with this group, in this language, that they want to wrestle it out.

A journalist from one of the Afrikaans newspapers, *Beeld*, reminds me: "Do you remember that the finalizing of the legislation by the core committee was done in Afrikaans?" I frown. "It was Johnny de Lange as chair, Willie Hofmeyr from the ANC, Dene Smuts of the DP, Koos van der Merwe of the IFP, Danie Schutte for the NP, and Corné Mulder for the Freedom Front. I like it," he says, "those responsible for the past working to rectify it."

It is late afternoon when Johnny de Lange concludes the debate. What makes this piece of legislation so unique, he says, is that it really is a patchwork of all the viewpoints of the country. "I can point out a Dene Smuts clause, a Danie Schutte clause, a Lawyers for Human Rights clause, a victim clause, a police clause—and for this all of us should proudly take credit." All but Jacko Maree, says De Lange, who used the committee discussions only to get cheap publicity.

Then it is time to vote. All those *for* the legislation should put their cards in the slots in front of them and push the buttons.

Everybody does it.

"Something is wrong," says the Speaker. All cards to be taken out. Put back in.

It seems the electric current that has to register the cards isn't working. The Speaker asks members to wait a few minutes.

Finally, the Speaker asks those members in favor of the legislation to put up their hands in the old-fashioned way to be counted—those who say yea (African National Congress, National Party, and Pan-Africanist Congress) and those who say nay (Freedom Front). The Inkatha Freedom Party abstains.

Then the legislation flails around for some time in the Senate. To prove that they are not mere rubber stamps of the Assembly, the senators insist on some changes. They want two non–South Africans on the commission; they want blanket amnesty to be discussed.

Through clenched jaws, the civil service law-writer hisses: "It's a web of a law—a *moerse* web. If you change anything, you have to change every single clause."

It is Dullah Omar's task to get the legislation passed by the Senate. When a colored National Party member tells how he was tortured and hung upside down by the security police, ANC members shout him down. Crying, he relates how he was repeatedly thrown on the cement floor. Amid raucous laughter, an ANC member shouts, "That's where you got your brain damage from."

Omar stands up. "We can make a distinction among perpetrators, but I hope this law will teach us all that we cannot make any distinction among victims."

At last the legislation finds its way to the Department of Justice in a building previously known as the Verwoerd Building. A building where most of the civil servants are white and speak Afrikaans. And those blonde ones with the orange-peel nails—you can't find better secretaries, a deputy minister confides—it is they who process the legislation. And it is the middle-aged Afrikaner men with their slumping shoulders, making bitter jokes in the elevators . . . "See you later?" *"Ja,* God—and the Constitution—willing" . . . who get it to the minister, the president, and the printers.

The Truth Commission Bill was signed into law by President Nelson Mandela on July 19, 1995.

They come for breakfast—my two brothers. Laugh, talk, eat, and dismiss the night before as just another normal night. Their politics, I notice, are still moderate National Party.

"Who fired the shots?" I ask. But I know Andries is one of the best shots in the district.

They explain. Every week before full moon and every week afterward, they patrol the farm. Since the 1994 election, they have caught more thieves than the whole stock-theft unit of the Kroonstad police. Andries usually drives the bakkie. Hendrik stands at the back with the spotlight. The moment they see the thieves, they switch on the light.

"Then we shout: *'Staan of ons skiet!'* ['Stop or we'll shoot!'] Or something in Sesotho," says Andries. "But at this point, you are full of sickening fears. The greatest fear is that the thief is armed, that he will shoot unexpectedly; then you also fear the moment they decide to split and one runs for the farmhouse and the other to loot. Most of the time, they don't stop when you warn them."

It is quiet in the dining room. "But the moment they run away . . . it is then that I am overcome by an indescribable cold fury . . . He who is trespassing and breaking the law—by running away, forcing me to shoot him—he is forcing me to point a gun at another human being and to pull the trigger . . . and I hate him for that.

"First I try to shoot into the ground next to him. If he's close to a mealie patch where I won't be able to find him, I try to wound him in the legs . . . all the time petrified that I might kill him and then have to live with it, deal with it for the rest of my bloody life . . ."

Hendrik adds: "But the worst is that they don't think Andries is deliberately trying to miss them; several of them told us that Andries *couldn't* hit them because their *muti* was too strong!"

"What do the police say?"

"Man, the moment the police come, all is well for them—they go to the police station, tomorrow they get bail . . . Most of the time, they get a suspended sentence. You leave the court together. Or on your way home, you pass them on the road. I told the magistrate it is not the value of the things they steal, it is the value of my life they steal, the value of my farm, the value of my future plans, the value of my peace of mind . . ."

In one of the first Afrikaans novels written by a black man, two black vagabonds murder a Jewish shop-owner. When someone squeals on the murderers, the main character condemns the stool pigeon. I drive up to interview the author.

"Why does your main character condemn the splitter and not the murderers?"

"Because black people must always stick together."

"But the woman who saw a white man running away from Chris Hani's dead body didn't say, 'He was white, so I'll shut up.' She said, 'The deed is wrong, so I'll speak out.' "

He looks at me. "No one can destroy whites—they have survival in their bones. But for us, if we don't stand together no matter what, we'll be wiped out."

Hendrik touches the knuckles of his right hand lightly. They are swollen. "Do you hit them?" I ask, numb.

Hendrik nods. "At some stage, we realized we were catching the same thieves over and over again and we thought we had to do something, so that if they want to steal, they'll decide to steal on any other farm except this one."

My brothers tell me that stock theft on the farm has increased five-fold since the election.

"How long will you be able to take this?" I ask Andries.

My brother shakes his head. "I don't know. I become aware of things in myself that I never knew were in me . . ."

"Like what?"

"Like feeling daily how my family and I become brutalized . . . like knowing that I am able to kill someone with my bare hands . . . I am learning to fight, to kill, to hate. And we have nowhere to turn. Some years ago, we could pick up the phone and talk to the highest power in the country. Now my home town is run by a guy whose name I can't even pronounce."

"Ja, but it was always like that for millions of black people."

"Exactly . . . I thought what was coming was a new dispensation for all . . . what I see now is that the brutalization of ordinary people that was previously confined to the townships is not disappearing, but instead spilling over the rest of the country." He stops, but then flings it out: "When Mandela was talking about white and black morality, how whites only care when whites die, he should have added: blacks don't care if whites die . . . but what is worse, they also don't care if blacks die."

My last free weekend before the Truth Commission starts its hearings in the eastern Cape. Mondli Shabalala picks me up on the farm on his way to Johannesburg. Mondli is a colleague of mine at the South African Broadcasting Corporation.

"Mondli, Moshoeshoe's name means 'He who can steal as swiftly and silently as cutting someone's beard.' How can the deftness of stealing be a mark of honor? Why did Dingane ask Retief to steal back the cattle stolen by Sekonyela?[2] Why would Mandela write in his biography

---

[2]All names from the nineteenth century, when African tribes, Dutch settlers, and English colonists were competing for land in southern Africa. Moshoeshoe was the founder and first paramount chief of the Basothos; Dingane was a Zulu chief; Sekonyela was a Tlokwa chief, a rival of Moshoeshoe. Piet Retief was one of the Afrikaners who led the Great Trek into the interior to escape British rule; he was killed by Dingane in 1838.

about the cattle he and his cousin stole from his uncle? Do we understand the same thing when we talk about stealing?"

Mondli is silent for a long time. Then he says, "I don't know. But what I do know is that I grew up with the notion that stealing from whites is actually not stealing. Way back, Africans had no concept of stealing other than taking cattle as a means of contesting power. But you whiteys came and accused us of stealing—while at that very same minute you were stealing everything from us!"

I remember how my parents and I sat the whole Sunday behind closed doors. How we stopped talking when the dogs barked. "They prefer to come on Sundays . . . when they think you are in church," my mother said. Later, when I left for Johannesburg, I looked back to wave and I saw them standing in front of the sandstone house of my youth. And as we drove out, my father locked the gate and turned the dogs loose.

CHAPTER TWO

None More

Parted Than Us

A workshop is organized for journalists who will be covering the Truth Commission and their immediate editors. We are surrounded by German, Dutch, and Chilean journalists especially. More conspicuous even: only two black journalists—one from radio and one from the *Sowetan*. How are we to understand the absence of black journalists at everything related to the Truth Commission?

During the standard "I am so-and-so" introductory session, a German journalist says: "I think that South Africa is still too traumatized to really look at its past—you are still figuring out whether you have survived it, whether your economy is intact, whether you are going to make it." It soon becomes clear that overseas journalists are interested only in the amnesty-seekers and whether there will be important politicians among them.

Various topics are discussed: Why should the commission be reported? How will emotional exhaustion be prevented? How can viewers, listeners, and readers be involved? Should Truth Commission stories be confined to a special page? Won't people just skip over this section? How can we see to it that the past becomes front-page news? No newspaper has the means to cover the commission full-time—will television be able to broadcast the hearings daily so that people can follow them from their offices?

What is the role of radio with its access to all the language groups and impoverished communities? And do all eleven official languages have the words needed to cover the commission? A Zulu-speaking colleague loses his temper: "Of course! And if the words aren't there, we'll make them up." Make them up? He provides a list:

ambush: *lalela unyendale*—lying down waiting to do an evil act
hit squad: *abasocongi*—neck-twisters
massacre: *isibhicongo*—crushed down
politics: *ezombusazwe*—matters about the ruling of the land
right-winger: *untamo-lukhuni*—stiff-necked
serial killer: *umbulali onequngu*—addicted killer
third force:[1] *ingal'enoboya*—a hairy arm

"Hairy arm?" I ask.

"During third force activities," he explains, "people said a cuff some-times moved too high up, and the exposed arm was always hairy—that means belonging to a white man."

By late afternoon, we are discussing how you keep your own past out of your reporting. The journalist from the *Sowetan* stands up: "My newspaper's position is that it has actually always done TRC-type sto-ries and will not make any special effort now to cover the commission."

Willem Pretorius of *Beeld* is on his feet. "In the army, I was sent to cut off Radio Freedom's cables and take them off the air. What does that make me? Can I—or can I not—report on the Truth Commission?"

It is suddenly very quiet. After a day of journalistic clichés, we've struck an artery.

"I was a political journalist at the old SABC—it was I who would re-move the voice of someone like Archbishop Tutu from reports and in-sert sinister background music," says an ex–South African who now works in America. "I was eventually fired for my left-wing political views . . . what does that make me?"

A well-known English-speaking editor gets up with a sigh. "Really. This is so unnecessary. We have worked for years and years to get the Afrikaner on board. And now we are working on the black editors . . . Experience has taught me that this kind of talk gets one nowhere. Nowhere at all."

Someone struggles up behind me. It's veteran journalist Hennie Ser-fontein, holding the microphone, beard and hands shaking so much I'm afraid he's having a heart attack. He stutters and gasps. "Everyone here

---

[1] Covert action during the 1980s by members of security forces and right-wing extrem-ists who aimed to ensure the failure of negotiations by stirring up hatred and distrust among South Africans. They used a variety of violent methods, including violent attacks on innocent people, clandestine elimination of ANC operatives, and assassinations.

is putting their past on the table, but you . . . your . . . getting-on-board!" he shouts. "My God, *julle Engelse* . . . whose *bleddie* board?" Hennie is on a roll, taking on the English press: dates, incidents, how information was changed by specific editors, how headlines were manipulated to suit the politics of the Nationalist rulers. He has the date; he has the names of the white English-speaking editors and businessmen who went to see P. W. Botha[2] with a blank check and said: "Demand of us what you will, but protect our interests."

Some journalists jump up and protest that they weren't even born yet when this happened; others loudly encourage Hennie. A black journalist walks out: the Anglo-Boer War all over again. The workshop ends in chaos. Only the adjournment for drinks and snacks restores some semblance of respectability.

On the way back from the workshop, my mind is swirling. Waiting at some traffic lights, I see a group of workers protesting outside an old-age home. Their strike action was front-page news this morning. One of them carries a placard: "Away with Jews."

Is it possible that a commission could find itself clinging to a morality that is respected nowhere else in the country?

And the idea of truth. Even if it's not spelled with a capital . . . Nadine Gordimer once asked a black writer: "Why do you always picture a white woman lounging next to a swimming pool? We are not all like that!" He replied: "Because we perceive you like that." Gordimer admits that she has to take cognizance of that truth.

One morning, when I was still a lecturer at a training college for black teachers, a young comrade arrived. He refused to enter my class. He called Afrikaans a colonial language. "What is English then?" I asked. "English was born in the center of Africa," he said with great conviction. "It was brought here by Umkhonto we Sizwe." That was his truth. And I, as his teacher, had to deal with this truth that was shaping his life, his viewpoints, his actions.

Will a commission be sensitive to the word "truth"?

If its interest in truth is linked only to amnesty and compensation, then it will have chosen not truth, but justice. If it sees truth as the widest possible compilation of people's perceptions, stories, myths,

---

[2] Pieter Willem Botha, former head of the National Party; prime minister, then president, of South Africa from 1978 to 1989.

and experiences, it will have chosen to restore memory and foster a new humanity, and perhaps that is justice in its deepest sense.

According to the law, the president must appoint the seventeen wise men and women who will serve on the commission in consultation with the Cabinet. The commissioners must be highly regarded in the community and must not have a high political profile.

There are various ways of proceeding, each likely to bring new names to the fore. First, the president could compile his own list and then discuss it with Cabinet. Second, the president and Cabinet could compile a list together—bringing in the obvious danger of political horse-trading. Third, candidates could be nominated by nongovernmental organizations, churches, and parties, and interviewed in public by a panel. Then the president and Cabinet could choose from a short list. The advantage of the last option is that political participation would be minimal, and there would be little opportunity to plant on the commission someone tasked with undermining its work. Public hearings would also rekindle interest in the commission, which has died down as the drafting of the legislation turned into a political fight.

The third option is chosen.

The president appoints a panel that includes Professor Fink Haysom, Jody Kollapen, Jayendra Naidoo, Baleka Kgositsile, Professor Harriet Ngubane, Senator Rossier de Ville, and Bishop Peter Storey.

The public hearings start on the morning of November 13 in the Good Hope Centre in Cape Town. There are forty-six nominations on the list. The first to appear are Professor H. W. van der Merwe, Glenda Wildschut, Dominee Murray Coetzee, and Archbishop Desmond Tutu.

The questions follow a set pattern. What kind of people should serve on the commission? What kind of contribution can the candidate bring to the process of reconciliation and truth? "I'm looking for someone who paid a price for his beliefs," says panel member Peter Storey, the Methodist bishop.

But it is Archbishop Desmond Tutu who has the panel eating out of his hand within moments.

"What should one call you?" asks Professor Ngubane. "Wouldn't people find you intimidating?. . . Here I am and I don't know whether I should say 'Your Highness' or 'Father' or 'Bishop' . . ."

"You can call me anything as long as you don't call me 'Your Graciousness,' " he laughs. "No, I don't think I intimidate people, I hope they think I'm fun."

What kind of people would he like to see on the commission?

"People who once were victims. The most forgiving people I have ever come across are people who have suffered—it is as if suffering has ripped them open into empathy. I am talking about wounded healers. A commissioner should be buttressed by spiritual life."

Tutu is asked to react to a remark made by General Tienie Groene-wald: "I confess to God, not to Tutu."

"*Jong*, if you've had a fight with your wife, it is no use you only ask forgiveness of God. You will have to say to your wife you are sorry. The past has not only contaminated our relationship with God, but the relationship between people as well. And you will have to ask forgiveness of the representatives of those communities that you've hurt."

Most of the candidates are clearly conscious that they may face political pressure and that they will be walking a tightrope between victims and perpetrators. Van der Merwe says that punishment is an inherent part of the moral and legal codes of this country and perhaps one should regard the transparent and open process of the commission as already a kind of punitive method. If Magnus Malan, our former minister of defense, says he feels humiliated after being charged in court for a massacre in KwaZulu-Natal, that is already a form of retribution.

All the women are asked whether they feel there should be women on the commission. No man is asked whether he feels there should be women on the commission. Nobody is asked whether they feel there should be men on the commission.

Glenda Wildschut says people should feel comfortable when they appear before the commission. If a woman had to appear before men only, or a black person before whites only, then people would not feel at ease. How the commission is going to listen to people will determine how acceptable it will be to the majority.

Mary Burton says the beneficiaries of the past system will be prepared to contribute to compensation only if they experience a complete change of heart, and that can happen only when people have information about the past.

Hlengiwe Mkhize reminds the panel that African culture has its own rituals of reconciliation and needn't depend solely on the Christian terminology of confession and forgiveness. Another candidate talks about the *"ilala"*—a grass blade milked for palm wine. When two people have had a fight, they sit opposite each other milking this blade while they confess. "The emptier the blade becomes, the emptier the heart of anger."

"Will you be able to bring right-wing Afrikaners on board?" Advocate Chris de Jager is asked.

"Don't appoint me to the commission as a token Afrikaner," De Jager says. "And if this commission becomes a witch-hunt, I want to warn you beforehand—I'm a pathetic hunter."

Alex Boraine underlines the importance of effective administration. If the three committees, the staff, the publicity, the financial administration, do not function efficiently, the commission need not even start its work. Not only will it become an international embarrassment, but the victims will be failed once more. The commission will have to find its way in uncharted territory. He also warns against having too many theologians on the commission—"It could end up as the Church Commission."

Deal carefully with the concept of collective guilt, says Professor Jaap du Randt. People must realize: there but for the grace of God go I. One person's vigorous search for truth is another's witch-hunt.

Considering the enormous task ahead, it is clear that Adam Small's ambivalent rambling is not appreciated by the panel: "I am a man of two hearts and not of this world. This Truth Commission thing is useless—it wastes hard-earned money to listen to a bunch of crooks. Only literature can perform the miracle of reconciliation."

After three-quarters of an hour in this vein, Fink Haysom asks: "But you are so critical—do you *want* to serve on this commission?"

"If there is space on the commission for an independent, critical, stubborn, sometimes naughty voice, then I will be there with my heart—but I will always remain critical."

Most of the candidates say they were initially opposed to the commission, but that the long court case of Vlakplaas commander Eugene de Kock changed their minds. They realized that a commission could provide more answers to more people at a lower cost—and arrive at a fuller picture of what happened in the past as a bonus.

The last of the forty-six candidates is the Reverend Frank Chikane.

"The Truth Commission should bring a new morality to this country . . . People demanding punitive justice are ignoring the greater justice a new morality could bring—a shared morality, freed from colonialism, oppression, and greed . . ."

Simultaneously, the beepers hooked to our belts start to vibrate viciously. We press the buttons: "Pls phn edtr." Manelisi leaves the room to phone. When he gets back, he passes me a note: "Editor says we must leave for Pretoria immediately, otherwise we'll be late for the Mandela dinner."

But we're waiting for the litmus test. It has developed gradually over three weeks of interviewing. An aspiring commissioner is asked: What will you do if you discover information that concerns the highest positions in the new government? Most candidates answer that the stability of the Government of National Unity is important for the survival of everybody. South Africa's democracy is young and fragile. One would treat such sensitive information with care.

But we have to go. We switch off our machines. We try to pull our equipment unobtrusively across the table toward us. We see Chikane's eyes following the two microphones gliding in pas de deux to his left, toppling from the table into our laps. We pack up—we roll up meters of cable. Our beepers urge: "Get to Pta NOW."

Manelisi holds up his finger. Here it comes. The litmus test. And Chikane says: "I believe unequivocally that all information needs to be treated in the same manner. Whether it touches the highest trees or the most ordinary shrubs. Should we treat information about important politicians differently to that about ordinary people, we immediately create a new injustice as bad as the previous one."

We leave. Outside the hotel, it is Johannesburg, it is Friday, it is five o'clock, and it is raining.

In the car, we send through our reports. The car windows steam up. We drive. We work. The cell phone rings. It's Radio Tswana. With his feet on the accelerator and brakes, Manelisi does a "Question and Answer" about the prospective Truth Commissioners. I hold the wheel. We experience in symbiosis the dodging of cars. A close shave manifests only in Manelisi's intonation: "The candidate said that the commission should bring a . . . [his voice suddenly revving] nnneww! [swerving] morality." We clean the windows with our notes, with our socks.

I do a Q and A with Radio Lotus from Durban, then PM Live on SAFM. We open some windows—we get soaked; we drive; we work.

The cell phone rings: "I'm hearing you on the radio . . . where the fuck are you? All of us are waiting outside the presidential gates."

The boss. I give the phone to Manelisi. I do the gears; he does the explanation. "We don't know . . . it's raining, we can't see anything, but we must be close to Pretoria."

We calculate. It's ten to six. He has to iron his shirt. We are not going to make it.

Radio Xhosa phones; Radio Lesedi waits on the line. We pass an accident—sirens and red light splashed on wet tar. While the cars slowly crawl ahead, I move across the gearshift, Manelisi slips underneath, and I am behind the wheel, foot on the gas. Sweat and rain covering us . . . here's the Voortrekker Monument . . . Unisa . . .

Six o'clock the cell phone rings.

"We're in Kerkstraat."

"Okay, we are on the steps here. Parks is waiting for us. We'll go in . . . don't dress up, just come, so that we can all be seated by ten past."

Against all odds, we find ourselves in front of the gates of President Mandela's official residence—"the house with the name that whites cannot remember." The guards stop us. We open the window and explain in four different languages who we are. They let us through. We speed up to the house in lanes of water and stop neatly in the last parking spot. We jump out. We open the trunk and grab our clothes. I open the back door and, in the pouring rain, unfasten my belt. Manelisi's T-shirt is halfway over his head when:

"Wait . . . wait! You cannot. You cannot undress here—the whole house overlooks the parking lot." It's the guard. "Just go deeper into the garden," he begs.

We take our clothes and stumble into the wet, muddy, dark garden, while our beepers go berserk. The ground is wet; everywhere there are pools of water and mud. I clasp my clothes together while I take off my jeans. I put them on the wet ground. I put my clothes on top. Manelisi does the same. I pull on stockings and shoes, and just when I'm busy washing under my arms with water dripping from the leaves, we hear voices. A flashlight falls on Manelisi in his red underpants, leaning slightly forward, shaking out his shirt. Absolute silence follows. The frozen moment is loudly broken by Manelisi. As if he is the president himself, he lifts his hands in annoyance: "Hey, guys, please. People are dressing here. Respect our privacy."

Upon which the guards obediently switch off the flashlight, make an about-face, and march away. Nine minutes past six. We run up the steps and slip into line just in time to greet the president. Our boss glows. "It's wonderful that you are here." She hands me a tissue to wipe my lenses and asks the doorman if Manelisi can nip out quickly to scrape some mud from his shoes.

In November, a list of twenty-five names is submitted to the president. Behind the scenes, it's said that, with one or two exceptions, the cream of the people with a human rights profile have already been taken up into the ranks of the ANC government and its various commissions.

Many of the names are unknown to the majority of South Africans. Some of them will remain unknown until the end of the process.

But before the final list can be compiled, the panel and the president have to clarify several things. Should a victim of gross human rights violations serve on the commission? What about someone like Father Michael Lapsley? How impartial can a person be who has lost both hands in a bomb attack? Would black victims identify with a white victim? Moreover, should people on the list be representative of a type of morality, or do they need to represent gender, politics, race, province, language, and so forth? To put it another way: Which Afrikaners will be on the commission? Those who paid a price in the past for their stance against apartheid or those who can now draw in the support of the National Party and right-wingers? And how can a former right-wing Afrikaner take moral decisions about people whose sentiments he shared?

Which black people will serve on the commission? How does one differentiate between people who got involved in the struggle because they were against the inhuman system of apartheid and those who got involved because they wanted the same material comforts as whites? How many black people will have the courage to take a critical public stance toward the new government? Should the Muslim as well as the Hindu religion be represented, and what about the Cape Muslims?

It's difficult to gauge exactly what the panel was thinking when they drew up the short list. Two additions, though, show how the wind is blowing. The Reverend Khoza Mgojo was added to give better representation to KwaZulu-Natal. Advocate Denzil Potgieter was added because of apparent unhappiness over the absence of colored people on the list. What about Glenda Wildschut, she's colored isn't she? . . . Yes, yes, but everybody knows "people" means "men."

The rest of the list one could more or less have predicted. The Afrikaners are Wynand Malan and Advocate Chris de Jager. The English commissioners are Alex Boraine, Mary Burton, Wendy Orr, and Richard Lyster; and the Indians, Dr. Faizel Randera and Yasmin Sooka. The black commissioners can be divided into two groups: those who will eventually be referred to as the Nguni Bloc or Black Caucus—Dumisa Ntsebeza and Bongani Finca—and the women, Mapule Ramashala, Hlengiwe Mkhize, and Sisi Khampepe.

This then is Tutu's team. And they have nothing to start off with. Not a chair, not a telephone, not a budget. Just a law.

The speed with which the commission gets on its feet is watched with envious eyes. A government spokesperson confides: "The Truth Commission is the ideal for all of us. Within a few months, it set up four offices, its internal communication is astonishingly up-and-running, the publicity it generates is better than textbook-perfect, it doesn't let itself be paralyzed—neither by bureaucratic red tape, nor by the government or any political party. Everyone knows that they are navigating a tight financial ship. They work on a contract basis. They evaluate their own activities and their personnel. The commission is an example of how things *can* be done."

On the insistence of Archbishop Tutu, the commissioners gather at the end of January 1996 for a retreat under the guidance of Father Francis Cull, Tutu's spiritual adviser.

"What lies ahead is a very difficult task. They have been called to do something for the whole of South Africa and, of course, one feels inadequate to deal with an immense job like this," says Cull. He explains how commissioners will not be allowed to talk during the retreat, even during mealtimes. "In the military sense, a retreat is a time when you withdraw in order to regroup and recoup. So, in a religious, spiritual sense, it is a time when you go into a place of solitude and silence, where you can be still and where you can come to terms with your inner journey. Where you can concentrate and focus on your own resources and the task ahead."

Through the luxury suburb of Bishop's Court, I follow the directions to the house of the archbishop, for the Truth Commission's first photo session. Even though a radio journalist cannot do much with a photograph, the chance to look around the official residence of an archbishop is too good to pass up. Guards block the way; there are dogs and demands for ID books, because the first death threats have already been made against some commissioners.

But as you take the garden path, seamed with shoulder-high hortensias, up to the big house, you get a feeling of transition—of transformation—of the have-nots occupying the world of the haves. It's a densely overgrown property, rich with trees and plants. But you can tell immediately: whatever is growing was planted long ago. No fine garden, no expanse of lawn—cut a little here, trim a little there, and that's it. You arrive in a courtyard that leads to the main house, the offices, and other buildings. Three children splash around in a half-empty fountain. Several families are obviously living in the outbuildings on the extensive property.

We journalists are taken to the dining room. A gigantic, elaborate table with carved chairs. On the wall hangs a skewish tapestry, woven with love for the archbishop by the women of Boitumelo. The study has heavy timber bookcases from floor to ceiling, partly filled with row upon row of leather-bound volumes. On other shelves lie stacks of alternative magazines, church pamphlets, and theological works out of Africa that could only have been printed on local presses. A series of gold-framed portraits of previous pink-and-chubby archbishops hangs next to homemade presents and badly taken photographs, testimony to the first black archbishop's lifetime of service to people once neglected and now eternally grateful. A handmade cross rests against the wall—Jesus looking more like an amnesty-seeker than a victim.

While we wait, a colleague tells us this story. "When Tutu comes to preach in Namaqualand," he says, "it's so hot, it's always hot on a Sunday. And when the service is finished, Tutu comes to my grandmother's house to lie there under the tree—she has such a dense, shady tree. And then for the next week the people talk of nothing else but that holy man . . . the Lord's chosen one . . . who lies under a tree—just like an ordinary person."

The door opens and the seventeen commissioners walk in. The media suddenly go wild, popping and flashing. Photographers elbow each other out of the way; the TV crew begs people not to crowd the camera angle. Somebody trips over my recording equipment with a tooth-shattering *klap*. While the commissioners are still busy seating themselves, a journalist calls out: "When is your first hearing?"

But something is happening. Absolutely focused, they seat themselves and Tutu bows his head and starts to pray: ". . . that we may have the strength to listen to the whispers of the abandoned, the pleas of those afraid, the anguish of those without hope." Whereas at their first gathering the commissioners looked either shy or too pleased with themselves, now there is a purposefulness in their bearing that suddenly has nothing to do with religion or group representation.

"This is just a photo session," Tutu says, "because the newspapers asked for a head-and-shoulders shot of each commissioner. After that, you may leave."

With just two weeks to go to the first hearings, challenges are launched against the Truth Commission legislation on constitutional grounds. Earlier, police general Johan van der Merwe has said that refusing amnesty would be unconstitutional. The interim Constitution clearly states that there *will* be amnesty. Hot on his heels are the families of Steve Biko, and Griffiths and Victoria Mxenge. They say that amnesty will take away the right of the ordinary citizen to a civil claim. During the first months of its life, the commission is constantly in court trying to clear up aspects of the legislation.

At a press conference, Deputy Chairperson Alex Boraine says: The commission has encountered opposition from day one—chiefly from the right wing. The head of the investigative unit, Dumisa Ntsebeza, says: Steve Biko's death[3] happened almost twenty years ago, it was not the commission that stopped the families from going to court. Moreover, Biko's family accepted an out-of-court settlement in which they received 65,000 rand [about $11,000]. According to Tutu, all the narratives around the commission are important; he insists that families have the right to strive for justice. But the commission has a far greater task, he says, which is "to listen to the unknown victims—those who have never received any attention from the authorities or the media— and to provide a forum for the exposure of their experiences."

Suddenly people seem to find the idea of amnesty repugnant. And Tutu is the one who has to explain: "*We* did not decide on amnesty. The political parties decided on amnesty. Amnesty made our election possible. The amnesty clause was inserted in the early hours of the morning

---

[3] Political activist Steve Biko, leader of the black consciousness movement that arose in the 1970s, died in 1977 of massive head injuries after twenty-six days in police detention.

after an exhausted night of negotiating. The last thing, the last sentence, the last clause, was added: amnesty shall be granted through a process of reconciliation. And it was only when *that* was put in, that the *boere* signed the negotiations, opening the door to our election." Tutu repeats this story in all the languages he can muster.

According to Johnny de Lange, the legislation was carefully checked by constitutional experts, and he has no doubt that it falls within the framework of the Constitution.

Meanwhile, the Mxenge family announce that they will sue security police assassin Dirk Coetzee for 1 million rand (about $167,000). Says Coetzee: "I am back in the country for six years already. It is strange that for all these years they have not charged me, but now that I am asking for amnesty, they have a problem. And this after I was prepared to testify for them in 1992 in a civil case against the old government."

"Do you have a million rand?" I ask.

"No, I do not even have a million cent, I have nothing . . . I have lost everything. I live in a rented house, with furniture that I got from my parents; I drive my mother-in-law's car."

A commission for truth? Long before the idea took shape in Parliament, it was discussed at two conferences, both organized by Dr. Alex Boraine. The first one took place early in 1994. Highly skeptical, I found a place at the back of the hall. The only images of righteousness I had to go by were of German geriatrics with cancer in overseas docks. What would be the effect of a manacled P. W. Botha, stripped of his little hat and forefinger, on his way to long-term imprisonment, other than astonishment that anyone could regard this as the final proof of justice?

But immediately I'm ashamed. Of course crimes against humanity should be punished.

It takes the Chilean philosopher and activist José Zalaquett, who served on the Chilean Truth Commission, precisely seven and a half minutes to convert me to the idea. The Nuremberg and Tokyo trials could work the way they did only because the guilty lost their political power and their guns. Their defeat was complete and the conquerors needed only to wrestle with their own sense of justice. But in Chile, as in South Africa, the overthrown regime is part of the new government and still has enough power to obstruct the inquests into any abuses or to start a new civil war.

Ideological purists, says Zalaquett—and every sentence he utters could serve as a maxim—maintain that it's better to suffer longer under a tyranny when there is hope for a politically purer outcome than to progress by messy compromises.

One cannot expect morality from politicians, but one can hold them to the ethics of accountability.

A policy that wants to make a difference has to prevent a repetition of past abuses and compensate for what has happened where possible.

It will sometimes be necessary to choose between truth and justice. We should choose truth, he says. Truth does not bring back the dead, but releases them from silence.

A community should not wipe out a part of its past, because it leaves a vacuum that will be filled by lies and contradictory, confusing accounts of what happened.

Perpetrators need to acknowledge the wrong they did. Why? It creates a communal starting point. To make a clean break from the past, a moral beacon needs to be established between the past and the future.

"The most important lesson the struggle taught me and my friends is that no one is endowed with remarkable courage. But courage is another name for learning to live with your fears. Now, after eighteen years and the Chilean Truth Commission, courage has again evolved a new definition: the guts not to give in to easy justice. To live within the confinements of reality, but to search day after day for the progressing of one's most cherished values. Merciless. Accountable."

Identity is memory, says Zalaquett. Identities forged out of half-remembered things or false memories easily commit transgressions.

Everybody seems excited about the presence of the Polish philosopher Adam Mischnik. He quotes Jürgen Habermas: Collective guilt does not exist. Whoever is guilty will have to answer individually. At the same time, there is such a thing as collective responsibility for a mental and cultural context that makes possible crimes against humanity. One should be aware of the fact that traditions are ambivalent and that one should stay critical about traditions and be very clear about what should be continued. The violations in Germany should have the effect that a specific mistrust exists about German tradition and cultural contexts. Like Germany, South Africa will always need to question its mentality, while communities with a stronger democratic culture need not do it so often.

"Here in South Africa it's reconciliation with a gun against your head. You choose negotiations when you choose the logic of peace. But the moment you get up from the negotiation table, you have to defend your erstwhile enemy—he is now your partner. He becomes your political and moral burden." Mischnik warns: "If you look for a scapegoat, and you find one and you make him the devil . . . then you yourself become the angel . . ."

". . . and then you wake up . . . lost," the interpreter says tentatively. Mischnik nods his head vigorously.

Kader Asmal quotes Aleksandr Solzhenitsyn: "By not dealing with past human rights violations, we are not simply protecting the perpetrators' trivial old age; we are thereby ripping the foundations of justice from beneath new generations."

FIRST
HEARINGS

CHAPTER THREE

Stretched Thinner and Thinner
over Pitches of Grief

Tension is plain to see in the faces and body language of all the commissioners. Archbishop Tutu is continually rubbing his right hand; shoulders are tensely set; faces look tired and drawn beneath two big South African flags and Truth Commission banners. The city hall of East London is packed from wall to wall.

Last night, the archbishop says, he had butterflies in his stomach: "We were aware from the beginning that the commission could go terribly and horribly wrong. But this first victims' hearing is the making or breaking of the commission."

"So what are your worst fears?"

He laughs nervously. "Silly things, like the microphones not working, security problems . . . or terrible things like victims not showing up or violence breaking out."

Commissioner Bongani Finca starts with the well-known Xhosa hymn: *"Lizalise idinga lakho"* (The forgiveness of sins makes a person whole). As the song carries, the victims file into the hall and take their seats at the front.

Archbishop Tutu prays. But untypically he sounds as if he is praying from a piece of paper: "We long to put behind us the pain and division of apartheid, together with all the violence which ravaged our communities in its name. And so we ask you to bless this Truth and Reconciliation Commission with your wisdom and guidance as a body which seeks to redress the wounds in the minds and the bodies of those who suffered."

Everyone stands with heads bowed while the names of the deceased and disappeared who will come under the spotlight today are read out.

A big white candle emblazoned with a red cross is lit. Then all the commissioners go over to the victims to greet and welcome them, while the audience stays standing.

But the journalists in the media room are hardly aware of this consecration of space. Frantic shouting accompanies the attempts to tune in TV monitors, establish clear sound reception, and set up laptop computers. Radio has its own small room. We have a whole newly appointed team, which has to cover the event in all eleven official languages. Today's hearings will be broadcast live, after an hour-long program on the meaning of the legislation, the origin of amnesty, the workings of the commission, and an interview with the minister of justice. Somewhere in a corner, foreign journalists are being briefed on the history of the eastern Cape, how to pronounce "Qaqawuli" and "Mxenge." Like people possessed, they take down notes. The locals watch them from a distance.

To seize the surge of language by its soft, bare skull

Beloved, do not die. Do not dare die! I, the survivor, I wrap you in words so that the future inherits you. I snatch you from the death of forgetfulness. I tell your story, complete your ending—you who once whispered beside me in the dark.

"When I opened the door . . . there was my closest friend and comrade . . . She was standing on the doorstep and she screamed: 'My child, my little Nomzamo, is still in the house!' . . . I stared at her . . . my most beautiful friend . . . her hair flaming and her chest like a furnace . . . she died a day later. I pulled out her baby from the burning house . . . I put her on the grass . . . only to find that her skin stayed behind on my hands. She is with me here today."

"I was trying to see my child. Just when he was about to open the police van at the back, I heard a voice shouting, saying: 'No, don't show her anything—*hou die meid daar weg!*' ['Keep the *kaffer* girl away from there!'] But I managed. I pulled a green curtain . . . I saw . . . my . . . child . . . sleeping among tires . . . and he was foaming in the mouth and he was . . . already dead . . . Then they pulled him out and threw him on the ground . . . And I looked at him . . . And he was dying . . . and they won't allow me to hold him . . ."

"This inside me . . . fights my tongue. It is . . . unshareable. It destroys . . . words. Before he was blown up, they cut off his hands so he could not be fingerprinted . . . So how do I say this?—this terrible . . . I want his hands back."

"It was Sunday. And cold. He came into the kitchen. 'Make me some bean soup.'

" 'It's Sunday, *jong*, I want to cook special food.'

"But he wanted bean soup.

"While dressing for church, we heard the noise. The youths were coming down the road. We were standing in our bedroom. We were not talking. We were not moving. They surrounded the house and they shouted: 'Let the spy *die*, let the spy *die!*' They threw stones through the window. When they left, he said to me: 'Don't cry, Nontuthuzelo. A person dies only once, not many times. I know now where these things are leading to. Come, let's make soup.' We went to the kitchen and put the beans in a pot.

"Then someone we knew knocked at the door. 'The comrades are burning your shop, Uncle Mick!'

" 'I'll be back for lunch,' he said to me.

"They told me afterward. He walked up to the door of his shop, he didn't look back . . . someone in the crowd shot him in the back . . . They told me afterward Craig Kotze had said my husband was the one who betrayed Steve Biko."

"Two policemen got on either chair and they dragged me to the window, and then they said I can now jump . . . I refused . . . they grabbed me by my shoulders and lifted me physically up and pushed me out of the window . . . and they were holding me by my ankles . . . each policeman holding one ankle. All I could see was the concrete floor at the bottom—we were three floors up, and all of a sudden one would let go of one foot—as he's about to catch my foot, the one he had released, the other chap lets go—and they played like that . . . and, you know, you thought: God, this is the end."

"They held me . . . they said, 'Please don't go in there . . .' I just skipped through their legs and went in . . . I found Bheki . . . he was in pieces . . . he was hanging on pieces . . . He was all over . . . pieces of him and brain was scattered all around . . . that was the end of Bheki."

"At Caledon Square, I heard a loud sound. Policemen were celebrating. They said: 'We've got Looksmart!' I was in my cell when I saw Looksmart being dragged up a flight of stairs by two policemen. They were beating him as he went up the stairs. I noticed that his beard had been pulled out . . . one by one . . . on one side of his face. He was bleeding heavily from the mouth. Two days later, they took him again—his hands handcuffed behind his back. That was the last time I saw Looksmart Ngudle."

"And the man there sitting next to the ambulance driver—he stood there with my son's intestines in his hands and he was actually holding it and carried it into the ambulance."

"In the mortuary—after the Queenstown massacre—I had to identify my son. We waited in front of the mortuary . . . a thick black stream of blood was running from under the door . . . blocking the outside drain . . . inside, the stench was unbearable . . . bodies were stacked upon each other . . . the blood from my child's body was already green."

"This white man with the red scarf, he shot into the outside bathroom where Sonnyboy was hiding . . . I was standing in the kitchen . . . I saw him dragging my child. Sonnyboy was already dead. He was holding him by his legs like a dog. I saw him digging a hole, scraping Sonnyboy's brains into that hole, and closing it with his boot. The sun was bright . . . but it went dark when I saw him lying there. It's an everlasting pain. It will stop never in my heart. It always comes back. It eats me apart. Sonnyboy, rest well, my child. I've translated you from the dead."

"I asked them, 'Show me the mark on his chin, then I will know it's my son.' They showed me the mark on his chin, and I said: 'It's not my son.' "

"When Fuzile didn't come home that night, I went to look for him. Now this makes me mad, really. My son was shot and nobody told me. I looked everywhere and nobody told me my son was in the mortuary . . . they later gave me his clothes. His T-shirt looked as if it had been eaten by rats."

"As she had a baby, the police said that the corpse could breast-feed the baby."

"Barnard was a frightful man—the cop we couldn't kill. He always drove this red Valiant and wore this red *doek*. Rambo of the western Cape, he called himself. Whenever his car appeared on the shimmering horizon leading the yellow Casspirs, we knew: someone dies today. We will remember the man with the red scarf who shot dead our sons."

"This was the last thing I saw: Barnard standing next to his car. He spoke Xhosa like a Xhosa. He pointed his firearm at me. I felt something hitting my cheek. I felt my eyes itching. I was scratching my eyes and yelling for help. Since then I've been blind . . . and unemployed . . . and alone and homeless. But today . . . it feels as if I can nearly see . . ."

"I heard shots . . . I ran . . . slipped and fell . . . I crawled out at the front door . . . On the steps, my son sat . . . with his father's face in his hands . . . He was covered in blood . . . He cried over and over: 'Daddy, talk to me . . .' Today he is twenty-one years old. I am still woken at night by his cries: 'Wipe the blood . . . wipe the blood from my father's face.' "

"That morning I did something I had never done before. My husband was still at his desk busy with the accounts of our business. I went up to him and stood behind his chair. I put my hands under his arms and tickled him . . . he looked surprised and unexpectedly happy.
" 'And now?' he asked.
" 'I am going to make tea,' I said.
"While I poured water on the tea bags, I heard this devastating noise. Six men stormed into our study and blew his head off. My five-year-old daughter was present . . . That Christmas I found a letter on his desk: 'Dear Father Christmas, please bring me a soft teddy bear with friendly eyes . . . My daddy is dead. If he was here, I would not have bothered you.' I put her in a boarding school. The morning we drove there, we had a flat tire. 'You see,' she said, 'Daddy does not want me to go there . . . He wants me to stay with you . . . I have watched him die, I must be there when you die . . .' She is now a teenager and has tried twice to commit suicide."

In the beginning, it was seeing. Seeing for ages, filling the head with ash. No air. No tendril. Now to seeing, speaking is added and the eye plunges into the mouth. Present at the birth of this country's language itself.

And it wipes us out. Like a fire. Or a flood. Tears are not what we call it. Water covers our cheeks and we cannot type. Or think.

> "We should all be deeply humbled by what we've heard,
> but we've got to finish quickly and really turn our backs
> on this awful past and say: 'Life is for living.' "

—ARCHBISHOP DESMOND TUTU,
after the first day of testimony in East London

MS. GOBODO-MADIKIZELA: Baba is going to present to us what he says is the work of the man who came to be known as the Rambo of the Peninsula. The police officer who is known by the name of Barnard. Good morning, I am just going to explain to you how this house is arranged. If you face toward your right, that is now the whole house, people in this house are approximately two hundred to two hundred and fifty. You are now seated on the platform. And our small tables are arranged as a horseshoe. Right in the middle of the horseshoe is Archbishop Tutu, next to him is Dr. Boraine, I am right at the extreme end of this horseshoe. I am seated directly across from you, we are facing each other. We are now going to start to talk to each other, Baba.

Could you please tell us, Baba, what happened on that day of this incident, could you please explain to us.

MR. SIKWEPERE: . . . A van approached—it was a white van and it was driven by Barnard. When he had just passed, he asked us all to disperse within five minutes. Now the communities asked, "How can he ask us to disperse, because this is just a small meeting?"— we were just twenty to twenty-five.

I wanted to find out what was the response from this white man. When I saw that the van now was stationary, I went to it. I was just standing for two minutes next to the window . . . now this white man opened the door and withdrew his gun. Now I wanted to find out what is the story going on, on the other side of this car. I tried to peep and I was looking straight into him, straight to him. While

I was still looking at him, these people asked him, "How can you ask us to disperse?"

This white man said this in Afrikaans—"You are going to get eventually what you are looking for. And I am going to shoot you." I was shocked at what this white man said to me. He said in Afrikaans, *"Ek gaan jou kry."* Now I wanted to find out why is he talking to me like this . . . I saw people surrounding this van—I was now wondering, Where do these people come from surrounding this van, all of a sudden?

After that I heard a loud noise, it sounded like a stone hitting a sink. But I decided not to run, I decided to walk. Because I knew that if you ran, you were going to be shot, so I decided—let me just walk into a safe place where I can just start running . . . When I arrived at the place where I thought now I am safe, I felt something hitting my cheek. I couldn't go any further, I stayed right there only to find out I had been hidden by a corner of a house. I felt my eyes itching, I was scratching my eyes. I wasn't quite sure what happened to my eyes at that particular time. I felt somebody stepping on my right shoulder. And saying, "I thought this dog had died already." I felt both my eyes—I was just waiting that these people are going to take me to a prison.

MS. GOBODO-MADIKIZELA: Baba, do you have any bullets in you as we speak?

MR. SIKWEPERE: Yes, there are several of them. Some are here in my neck. Now on my face you can really see them, but my face feels quite rough, it feels like rough salt. I usually have terrible headaches.

MS. GOBODO-MADIKIZELA: Thank you, Baba.

MR. SIKWEPERE: Yes, usually I have a fat body, but after that I lost all my body, now I am thin, as you can see me now.

MS. GOBODO-MADIKIZELA: How do you feel, Baba, about coming here to tell us your story?

MR. SIKWEPERE: I feel what—what has brought my sight back, my eyesight back is to come back here and tell the story. But I feel what has been making me sick all the time is the fact that I couldn't tell my story. But now I—it feels like I got my sight back by coming here and telling you the story.

(Lucas Baba Sikwepere)

Instinctively, one knew that some people would deliberately cut themselves off from the Truth Commission process. But very few people escape news bulletins—even the music stations have a lunchtime news report. So it is crucial to us that the commission and its narratives be captured as fully as possible on ordinary bulletins. Even people who do no more than listen to the news should be given a full understanding of the essence of the commission. This means that the past has to be put into hard news gripping enough to make bulletin headlines, into reports that the bulletin writers in Johannesburg cannot ignore. To do this, we will have to use the full spectrum of hard news techniques and where necessary develop and reform them.

A bulletin generally consists of three audio elements: ordinary reporting read out by a newsreader, twenty-second sound bites of other people's voices, and forty-second voice reports sent through by a journalist. How can these elements be molded to our aims? An expert needs to come help me, I plead. And they send Angie.

I sit next to her in the media room. It is the first day of the hearings. Angie types codes and passwords into her laptop computer to log on to the network. We wait: little lights flash and scratchy shrieks issue from the modem—sounds of broken glass. For the rest of my life, I will remember this scene: the members of the radio team, each wearing earphones, recording the translation of their assigned language, and Angie on a cushion, so that she can reach the high table, making a furious assault on the day's first news story—furious, because Angie is someone who types with all ten of her fingers. And as those pinkies squirrel away on the keys, the testimony of the first victim of the first day, Nohle Mohape, goes through to Johannesburg—in time for the eleven o'clock bulletin.

Thus our labors over the next two years will be structured. We do short packages, text with sound bites or live interviews, for the afternoon programs, and in the evenings we work on longer pieces for the following morning. Meanwhile the bulletins keep flowing through. Stories, complete stories with beginnings, middles, and ends, are told for the first time: in a forty-second report, we relate how Phindile Mfeti told his wife that he was going to have his jeans shortened, then disappeared without a trace. How she later found on his desk the glasses and pipe that he always took with him. How she asked the commission for something to bury—even if it was just a piece of bone or a handful of ash.

We also learn quickly. For words like "menstruation" or "penis," there is no place on the news; a phrase such as "They braaied [barbecued] my child on a fire" is out of the question. We are told that the writer Rian Malan has complained that he doesn't want to mix "breakfast and blood" in the mornings. This is just the encouragement we need. We write the first lines of the hard copy: "The missing hand of ANC activist Sicelo Mhlawuli dominated the testimonies before the Truth Commission hearings in East London today. Mhlawuli's hand was last seen by a fellow detainee." Then the recorded comment: "I saw the severed hand of a black activist in a bottle at a Port Elizabeth police station. The police told me it was a baboon's hand. They said to me: 'Look here, this is the bottled hand of a communist.' But I know that Sicelo Mhlawuli . . . was buried with his hand missing." This is a perfect sound bite. (How quickly our own language changes—"fantastic testimony," "sexy subject," "nice audible crying." We also insist on the use of "Truth Commission" rather than "TRC," which would conceal the essence of the commission behind a meaningless abbreviation.)

We pick out a sequence. We remove some pauses and edit it into a twenty-second sound bite. We feed it to Johannesburg. We switch on a small transistor. The news comes through: "I was making tea in the police station. I heard a noise, I looked up . . . There he fell . . . Someone fell from the upper floor past the window . . . I ran down . . . It was my child . . . my grandchild, but I raised him."

We lift our fists triumphantly. We've done it!

The voice of an ordinary cleaning woman is the headline on the one o'clock news.

Week after week, voice after voice, account after account. It is not so much the deaths, and the names of the dead, but the web of infinite sorrow woven around them. It keeps on coming and coming. A wide, barren, disconsolate landscape where the horizon keeps on dropping away.

And this is how we often end up at the daily press conferences—bewildered and close to tears at the feet of Archbishop Tutu. By the end of four weeks, they are no longer press conferences. He caresses us with pieces of hope and humanity. We ask fewer and fewer critical questions. Perplexed, we listen to the sharp, haughty questions posed by foreign journalists—those who jet into the country, attend one day's hearings, and then confront the commission about its lack of judicial procedures and objectivity.

The first sign of the International Journalist in your midst is the subtle fragrance. Male or female, overseas journalists can obviously afford a perfumery that you won't find on the shelves at Pick 'n Pay. The second sign is the equipment. Microphones like cruise missiles on launching pads appear in front of interviewees, and you have to find space next to them for your humble little SABC mike. They are equipped with recorders that produce fully edited sound bites and reports at the push of a button, computers they can carry in their inside pockets, and cell phones no bigger than lipsticks. And they know something really big is happening in East London, they pick up the vibes—but nothing fits into their operating frameworks. "How can you report *anything?*" A Belgian journalist struggles to keep the skepticism out of his voice. "South African journalists keep on bursting into tears all around me in the hall."

The Story of the Century, they tell us. With heroes and villians, well-known and unknown characters, the powerful and the powerless, the literate and the illiterate. Hung with laptops, tape recorders, bags, notebooks, and reels of cable and tape, we limp into hotel foyers long after midnight.

Why the eastern Cape—why start at this scalp of green silence?

This part of Africa was the first frontier between black and white, between the terrestrial endeavor of Africa and the maritime endeavor of Europe, says Noel Mostert in his book *Frontiers*. The eastern Cape opened between white and black a relationship beyond that of master and slave. Its landscape provided a dramatic backdrop for the moral struggles around colonialism, expansionism, race, and freedom.

According to Mostert, the indigenous people of the eastern Cape found themselves selected by history to bear for centuries the brunt of contact with the outside world. Despite the fact that these were peaceful farming and cattle-herding communities, the area became known for its fierce resistance to oppression. The Xhosas originally consisted of three main groups: the Pondo, to which Winnie Madikizela-Mandela belongs; the Thembu house, of which her former husband is a prince; and the Xhosa group, which produced Steve Biko.

Resistance in the eastern Cape was complemented by excellent missionary schooling, which enabled the oppressed to put forward a refined political argument in English, thus breaking new ground in black political thinking internationally. The eastern Cape also saw the beginnings of the Pan-Africanist Congress and Black Consciousness. From the sixties onward, with the cream of its leadership either in jail or in exile, the eastern Cape endured an unprecedented escalation of human rights abuses, many of them notorious. These included the detention and death of Steve Biko, the assassination of the Cradock Four and Pebco Three, the massacre at Bisho, and the Motherwell bomb incident.

Of all those detained without trial in South Africa, one-third came from the eastern Cape. Why? Because the region was also the dumping ground for those soldiers who got out of hand during the bush war[1]— the veterans, black and white, of Koevoet and the notorious 101 and 32 Battalions. These men had to be kept out of the glare of the media, and at a distance from Parliament and human rights organizations. And their names cropped up during the first week of hearings in East London, always in connection with torture and murder: Gideon Nieuwoudt, Albert Ntungata, Eric Winter, Chris Labuschagne, Spyker van Wyk, Gert Strydom.

It was apparently assumed in security circles that whoever crushed the eastern Cape would control the country. The region still lives with the consequences. Despite the fact that Xhosa people dominate South African politics, this is the second poorest of the nine provinces, with 65 percent of the economically active population unemployed.

True to its spirit of resistance, the first attempts to stop the Truth Commission emanate from the eastern Cape. The Biko family file several cases to prove that the legislation is unconstitutional, while perpetrators from Port Elizabeth succeed in preventing the Truth Commission from allowing victims to name them.

It has to be this part of the country that turns us inside out, that renders us: bare lips. It has to be this region of fierce opposites—meadows and plains, waterfalls and *dongas*, ferns and aloes—that sparks from a

---

[1] During the late 1970s and through the 1980s, South Africa was almost constantly at war with the forces of SWAPO—the South West African People's Organization, dedicated to independence for Namibia. Koevoet was the name of a plainclothes police unit whose unorthodox methods against SWAPO won it a reputation as a killing machine doing the secret bidding of the South African Defense Force (SADF).

speechless darkness the voices of the past. And at long last, we can weep in the certainty of this April, in the assurance of the testimony of fellow South Africans.

It was the end of October—10 October 1985. She was on her way to work, two young men approached her. Now they were five. When they saw her, they chased her. She went to hide in another house, and now they took her out of that house.

They took her overall, and they poured gasoline over her. One of them held her feet and then they started igniting her feet. They were beating her up. There was nobody who could stop this, the police were looking for her, but they were lost and they couldn't find her. She tried to [take the police] to them . . . to the people who tried to hurt her, but they couldn't [understand her] because she didn't have a voice. The police took her to Bloemfontein.

In Bloemfontein she stayed for three days, and she started to mention everybody who did this to her. Then after that, she died. They didn't allow her to be buried in Colesberg, because they said she was an informer. They said if she was buried there, they were going to burn the church. Then she ended up being buried in Pilonome Hospital. That's where I will stop for a moment.

ADV. POTGIETER: Was there any truth in this allegation that she was an *impimpi*, an informer?

MRS. MALITI: That's how they got her, but the reason why they burnt her is because my uncle is a policeman.

ADV. NTSEBEZA: You said while this happened there was a boycott of the shops that time. Your mother's main offense was that she went to buy meat from the butchery—you will correct me if I am wrong . . . She tried to clear her name?

MRS. MALITI: Yes sir.

ADV. NTSEBEZA: According to the report that you gave to the people who were taking the statements earlier, she paid 100 rand.

MRS. MALITI: Yes.

ADV. NTSEBEZA: Where did she send this R100?

MRS. MALITI: She sent it to the comrades and the comrades announced it, that she did pay this R100 trying to ask for forgiveness for buying meat during a consumer boycott. They said they forgive her. Now she took this letter to the township.

ADV. NTSEBEZA: When she came back to the township, she was under the impression that she was forgiven?

MRS. MALITI: Yes.

ADV. NTSEBEZA: In other words . . . she was killed while she was still under the impression that she was safe, knowing that she was forgiven?

MRS. MALITI: Yes, that's so.

ADV. NTSEBEZA: When did the police come in?

MRS. MALITI: The police arrived when she was burnt already. When the police came in, they could—they were trying to find out where she was, but they could hear her crying. They saw her in the main road, she was already alight.

ADV. NTSEBEZA: Did she run after she was burnt?

MRS. MALITI: No, she couldn't run, she was just walking slowly, her clothes were burning. She went in the direction where the police were . . .

ADV. NTSEBEZA: Were the people afraid to help her?

MRS. MALITI: No one was allowed by the comrades to help her, so she went alone to the van.

ADV. NTSEBEZA: Were these comrades who were chasing people away?

MRS. MALITI: There were five of them—at the beginning there were too many, but at the end they were just five. One of them was Tifo Sihlaba . . . it was Tabo Gusha, Pinkdyaan Kelem, Toto Mayaba, Tembile Falati.

ADV. NTSEBEZA: What about Zolile Silwayane?

MRS. MALITI: Zolile Silwayane is the one who actually accepted the money, he is the leader of this whole situation. Yes, he is the one who announced that he had received the money, and he was the one who actually went back again and said she must be ignited.

ADV. NTSEBEZA: This is a very unique case from all the cases we have heard. We've been listening to cases where our people were being killed by police and the government, but now this is unique because our people are being killed by our own people at the same time. Do you know the husband to the deceased?

MRS. MALITI: Yes, I know his name is Doti. That day—he doesn't know anything because he ran. He ran to Crossroads, and even today he is not well since then.

ADV. NTSEBEZA: Just to clear something up, are you trying to say he was never well again mentally?

MRS. MALITI: Yes, that's what I am saying.

(Thomzama Maliti, testifying on the death of Nombulelo Delato)

The word "truth" makes me uncomfortable.

The word "truth" still trips the tongue.

"Your voice tightens up when you approach the word 'truth,' " the technical assistant says, irritated. "Repeat it twenty times so that you become familiar with it. *Truth is mos jou job!*" ("Truth is your job, after all!")

I hesitate at the word; I am not used to using it. Even when I type it, it ends up as either *turth* or *trth*. I have never bedded that word in a poem. I prefer the word "lie." The moment the lie raises its head, I smell blood. Because it is there . . . where the truth is closest.

The word "reconciliation," on the other hand, is my daily bread.

Compromise, accommodate, provide, make space for. Understand. Tolerate. Empathize. Endure . . . Without it, no relationship, no work, no progress, is possible. Yes. Piece by piece we die into reconciliation.

However—neither truth nor reconciliation is part of my graphite when sitting in front of a blank page, eraser close at hand. Everything else fades away. It becomes so quiet. Something opens and something falls into this quiet space. A tone, an image, a line, mobilizes completely. I become myself. Truth and reconciliation do not enter my anarchy. They choke on betrayal and rage; they fall off my refusal to be moral. I write the broken line. For some brief moments of loose-limbed happiness, everything I am, every shivering, otherwise useless, vulnerable fiber and hypersensitive sense, comes together. A heightened phase of clarity and the glue stays . . . and somewhat breathless, I know: for this I am made.

I am not made to report on the Truth and Reconciliation Commission. When I was first told to head the five-person radio team covering the Truth Commission, I began to cry, inexplicably, on the plane back from Johannesburg. Someone tripped over my bag in the aisle. Mumbling excuses, fumbling with tissues, I looked up into the face of Dirk Coetzee. There was no escape.

After three days, a nervous breakdown was diagnosed. Two weeks later, the first hearings on human rights violations began in East London.

The months that have passed have proved my premonition right—reporting on the Truth Commission indeed leaves most of us physically exhausted and mentally frayed.

Because of language.

Week after week, from one faceless building to another, from one dusty, godforsaken town to another, the arteries of our past bleed their own peculiar rhythm, tone, and image. One cannot get rid of it. Ever.

To have the voices of ordinary people dominate the news. To have no one escape the process.

We sleep between one and two hours a night. We live on chocolate and potato chips. After five years without cigarettes, I start smoking again.

In the second week of hearings, I do a Question and Answer on a current affairs program. I stammer. I freeze. I am without language. I put the receiver down, and think: Resign. Now. You are clearly incompetent. The next morning, the Truth Commission sends one of its own counselors to address the journalists. "You will experience the same symptoms as the victims. You will find yourself powerless—without help, without words."

I am shocked to be a textbook case within a mere ten days.

"Exercise regularly. Take photographs of loved ones with you to come home to in the hotels. Take your favorite music with you. And talk to one another . . . be one another's therapists."

We develop techniques to lessen the impact. We no longer go into the halls where the hearings take place, because of the accumulated grief. We watch on the monitors provided. The moment someone starts crying, we start writing/scribbling/doodling.

One hotel room drifts into another. One breakfast buffet provides the same sad fruit as another. One sorrow-filled room flows into another. One rental car smells like another . . . but the language, the detail, the individual tone . . . it stays.

"I'm going to take the tale of Nomonde Calata and make a comic out of it," says my friend Professor Kondlo, the Xhosa intellectual from Grahamstown. "I will call it 'The Contestation of Spaces.'" It is late at night. We sit and drink in the sultry eastern Cape midnight. Outside the window, the dark sea pushes past white trails of mist.

"The first page of my comic will carry the headline 'The Past,' and it will have two drawings. In the one frame, I will write 'Male Storyteller (Historian)' and draw a group of men sitting in the traditional *kgotla* or *kroro* or *motse*—whatever you want to call it, that glamorous space in which men and boys meet each other. Where stories are told of where you come from, who you are, the structure of the group's male ancestry, who your role model is. The tales which interpret your world for you, and help the male tellers to take decisions about economics, politics, history.

"Frame two will have the caption 'Female Storyteller (Socializer of Children).' This drawing will show a space where food is prepared. Children of both genders sit and listen to the stories of make-believe. A flowing gallery of magical and bizarre moments that cut into everyday life. 'Are you awake? Are you listening?' asks the grandmother. The children must react and interact with the multidimensional performance. Unlike the stories of the men where boundaries are set, these stories undermine boundaries: men turn into women and vice versa, animals become people, women fall in love with animals, people eat each other, dreams and hallucinations are played out."

"I don't get it. The wife of Fort Calata really doesn't fit the stereotypical storytelling grandma by the *pappot* and the fire that you want to put in your comic."

"Exactly," says Professor Kondlo, and thumps his fist on the table. "Over these drawings, I rubber-stamp: MIGRATION, URBANIZATION, FORCED REMOVALS. And then starts the actual story of Nomonde Calata as a woman, sitting in the male space of the British colonial city hall of East London and relating a story as part of the official history of this country. It's bloody amazing!"

"Your introduction only handles the cultural aspect," I say. "Maybe you should draw Nomonde arriving at the city hall accompanied by the police who once persecuted her? Now her space is protected and officially demarcated for her—here she is safe. Then you start immediately where she testifies how the police burst into her house and arrested her husband . . ." I dig through my notes, but he is already playing the cassette:

NOMONDE: My husband was in the room, he already had his clothes on, and he was wearing very warm clothes. Three policemen I can remember—Mr. Venter, Mr. Caio was a black man, it was Mr.

Strauss who was wearing a uniform. He had a small stick in his hand. They were not very patient with him, they were pushing him . . . they were really making him to hurry. I merely requested, "Please, do not push him, do not handcuff him, because he's got a . . . chest . . . problem . . ." *[pause . . . a sob . . . an audible shuddering]*

JOHN SMITH: Would you like some time, Mrs. Calata? Are you fine? . . . Let me assist you with this whole . . .

NOMONDE: After leaving with him, they handcuffed him to the back, leaving with him *[clears throat]* because I was also waiting for a trial—the trial for wearing a T-shirt—I didn't know where he was taken to, I didn't know where they had taken him to . . .

"Why do you think she cried here specifically?" I ask.

"Maybe remembering her husband as vulnerable. Because one picks up from the testimony that they had a special relationship—he confided in her, they discussed everything, and when he didn't turn up on time that night, she knew at once that something was wrong. When she cries at the end, it is also because this friend of hers, the wife of Matthew Goniwe, is crying."

"But now this new space that Nomonde is sitting in—it isn't only physical, it's also metaphorical."

The professor smiles. "Yes. We're talking about two different social spaces: one in which violence was justified in the past. And the other, in the present, where abuses of human rights are condemned as immoral and wrong. By choosing the city hall in the center of town and not a community center in the township, the Truth Commission wants to portray a symbolic break with the institutional frameworks of the past. This city hall is no longer the official domain of whites and perpetrators: it now belongs to all of us."

NOMONDE: In May, Fort was not around, he was in Johannesburg to see a physiotherapist, because he had this frozen shoulder. On 27 May in the early hours, I was woken up by the knock and the lights, the flashlights that were right in the house. And I went to open the door. Opening the door, I saw Mr. Venter and Mr. Gouws—and many other policemen, there were horses, SADF, it was just full. They entered my house and said they wanted to search. They got into my bedroom, they searched . . . they were looking for documents, UDF documents, they took everything. In their search, Mr.

Venter he asked me: "Where's your husband?" I said to him, "My husband is not here, he is in Gauteng." He was asking this in Afrikaans. *"Jy moet vir jou man sê, hy kan maar wegkruip en jy kan hom maar wegsteek, die dag as ons hom kry . . . dan sal hy kak."* ["Tell your husband he can hide away, you can help him to hide, but when we find him . . . he's going to shit."]

I was worried and I was scared. And at the same time, I was brave. I kept quiet and I looked at him. *"Jy sit op my bed—staan op."* ["You are sitting on my bed—get up."]

He stood up and he said, "What is this bed after all?" After that they left my house.

Matthew Goniwe arrived after the police had left. He said they visited all the executive members; they took all the documents from the members.

"After this testimony," says Kondlo excitedly, "I draw a page from a CIA handbook used in the early eighties to teach Latin American security forces how to extract information from prisoners. The purpose of this will be to explain the psychological underpinning of torture. The first step is to bring in a superior outside force. One of these outside forces is time: a person should be harassed at a time when he least expects it and when his mental and physical resistance are at its lowest—ideally in the early hours of the morning. When confronted at this time, most subjects experience intense feelings of shock, insecurity, and psychological stress and have great difficulty adjusting to the situation."

"What I find fascinating is the interaction with Venter about the bed. He invades her privacy, he sits on her bed—something only very intimate guests or children would usually do. While he's sitting there, he threatens her husband. Then she reclaims her space: you can do this and say that, she says . . . but you will *not* sit on my bed. Although he scoffs at it, he indeed gets up from the bed—despite himself, he respects their space!"

NOMONDE: In April, before Fort went to Johannesburg for this physiotherapist treatment, he arrived from a UDF meeting. It was at night. I was already in bed, but he woke me up. He said, "Nomonde, I have to tell you this." I said to him, "Speak." And he said: "We were detained with Matthew for a few hours in Port Elizabeth. We left Sparrow in the car, because we didn't want the car to be seen . . . A Security Branch [man] was sitting there . . . they were waiting for us. There was one of them who asked: *'Luitenant, moet ons dit nou doen?'* And he answered: *'Dis nog nie die regte tyd nie.'* ['Lieutenant, should we do it now?' . . . 'It's not the right time yet.'] They asked questions. At the same time, Matthew was being asked such questions . . ."

SMITH: Did your husband tell you what he understood those words to mean?

NOMONDE: Yes, he was able to explain, and said, "I think they plan something very big about us." They took it lightly, but they were unhappy and uncomfortable . . . And he expressed his shock about what he had heard.

"I wonder why Fort said: 'They plan something very "big" '? He makes it sound like a launch or something instead of a death."

"Maybe the translation is off the mark. But note that Nomonde is now testifying in a space made safe for her by the same police."

"You know, it's not necessarily the same policemen. I interviewed Sydney Mufamadi of Safety and Security and he said the regions were ordered to put together new groups to deal with security around the Truth Commission, people who are positive toward the new dispensation and not linked at all to past abuses."

"So: the inside of the hall. I will draw all the Truth Commission posters and that massive banner—all of this signifying to Nomonde that this space is owned by the commission and therefore safe and official. Safe for a political activist, safe for a woman and wife, official in its acknowledgment of her story as the truth and official in giving her the space to become a historian, a custodian of history despite her gender."

"We haven't even begun to understand what we're hearing. Do you remember where Nomonde describes waiting on the night of 27 June, when Fort, Matthew, Sparrow, and Sicelo went to a briefing in Port Elizabeth? How the abnormal situation with police watching the house has become normal, and when they're *not* there, it's abnormal?"

NOMONDE: At eleven I was anxious . . . I was unable to sleep because my husband was not yet back as he had promised. I knew that he was always being followed and harassed even when he went to the OK, wherever he went he was harassed by the police. There was a reverend who visited our place on that weekend, and I woke him up and said I was uneasy . . . I went to the reverend's room and said: "I'm anxious because my husband is not yet here." He reassured me and said that probably he would be coming tomorrow morning because it was very late. Still I felt that, no, this was not the situation. He always reports when he is going to oversleep somewhere . . . He doesn't just do something without informing me. So I kept on. I was awake, I had insomnia. Usually when I looked out, there were Casspirs, there were vans, there were Casspirs even on the other streets, but that evening it was *[whispers]* quiet—there was not a car moving around as they usually do . . . but this was also an indication that something was wrong . . . I had this premonition, and I was highly expectant at the time. I still had insomnia. The following day, I woke up, but I was working under pressure because I was hopeful that probably the reassurance of the reverend might be true.

"But the way Nomonde found out about the death of her husband surpasses all fiction . . ."

NOMONDE: We [Nomonde and Nyameka Goniwe] were unhappy and we slept without knowing on Friday what had happened to our husbands. Usually the *Herald* was delivered to my home because I was distributing it. When the *Herald* was delivered, I looked at the headlines and one of my children said: "Mother, look here in the paper . . . the car belonging to my father has been burnt." At that moment, I was trembling, because I was afraid what might have happened to my husband—because if his car is burnt down like this, I was wondering what happened to him. I started distributing the papers as usual, but I was very upset during this time. After a few hours, some friends came in and took me and said I must be among the other people, and they said I must go to Nyami. Nyami was always there for me and I was only twenty at the time and I couldn't handle this . . . so I was taken to Nyami's place *[cries loudly while interpreter finishes]* and when I got there, Nyami was crying terribly . . . it affected me also . . .

SMITH: May I request the commission to adjourn maybe for a

minute . . . I don't think the witness is in a condition to continue presently . . .

TUTU: Can we adjourn for ten minutes, please.

"For me, this crying is the beginning of the Truth Commission—the signature tune, the definitive moment, the ultimate sound of what the process is about. She was wearing this vivid orange-red dress, and she threw herself backward and that sound . . . that sound . . . it will haunt me for ever and ever."

"It's significant that she began to cry when she remembered how Nyameka Goniwe was crying when she arrived at the Goniwes' house. The academics say pain destroys language and this brings about an immediate reversion to a prelinguistic state—and to witness that cry was to witness the destruction of language . . . was to realize that to remember the past of this country is to be thrown back into a time before language. And to get that memory, to fix it in words, to capture it with the precise image, is to be present at the birth of language itself. But more practically, this particular memory at last captured in words can no longer haunt you, push you around, bewilder you, because you have taken control of it—you can move it wherever you want to. So maybe this is what the commission is all about—finding words for that cry of Nomonde Calata."

"When the hearing resumed, Tutu started to sing: 'Senzeni na, senzeni na . . . What have we done? What have we done? Our only sin is the color of our skin.' I was at a meeting once where ANC leaders rejected this song because it perpetuates the idea of being a helpless victim. But when it was sung this morning, I cried with such a sense of loss and despair I could hardly breathe . . ."

"Listen how tired and resigned her voice sounds when she goes on with her story." Kondlo presses a button on my tape recorder.

NOMONDE: When I was at home, the reverend from my church visited me. He was there to explain that the bodies of Fort and Matthew were found. Well, we settled. At the time, I had my second child. This child was very close to the father—after hearing this news, the child was sick. I was pregnant at the time . . . I left that child that was inside of me . . . I don't know what happened on that day.

"At first I thought she was saying she had a miscarriage—but she obviously means this in a metaphorical sense. Because she mentions later that all her children were born in a natural way, but that this last one, a son, was a cesarean."

"And when she describes her visit to the doctor, she puts on this brave face again in front of the security police waiting for her there."

NOMONDE: He said to me, "Sister, you have to clean your face, you have to wipe out the tears, you have to be brave"—and I listened. And when they saw me, they saw a very strong person. I saw the doctor and then went home. Mr. Xoliwe is the man we asked as families to go and identify the bodies. He said, "Yes, we've seen the bodies, but I've discovered that the hair was pulled out. His [Fort's] tongue was very long. His fingers were cut off. He had many wounds in his body." When he looked at his trousers, he realized that the dogs had really bitten him very severely—he couldn't believe that the dogs had already had their share . . . Well, the funeral went on . . . I'm sure the chairman of this committee knows exactly the function . . .

Kondlo nods his head. "The funeral of the Cradock Four on 20 July 1985 changed the political landscape of this country forever. It was like a raging fire. ANC and SACP flags were defiantly displayed, buses and buses full of people turned up—a state of emergency was declared. But in a sense it was the real beginning of the end of apartheid."

"Two days after Mrs. Calata—why do I call her this now, when we've talked the whole time about Nomonde? Is it the horror of her testimony that has distanced her from me or do I simply feel humbled? Anyway, after the birth of her child, the security police turned up."

NOMONDE: The leader of those police was Mr. Labuschagne. He said: *"Hau . . . jy't 'n baba, sonner 'n pa . . . wil jy nie hê ons moet die pa wees van die baba nie? Ons kom deursoek die huis."* ["Hau . . . you've got a baby, without a father . . . don't you want us to be the father of the baby? We've come to search the house."] I kept quiet, I didn't give them an answer, but after a few minutes they came back. They said, "We want to evict you out of this house, because you don't have money to pay for your rent and we know for a fact that you don't have money . . . even in Fort's account there is no cent left." I didn't indicate whether I will move out or not. They repeated this. I said to them: "No, I'm not going out of this house, you will have to take your gun and shoot me and take me out of the house." Well, they stood up and left.

We had an inquest at New Brighton. The finding was that the court agrees they were killed, but there is not enough evidence as to who killed them. We stayed at home with no knowledge of what was happening until 1994—then there was a report in the *New Nation* newspaper and the inquest was reopened.

SMITH: Are you referring to the note where instructions were given for your husband to be removed from society—your husband and the other three?

NOMONDE: Yes. "They should be permanently removed from society as a matter of urgency . . ."

SMITH: Was the finding of the inquest that the security forces were responsible for the deaths, but it could not apportion blame either to the army or to the police?

"How could we lose our humanity like that? The word 'apartheid' suddenly sounds like a euphemism!" I battle with my voice.

"Whites," says Kondlo, throwing back the last of his drink with a grimace, "have no *ubuntu* . . . they choke on all their rights, but they have no human compassion. Look at this poor guy Webber who lost his left arm in an APLA attack. Why does he come alone every day? All the black victims are accompanied by their families and people from their communities. And Webber? Is it because he really has no one in the world, or is it because whites do not care about each other?"

Wordless, lost. While Afrikaner surnames like Barnard, Nieuwoudt, Van Zyl, Van Wyk, peel off victims' lips. The question they keep asking: What kind of person, what kind of human being, keeps another's hand in a fruit jar on his desk? What kind of hatred makes animals of people?

It is ordinary people who appear before the Truth Commission. People you meet daily in the street, on the bus and train—people with the signs of poverty and hard work on their bodies and their clothes. In their faces, you can read astonishment, bewilderment, sown by the callousness of the security police and the unfairness of the justice system. "We were treated like garbage: worse even than dogs. Even ants were treated better than us."

And everyone wants to know: Who? Why? Out of the sighing arises more than the need for facts or the longing to get closure on someone's life. The victims ask the hardest of all the questions: How is it possible that the person I loved so much lit no spark of humanity in you?

A mother stumbles onto the fact that her child is dead. She sends one child to go and buy fish. He hears on the street: "They shot your little brother just now."

The abnormality of South African society strikes Commissioner Mary Burton. "In a normal society, if your child is not at home on time, you think he might still be at his friend's. But under apartheid, you go and look at the police station, then at the jails, then at the hospital, and eventually at the morgue."

What gradually becomes clear is that the apartheid system worked like a finely woven net—starting with the Broederbond, who appointed leaders. In turn these leaders appointed ministers, judges, generals. Security forces, courts, administrations, were tangled in. Through Parliament, legislation was launched that would keep the brutal enforcement of apartheid out of sight.

It is striking that no politicians attend the hearings. Is it because they respect the independence of the commission, or do they simply not want to know what price ordinary people paid for the end of apartheid and the new dispensation? Many of those testifying are unemployed and live in squatter camps.

Now that people are able to tell their stories, the lid of the Pandora's box is lifted; for the first time, these individual truths sound unhindered in the ears of all South Africans. The black people in the audience are seldom upset. They have known the truth for years. The whites are often disconcerted: they didn't realize the magnitude of the outrage, the "depth of depravity," as Tutu calls it.

Where does the truth lie? What does it have to do with reconciliation and justice?

"For me, justice lies in the fact that everything is being laid out on the same table," says my colleague Mondli. "The truth that rules our fears, our deeds, and our dreams is coming to light. From now on, you don't only see a smiling black man in front of you, but you also know what I carry inside of me. I've always known it—now you also know."

"And reconciliation?"

"Reconciliation will only be possible when the dignity of black people has been restored and when whites become compassionate. Reconciliation and amnesty I don't find important. That people are able to tell their stories—that's the important thing."

"For me, it's a new beginning," I say. "It is not about skin color, culture, language, but about people. The personal pain puts an end to all stereotypes. Where we connect now has nothing to do with group or color, we connect with our humanity . . ." I keep quiet. Drunk or embarrassed.

"Let us drink to the end of three centuries of fractured morality," says Mondli, and lifts his glass. "Here people are finally breaking through to one another and you and I are experiencing it."

"And maybe this is how we should measure our success—if we manage to formulate a morality based on our common humanity."

Mondli laughs and says: "We're all starting to talk like Tutu."

Time and time again the name crops up: the A-Team of Tumahole, the township at Parys on the banks of the Vaal River. "I only heard there was this thing called the A-Team. They were people against the UDF. They used to drive through the township in their cars—they started this A-Team to work with the police. At night we saw police vans delivering booze to their houses. The A-Team wore their names on their chests, they carried hammers, pangas, and guns to bring death to their own community."

According to witnesses, the activities usually started on a Saturday afternoon. After drinking and taking some drugs, they would target their prey. Torture and killing were never part of their vocabulary; instead they took their victims to what they called "the Open Field"—all in the name of discipline.

David Nhlapo, an ordinary resident of Tumahole, says the A-Team picked him up one evening. They took him from Parys to Sasolburg. "That's where they put a tire on me, poured me with petrol, and they said I should be naked. I undressed myself and they said, 'You are now going to feel the pain the other policemen felt.' They sliced my friend's neck with a spade."

In stories about KwaZulu-Natal, the name of another gang often comes up—the Amabutho. They also had special attire that singled them out—balaclavas and colorful overalls. Their weapons were

knobkerries, spears, and axes, and they worked with Inkatha and the
SADF. Their rituals were steeped in tradition. Before going after their
victims, they drank and splashed on war potions to make themselves
invincible. They also didn't speak of "killing," but used euphemistic
phrases like "to remove obstacles" and "to purify the fields."

A survivor of one of their attacks remembers: "And one of the Am-
abuthos said: 'Let me see who has an ax . . .' and I heard they were
chopping down our door and they were coming inside . . . I don't know
when Kumbolani died because at that stage I was hiding. I wasn't hiding under the bed, because I realized if they find me under the bed, they
will kill me more cruelly, they must kill me standing. So I stood behind
the door and I was hiding, and they got inside, they chopped him . . .
they chopped him in his face with an ax and on his chest . . . they
opened up his chest with an ax."

The Amabutho often removed body parts to brew a concoction with
which to cleanse themselves of the murder. The operational tactics of
both the A-Team and the Amabutho echo some of the Vlakplaas rituals
described by Dirk Coetzee. Men bonding in groups. Drinking, choosing a
victim, arming themselves, and then getting together to make the Big Kill.

Tutu reads an anonymous letter in Afrikaans sent to the commission
during the second week of hearings: *"Dan huil ek vir dit wat gebeur het, al
kan ek niks daaraan verander nie. Dan soek ek in my binneste om te verstaan
hoe is dit moontlik dat niemand eenvoudig geweet het nie, hoe is dit moontlik
dat so min iets daaraan gedoen het, hoe is dit moontlik dat ek ook maar baie
keer net toegekyk het. Dan wonder ek hoe is dit moontlik om met daardie skuld
en skande van die binnekant te lewe . . . ek weet nie wat om te sê nie, ek weet
nie wat om te doen nie, ek vra u hieroor om verskoning—ek is jammer vir al die
pyn en die hartseer. Ek sê dit nie maklik nie. Ek sê dit met 'n hart wat stukkend
is en met trane in my oe . . ."*

("Then I cry over what has happened, even though I cannot change anything. Then I look inside myself to understand how it is possible that
no one knew, how it is possible that so few did something about it, how
it is possible that often I also just looked on. Then I wonder how it is
possible to live with this inner guilt and shame . . . I don't know what
to say, I don't know what to do, I ask you to forgive me for this—I am
sorry about all the pain and the heartache. It isn't easy to say this. I say
it with a heart that is broken and tears in my eyes . . .")

. . .

The texts grow next to one another in the vapor of freshly mown language. Nomonde Calata, Priscilla Zantsi, Isabel Hofmeyr, Nontuthuzelo Mpehlo, Nqabakazi Godolozi, Elaine Scarry, Feziwe Mfeti, Nohle Mohape, Art Spiegelman, Govan Mbeki, Phyllis Maseko, Ariel Dorfman, Lucas Sikwepere, Abdulhay Jassat, Johan Smit, Ms. Mkhize and Ms. Khuzwayo, Marta Cullberg Weston, Cyril Mhlongo, Bheki Mlangeni's mother, Colette Franz, Yehuda Amichai.

Some journalists ask to be deployed elsewhere. Others start to focus on the perpetrators. Some storm out enraged at parties, or see friends fleeing from them. Some drink deep gulps of neat brandy; others calm themselves with neatly rolled *daggazolletjies*. After four months, most of us who travel frequently become ill—lungs and airways. The chairperson has bronchitis; the deputy chairperson, pneumonia. It's the planes, someone says, they are germ incubators. No, it's the constant adapting to different climates and altitudes. We are becoming a family. I board a tiny propeller plane and sit next to one of the interpreters. In the back sits the archbishop with his Anglican bodyguard. While we ascend shakily, I see how Tutu bows his head and prays, and I just know, somehow, we're going to be fine.

I walk into my home one evening. My family are excitedly watching cricket on television. They seem like a happy, close-knit group. I stand in the dark kitchen for a long time. Everything has become unconnected and unfamiliar. I realize that I don't know where the light switch is.

I can talk about nothing but the Truth Commission. Yet I don't talk about it at all.

Until the day in Queenstown. It is bitterly cold. Coated, scarved, we listen to one necklacing[2] experience after another—grim stories, a relentless procession of faces in a monotonous rhythm.

A man testifies about a bomb explosion in his restaurant. He says,

---

[2] "Necklacing" was a form of black-on-black violence that emerged in the mid-1980s. The "necklace" was a gasoline-filled rubber tire, first forced over the victim's head and shoulders, trapping his arms, then set on fire. It has been said before the Truth Commission that the first necklacing—of Maki Skosana—was instigated by third force elements, because there were television cameras on hand that immediately broadcast this terrible brutality around the world.

"The reason why only one person died that day is because of the top-quality tables that we have at the Spur."

And I start to laugh.

"My friend came to me and said: 'Lucas, I wanted to come to you . . .'"

". . . But I couldn't find my legs," I say to myself, and collapse with laughter.

A local journalist puts some tea in front of me and asks tentatively: "Have you been covering the commission for long?"

I take two weeks leave.

We tell stories not to die of life

The man sits alone. He is wearing a cheap jacket. In a formal, old-fashioned Afrikaans, he says he cannot tell the story of how an ANC bomb wiped out his family and friends.

"I can deal with it only in the form of questions. Do you know, you the Truth Commissioners, how a temperature feels of between six and eight thousand degrees? Do you know how it feels to experience a blow so intense that it forces the fillings from your teeth? Do you know how it feels to look for survivors and only find the dead and maimed . . . Do you know how it feels to look for your three-year-old child and never, Mr. Chairman, never to find him again and to keep wondering for the rest of your life where he is?"

Toward the end of the eighties, the Van Eck and De Neyschen families went on holiday on a game farm near Messina on the northern border of South Africa. One afternoon the two families went out in the bakkie to look for game. The back wheel on the right—the exact spot where the three-year-old Van Eck boy was sitting—struck a land mine.

"We were immediately in flames. When I came to myself, I saw my baby boy of eighteen months was still alive . . . he was lying still, but looking at me. Mr. De Neyschen was lying on his steering wheel . . . his hair burning, blood spouting from his forehead."

Van Eck pulled them all through the window, and then he went to look for survivors.

"Right behind the vehicle, I found my wife and Martie de Neyschen. Both severely maimed and killed outright. I searched further. I came upon little Kobus de Neyschen, who had some life in him. I went back to his father and said: 'The child is still alive, but severely maimed and burnt.' His father asked there on the scene to let his child go . . . which is what happened. Then I noticed Mr. De Neyschen's daughter Lizelda walking toward us out of the veld . . . She had a cut across her face and she limped. Then I searched further for my son of three years, but could not find him . . . until today I could not find him . . . I and my son buried our two family members and the next day our two friends. Since then it has been down the hill for me all the way. I sit for days . . . I simply sit . . . I lost my business. I am reduced to a poor white."

The small side-hall accommodates the electronic media. The translation is channeled to our tape recorders. We see Van Eck on the monitor. I write the news copy. I decide on a sound bite. I dictate the hard copy over the phone. I read: ". . . and never comma Mister Chairman comma never to find . . ." A catch in my voice . . . My throat throbs heavily. My breast silts up, speechless.

I give the phone to a colleague and flee blindly among the cables and electronic equipment . . . out onto the veranda overlooking Nelspruit. I gasp for breath. Like two underwater swimmers, my eyes burst out to the horizons . . . the mountains lit in a blushing light-blue hedge of peace. I am drowning. My eyes claw at the trees, the kloofs . . . see, smell . . . the landscape of paradise and a language from paradise: *"Mispel, maroela, tarentaal,"* I whisper. The air is drowsy with jasmine and *kanferfoelie.* I sit down on the steps and everything tears out of me. Flesh and blood can in the end only endure so much . . . Every week we are stretched thinner and thinner over different pitches of grief . . . How many people can one see crying, how much sorrow wrenched loose can one accommodate . . . and how does one get rid of the specific intonation of the words? It stays and stays.

I wake up in unfamiliar beds with blood on my flayed lips . . . and sound bites screaming in my ears.

I receive a call. "They say the story is really powerful . . . Can we possibly send another sound bite? Shall we send the one about the fillings or the one about the daughter coming toward them?"

I wipe my face. "Send the one about how he just sits—and remember to add that the newspapers of the day said pieces of his son's hair and eyes were found in a tree near the bakkie."

My hair is falling out. My teeth are falling out. I have rashes. After the amnesty deadline, I enter my house like a stranger. And barren. I sit around for days. Staring. My youngest walks into a room and starts. "Sorry, I'm not used to you being home."

No poetry should come forth from this. May my hand fall off if I write this.

So I sit around. Naturally and unnaturally without words. Stunned by the knowledge of the price people have paid for their words. If I write this, I exploit and betray. If I don't, I die. Suddenly my grandmother's motto comes to mind: When in despair, bake a cake. To bake a cake is a restorative process.

I snip into a bowl glacé pineapple, watermelon, ginger, green figs, dates, and walnuts. Big red and green cherries, currants, sultanas. I let it stand in a cool, dark cupboard—a bowl full of glistening jewels soaking in brandy. I relish the velvet of twelve eggs, butter, and sugar. I bake a fruit cake and eat small fragrant slices in the blinding blue Cape summer heat.

And I think up delicious lines of lies and revenge.

CHAPTER FOUR

The Narrative of Betrayal Has to
Be Reinvented Every Time

DR. BORAINE: Mr. Snayer, Basil—where did Anton stay before he was killed?

MR. SNAYER: At the house next to mine.

DR. BORAINE: So you at that time—on that night in November 1989, early morning—you didn't really know that he was there?

MR. SNAYER: No, I had no idea.

DR. BORAINE: Okay, thank you. Now you have told us that you heard shots being fired—approximately what time was it when you first heard that?

MR. SNAYER: It must have been between about twelve-thirty and twelve forty-five in the morning. I remember that because I had been out rehearsing with the band I play for. Until about twelve o'clock. I came home, found my wife in the kitchen baking cookies, because that was the day of my eldest daughter's birthday, eleventh birthday. *Ja*, I was terrified and, of course, one immediately reacts to that, and the proximity of the sound immediately made me and my wife fall flat on the kitchen floor and I made my way to the telephone—phoned my neighbor. His response to me was that there could be a shooting—between people either in his backyard or just outside in the street. My wife, while I was in the bedrooms of my children, taking the boys out of the room which was the closest to where I heard the shots, and taking them away from there to a back room where my daughters were—my wife had phoned the Athlone police station and the response from the police station was that she needn't worry, they knew all about what was going on.

And that obviously made me more terrified because of how I began to interpret things from that point onward. I made my own deduction it could be one of two things at that point. It could have been a possible perpetrator of the—or offender of the law, who had been cornered; or it could have been a freedom fighter who had been surrounded by the police. I then went back into the back room where my family was with our housekeeper.

And, of course, they were—they were shivering there . . . my children were at that time thirteen, eleven, and four years of age . . . and crying incessantly and probably wondering when the next shot was going to hit their bedroom door. The shots were just going on and on and on. And I then started crawling around, moving toward the back of the house, where most of the sound was coming from, and I managed to open the back window very, very slowly and slightly, and on peeping through, I saw feet moving about in my backyard, and then with the amount of vision that I had, I could clearly see that my back gate was wide open and I know that it's a practice of mine to lock it.

I then became aware of people walking around in the back street, in and out of the gate, in my backyard past that window, and everybody was armed. Some had taken position on the property opposite my house, opposite the street in the back, also armed and shooting. I then closed the window and proceeded to go to the front of the house, and at that point I—my thought was to evacuate my house for the safety of my family. By this time, it was about possibly three o'clock in the morning. And the shooting hadn't abated. I then went back to the back of the house, opened that same window, and I think it could have been around three o'clock or just before when I saw a Casspir vehicle coming down Denton Road, which is that road at the back.

It's a cul-de-sac, and I suppose with no space to turn, the vehicle that had gone past reversed again out of the street. It must have made a turn, and minutes after that it came back, this time reversing past the window again, and I was watching all of this.

Then at around that time, when the vehicle had gone past again, I then heard it revving up. It speeded up and rammed the wall of Mr. Noordien, my neighbor next door, rammed the wall. About three attempts were made before the wall gave, and the Casspir then parked right opposite, in very, very close proximity to the apartment where—where Anton was apparently living. It was at that time there was an increase in the gunfire and also in the type of sound that I heard. Only to discover afterward, of course, that there were huge holes in the wall, both outer and inner walls, right through the wall.

Soon after this exercise of the Casspir, I went back to the room to report to my wife what was happening. And then I heard the front doorbell ringing and I went to see who was there. A person who identified himself as either Sergeant or Captain Brazelle. He said to me that I should open the door because there is a terrorist in the house next door and they needed to come in. I protested and said my family had been terrorized right through the night already, and that I didn't think it was a wise thing for them to come and use my house as an advantage point from which to fire heavy artillery. They were all very heavily armed. He said to me he didn't need my permission. I then felt quite helpless and frustrated.

I opened the door and he barged in, with about four or five policemen in uniform following him with guns at the ready. They took various positions, two in the kitchen, at the kitchen window opposite the apartment, and two in the bathroom next to the kitchen, also opposite the apartment. I was ordered for my own safety to go into the room where my family was and not to come out. I didn't obey that, I went into the room and kept the door open. And I then saw that the two policemen who were at the kitchen window bashed the kitchen windows out . . . it sounded as if the house was blowing up.

I—I began to feel increasingly compromised by a situation over which I had no control.

I heard voices outside shouting, *"Kom uit, jou vark* [Come out, you pig], today is your last day—today you are going to die." I—I didn't—I really didn't know why this was happening. And every time the voices or voice said, *"Kom uit, jou vark,"* which to my mind meant they were only fighting one person. The shooting didn't—didn't stop.

Then I went into a room adjacent to the back room where I—where I had spent much of my time that morning, and at around seven forty-five that morning, about—*ja,* about quarter to eight, I became aware of a policeman on the roof, lying or crouching, and a hand or arm movement which could have been either trying to catch something that had fallen or throwing something.

Very—I mean almost immediately after that, there was a loud, very, very loud explosion. And then everything just went quiet and minutes after that, I heard someone saying, "You may come out now, it's all over."

No one was allowed into—into that apartment until the police had done what they—whatever they were doing inside and whatever was—or whoever was carried into an ambulance. But when we—when people who were surrounding the place were finally allowed in by Mr. Noordien, we saw the effect of whatever had been—had been shot into the room or whatever explosions occurred.

There were bits of clothing on the floor, against the wall—the walls and ceiling were blood-spattered all—all over. Bits of what I—I can only describe as hair of some sort and flesh were also strewn around and—and smeared or whatever onto the wall.

And that—that ended a—I suppose, an episode in our lives as a family which we will never forget.

But I want to end by saying that I agreed to testify here today not simply because the truth must be told.

I also agreed because of the impressions created by claims that young cadres like Anton and Ashley Kriel, Robbie Waterwitch, Coline Williams, and many, many others were communists or young people misguided by communists. That myth should be exploded once and for all. I believe that a brave soldier died in the service of his country. I also believe that I owe it to the family, who were not given the chance to say good-bye.

(Basil Snayer)

I've been a stranger in my country for a long time. My full name was Mark Henry. In 1991, I changed it to Yassir Henry. Because Mark was the name I could no longer live with—it was much more than religious grounds. Mark was a name that brought me ostracization, that brought me shame and brought me great danger. I am twenty-six years old now . . . I want to recapture my experience at the hand of the state that has scarred me for life and has caused me psychological trauma.

I tell this in order to have some kind of continuing and I hope that by telling it I may wake up from this nightmare that I've lived ever since 16 November 1989.

I became politically active when I was fifteen years old. In 1986, myself, Ashley Forbes, and Peter Jacobs went into exile with the strong belief we would return stronger to protect our people from the brutalities of the state . . . The plan was that they would come back and set up structures and I would follow with expertise. We went to Swaziland, and we formally joined the ANC in Maputo. In Lusaka we were screened, accepted, and sent to Luanda. We were split up—I went to "the East" for military training. After two months, I was taken up in the security structures of the ANC. I was selected to specialize in military engineering. At the age of seventeen, I was sent to the Soviet Union for ten months.

There I specialized in special intelligence and military combat work. During that time, I was appointed military commissar of ten combatants. For me this was a very great honor and responsibility . . . I was thrust from boyhood into a world that demanded constant vigilance, maturity, discipline. I returned to Luanda and was appointed to work with the Soviet person responsible for training cadres in the underground of South Africa who came for short periods of training to Luanda. When the Soviet person left, I was given the full responsibility for his work. End 1988, I was called to Lusaka and informed that I will form part of the technical working group subordinated to Ronnie Kasrils—then head of the Military Political Council. I found that this assignment did not fulfill my objective that I initially went into exile for, namely to receive specialized training and return to the country.

In 1989, together with Anton Fransch, known to me only as Mahomed, I was infiltrated back into SA . . . Contrary to my expectations, there was no clear briefing of what we were supposed to do in Cape Town. Instead we were told that we were to be debriefed. We had to give details of our training—the process that unfolded was extremely confusing, exacerbated by the fact that we were charged to household chores. We were restricted to certain areas of the house only and were openly treated with suspicion. Our personal relations became so strained that there was open hostility. After a month, I decided to leave—I felt there was no longer trust. I felt that my life was at risk. I left and contacted my sister, who helped set me up somewhere else as a student. *[long silence—sighs audibly before continuing]*

One day, purely by chance, I met Mahomed in a shop. We spoke frankly. I conveyed to him my concerns and said that I was prepared to meet them for a discussion. His opinion was that since I left in the manner I did, I did not have the right to meet them on neutral ground and I should go back with him. I truly begged him not to show me where he stays . . . But he coerced me into going with him. Then there he refused to let me go, unless I told him where I stay. Following this, I felt compelled to relocate. I felt particularly vulnerable, as the distrust between me and other comrades had not been dispelled. But I was running out of funds and decided to relocate to my family home for three days while organizing alternative accommodation. But the second day at my parents' home, about three-thirty I heard a commotion at the front door and several security policemen holding my father as a human shield with a gun against his head . . .

Outside they were laughing, shaking hands, and congratulating themselves, saying: *"Die skaap is in die kraal."* ["The sheep is in the pen."] In
my mind, I thought this would be my end. I was taken by car and they
started asking me about my weapons and about Mahomed. They took me
to Grassy Park and then to Culemborg. They interrogated me: weapons
and Mahomed and whether it was Anton Fransch. They showed me photographs of myself, they showed me photographs of Mahomed, they
showed me computer printouts with information about our infiltration
into the country. At one stage, one just walked in and said, *"Wat praat julle
nog met die fokken donner?"* ["Why are you still talking to the fucking bastard?"] And he hit me twice on the chest . . . I kept on saying I had no
weapons, I don't know Mahomed. Then they informed me that my father
was arrested as well. I told them that Mahomed and I had disagreements
and we had broken contact. Liebenberg told me that unless I cooperated
they would kill my mother and nephew, who was only four. At the time,
I didn't see this as an empty threat . . . I was nineteen. I don't think any
nineteen-year-old should be given such a choice . . . I had no choice. I
agreed to tell them on condition that they release my father and leave my
mother alone. I tried to stall for time and pointed it out on a map. They
showed me a very big map. I took a while and then I showed them . . .
[cries] I showed . . . them . . . where he stayed. They took me . . . with a
large . . . contingent of police to the house . . . With the confirmation
that this is the house, many more police came . . . I was then forced onto
the floor of the car with my head between my legs and my hands handcuffed behind my back . . . *[sobs]* I thought that . . . that—that—that they
would arrest Mahomed . . . *[sobs]*, but they entered the premises without
warning . . . I heard gunshots. I could hear that the police were afraid.
They were running up and down, someone shouted that one of them had
been shot. They started shouting at Mahomed to come out. What followed was a fierce exchange of gunfire. I heard a grenade . . . I think it
was then that I knew it was not about arresting him . . . somebody
shouted that they couldn't get in and that he had grenades . . . I heard a
very big explosion, it sounded like a rocket had been launched, and then
. . . *[whispers]* there was silence . . . And they shouted that it was over. In
my head, I heard all the time, and even now—although now I am asking
the same question: Who sold me to the police? Who sold me to the police? . . . *[cries]* Anton died! . . . With that question on his mouth . . . And
I wake up night after night with the same question! *[cries]* No . . . no . . .
Thereafter I was taken back to Culemborg and the questioning continued

. . . the questioning continued . . . with hours of silence in between. They showed me thousands of photographs of people in exile. I was shown an album. All the other albums, they did the paging. But this one they asked me to page and at the fourth or fifth page . . . I saw something that to this day I have nightmares about. The photograph was that of a severed head of someone I personally trained in Luanda. His lips and kidneys were all up alongside his neck. His eyes were open and there was dried blood on his lips. The rest of the album contained photos of his body parts strewn across a street . . .

Where does culpability rest? I believe I cannot be held solely responsible for the death of Anton Fransch. And the role played by the security police must be exposed. *[cries out]* I wish! To be recognized! For who and what I am! So that the falsification of my history can be rectified. I want to know who the person was who informed on *me*. Only then will I be able to reconcile myself with my experience and with the death of Anton *[voice breaks completely]* that the ANC acknowledges their role in my pain! That they restore my military rank. And that the TRC will grant me the possibility to wake up from this nightmare with which I've been living for so many years, so that I too can share in the process of healing taking place in our country.

ARCHBISHOP TUTU: Yassir—there is not much one can say . . . those of us who have not undergone this kind of experience can sometimes be very glib. But what we realize is the incredible cost, the heavy price paid for getting us where we are. Especially by young people like yourself . . . We hope that this moment has lifted some of this heavy burden from you . . .

(Yassir Henry)

CHAPTER FIVE

The Sound of
the Second Narrative

For six months, the Truth Commission has listened to the voices of victims. Focused and clear, the first narrative cut into the country. It cut through class, language, persuasion—penetrating even the most frigid earhole of stone. And it continues. Somewhere, in some dusty community, from week to week, the tale keeps on being plaited.

She is sitting behind a microphone, dressed in beret or *kopdoek* and her Sunday best. Everybody recognizes her. Truth has become Woman. Her voice, distorted behind her rough hand, has undermined Man as the source of truth. And yet. Nobody knows her.

The truth and the illusion of truth as we have never known them.

Yet something is amiss. We prick up our ears. Waiting for the Other. The Counter. The Perpetrator. More and more, we want the second narrative. And it had better be good. It had better be powerful. It had better display integrity. And it had better bring acute personal detail, grief, and bewilderment.

There can be no story without the balance of the antagonist. The ear and the heart simply cannot hold their heads above a one-way flood. In time, the victims' hearings are reported more sketchily, read less avidly, scheduled less frequently. Who would want the truth when the truth has turned its back? Who would wish to confess before commissioners with as little power as themselves?

Now and then, the muffled sound of a perpetrator is heard in a court interdict or press release. At the political submissions in August, no politician rises to the occasion. There is not a single moment of frank personal feeling. When F. W. de Klerk says: "I stand here before you to-day . . ."—he is not even standing, he is sitting down.

After six months or so, at last the second narrative breaks into relief from its background of silence—unfocused, splintered in intention and degrees of desperation. But it is there. And it is white. And male.

The starting point of the human rights hearings was the indefinable wail that burst from Nomonde Calata's lips in East London. The starting point of the perpetrators' narrative is the uncontrollable muscle in Brian Mitchell's jaw. Mitchell is seeking amnesty for his part in the Trust Feed massacre, in which eleven people died. When Judge Andrew Wilson asks him during his amnesty hearing: "Would you say you suffered a lot?" the only answer Mitchell can muster is a frantically quivering jaw muscle.

Two main voices will be heard in one week: the army generals and the police generals.

I phone army headquarters: "May I please interview General Georg Meiring?"

"About what?"

"About his submission, Monday."

"The general speaks to no one. He stands by his submission. He has nothing more to say."

"But I want to know why Meiring is not presenting the submission of the old SADF."

I'm told to get lost in the *ons-is-nog-steeds-baas-al-dink-jy-nie-so-nie* tone. [The we-are-still-the-boss-even-if-you-don't-think-so tone.]

It is Monday morning. The military squad marches into the venue in Cape Town for Operation Shut Up and Deny. And one has actually forgotten how they look: the clipped little mustaches, *snorretjies;* the shifty eyes; the arrogant circumnavigation of questions. When General Deon Mortimer opens his mouth, a chill runs down my spine. I have forgotten the worst: the brutal Afrikaner accent and the unflinching tone. The relish with which he pronounces the words "ban" and "banning," the contemptuous use of the word "terrorist," the cold-blooded smugness of the statistics. The *oordaad,* the excessiveness: "Mozambique: 23 May 1983. Operation SKERWE took place, using twelve Impalas and two Mirage F1 AZs, to attack known ANC facilities in the Matola suburb of Maputo in retaliation for the car bomb detonation outside air force headquarters, Pretoria, on 20 May. Two ANC houses and a headquarter were attacked." No press conference, no interview.

And it is this performance, more than anything else, that changes the tone of the commission. Alex Boraine leans so far forward that only his head and neck are visible above the table as he slashes at their submission before their eyes. The Reverend Khoza Mgojo stammers in anger: "You reel off these statistics as if it's nothing. People, human beings, died there. People whose families we've been listening to for the past six months." The commission seems to be saying: "Before we are through with you, you will see the human faces behind these figures."

That same day in Johannesburg—police general Johan van der Merwe walks in. He might not have much to say, but at least he identifies himself with his underlings, something no powerful person from the old regime has done yet. He also spells out the difference between the politician and the soldier: the one takes the decision; the other carries it out. The better you carry it out, the better soldier you are.

Unexpected overtones accompany the second narrative at the launch of the book *Reconciliation through Truth* by Kader Asmal, Louise Asmal, and Ronald Suresh Roberts.

The book states very precisely: the Truth Commission will not be able to fulfill its implicit mandate to create a new moral order if it does not make a distinction between those who fought against apartheid and those who defended it. This is an old debate, but these writers give it a new dimension. They spell out that, contrary to the claim made by the commissioners, there is no imperative in the legislation not to make any distinction between the perpetrators and the victims of the two sides. It is not a question of bad apples on both sides, says Kader Asmal, it is a question of a bad tree, a weed, on the one hand, and an apple tree on the other. The book asks: If the Truth Commission cannot distinguish between right and wrong, how can it weave a moral fabric?

The night of the launch also provides an opportunity to hear Deputy President Thabo Mbeki's thinking on reconciliation—an issue he seldom dwells on.

"Apartheid forced the individual to abdicate his or her personal morality," he says. "The only thing that will heal this country is large doses of truth . . . and the truth is that apartheid was a form of genocide and a crime against humanity . . ."

It is obvious from the well-formulated speech that the days of visiting Betsie Verwoerd and drinking tea with Afrikaner *tannies* are over. The days of bending over backward to accommodate, of gritting the teeth in tolerance, are over. Reconciliation will be possible only if whites say: "Apartheid was evil and we were responsible for it. Resisting it was justified—even if excesses occurred within this framework." Mbeki says that if this acknowledgment is not forthcoming, reconciliation is no longer on the agenda.

Although this political line is timely, it also freezes the debate in tones of black and white and gives no guidance on how the individual can move forward.

The hearings on human rights violations have forced the Truth Commission to formulate a different position on reconciliation—in a way that takes it out of the color code and makes it available to all South Africans as a future guideline. The human rights of black people were violated by whites, but also by blacks at the instigation of whites. So the Truth Commission was forced to say: South Africa's shameful apartheid past has made *people* lose their humanity. It dehumanized people to such an extent that they treated fellow human beings worse than animals. And this must change for ever.

These contending positions on reconciliation and change vie for supremacy.

While debate flourishes around the question of amnesty for ANC members, some ripples stir the waters of the Wilderness. As the Crocodile flounders, a secretary, Mrs. Hartman, focuses attention on its last remaining teeth: Mr. Botha is deeply religious, she tells a journalist. He knows his Bible. He will speak when the time is right. She also says: Mr. Botha walks around with a big smile on his face. He says people also said bad things about Hitler.

After weeks of pressure, questions, and criticism, the second arm of the Truth Commission at last goes into action. The first amnesty hearing. It takes place in the Bafokeng Civic Centre on the hill overlooking several well-known casinos. The building houses the offices of King Lebone Molotlegi XIV—tribal leader of the Bafokeng-Bakwena, the richest tribe in Africa with a yearly income of R75 million from local platinum mines. However, the money has always been controlled by trustees: first the old regime, then Lucas Mangope, and now the new government. The civic center is decorated with doorknobs in the shape of crocodiles—the genealogical totem of the tribe. Bafokeng-Bakwena means "People of the Dew and the Crocodile."

Early in the morning, a group of people file down the slopes toward the venue. The Amnesty Committee consists of three judges who are not members of the seventeen-person Truth Commission: Judges Hassen Mall, Andrew Wilson, and Bernard Ngoepe. Accompanying them are Commissioners Sisi Khampepe and Chris de Jager. And the judges are difficult. They want nothing to do with the media. They refuse to make statements. They refuse to give interviews. They refuse to hold a press conference. Despite clinging to legal decorum, they don't seem to get going. We all stand around. The chairperson and his deputy Boraine eventually arrive, but the doors remain closed. Now and then, someone storms out, glances back into the hall, grabs some furniture, and drags it back inside.

"What is the problem?" I ask. The problem is the seating arrangements. The judges are used to such matters being resolved by the architecture of a courtroom. Now they have an ordinary hall, and it seems from the human rights hearings that you make a Statement with your seating arrangement. You project a symbolic message. In a nutshell—the site of a seat can influence amnesty!

Now where should the perpetrators sit? On the same raised level as the judges? And the victims? Down among the audience? Most of the perpetrators are still in prison and are guarded by a whole troop of warders. And where should Tutu and Boraine sit? The Amnesty Committee is independent. In no way can its decisions be influenced by the Truth Commission.

A table is moved off the stage. Then the chairs. To the great annoyance of the camera and technical personnel, who rush around setting up their equipment in new positions. Out of pure boredom, we produce a short report for the news, on how the learned judges have the same problem as an uninitiated hostess on a Saturday evening. Who sits where? This tongue-in-cheek story is no sooner broadcast than the judges march sulkily into the hall. In a piqued voice, Judge Mall asks the media to be aware of their responsibility and not to send utter nonsense out into the world. The late start has nothing to do with who is sitting where, but with the demands of Correctional Services. Later we hear that one of the judges' wives is a dedicated radio listener. After the news, she phoned her respectable husband on his cell phone: "Don't make asses of yourselves."

An Afrikaner son from a National Party home. God has given South Africa to the Afrikaner. Willing to die, but also willing to murder, for this land.

It was Dirk Coetzee's dream to become a member of the elite corps, the cream of the crop, the handpicked core of the security forces. When he was eventually assigned to Vlakplaas, the unit was nothing more than a dormitory for askaris being paid R200 (about $35) a month. Coetzee immediately improved the living and working conditions— changed it into a place where the *manne* could relax, a farm for "the guys." Even though the official task description for Vlakplaas was simply to track down and arrest guerrillas, in the eighteen months of Coetzee's stay, there was only one arrest. Nevertheless, and despite spending millions of rands at the taxpayers' expense, the unit was never criticized or accused of wasting money.

The reason is obvious: the unofficial task, namely to train a hit squad that could be called out to take care of activists, was carried out perfectly. The orders were given orally, one to one. No diaries, no written reports. "Amongst ourselves," says Coetzee, "we developed our own body language. The wink of an eye, the nod of a head, could spell someone's end."

Dirk Coetzee has often been accused of stretching stories and fabricating details. Yet it is precisely these details that make it difficult to dismiss his evidence ... because they exude intimate and authentic knowledge. Testifying about the torture of teacher Joe Pillay, Coetzee had Nazi-like scenes unfolding in an underground bunker near Fort Klapperkop in Pretoria. Neither the torture nor the information sought was important, but the experiment preceding the death—*that* was what counted.

"They eventually decided then to bring in an army doctor in a brown uniform with a drip and the so-called truth serum ... they put Pillay on a stretcher and the doctor controlled the drip in his arm. He lost control over his thinking. It made him fall into a kind of relaxed position."

Coetzee describes the layout of the buildings, the high brass, among them Jonas Savimbi, attending discussions. They weren't allowed to drink, he says, because of these important presences.

"The drops have an effect. Four drops for not too big a person . . . and if you give more, it's like administering chloroform . . . more would bring such a deep sleep that one would die. We were all drinking. We gave Kondile his spiked drink. After twenty minutes, he sat down uneasily . . . then he fell over backward. Then Major Nic van Rensburg said: 'Well, chaps, let's get on with the job.' Two of the younger constables with the jeep dragged some dense bushveld wood and tires and made a fire . . . A man, tall and with blond hair, took his Makarov pistol with a silencer and shot him on top of his head. His body gave a short jerk . . ."

Coetzee is an expert on banal statistics.

"The burning of a body on an open fire takes seven hours. Whilst that happened, we were drinking and braaing next to the fire. I tell this not to hurt the family, but to show you the callousness with which we did things in those days. The fleshier parts of the body take longer . . . that's why we frequently had to turn the buttocks and thighs of Kondile . . . by the morning, we raked through the ashes to see that no piece of bone or teeth was left. Then we all went our own ways."

What is there left to say? As part of his amnesty application, this man has handed in his unpublished manuscript on hit squads—copyright reserved.

IMRAM MOOSA (on behalf of Charity Kondile, the mother of Sizwe): You have said you would like to meet Mrs. Kondile and look her in the eye. It is an honor she feels you do *not* deserve. And that if you were really remorseful, you wouldn't apply for amnesty, but in fact stand trial for what you did . . .

COETZEE: I respect Mrs. Kondile's feelings as far as she doesn't want to see me. But I feel that I should not be made an isolated case. I am also entitled to the rights of the laws of the land.

After this showdown, there is a long, uncomfortable silence in the hall. The amnesty panel, the legal representatives, the audience, the Kondile family . . . the only movement is Dirk Coetzee's gulping Adam's apple.

. . .

A journalist enters the media room of the Durban Christian Centre. "Someone, a young boy who speaks English with a heavy Afrikaans accent, put a big black bag down next to me and asked me to keep an eye on it. Do you think I should tell the police?"

"Of course," we urge him. Since Coetzee's amnesty hearing started, security has been clamped tightly around the event. At one point, a death threat was received, and after that there were apparently sharpshooters on the roof. Coetzee himself has a phalanx of bodyguards who precede him into the hall, to check the chair in which he will sit, the toilet he will use.

The journalist calls the police and shows them the black overnight bag against the wall. In a flash, they go into action. The area around the bag is cordoned off. The media room is evacuated—under a drooping awning, we all stand smoking while the bomb squad is called by radio. They arrive with a sniffer dog. Now they need three more bags so that the dog can have a choice. Three of us offer our bags, and they are put next to the black one. The dog starts sniffing, then sits down next to the black bag. There is something in it. Now we are moved to the other side of the building.

Inside the hall, it is David Tshikalange's turn. Tshikalange started out as Coetzee's gardener and ended up as a member of the Vlakplaas hit squad.

Everybody is still busy working out how to open the bag and defuse the bomb, when a side door of the hall opens and one of the cute young translators trips out. Before anyone can move, she picks up the black bag, throws it over her shoulder, and walks off—without even noticing the astonished faces of the bomb squad. She turns out to be the Tsonga translator, specially flown in this morning from Johannesburg to translate for Tshikalange, who has sounded like an imbecile the past three days because of poor translation. Her flight was late and she went straight to the translation booth. In passing, she asked somebody to put her bag in the media room. And why did the dog sit down next to it? There was indeed something suspicious inside it. Bullets. A package of cartridges that she forgot to take out after her last trip to the shooting range.

While Dirk Coetzee tells of how Griffiths Mxenge was stabbed, how the knife was twisted in behind his ribs and couldn't be pulled out, how his throat was cut and his intestines jerked out, his security men sit behind him, half concealed by a curtain. One of them is Klein Dirk. His blond girlfriend is with him today. She is wearing a little black foliage of a dress with thin straps. As Coetzee is relating the details, to gasps of horror from the audience, she is busy lacquering her nails. Her left hand is splayed on Klein Dirk's thigh—he holds the bottle while she applies neat layers of dark polish to her nails.

The Truth Commission starts its work in 1997 with the continuation of the amnesty hearing of Dirk Coetzee, Almond Nofomela, and David Tshikalange in Johannesburg. But the hearing soon settles into a half-hearted pace.

The hearing is supposed to start at ten. At a quarter past ten, the Truth Commission banner is still being hammered into the wooden paneling of the council chamber. At half past ten, the first testimony begins. At eleven, it's tea time. The committee adjourns. We wait. And wait. It's twelve o'clock. At half past twelve, Commissioner Chris de Jager appears in the passage. They've devised a way to shorten the hearings.

"Why didn't you devise it yesterday?" an angry journalist asks.

"How do you foresee dealing with thousands of applications when you've barely managed half an hour this morning?" growls another.

"It's ridiculous!" shouts a third, beside himself. "You refuse to start before ten o'clock in the morning, you adjourn for tea, for lunch, for the demands of nature and the menopause, and, oh boy!—you never work later than four o'clock. You handle the proceedings as if you're in court—but unlike a court, you have a specific time span and *you'll never make it at this pace!*"

All the journalists are edgy. Deadlines are coming up, and not a single line of argument has been sustained, nothing was said, nobody was seen long enough to churn out even a funny kind of story. But more worrying—this seems like a deliberate slide toward general amnesty.

David Tshikalange and Almond Nofomela wanted to buy some diamonds in Lesotho. They asked Coetzee for money (he says). He in turn borrowed R5,000 from his mother-in-law and lent it to them.

"They returned a day later, with five little small diamonds the size of a matchstick, stained, cracked, and one a little bigger—like the nail of my small finger—a yellow one, which I later learned is called 'canary yellow.' To me as a layman, I could see that they were cheated—if one just thinks of your wife's engagement ring. And I send them to return the man's diamonds and bring my money back."

Coetzee ordered Joe Mamasela to go with them. Little did the Lesotho diamond dealer know that the men he took for stupid opportunists were in fact three of South Africa's most ruthless killers. He was lured out of Lesotho, killed in a blue gum plantation near Lindley, and his car taken in exchange for the diamonds. When the three showed up at Coetzee's, he realized that a dead body in a plantation near a platteland town spelled trouble. Coetzee, who was on his way to oversee the murder of lawyer Griffiths Mxenge in Durban, rushed back to Lindley that same night. They put the body in a funeral parlor's body bag and it was later burnt. The car was stripped and sold at the border for the R5,000 Coetzee got from his mother-in-law.

So where's the political motive?

"It would have been disastrous if a sensitive source like Joe Mamasela was uncovered. Secondly if I, or Joe, or Almond, were charged for diamond stealing, it would embarrass the security forces, and Vlakplaas would be exposed."

Vlakplaas had it in for Lindley.

A jolly drinking session. Singing, with their arms out of the windows, five black men in their blue Ford Escort turned onto the national road toward Lindley. Unbeknownst to them, they swerved right in front of the deadly Vlakplaas contingent back from an operation. "They were a danger! They ignored the solid white line," says Coetzee; he tried to force them off the road. They refused and found themselves under fire from the car behind Coetzee's. That was Joe Mamasela emptying his Tokarev pistol, wounding four of them, one seriously. The men then stopped.

"Joe and Almond pulled the people in the vehicle out of the car. Joe, of course, in the normal manner, kicking karate and fisting them down. At the time, a pastor, an Afrikaans *dominee*, stopped with his wife and asked if everything was okay, and I was just worried to get this member of the public out of the way and I said: there's nothing to worry about, everything was under control—I was from the police."

At the time, Mamasela had infiltrated the ANC in Botswana and his links with the security police could not be made known, especially not when he was carrying a weapon of Russian origin. So they picked up all the empty cartridges and Coetzee ordered Nofomela to fire some shots with his own service pistol. They left the wounded there and reported the incident at Lindley.

Then Nofomela refused to take responsibility for Mamasela's wild bout of shooting. However, no problem was really insurmountable at Vlakplaas.

"From security headquarters, Brigadier Jan du Preez, with the consent, I can assure you, of General Johann Coetzee, through the divisional CID [Criminal Investigation Department] officer, Brigadier Van der Merwe in Welkom to the attorney general's office in Bloemfontein—Advocate Tim McNally. They cooked the whole thing."

Coetzee sits back: another episode in the life and lore of Dirk Coetzee.

After the hearing, Mamasela phones a Sesotho-speaking colleague and tells him Coetzee is talking a lot of nonsense. It was Coetzee himself who wanted the diamonds, that's why he borrowed the money from his mother-in-law. When he saw that he had been cheated, he sent Mamasela along to get his money back. According to Mamasela, he, Nofomela, and Tshikalange sat at the Lesotho border for hours. What could they do? They were between the devil and the deep blue sea. The diamond dealer would never return the money, but they couldn't go back to Coetzee with empty hands. Then they decided to pull off the first and best person driving by and take his car, and give that to Coetzee in place of the money. And so they killed the next man who came along: "In his car, we found a milking logbook from a dairy farm; he worked for one of the biggest dairies in Lesotho. We took his car to Coetzee."

My colleague reports this story on the radio. At the end of the broadcast, some people phone from Lesotho: "Thank you, Radio Lesedi, thank you, Mamasela—we've been wondering for years what happened to our father."

It was an ordinary weekday. Japie Maponya went about his work in a building society in Krugersdorp, oblivious of the fact that two Vlakplaas askaris were watching him through the plate glass windows. His sin? His brother, Odirile Maponya, was an ANC guerrilla and had been responsible for the death of a black policeman. When Japie left for home at closing time, he was confronted by two men who said they were investigating a case of fraud against him. He should come with them to a police station. Kidnapped, Japie was taken to Vlakplaas, where he was assaulted by Eugene de Kock.

"De Kock was angry and was shouting and assaulting him," one of the askaris testifies. There are ways to make a man talk. "De Kock wanted a canister of tear gas . . . I think he went to fetch it from the back of his car and we blindfolded him, myself and Johannes Mbelo . . . there was a combi[1] similar to these that sell ice cream that we called the A-Team because it didn't have any windows. We then put him into this combi. De Kock then took this canister of tear gas and sprayed it on his nose and closed his nose and he remained inside coughing in the combi. After a while, he opened up the combi and dragged him out and threw him on the ground. He was not talking at that stage. De Kock asked me if this person would be able to recognize me at a future stage and I said yes. And he told me: 'Do not worry, my china, he won't see you again.' "

Three years after the death of Japie, the very same brother on whose behalf he was tortured to death planted a bomb at the Sterland cinema complex in Pretoria, but something went wrong with the fuse and Odirile Maponya blew himself up.

The family asks the Truth Commission to lead them to the remains of Japie, so that the two brothers can rest in peace.

Nofomela suddenly becomes very talkative, spilling over with details, when he gives evidence about the murder for which he is sent to spend the rest of his life in jail.

In the beginning, Nofomela's problem was a very common one: money. "I could no longer claim traveling expenses at Vlakplaas—but I had a big family, new house, new furniture, and my car was in the garage," says Nofomela. And cars play a crucial role for the *manne* at Vlakplaas. They never just say "car"—it's always: "a light-blue and white Opel Laurel" or "a gray Cortina with a white bonnet."

"Then Johnny Mohane suggested that we steal money from the Lourenses—they have lots and lots of money lying in a bag in the house."

Late that afternoon, when they stalked the house from the back, they found Hendrik Lourens sitting on his veranda. When he saw them, he asked: "What are you kaffirs doing on my farm?"

---

[1] A minibus.

"That annoyed me! The fact that he called me a *kaffer*—especially if I thought about the way I worked at Vlakplaas . . . Because quite often I worked *for* whites who were oppressing blacks and today here a white man is calling me a kaffir. This term that I absolutely resented."

And that, says Nofomela, is his political motive.

The brother of Ace Moema sits motionless as Dirk Coetzee testifies that Ace asked too many intelligent questions about the structures of Vlakplaas. He must be an ANC plant, Vlakplaas operatives believed, because he didn't fit in with the other askaris. "He was a thinker," says Coetzee, "always reserved. A nondrinker. A nonsmoker." Ace was discussed, and Brigadier Schoon told Captain Koos Vermeulen—who hated blacks fanatically, according to Coetzee—to do with Ace "as he saw fit."

After the testimony, Ace Moema's brother addresses the committee and conjures up the haunting image of his mother at home, at this very moment, waiting. Waiting for him and waiting for solace. "My mother . . . is not here today, my father is late. When we left this morning, she said she cannot stand the pain of listening to the proceedings about how gruesome a death her son died . . . 'So,' she said, 'go and listen and reflect on what the proceedings are . . .' Now she is waiting at home, she doesn't know what is happening—she expects us to get back and tell her something . . . I'm not quite sure when I get back home what is it that I tell her to ensure that . . . she finds solace in whatever I say to her . . .

"If being intelligent, being quiet, is a criterion for one to die, then it really brings to light the kind of anarchy that reigned at the time at Vlakplaas. In 1991, at the time of the Harms Commission,[2] I was called to give evidence and I went through this and I'm going through this again. What was clear was . . . the ineptitude, the obvious lack of sensitivity . . . of the pain that one was going through . . . And clearly from the word 'go' the Harms Commission was a farce . . . one would expect much more from the proceedings that are going on here.

"My mother would like to know where her son is. Why was it that he had to die? I am here to express the deepest . . . [*cries . . . drinks some water—sits for a long time with his slender left hand covering his forehead*] . . .

---

[2]Allegations by Dirk Coetzee and others that police "death squads" had assassinated leading dissidents led to nationwide calls for investigation. In 1989, Supreme Court Judge Louis Harms was appointed to head a commission of inquiry. He could find no evidence of death squad or third force activities.

Your Honor . . . I . . . left the country because of the pain I'd gone through. I've lived in exile, I've lived under very harsh conditions, but this is one of the worst moments for me to be sitting here, to try to say how the family feels about what has happened . . . and . . . Can I round off by asking two questions, just two questions, so that my mother at home could sleep in peace?

"Can somebody go to her and say: 'I've committed the murder, I'm sorry'?

"Can somebody take her to say: 'This is where your son is . . .'?"

The attorney general of KwaZulu-Natal, Tim McNally, announces that he is going to arrest Dirk Coetzee and put him on trial for the murder of Griffiths Mxenge.

Of course. It's the season . . .

In the long grass, they walk carefully . . . test the wind, follow the spoor . . . the rifle held reassuringly against the body.

And they are not out for a bit of liver or a slice of biltong. They want one of the Big Five for a trophy on the wall.

Under the thorn tree, things are getting uneasy. Battered rhinos, a one-toothed elephant, scarred buffaloes, and a tiger. Truly—out of sorts, out of habit, out of habitat—tittering on the fringes of their *keelvelle.*

Why would an animal become a hunter? Because justice changes its spots, says the hunter, sighting through his telescope.

In the light of campfires, rumors ferment. A lion rumbles in the dark and everyone gets excited. Will he or won't he appear? Who will be the first to put a bullet in the heart? Who will hang the trophy above his bar counter? What infamous name can become part of our personal hunting statistics? One can virtually hear the hunters closing in on the erstwhile big game.

But of late it seems that the Truth Commissioners themselves are developing a lust for hunting. They threaten here, they subpoena there, but they are amateurs . . . the meat hooks next to the fire remain empty . . . In a dapper Boy Scout group, the amnesty judges are scaring up small game—meticulously recording cases where skunks are camouflaged as antelopes.

Who is going to outwit whom?

Is there no rescue for a threadbare old animal during this hunting season? Yes, says the taxidermist, wander over to the new camp on the other side of the game farm . . . a crocodile is not regarded as one of the Big Five there. What is more: they do not distinguish between the hunter and the hunted.

Behind Coetzee's legal team is a wall of files. Their spines are labeled "Lindley Incident," "Lothar Neethling," "Harms Commission Transcript," etc. The blond ponytail of Coetzee's young advocate lies motionless on his back as he navigates the evidence. He puts sharp and critical questions to Coetzee—to which his client responds with practiced fluency. This is calculated to make the Amnesty Committee assume that the most difficult ground has already been covered. While the advocate speaks, the attorney next to him runs a highly efficient factory line of files, documents, and letters—passed on quietly by an assistant at the slightest nod of the head.

Dirk Coetzee is an industry.

Not so Nofomela. He is defended by a one-man team with a two-file argument. On the third day of the hearings, the press still don't have copies of Nofomela's application. The lawyer sits by himself and seldom asks a question. As a result, Nofomela is subjected to endless cross-examination. When he speaks about anything in which Coetzee is involved, he is vague. When he speaks about the murder for which he is serving a life sentence, he is verbal, exact, and even offers dates and details like "late afternoon" and "by midday."

An unforgettable image: we are busy loading our laptops, notebooks, machines, and cables into an Avis car, when a Mercedes of the latest design glides past us like a swollen foot. The tinted windows slip open and Dirk Coetzee's legal team wave regally at us. Behind them scuttles the clapped-out diesel Mercedes of Almond Nofomela's lawyer.

Dirk Coetzee walked from the darkness into *Vrye Weekblad* ("Free Weekly"), an Afrikaans newspaper with an editorial policy strongly critical and well to the left of the apartheid government. He was not the average Afrikaner, nor was he one of the greatly misled. He was also not a hero. He was just a person who, like the rest of us at that time, didn't necessarily know what was right, but did know what was wrong. And as he was rejected and insulted over the years, as his reactions veered between paranoia and psychopathy, he never weighed on your conscience. Coetzee was just an Afrikaner who, for whatever reason, decided to walk a certain path. And to pay the price for it.

CHAPTER SIX

The Wet Bag and Other Phantoms

"I stand before you—naked and humble. I have decided to stop apologizing for apartheid and to tell the truth. With this I will betray my people and I will betray myself. But I have to tell the truth. I have made peace with God and the time has come to make peace with the people of KwaZulu-Natal. To make peace with myself. It is this audience which haunts me in the back of my head. Maybe among you are those whom I assaulted, whom I left behind for dead in the field."

Constable William Harrington testifies about the Seven-Day War in the area around Pietermaritzburg in the early nineties, when two hundred people died, hundreds of houses were burnt down, and thousands of refugees were left homeless. He admits that he assaulted more than a thousand people during his short service period of two years and eight months in the police force. This works out to more than one person every day.

Harrington was eighteen years old and had been out of the Police Training College for barely a week when he was sent to track down ANC combatants in the dark.

"Richard said I should stick close to him. I was so afraid. We entered an ANC/UDF area. Rick pointed out Dallies—he was fired at by the ANC the previous week. When we descended into a dark valley, whistling started two hundred meters from us—it was echoed into the valley. 'They know we are here,' whispered Rick. I tried to run, but it was difficult—with the *haelgeweer* and belt around my waist, trying to prevent the flares and bullets from falling out of my pocket."

In the darkness, they came across a group of men, down on their knees to keep out of sight, and signaling to one another by making clicking sounds with their tongues. The unit Harrington was in crouched down silently and crept closer, making the same clicking noises. Five meters from them, someone suddenly shouted, *"Amapoyisa!"* ["The police!"] and everybody started to shoot in all directions.

"It was like a movie imprinted on my memory. Flares were fired, people tumbled as they were shot . . . it was like a herd in flight."

After this baptism, Harrington learned quickly. At night, disguised in balaclavas, his unit sowed destruction in ANC areas. They went from home to home, searched for weapons, demanded to see Inkatha Freedom Party membership cards. If the house was without one, it was burnt down. "I fired on any ANC house or group from my vehicle, I distributed weapons to IFP chiefs, I transported Inkatha members and ammunition. It was days of death and blood.

"It was my war, my personal war against the ANC. My superiors told me: 'You act as if you are a little God.' And they were right. I did exactly as I pleased. At the age of twenty, I made my own choices as a constable. I aligned myself with the IFP and up to this day, I never had a lecture, letter, or pamphlet informing me the ANC is no longer a lot of terrorists."

Harrington's hero was Major Deon Terreblanche—notorious for his killing sprees. "He was actually like my father. He was interested in my work. He always wanted to know how I was. He told me I personally have to fight against the ANC, because they were communists. He said he would see to it that I never get into trouble."

But a *kitskonstabel* with ANC sympathies killed Terreblanche.

"I cried constantly. I drank to forget. I grieved for that man. I carried him at his funeral—how could I not have loved that man? But when I look at what he did, then I know I should not have loved him, but when I think of him with my heart, then I know that man was my father . . . that man I loved."

And his mother?

"At that stage, she was dying of cancer."

The camera picks up the thin line flowing from the corner of Harrington's left eye over his cheek. He raises his right hand stiffly and tries to wipe it inconspicuously from his face.

"I grew up in jail. I was just twenty-one when I was sentenced. But my fear now belongs to the past. As I leave this stage here today, I will be a marked man for the rest of my life. I have just betrayed the police motto: One for all and all for one. I will be stigmatized as a traitor because I have named every individual who worked with me—and when you fight like that, the only thing you have is trust. You trust on each other for your life. And I have betrayed them—all of them . . . but I beg you for forgiveness and peace."

When Harrington leaves the stage, he bursts uncontrollably into tears. He is immediately taken to a special room for psychiatric support.

William Harrington was refused amnesty.

Amnesty application of policeman Hendrik Johannes Petrus Botha

"Under the pretext that he had toilet paper in his backpack, Laurie retrieved his backpack with the weapons and black bag from the combi. The five of us walked through the thick bushes to an opening on the Tugela riverbank. Laurie put down his backpack and whilst Laurie, [Mbuso] Shabalala, and Charles [Ndaba] were urinating at the riverbank, Sam and I took the two silenced weapons out of the backpack.

"In the meantime, Laurie had made Charles and Shabalala sit flat on the ground facing the direction of the river. Laurie told them we are taking them to a safe house in northern Natal. Sam and I came from behind and shot them in the back of the head. After they had fallen, we each shot a second time into the body. I shot Charles, and Sam shot Shabalala. Sam and I removed their clothes, while Laurie returned to the vehicle to get concrete poles, hessian, and wire.

"Laurie cut the wire into lengths and Sam rolled Charles and Shabalala separately in hessian after the concrete pole had been placed over their chest and legs. The wire was then tied around their bodies to keep the hessian and poles in position. Laurie and I then threw Charles's body into the river from the bank. I then assisted Sam in doing the same to Shabalala's body. We put the clothes into the black bag. Branches were broken off the trees and the bloodstains wiped away. We spent about an hour making sure that the area was clean and that the bodies had sunk."

Extract from Darren Taylor's radio interview with Lourens du Plessis

What is of utmost importance is to examine the backgrounds in which we grew up. I mean that's where we were molded. I'm not accusing anybody, but people were placed on a pedestal . . . not, I

think, by intent, but it was carried over from the family conversa-
tions . . . What I would have liked to have done is to follow my conscience, because I really did have . . . the knowledge that we were
doing wrong. I could figure it out for myself . . . those who never experience a prick of conscience haven't got a conscience. I would really like to have the courage . . . to live according to my convictions,
because during the seventies, I started feeling uncomfortable about
things. I said on many occasions to my colleagues: "You know, we're
wrong! We're oppressing these people." But this is as far as it went.
I must say that I had a family to feed . . .

   (Du Plessis is a former SADF colonel. His name appears on the
"death signal" calling for the permanent removal from society of the
Cradock Four.)

Extract from Darren Taylor's interview with Gerrie Hugo

An experiment was done to test the strength of motherhood with a
baboon, a female baboon with a baby . . . where it was put in confinement and the floor started heating up, so as to test how strong
motherhood is, to check how far it will go before the baboon drops
the baby . . . and gets on top of the baby to get away from the heat. In
the end, the baboon couldn't take the pain anymore and dropped the
baby and got on top of the baby to get away from the heat. And I feel
this is happening within the rank and file of the security forces . . .
where the baby, being the operative, honestly believes that he will be
protected by the powers that be, but the powers that be, the design-
ers of the system and the planners, are starting to feel the heat and
eventually . . . they drop the baby . . . and the operative must take
that in mind, that that is going to happen to you. And the only way
that you can protect yourself is to come forward now and come clean.

   (Hugo is a former military intelligence operative in Namibia and
South Africa.)

Shame strangles the remembrance of you

It was different before. Victims told their stories to the Truth Commission. In another hall, at another time, in front of another commit-

tee, perpetrators explained their deeds. But the amnesty hearing of police captain Jeffrey Benzien seizes the heart of truth and reconciliation—the victim face to face with the perpetrator—and tears it out into the light.

Never before had the double-edged relationship between the torturer and the tortured been depicted as graphically as it was that week in the small, stuffy hall of the Truth Commission in Cape Town. Initially the body language of the tortured was clear: "No one else counts, not the Amnesty Committee, not the lawyers, not the audience—what counts today is you and me. And we sit opposite each other, just like ten years ago. Except that I am not at your mercy—you are at mine. And I will ask you the questions that have haunted me ever since."

But it isn't that easy.

The first indication of the complexity of the relationship between an infamous torturer and his victim is the voice of Tony Yengeni. As a member of Parliament, Yengeni's voice has become known for its tone of confidence—sometimes tinged with arrogance. When he faces Benzien, this is gone. From where I sit taking notes, I have to get up to make sure that it really is Yengeni speaking. He sounds strangely different—his voice somehow choked. Instead of seizing the moment to get back at Benzien, Yengeni wants to know the man.

". . . What kind of man . . . uhm . . . that uses a method like this one with the wet bag to people . . . to other human beings . . . repeatedly . . . and listening to those moans and cries and groans . . . and taking each of those people very near to their deaths . . . what kind of man are you, what kind of man is that, that can do . . . what kind of human being can do that, Mr. Benzien? . . . I'm talking now about the man behind the wet bag."

At Yengeni's insistence, Benzien demonstrates the wet bag method. "I want to see it with my own eyes." The judges, who have come a long way from meticulously sticking to court procedures, jump up so as not to miss the spectacle. Photographers come running, not believing their luck. And the sight of this bluntly built white man squatting on the back of a black victim, who lies face down on the floor, and pulling a blue bag over his head will remain one of the most loaded and disturbing images in the life of the Truth Commission.

But for this moment, Yengeni has to pay dearly.

Back at the table, Benzien quietly turns on him and with one accurate blow shatters Yengeni's political profile right across the country.

"Do you remember, Mr. Yengeni, that within thirty minutes you betrayed Jennifer Schreiner? Do you remember pointing out Bongani Jonas to us on the highway?"

And Yengeni sits there—as if begging this man to say it all, as if betrayal or cowardice can only make sense to him in the presence of this man.

"A special relationship" is what Benzien says existed between him and Ashley Forbes. Forbes, biting his upper lip, tries to get Benzien to admit to acts that had clearly plunged him into months of hell, driving him to the point of suicide.

> BENZIEN: You I can remember especially because I think that the two of us, after weeks of your confinement, really became quite close . . . I may be mistaken, but I would say relatively good friends in a way . . . I assaulted you that first day . . . but then I took you on a trip . . . and I'm not saying this flippantly . . . you said that it is the most Kentucky Fried Chicken you've ever ate . . . and then we went to the Western Transvaal, where you pointed out arms caches . . . Do you remember the time when you saw snow for the first time . . . what happened in the snow next to the N1 . . . and the trip to Colesberg, how you braaied with me?
>
> FORBES: Is it true that you tortured me every month on the sixteenth as a kind of anniversary of when you arrested me?
>
> BENZIEN: In the spirit of reconciliation, you are making a mistake . . .
>
> FORBES: On the second occasion, I was wrapped in a carpet . . . my clothes were removed and the wet bag method used on me . . . Do you remember that you said you were going to break my nose by putting both your thumbs into my nostrils, ripping them until blood came out of my nose?
>
> BENZIEN: I know you had a nosebleed, but I thought that was as a result of the smack I gave you.

Benzien reminds Forbes that he always brought him fruit on Sundays, and how at great risk he smuggled Westerns—Forbes's favorite reading material—into the cell. The images of snow and fruit blend into the relationship of the protector and the vulnerable—a union in which both could live out fantasy and nightmare. When Forbes mentions anal penetration, Benzien purses his lips disapprovingly: "I deny that, and I'm deeply disappointed that you say that."

All this time, Ashley Forbes's wife is sitting in the row behind her husband's torturer. When Benzien mentions the kind way she greeted him that morning, he is overcome with emotion.

A torturer's success depends on his intimate knowledge of the human psyche. Benzien is a connoisseur. Within the first few minutes, he manages to manipulate most of his victims back into the roles of their previous relationship—where he has the power and they the fragility. He uses several techniques to achieve this during the amnesty hearings. He sits alone, for three days, in the same gray suit and tie. At a press conference afterward, the victims remark how strange it was to see him so alone. He constantly drinks water. He tells how in the past his children had to be escorted by police because he was such a hated man. How they knew about the wet blanket kept in the bath in case of a petrol-bomb attack on the house. Benzien remembers his victims' code names, the exact words they spoke, their unique mannerisms. All of them confirm that he was feared nationally—he could get the information he wanted in less than thirty minutes.

"Cape Town had the same potential as Johannesburg, Pretoria, and Durban for shopping-mall bombs—but I, with respect, Mr. Chairman, did my work well."

Gary Kruser is now a director in the police force, in command of the VIP protection unit. Neatly and professionally, he asks Benzien: "What happened after you arrested me?"

"I didn't arrest you, sir," says Benzien. "Perhaps you confuse me."

Kruser snaps: "*I know you.* It was you!"

But Benzien does not remember.

KRUSER: Is it not true that you and Goosen assaulted me throughout the trip in the combi . . . that you sat on my head . . . after you arrested me outside the bioscope?

BENZIEN: I cannot remember the arrest . . . but if you say we assaulted you in the combi, then I would concede that in all probability we did . . . I don't know how, though . . .

KRUSER: Do you remember when we arrived at Culemborg you hung me up?

BENZIEN: Hung you up! What you refer to as "hanging up"—is that handcuffing you to the burglar-proofing?

KRUSER: Yes . . . so that my feet do not touch the ground, and then hitting me in the stomach . . .

Then Kruser breaks down and the protruding eyes of Benzien look concerned that this man, who is now his boss, is crying. Considering the whole state of affairs—Benzien's expression might be saying—what happened to you does not seem so bad.

But for Kruser it is too much for flesh and feelings: that this experience, which has nearly destroyed his life, made not the slightest imprint on Benzien's memory.

KRUSER: *[in a stern voice]* Did you ever get information out of me?
BENZIEN: *[snappy]* No sir!
KRUSER: Was anybody ever arrested because of me?
BENZIEN: No sir!

Then Kruser sits up straight—the way he was sitting before the hearing started.

Behind Benzien sit the victims of his torture—in a row chained by friendship and betrayal. Yengeni betrayed Jonas; Jonas pointed out people in albums; Peter Jacobs betrayed Forbes; Forbes pointed out caches; Yassir Henry betrayed Anton Fransch. During the tea break, they stand together in the passages with their painful truths of triumph and shame. As everybody is leaving, Benzien grabs the hand of Ashley Forbes tightly in both his own—Forbes smiling shyly under his thin mustache.

SB/TRC/JACOBS

Police captain Jeff Benzien's first torture victim, Peter Jacobs, has accused him of not making a full disclosure to the Amnesty Committee. Jacobs—now a National Crime Intelligence superintendent—says Benzien has only conceded to the truth about his other torture methods following information from his former victims in cross-examination. Antjie Samuel reports:

Benzien has not come out with the whole story, says Peter Jacobs. During cross-examination, Benzien admitted that he had shocked Jacobs with an electric device in the nose, ears, genitals, and rectum. He also described the so-called "watch ruse," when policemen changed the time on their watches to give Jacobs the impression that he had been interrogated until the afternoon. Benzien said that when they told Jacobs they would continue the next day, he volunteered to show where Ashley Forbes was hiding. Jacobs knew Forbes would be gone by the afternoon. Benzien also admitted telling Jacobs: "I'll take you to the verge of death as many times as I want to." (Antjie Samuel, SABC Radio News, Cape Town, transcript of voice report.)

"Beyond the Grape Curtain" by Sandile Dikeni (Cape Times)

> And so continues the torture of Tony Yengeni. Yengeni broke in under thirty minutes, suffocating in a plastic bag which denied him air and burnt his lungs, under the hands of Benzien. In the mind of Benzien, Yengeni, freedom fighter and anti-Apartheid operative, is a weakling, a man that breaks easily . . .
>
> I said I am not gonna write no more columns like this, but the torture of Yengeni continues, with some of us regarding him as a traitor to the cause, a sell-out, a cheat and, in some stupid twist of faith and fate, his torturer becomes the hero, the revealer, the brave man who informed us about it all.
>
> Tony Yengeni in my eyes remains the hero. Yengeni is one of the many people in the ANC executive who stood by the TRC, knowing that certain issues about the ANC would be revealed in the most mocking and degrading way by their torturers. In my eyes, Yengeni of Guguletu is one of the people who still gives me hope amidst the caprice of the present.
>
> And not only Benzien, but many of us, owe him an apology.
>
> And now, as I look at Yengeni, yes, I see blood, his own blood on the hands of Benzien and the Apartheid state. I see blood. The blood of Yengeni's friends and comrades crushed and sucked out of their lungs by the heroes of Apartheid—in under forty minutes, says the torturer, in his clinically precise 'full disclosure'.
>
> I said I am not gonna write no more columns like this.
>
> I made a mistake.

For the first time, the Amnesty Committee calls and cross-examines a psychologist. Ria Kotze, who testifies on the psychological aspects of Captain Jeffrey Benzien's personality, has been counseling Benzien since 1994, when he had a nervous breakdown. Initially Kotze was treating Benzien's wife for depression, but she was called in to treat him too after an attack she describes as an auditory hallucination.

I go to speak to her after her submission. What does "auditory hallucination" mean?

"It means he heard voices, but more I cannot tell you. This was the only thing that Benzien asked me *not* to talk about."

"Now why was that?"

"It's the only thing he has left—this little incident—and it is his pride that he has kept it to himself."

When Benzien comes out for a smoke break, I ask him about the term.

"I can't tell you, except that I thought I was going out of my mind." He smokes shakily.

"But is it accusing voices, new voices, familiar ones . . . ?"

He walks off: "Leave me . . . God, just leave me alone."

The clearest description of what Benzien was experiencing comes from Kotze's testimony. She says Benzien was sitting on his veranda one evening, smoking a cigarette, and then he had a flashback—so intense and real that he burst into tears. His wife called Kotze and told her that when she asked Benzien what was wrong, he kept on saying: "I cannot tell you—I'm too ashamed." Kotze says Benzien suffers from a severe form of self-loathing.

The Amnesty Committee uses the opportunity of Kotze's appearance to explore the issue of memory loss. Several perpetrators claim not to remember certain things and the committee obviously is not sure whether people are genuinely traumatized or whether they are deliberately hiding information and so do not fulfill the amnesty requirement of full disclosure.

The first issue raised by the victims' advocate is the textbook definition of posttraumatic stress: it can be experienced only by a victim. And the fundamental characteristic of the victim is a feeling of helplessness, intense fear, and powerlessness. Surely Benzien cannot be classified as a victim?

(If this definition is accurate, why do the commissioners, the briefers, the statement-takers, the journalists, all get psychological treatment?)

Benzien was a victim of his inhumane working conditions, Kotze says. He was a good cop at Murder and Robbery. But he was so good that he was moved to Security, where he had to create these torture methods to fulfill the expectations about him. This destroyed his whole sense of self.

The Amnesty Committee wants to know how Benzien can say one minute that he does not remember and insist the next minute that something did *not* happen. Is it possible to forget and be quite sure at the same time?

All of this centers on what Advocate Robin Brink describes as "the nasty broomstick episode." Famous western Cape MK[1] member Nicla Pedro was caught on his way to Lesotho, where he was supposed to meet with MK cadres. Their names were in a letter that he was to open only after he had crossed the border. When he was caught, he told the security police he had swallowed the letter—"I lied," says Pedro. Benzien then took him to a separate room, spread a newspaper, and ordered him to defecate. Then the nationally famous torturer put on surgical gloves and worked through whatever was on the newspaper. When nothing was found, he pushed his finger up Pedro's anus. Then he took a broomstick and told Pedro: "I'll find the letter, even if I go up to your stomach."

Pedro, just released from an institution for alcoholics, testifies in tears before the Amnesty Committee. Benzien emphatically denies that he ever used a broomstick. He looks quite shocked when the claim is made. He denies it, over and over.

To reconstruct your memory, to beautify it, is an ordinary human trait, says the psychologist. Most people do it. But there are probably three kinds of memory loss. The first is voluntary—you change your memory because you are under threat, because you cannot bear to live with the reality. The second is involuntary—something is so traumatic that it rips a hole in your memory, and you cannot remember the incident or what happened just before and after it. But there is also a third kind of memory loss and that occurs when you testify in public. Kotze says Benzien's stress levels were so compounded by having to testify and his anxiety about how this might affect the last bits of life he has with his wife and children that it is quite possible he remembered even less than usual.

How to distinguish between lies and memory loss?

Slowly, as if speaking to herself: "In my job, there are, in a sense, no lies—all of it ties in, reacts to, plays upon, the truth . . ."

---

[1] Shorthand for *Umkhonto we Sizwe*, the military branch of the African National Congress.

CHAPTER SEVEN

Two Women: Let Us Hear
It in Another Language

The previous day, it was Christmas. We saw these people with white scarves, the *witdoeke,* and other people who were blowing whistles.

When I came home, I saw there were many white men, they kicked my door, they kicked it and they went in. I am sure I nearly died that day. They missed when they shot—they missed me on my forehead. Another soldier approached—the soldier was sitting on top of the car and he was pointing at me. He started shooting at me while I was trying to open the door. Now these bullets looked like pellets and they were black. Then I went in next door and I tried to wonder how did my children survive.

During that time, Mr. Ndamana couldn't run away, he was too old. He threw a stone on the house, then he cried, "Oh! How can they kill Jackson like that!" After they killed my husband Jackson, they threw him in the garden. These people with white scarves came into the house.

Now these men came in and one of the women knelt down to pray. Some of the houses were on fire. There were white men all over and they were shooting. We heard them, that they were going into the toilet—my God, help me!—and I closed the door. I heard bullets going into the toilet, somebody hit my door, one of the children said, "Mama, let's leave, let's go out, my father is coming, he's calling us."

Apparently that was the last time he spoke. The white-scarf people axed him, houses were on fire, there was just fire all over. There were bullets flying all over, I don't know what was going on there. Around four P.M. I thought we were all dead already, it was just dark and there was smoke. Apparently now they were leaving, around four. We were tramping over dead bodies, there were lots of them. Some of these children were put on fire. When they put me in the van, this van was already full of people. I was taken to Tygerberg.

My fifteen-year-old son, Bonisile, ran away with his sisters. When they arrived, they found out that their father was already dead. They cried. Some of the men who survived that day came to my house, now these men picked up my husband. He was—he was put on top of his own son . . . This child, who was also full of blood, kept on asking—"Daddy, can you see me, can you see me? Daddy, can you see me?" Now I heard when they got there at Conradie Hospital, when they were in this passage on their way to Conradie, he died.

. . . These bullets in me feel like steel thorns . . .

The undertaker took us to his mortuary. I saw him, I was with my elder daughter. When we got there, his eyes were hanging, we could see that there were dots, black dots all over his body. And we could see now the big gash on his head, the gash caused by the ax.

I am still sick . . . my feet were rotten and my hands were all rotten, I have holes, I can't sleep well.

Sometimes when I try to sleep, it feels like something is evaporating from my head until I take these pills, then I get better. All this is caused by these bullets that I have in my body.

My son Bonisile, who was smeared with his father's blood on him, was never well again after that, he was psychologically disturbed.

MS. GOBODO-MADIKIZELA: He passed Standard Six with symbol A, symbol B, and C . . . I can't see this clearly, but from this certificate it looks like he has sixty, seventy, and eighty percent. It looks like before he saw this horrible sight of his father, he was a good son. Thank you, Mama, I am going to let you go now.

(Elsie Gishi)

It was our Christmas party . . . I suddenly became aware of something that sounded like firecrackers. I saw Rhoda Macdonald throw back her arms and die, and Ian did exactly the same thing. I swung around to look at the door to see what was happening and I saw a man there with a balaclava on his head—but not over his head—with an AK-47, and my immediate reaction was, "Oh my goodness, this is a terrorist attack!" After that I blacked out and I don't remember anything else until I was on the helicopter being flown to Bloemfontein, when I was aware of somebody telling me, "You've been in a terrorist attack and we are taking you to an [intensive care unit]."

The next moment I became conscious was actually in ICU, I was aware of my family and friends around me. And the most terrific experience to me in the intensive unit was the fact that every evening as dusk fell this man would appear at the window. I initially thought it was a security guard. I couldn't communicate with my family except through writing, because obviously I had tubes everywhere, and I just used to write to them: "Please tell them to take the man away from the window." [Tape ends.]

Eventually my eldest daughter was very clever and after about two weeks . . . my daughter brought a photograph of one of the suspects . . . and it was . . . this face at the window . . . and this was the gentleman at the door with the AK-47 . . . So that actually was a tremendous healing thing for me, because suddenly I'd found him and I knew who that hallucination was at ICU.

I spent a month in ICU. It was quite traumatic, I had to learn to walk again. I came home. My children were unbelievable, they used to fight over who was to bathe me, who was to dress me, who was to feed me. I don't know whether I could ever have made it without them. I had open-heart surgery—I had a hole in the aorta and I actually stopped breathing. And I also had half my large intestines removed. I've got really very ugly scarring up the middle and I have a damaged thumb from the shrapnel. I've still got shrapnel in my body, but all it means is that the bells ring when I go through the airport, and that makes life exciting. And I have an injury on the knee. But all in all, what I must say is, through the trauma of it all, I honestly feel richer. I think it's been a really enriching experience for me and a growing curve, and I think it's given me the ability to relate to other people who maybe go through trauma.

But while I was in hospital I was really quite touched that members of the ANC did come to visit me, just popped in to see how I was doing. I thought that was very touching, and of course Bloemfontein, and really the whole world, sent out messages, and in fact I was quite spoiled.

(Beth Savage, testifying on the King William's Town Golf Club attack)

CHAPTER EIGHT

Guilt Is on the Move
with All Her Mantles

It is a quarter to six. Monday in the first week of March. The Amnesty Committee has already adjourned. In a deserted part of Pretoria's Munitoria Building, only the radio team is still working. I have a report to file, but my mind is working overtime: What is a narrative? Two versions of the murder of policeman Richard Mutase and his wife in November 1987 were put before the committee today by the amnesty applicants. Roland Barthes said: "Narrative does not show, does not intimate . . . [Its] function is not to represent, it is to constitute a spectacle." Does this mean that the narratives about the Mutase killings are not true but simply spectacles for an occasion? And the occasion happens to be amnesty?

I transcribe Captain Jacques Hechter's version:

> We got out a distance from the house. We were wearing dark clothes and balaclavas. Mamasela's wasn't over his face, just rolled down low. He knocked on the Mutases' door and asked if he [Richard] was in. We were standing around the corner and listening. When Mamasela told us that Richard's wife was expecting him, we decided to wait for him inside. Mamasela knocked on the door again. When the woman opened the door, Mamasela pushed her with a gun to a back room, where he had to keep her from seeing us. We switched off the lights, but left the television on so that it seemed that someone was there. We then hid behind the couch. Then a vehicle arrived: his Mazda. He came to the door and found it locked. He was struggling with the lock when we jerked him in-

side. He immediately realized there was trouble. He struggled violently—he fought like a tiger and he shouted wildly. To bring him under control, I started to strangle him—

I switch the tape recorder off—will I ever again hear the word said like that, with such apparent relish? Through clenched teeth, Hechter says: *"Ek het hom gewurg . . ."* but the "r" is rolled half a second longer than usual and the dry, scraping "g" catches in his throat.

—and Van Vuuren smothered him with a pillow over his face. He then fired four shots with his AK-47—the pillow was a silencer. Loots was also present and he accidentally hit me with the stock of his AK-47 against the arm. Then we called Mamasela: "Come on! We're finished." Just as we were walking out, we heard a shot from inside the house. When Mamasela joined us, we asked what the shooting was about. He told us that he killed the woman because she saw his face. It was also only afterward that we learned that there was a child in the house.

Angie, with earphones on and eyes closed, is editing sound bites. Somewhere something rings like a doorbell, but since we're visitors, we ignore it. Suddenly she pulls off her earphones and crinkles her nose: "Something is burning. When my eyes are closed, my sense of smell is very good."

I leave the media room, go down the passage, winking as I pass one of my ancestors in a portrait: Magistrate Krog—thick, hairy-necked, and framed in golden tresses against the wall. And then I see it: a heavy stream of smoke billowing around the corner down the passage. I run back. "There's a fire burning at the end of the corridor!" Angie calmly carries on working. I run to the lift to go and warn security that something is burning. As the doors close, the often-repeated warning against using the lift during a fire strikes me. Too late. The lift is already descending. I break into a sweat. I have never been afraid of anything, but always stupid, stupid, stupid! "The SABC's inimitable Crispy Krog!" one of my colleagues jokes later. When the doors finally open on the ground floor, the air is thick with white smoke.

"Get out, you stupid bloody woman—the whole place is burning!" screams one of the guards as he yanks me out of the lift.

"But my colleague is still working up there on the third floor." I cough and make for the stairs.

"The fire brigade will save them . . ." but we both shoot up the staircase.

Upstairs—what do we take, what do we leave behind? Certain that the fire will soon be under control, we leave behind our laptops, the tape recorders, notebooks, a new packet of cigarettes. We take our bags and cell phones. Outside the sirens blare. We see smoke in a wide range of whites, grays, and blacks, but no flames.

On the pavement, I take from my bag an Afrikaans novel that contains a fictionalized account of the Mutase murders. The writer John Miles based his novel *Kroniek uit die doofpot* on documentation that was given to him by Mutase's lawyer.

I read John Miles's version:

(At the front door he walked straight into the trap. The next morning the packets of take-away food still lay on the ground next to his half-open car door.)

He shut the front door behind him. The light switch did nothing but click. The mains, he thought—I have to get to the back of the settee, to the pistol I hid there.

But he fell over the settee as his head snapped to the left: it was the first glancing blow. Someone caught him round the shoulders, someone around the thighs. Fiercely they fought. He kicked out and knew he'd found a mark. He bit the fingers over his mouth . . . My eye! he thought desperately, as something sank deep into it . . . he was finished. There were too many of them. They fell. My eye! The same side as my dead ear. God, they're turning me into a half-person.

Had he heard . . . a laugh? The reek of stale sweat, he thought. How well he knew it! The smell of stale human sweat soaked into a uniform. Uniform sweat. You never forgot it.

'He was in the kitchen, in front of the new stove. He was pitch-black in the face; I'd never seen him so black and his face—what was left of his face—a huge hole in the back of his head on the sticky floor. They used a pillow as a silencer . . . pushed the pillow against his

head, shot through it, the place was full of feathers. And what a
mess! It looked as if a tornado had gone through the house: everything lying broken, the TV beyond repair, the kitchen cupboards
and chairs—everything except the new stove.'

Miles also offers the *Sowetan*'s version:

A former Bophuthatswana policeman and his nursing-sister wife
were shot dead in their home in Temba township, near Hamman-
skraal on Monday night . . . Their six-year-old son, Tshidiso [. . .]
who was unhurt, was left crying alone the whole night in the house,
apparently because he did not know what to do with the bodies . . .
Neighbors said they heard shots fired at night but they did not take
any notice. After the shooting three men were seen leaving the
scene in a blue combi.

I use a cell phone to call the current affairs programs from the pavement: "We are busy with a package for tomorrow on the murders of
Richard and Irene Mutase."

"Please brief us: Who are they?"

"Mutase was assaulted by a white superior—so badly that his
eardrum burst. He put in claims against this man as well as the minister of law and order, and shortly after that, he and his wife were murdered. Maybe you should line up the writer John Miles for tomorrow.
He wrote a book about the episode. He saw in Mutase's story a model
of the ordinary man's quest for justice in the apartheid era."

"What time will we get the package?"

"At the moment, we're sitting on the pavement in front of the Munitoria Building. We've been evacuated because there's a fire somewhere."

"Take a smoke break," laughs the producer. "And maybe mention the
fire in your last paragraph."

But the fire becomes much more than a postscript. Within an hour,
the area around Munitoria has been transformed into one of the biggest
fire-fighting actions in the history of Pretoria. And as the fire grows
from smoky to fiery, leaping from floor to floor, we report it blow by
blow to the news programs on our cell phones.

I phone the Amnesty Committee's Leader of Evidence: "The building in which the five policemen are appearing is on fire."

Silence on the other end of the line. "Come again?"
I repeat myself. "Can't you hear the sirens?"
He starts laughing hysterically.

Hechter and Van Vuuren each told their own story today. And their stories became part of a whole circuit of narratives: township stories, literature, Truth Commission testimonies, newspaper reports . . . The
murder was the clay. The political climate, the amnesty conditions, the
presence of Tshidiso Mutase and his grandmother, the lawyers—all of
these were the hands forming the clay. So there are actually two stories:
the story and the understory, the matrix, the propelling force determining what is left out, what is used, how it is used. And at the heart
of this force are the amnesty conditions. Today they gave rise to long
descriptions of who gave the orders—to create a context for political
motivation. And then the gory finer details of the murders—to create
the impression of full disclosure.

Certainly, the narrators walked a fine line between providing enough
detail to impress the legal teams and avoiding the more gruesome details for the sake of the Mutase family. Whereas Irene Mutase's mother
graphically described how something white protruded from Mutase's
ear after he was killed, and fixed her eyes on Van Vuuren and Hechter.

But there is also the invisible audience—the imagined audience on
the horizon somewhere—the narrator's family, colleagues, the new
government. And every listener decodes the story in terms of truth.
Telling is therefore never neutral, and the selection and ordering try to
determine the interpretation.

Truckloads of firemen are brought in. They file past us in their heavy
protective clothing—most of them can barely be twenty. From the outside, it doesn't look as if the fire has reached the media room, with its
expensive translating, sound, and television equipment.

Angie and I are called aside. National Intelligence is here. They have
orders to save the Amnesty Committee's documents. They have been
told that we are from the commission—do we know where the documents are? We look at each other guiltily. One evening when we were
working late, I went looking for some tea or coffee to plunder. The first
open room was the amnesty judges'—and, yes, a case of documents. I
sifted through them. Against the wall was a row of cabinets. In some of

them, there were stacks of confidential amnesty applications, but in one I found tea, coffee, and delicious cookies dipped in white chocolate.

"We're from radio, not from the Truth Commission," we mumble. "But the documents are on the third floor, the third room on the right down the passage, in the second, third, and fourth cabinets from the door."

This is Paul van Vuuren's version:

> There was a big noise, he was screaming terribly. And . . . me and Captain Hechter . . . *[sighs]* worked together without talking. Each knew what he had to do . . .
>
> I can just explain to you that at that stage in the operation . . . time is a factor and one only acts without thinking . . . On that specific night, we were not discussing whether the woman would see Mamasela. We did not take it into consideration, which was a mistake on our part, we should have considered it. But I knew that Captain Hechter's wife was divorcing him at the time and we did not put pressure on each other.
>
> After we fought with Richard Mutase and Captain Hechter put the pillow over his head, and I fired four shots with an AK-47, Captain Loots and Captain Hechter went out the door . . . and I can't remember if Captain Hechter told me to go and call Mamasela. I went to the room . . . if I remember correctly, the woman's head was under the blanket, or the sheet, but her head was covered. I told Mamasela: "You must come, we are finished"—and then I turned around and ran out. Heard shots. When I got outside, Mamasela was next to me. I said, "What did you do?" He told me that he shot the woman also because she saw his face. I just want to mention that at the time it was not strange that people would recognize Mamasela. Because Mamasela and I were reasonably big friends and he told me that he was going to get plastic surgery at the state's expense. He often spoke to me about his personal stuff. So as far as I'm concerned, Mamasela's face was to be changed later.

We file this report: "The fire in the municipal building, which broke out late yesterday afternoon, is still smoldering. But the hall in which the hearings of five former security policemen took place was apparently not touched by the blaze. National Intelligence personnel are still on the scene to ensure that the amnesty premises are sealed off. They were sent yesterday evening to retrieve sensitive and important documents. At this stage, it is not clear whether equipment belonging to the SABC or the Truth Commission was damaged by the blaze. But the fire department says that everything will be soaked with water and soot."

And this one: "Grocery trolleys full of documents of the Amnesty Committee are currently being pushed out of the damaged wing of the Pretoria Municipal Building. The documents, among which are court records, are either wet or scorched at the edges. Other documentation of specific cases—such as that of the KwaNdebele minister Piet Ntuli—has been drenched. Truth Commission personnel are standing around dismayed while an alternative location is being organized. Technical personnel say that the translating equipment will not be dry in time to continue the hearings today."

Our computers are warped from the heat and caked with soot. Our tape recorders are still working. The packet of wine-gums must have burst open because the table is covered with colorful blobs. Our bags smell of smoke.

"So does mine," says Judge Hassen Mall the next day. "It's almost a souvenir."

The smell lingers for months afterward.

In an interview some months after the fire, Joe Mamasela gave his version of the Mutase murders in an unbroken stream of words:

"I was talking to her [Irene Mutase—in the back room of her home] to lie to her that her husband was involved in robberies and stuff like that and I asked, didn't he bring in any money, and generally she was quite concerned that, no, the man did not bring any money, at the back of my mind you know I felt pity . . . I did not know what I can do to help her . . . and then all of a sudden, Hechter came in, and when they were fighting with her husband, she got concerned, she was calm all the time because I tried as much as possible to keep her calm, but during the struggle, myself I was disturbed, I was perturbed, and she was uncontrollably agitated, and Hechter came in and said: '*Jy staan en gaap, hoekom maak jy nie die vrou dood?*' ['You're standing there gaping, why don't you kill the woman?']

Then he took my revolver and *he* ordered her to get into the bed and he shot her about four times in the direction of her head, I could see the body, the blood . . ."

"And the child?"

"No, the child was in the other room. He was sleeping. *Then* he gave me the gun and said: *'Nou gaan maak die kind . . . gaan skiet daai kind.'* ['Now go and kill . . . go and shoot that child.'] So I took the gun and I opened the door where he was sleeping and I saw this innocent little thing, and his face mirrored the face of my own child . . . I just couldn't do it."

"So he slept through all the noise, all the bullets?"

"No, he slept through the noise . . . I had a gun in my hand, I could have killed the boy in cold blood. It was killing my own child . . . I then fired two shots in the direction of the bedroom, where the wife lay, then I closed the door. Then Hechter said to me, 'You did not shoot, I did not hear any shots.' I said, 'No, I shot.' He said, 'Bring the weapon here.' And he took the gun and opened it and I was glad that I managed to shoot at random, otherwise I would be killed for defying an order. So in a way, I believe I'm happy that I didn't kill the child whilst that thing was going to haunt me for the rest of my life. I don't think I would have retained my sanity the way I've retained it."

The stories stay with me. How they correspond. How they differ. The stylistic traits of the oral narrative. The story does not turn around a single climax. Rather, it collects smaller episodes: the murder is just as important as the arrival at the house; the strategy inside the house equals what happened thereafter.

And the iconic images: Hechter sketching the dark house with the flickering TV. Van Vuuren describing the struggle, the choking, and the shooting, without a word passing between the antagonists; adding a sensitive touch: "I knew his wife was divorcing him . . . I didn't put extra pressure." Miles, the writer, uses the take-away food abandoned next to the car and the feathers of the pillow sifting down like dust everywhere in the house after the shooting. Mamasela talking about the sleeping child. The stories often make use of direct speech, seldom have more than two characters per scene, and quickly switch from one episode to the next.

Every narrative carries the imprint of its narrator. Hechter draws pleasure from detail. He articulates crisply and rasps particular sounds. He also describes fighting like a tiger, struggling with the lock, Loots accidentally hitting him with the gun. By comparison Paul van Vuuren's tone is almost casual. His pronunciation has the bluntness of a working-class background hidden behind a careless, arrogant tone of voice. He insists on using proper titles, and stumbles when constructing long sentences. He also says: "after we 'fought' with Richard Mutase"—as if there was something equal about the contest. But in his story, he also presents himself as a friend—to Hechter and Mamasela. Mamasela's flow is a hasty stream full of well-worn clichés. But he portrays himself as a sensitive person: disturbed . . . no—*perturbed*—by death.

Oral narratives, the academics say, are driven by remembered core phrases and images that carry the distillation of the entire story. From these cores, the action, the characters, the conclusion, all unfold. And though the narratives may differ in the information they bear, the core elements stay the same. They overlap.

One such core moment is that of confrontation. Hechter, Van Vuuren, and Miles all focus on the moment Mutase entered the house. And they all use the kernel image of the pillow—initially it's a cushion from the couch. Hechter says that Van Vuuren used the pillow first to smother Mutase and then to silence the shots. Van Vuuren says Captain Hechter put the pillow over Mutase's head. In Miles's book, a family member tells of how a bedroom pillow was used and feathers, blood, and destruction were strewn all through the house. Mamasela tells of how Hechter shot holes in the blanket in an attempt to kill the woman. In all the stories, a landscape is created where the powerful are struggling with the powerless, the armed with the defenseless, and the landscape is filled with misunderstanding.

It's worth noting where the stories differ—on the question of accountability. No one will admit to killing Irene Mutase, because no political reason could possibly exist why an ordinary nurse had to be killed. According to Hechter, they called Mamasela, walked out of the house, and then heard the shooting. According to Van Vuuren, he went to the back room to call Mamasela. When he got outside, Mamasela was next to him telling him that he had to shoot her. Mamasela says Hechter and not Van Vuuren was with him, and Hechter shot Irene Mutase. Does the bond of friendship that Van Vuuren speaks of still exist between him and Mamasela?

"Hang on a second," a disparaging voice pipes up in my head. "What's the point of all this 'textual reading'? You're just neutralizing the story of the death of Richard and Irene Mutase. You're wrenching the heart out of the horror. You can live comfortably with the details, once they've acquired no more than academic relevance."

But I argue back. "The things revealed by such a reading aren't academic at all. What's 'academic' about the attempt by everyone involved to avoid responsibility?"

"Take this thing about the pillow, then. 'Here's the motif, class.' It's a literary trick."

"But doesn't it bring something important to the surface? The image of the Mutases, butchered under soft pillows and fluffy blankets, says so much about the brutality of the crime. And at the same time, it explodes a whole series of clichés—like the white fear of being killed in your bed, or the idea of living with your head in the clouds—under a sweetly scented pillow."

While a building is being destroyed in front of me by a beautiful, all-consuming fire—I argue with myself, I compare versions of truth.

Out of this must now be taken: The Truth?

It must be so.

The truth is validated by the majority, they say. Or you bring your own version of the truth to the merciless arena of the past—only in this way does the past become thinkable, the world become habitable.

And if you believe your own version, your own lie, how can it be said that you are being misleading? To what extent can you bring yourself not to know what you know? Eventually it is not the lie that matters, but that mechanism in yourself that allows you to accept distortions.

Either Hechter or Mamasela killed Irene Mutase. The truth does not lie in between. There cannot be a compromise between the two versions.

Is the truth known only to the dead?

Between the bodies, the child Tshidiso remains. Which truth does he inherit? It is for him that the truth must be found.

And so, if the truth is to be believed in this country, it must perhaps be written by those who bear the consequences of the past.

It is asking too much that everyone should believe the Truth Commission's version of the truth. Or that people should be set free by this truth, should be healed and reconciled. But perhaps these narratives alone are enough to justify the existence of the Truth Commission. Because of these narratives, people no longer can indulge in their separate dynasties of denial.

> We cannot Judge our homeland. The sword of justice
> will stick fast in our personal disgrace.
> —JOSEPH BRODSKY

> The reason I know I am NOT insane
> is because, unlike my brother,
> I feel guilt.
> The insane do not feel guilt.
> —FRANK BIDART

It's them! It's truly them . . . I go cold with recognition. That specific salacious laughter, that brotherly slap on the hairy shoulder, that guffawing circle using a crude yet idiomatic Afrikaans. The *manne*. More specifically: the Afrikaner *manne*. Those who call their sons *"pa se ou rammetjie,"* or *"my ou bul"* ("Dad's little ram" or "my old bull").

The nightmare of my youth.

The bullies with their wives—the chatty women with impressive cleavages and well-behaved children. The mustached men who, for decades, turned life on the platteland into a spiraling inferno of destruction, brutalization, and fear. The third force. *Ingal'enoboya.*

They stand in a group, the five: Cronje, Van Vuuren, Hechter, Venter, Mentz. The journalists, lawyers, victims, visitors, walking into the foyer of the amnesty venue in Pretoria give them a wide berth. We all know: they were the doers. Killing, for them, was not dressed in the official pastels of "eliminate," "remove," or "take out." Their task was not to make speeches or shuffle papers. Their task was to murder.

Aversion. I want to distance myself.

They are nothing to me.

I am not of them.

I find myself overcome with anger. Anger for being caught up in their mess. Watching them out of the corner of my eye, trying to act normally, laughing, smoking—a slushy fear invades me. Emanating from Paul van Vuuren with his sullen, fleshy face, his hard dark hair and mustache, his blank black eyes. The Afrikaans he speaks makes my tongue go dry—the tone, the delabialized vowels, and the thick, arrogant rhythms must be the undercurrent of every activist's nightmare.

When the amnesty hearing begins, I go sit in a bench close to them. To look for signs—their hands, their fingernails, in their eyes, on their lips—signs that these are the faces of killers, of the Other. For future reference: the Face of Evil.

1989. A rural suburban afternoon like any other. My youngest is sitting in the kitchen with me, reciting the route of blood through the body.

"Good, start again, from the lungs it goes . . ." The phone rings. The dog barks.

"24543."

"Is that Antjie?"

"Yes," I say. I cover the mouthpiece. "The kettle, switch off the kettle."

"Is that the one who spoke to the ANC?"

I am silent. It is that kind of sluggish Afrikaans.

"Do you know the Wit Wolwe? We're coming for you tonight. A traitor and slut like you must be shot like a dog." The phone goes dead.

I remain standing there. Suddenly I can see everything. I hear my blood. My heart beats messily like an overripe pear. A crumb, a Romany Cream crumb, on the table. Even the minute, almost invisible movements of my breath through my nostrils, I see. The house is suddenly invaded by an unbearable weight of jasmine. I replace the receiver. Make coffee with precise attention to detail.

I take the children out to the farm. I go back home. It is already dusk. Should I lock the door? Must we close the blinds? Switch on the lights?

Later I hear John in the study. He comes out with a forgotten gun.

"What the hell are you doing?"

"Well, I don't know about you, but I'm not going to let myself get killed in my own house by a fucking crazy racist."

"Are you off your head! Are you planning to spend the whole evening sitting in your lounge waiting, gun in hand, like a bloody Voortrekker!"

We both look at the gun. The barrel is rusted and spiders' webs are dangling from it. We laugh. "I don't even have bullets," he says. We sink down on the floor next to each other. Our legs have suddenly forsaken us.

He pours us each a drink. I open a packet of peanuts. It's already dark. My head is turned as if I'm listening for something. John locks the door. We go and sit in front of the TV. He turns off the sound: "You can't hear the gate."

"If the gun was working and I used it tonight, what would disturb you about that?"

"I would have despaired completely. If that man wants to shoot, he must shoot, then it's on his head. But I won't shoot another person."

"Jesus, woman, it's not you shooting, it's me. And I'll shoot anyone who wants to shoot me or my wife or my children."

Hysteria builds in me. "This is about a goddam principle—the only principle you and I actually have. If you shoot him, he can just as well shoot blacks, anyone can shoot anyone. Do you want to live in a place like that? Do you want your children to live in such a country?"

"Spare me your clichés about the struggle tonight. Get real. We're sitting here trapped in our own home and in an hour's time, we could fucking well be dead!"

The word hangs between us.

Nine o'clock. We wait. We drink, but it has no effect. If someone shot you from the veranda, he could hit your body. From the street, the angle would be less lethal. Every time a car goes past, we prick up our ears. The dog barks endlessly.

Ten o'clock. And I realize we're waiting for nothing but that sound. The final invasion. Perhaps that is what kills you—not the bullet, but the shock of having the fragile privacy of the body brutally destroyed, forever.

Eleven o'clock. We know this is nothing, absolutely nothing, compared to what other people in this country have endured. Still my whole being pleads for that sound. Let it happen; let it pass.

Twelve o'clock. Our bodies sore from listening. We go to bed. We lie next to each other. Our eyes scratch the darkness. When the sparrows start rummaging in the gutters, we fall asleep. Day breaks over the platteland town—like all other days.

For more than a month, the five security cops have been sitting opposite their victims and talking about their deeds. And unlike Dirk Coetzee, who was always only watching, these men did it. Every single gruesome detail, their hands did, their eyes saw, their brains sucked. Their testimony has changed the debate among white South Africans. Whereas before, people denied that atrocities happened, now they deny that they *knew* they were happening. As the weeks drag on, the toll becomes apparent. By the last week of hearings, most of the legal jargon and procedures have disappeared. Five exhausted men and five despairing Amnesty Committee members finally complete the process.

For me they have become more real than my own life.

I ask their lawyer whether I can interview each of them separately. I want to know (although I don't tell him this, of course) whether they are deranged freaks, murderers who committed crimes in the name of the government, or whether they are forcing the Afrikaner to confront himself. More to the point—what do I have in common with the men I hate the most?

Jack Cronje was the first one to catch me off guard. The way he sat, day after day, before the Amnesty Committee, in his gray suit and his inoffensive tie—he could have been my own Oom Albert from Reitz; he could have been sitting in the *ouderlingsbank* in Morewag Church. But Jack Cronje has resigned from the Hervormde Kerk. "I know what I did . . . and I don't want to burden the church . . ."

He is sixty years old. Sometimes he is completely confused when he testifies.

"His doctor is testing him for Alzheimer's," says the lawyer.

The judges, who are more or less his own age, find it difficult to slate him for contradictory evidence. Cronje has three children. His daughter is in the police. He doesn't want to disclose where his sons work. "I don't want them to be identified as the sons of Jack Cronje."

His mustache quivers. "This is what my life has come to . . . All that I have, my best years, all that I know of loyalty and honor, I gave to the police. Now I find myself disgraced by politics.

"When I drove back in the mornings after an operation, and people passed me on their way to work, I thought: I did it for you and for you . . . you could sleep safe and sound, because I was doing my job. This country would not have held a week if it weren't for the security forces . . . For myself I didn't do it, also not for my pocket. I did it for my country.

"Vlakplaas," he brags, "was different under me. You saw on television the looks of Eugene de Kock's men . . . a man with such long hair would not dare put his foot on my farm . . ."

I interview them one after the other in a quiet corner of the Pretoria Synod hall. "You know, your whole body language and tone of voice change when you are with these men," says an English-speaking colleague. "I couldn't hear what you were talking about, but there is a definite intimacy . . ." I say nothing. When I spoke to them, I did use all the codes I grew up with, and have been fighting against for a lifetime. But now I want a good story and I want to understand them. I take the interviews to psychiatrist Dr. Sean Kaliski of the Valkenberg psychiatric unit.

"You can't sit in this grand building and explain how things were in those times . . . the people stir around in our souls and they don't understand the circumstances of those days." Warrant Officer Paul van Vuuren nonchalantly swivels his chair while I interview him. "I talk to you because you smell nice," he tells me. Later I erase it from the tape.

"It is not easy to sit in this chair," he says. "You expose your soul to the nation of South Africa, white and black. And they look at me and they think I am a monster . . . for sure I can feel it . . . their attitude and the way they look at me . . . I can actually say that I see the fear in their eyes as well as the hatred . . . The victims' lawyer says we must talk to them, but it is difficult . . . because every time we say we're sorry, they shake their heads and say they don't accept it . . . and that is also acceptable to me . . . You know, you say you're sorry, but on the other hand, it is also empty words . . . Do you understand what I am trying to say? I mean here I walk up to a person I don't even know . . . and I say, 'Listen here, I'm sorry.' I mean isn't it just empty words?"

Kaliski calls it anomie. The norms you are used to following no longer apply and you, alone, are now called upon to explain your actions within a totally different framework. So it is with the five applicants. They are no longer buffered by an Afrikaner culture in power.

They have to explain themselves to a commission appointed by a new government. Three of the commissioners are black. Day after day, different groups of black victims file silently into the benches opposite them. Sometimes they are being challenged in sophisticated English by someone like the son of Fabian and Florence Ribeiro, the popular Mamelodi doctor and his wife. Other times, mothers and aunts shake their heads—uttering disgust in countless mother tongues.

Van Vuuren shot Richard Mutase, a fellow policeman and colleague, with an AK-47. Mutase's wife, Irene, was also shot that night. The couple's small son, Tshidiso, attends the hearing.

"I mean he sat there and he looked at me and I killed his father . . . and I [a long, slow sigh] can understand that he should hate me in his heart and his whole soul . . . But I didn't even see him that night . . .

There were tears in his eyes at the hearing today . . . that I saw myself . . . so I feel so sorry for him . . . I mean you can't get past that. I truly feel sorry for him . . . If I could do something for him and he calls me and says, 'Do something for me,' then I will do it . . . and if he says, 'Take me to Cape Town,' then I will take him . . . but I mean what the hell does one *do?*"

That cry has been echoing in my head ever since. What the hell does one do?

Kaliski talks about the legitimacy constructed in the past around these extreme forms of violence. The lawgivers made the laws, the lawyers executed them, and they were assisted by a whole lot of other professions. This created a normative structure that legitimized the killings.

And the basis was not a fear of Communism, Kaliski says. "We believed black people were not human; they were a threat, they were going to kill us all and then waste away the country until it was nothing but another African disaster area." He talks about a recently published book, *Bad Men Do What Good Men Dream.* While some men were out killing black people, many whites were busy dreaming of a life without black people: separate laws, separate amenities, separate churches, separate homes, separate towns, separate countries . . .

Of all the cops, Captain Jacques Hechter is the most inaccessible. I was warned beforehand that he does not speak to journalists. When I asked him for an interview, he swung around irritably on his crutches and barged off. I ran after him and barred his exit. I repeated my request. He hissed through clenched teeth: "I don't talk, it's sore, everything is too sore."

"But shouldn't people know about that?"

"Why?" he barked. "It's all games. The former politicians played games with us, and this whole Truth Commission thing is a game of the new government. I know that I will not get amnesty . . . The only thing I can tell you, I'm not going to jail."

"What will you do?"

He glared at me. "Think for yourself." And limped away.

According to a psychiatric report by Professor Jan Robbertse, Hechter suffered from dyslexia as a child. Dyslexics are often unable to integrate their needs and wishes with reality, and as a result find it difficult to form an enduring sense of themselves and others. This is why, says the report, Hechter has been a loner since childhood. The report also deals with Hechter's "personality disassociation." He has developed two personalities that do not associate with each other and alternate autonomously in the dominant position. And this helps to explain his reign of terror in the eighties. By day Hechter had the personality of a cop, a just man working in an office. By night he became a hangman. In his own words: "a white Afrikaner terrorist."

He worked alone. He would put on his balaclava, a pair of gloves, take one of his old cars, and go out to kill people in the township. He delivers his testimony about scores of murders without emotion. His pronunciation is crisp, with a particular relish in gutturals and occlusive consonants. Through it all, his green eyes stare straight at the table in front of him. Those eyes (he told the psychiatrist) are always open. He cannot close them—neither to sleep nor to pray.

Strangely enough, the two personas prevent Hechter from suffering any posttraumatic stress symptoms. The moment he becomes uncomfortable and tense in one persona, he switches to the other.

Hechter will be remembered for the deaths of Jackson Maake, Harold Sefolo, and Andrew Makupe. The fact that he allowed them to hold an ANC flag and sing "Nkosi Sikelel' iAfrika" before they were killed, says Hechter, is proof that he is a just man. He cannot remember electrocuting them, but he remembers other things:

> JUDGE BERNARD NGOEPE: Are you able to remember that on a certain day in 1987 on a farm near Pienaarsrivier, you electrocuted three people?
>
> HECHTER: I can . . . the electrocution . . . I can remember after it was told to me. But it was completely out of my thoughts . . . I consciously banned these things from my thoughts . . . I haven't thought about it for ten years . . .
>
> NGOEPE: But you remember trivialities.
>
> HECHTER: Yes, I remember terribly . . . I can remember the path . . . it was a white chalky road . . . and there were guinea fowl. I can remember things like that, but the really . . . the worse deeds . . . those I do not remember . . .

Common themes weave through the lives of the Vlakplaas five.

Most of them came from relatively poor families, and the police force (like the civil service) was a security net for poor and ambitious

Afrikaner boys. Other shared characteristics are their devotion to the church and the National Party and the role their fathers had in their lives. Both Colonel Roelf Venter and Captain Wouter Mentz do not talk of their fathers as *"Pa"*: they prefer the Old Testament term *"Vader"*—in Afrikaans a term reserved only for God. Another marker is hunting. Venter was taught to stalk from a very young age—he was so small, he had to be tied to his father with a rope so that he wouldn't get lost.

Venter says this about his actions: "Then I was not sorry because I thought it was right. Now I know that it was wrong and I regret my deeds." This sounds ordinary, but according to psychiatrists, Venter has made a crucial leap with this statement—allowing for a space where change is possible: then it was right; now it is wrong. What makes this a psychological breakthrough is that it is almost impossible to acknowledge that the central truth around which your life has been built is a lie. At the risk of the disintegration of your self-image, you would rather keep on denying any wrongdoing.

Venter's neighbors have asked him to move to another area—he has become a stigma. Dr. Kaliski describes this as a major disservice done by the Truth Commission. "Some individuals are targeted as the scapegoats for past atrocities. And that allows other citizens to deny any complicity."

Wouter Mentz seldom reads his evidence from papers. He answers in a soft, accommodating voice—the only sign of tension is the constant jerking of his legs and feet under the table.

"My circle of friends has shrunk, my family have distanced themselves from me, I have problems with relationships . . . I was engaged for three years to a lawyer . . . before that I was divorced. A sword is hanging over my head . . . I'm not a state witness of the attorney general and if I don't get amnesty here, I will be prosecuted . . . then I will have to go to jail, where they will surely kill me . . . so one cannot sleep at night . . . I live from the morning to the evening . . . I cannot plan anything for next week or next month . . . I cannot go and ask for work—who will give me work? If you walk into a place, people stop talking and look at you. That time, people slept safe while we were fighting terrorists . . . and now we are the criminals—I never stole money—I'm not Eugene de Kock."

Mentz, according to the psychiatric report, shows symptoms of shell shock. He was deeply marked by a traumatic childhood. Apparently his father used to kick open his door at four o'clock in the morning, shouting: "Why the fuck are you still sleeping?" Mentz had to take care of the chicken farming. He also suffers from trichotillomania—a compulsive affliction in which people pull out their hair. In an effort to be accepted into male culture, Mentz joined the police force and was keen to become part of the elite unit—one of the Vlakplaas *manne*.

How can you brutally kill someone and then go home and pick up your daughter and put her on your lap?

"*Ag*, many times I didn't even go home," says Mentz. "I only went back the next morning when I knew that my wife and daughter were already out of the house . . . because if I go just after . . . because you can't, you want to wash yourself six times to get it out of you . . . many times I didn't go home for two or three days . . . you can't go home and take a beer and pour some wine for your wife and then tell her that you saw this murder or that armed robbery—one cannot do that."

What do I do with this? They are as familiar as my brothers, cousins, and school friends. Between us all distance is erased. Was there perhaps never a distance except the one I have built up with great effort within myself over the years? From the faces alone, I can tell who was taken up in the Broederbond, who is a Rapportryer, a Ruiterwag, who is working class. The Mentzes, I know, have a musical bloodline. Whether your name is Jack or Paul or Johannes—it means something. In some way or another, all Afrikaners are related. If somebody says his father bought land here, or he grew up in Odendaalsrus or Welkom—then I know. From the accents, I can guess where they buy their clothes, where they go on holiday, what car they drive, what music they listen to. What I have in common with them is a culture—and part of that culture over decades hatched the abominations for which they are responsible.

In a sense, it is not these men but a culture that is asking for amnesty.

For days I am in a daze. I do a radio profile on each of the five. I try to find an entry point for each character. I use the music of Coenie de Villiers:

Calvyn de Wet van Zyl was 'n Boer in murg en been
met 'n sluimerende droom

van 'n land wat sonder skroom
onbesmet is deur 'n donker ideaal

Calvyn de Wet van Zyl was a Boer in bone and marrow
with a slumbering dream
of a land that is without shame
not tainted by any dark ideal . . .

Calvyn de Wet van Zyl knows the country is bought at a price
that is why he becomes more prepared
even carries a gun in the street
against the evil odds of the Black Danger

When Venter talks of hunting, Coenie de Villiers sings in the background:

My Dad was a hunter
he was a man of steel

Don't be afraid, my son,
don't disgrace your skin
you are Boer in bone and marrow
what more can you ask?

Moenie vrees nie, my seun,
jy kom jou vel te na
jy is Boer in murg en been
wat meer kan jy vra?

I am powerless to ignore what vibrates in me—I abhor and care for
these five men. I get up one morning with my face all swollen from a
rash. My scalp itches so much that I have to empty a bottle of cortisone
on it. The question haunts me: Why do I want to give evil a human
face?

Half an hour after the first profile is broadcast, the phone rings. Listeners are outraged. "You suggest that all Afrikaners are murderers."

"Those guys are psychopaths."

"I have nothing to do with all of this. I live on a farm in Hofmeyr and
I will not allow you to make me an accomplice."

"Jack Cronje conned you beautifully! Ask him who built the swimming pool in his backyard?" (And this, of course, is the call that upsets me most.)

Not just Afrikaans listeners. "Don't pretend it's whites. It's the work of Afrikaners and Nationalists."

"In my own humble way, I did my bit—don't classify me in your 'us.' "

I do a follow-up package on the four categories of guilt formulated by German theologians after the Second World War: criminal guilt—for the people who did the killings; political guilt—for the politicians and the people who voted them into power; moral guilt—for those who did not do enough, who did not resist, who were passive; and lastly, metaphysical guilt—if I survived while the other was killed, I am guilty of my very existence. I quote Karl Jaspers: "Thousands in Germany sought, or at least found death in battling the regime, most of them anonymously. We survivors did not seek it. We did not go into the streets when our Jewish friends were led away; we did not scream until we too were destroyed. We preferred to stay alive, on the feeble, if logical ground, that our death could not have helped anyone. We are guilty of being alive."

The dermatologist diagnoses a trauma-related rash. I get pills and ointment, and key into the Internet search engine: collective + guilt.

The cobblestone courtyard of the Cultural History Museum on Adderley Street: the National Party is entertaining journalists. The leader moves benevolently from circle to circle. Someone warns him: "This is perhaps not the most appropriate time to join this circle. We are discussing the Truth Commission."

"But I like talking about the Truth Commission," the leader says. "And I just want to reiterate that I am just as shocked and appalled by these things as you are."

(I've had this conversation before. With Roelf Meyer. Who also didn't know. I asked him: "The morning you switched on the radio and heard that Dulcie September had been shot—what did you think?" "Let me get you another glass of wine," he said charmingly.)

"Maybe so," I bite back, "but the five policemen say they did it for us."

He narrows his eyes in sincerity. "But I never asked anybody to commit these deeds in my name or in the name of my party."

My last reserves desert me. I walk up to him. I push my hand in his face.

"I spoke to them all. They were all members of your party. They all say they did the dirty work for you and for me. And all of us are trying to deal with that, with the responsibility of that, with the guilt of such a claim . . . and where are you? Where the fuck are you!"

The hasty arrival of a bodyguard and senior politicians brings me to my senses.

"You have fallen hook, line, and sinker for the ANC's attempts to put the blame on the Afrikaner. And I am sorry—I will not take the blame for people who acted like barbarians, who ignored the parameters of their duties. They are criminals and they ought to be punished."

I look at the man in front of me. He has aged. Where once his face was smooth and full, the skin is creased and his smile sticks in his cheeks. His nose seems to be made of a different substance. And I look at him as he stands there with his glass of whiskey and his cigarette and I think of my father. And other blood-nationalists like him. Ordinary people. Good people. And how they have been left on their own to deal with what they hear.

After Dr. Verwoerd was stabbed to death in Parliament, my mother wrote an essay picturing the Afrikaner psyche.

As long as I live, I will never forget that Thursday morning when I was far from the house alone in the veld. A clump of trees grows there that I water regularly. Everything was bitterly dry. I stood with my foot on the wire fence watching how the thin stream trickles over the cracked earth. Our farm lies on the route to the south—so we seldom notice the planes anymore. But suddenly I became conscious of a drone from the southeast. In one way or another, it was different from any other plane that I have heard. I looked up and remembered that I had heard over the radio that the coffin with the body of the Prime Minister would be taken to Pretoria that day. Could it be? And I looked again. But, no, I thought, this is only one plane. There should be a whole squadron of our most beautiful, noble air-giants to take this man to his last resting place. It was a lonely, heavy bomber. It flew lower than I have ever seen a plane before. And its motors, I don't know how, sounded muted. And its flight very still, as if it should be handled with the utmost tenderness. And I realized, it is so that I am standing all by myself on the pale Free State landscape, while the body of this great man passes me by. In this moment, the life of the man I only saw and admired from afar had touched my life. And I don't have the arrogance nor the confidence of the new generation to control such a touch. It moved in my soul. And I was wondering what I should do. Should I go out on the streets and call upon people to consider what is happening to our country? Should I call on them with the only call that I know—that of concentration camps, tears, and blood? . . . And I prayed that my hand should fall off if I ever write something for my personal honor at the cost of my people and what has been negotiated for them through years of tears and blood; that I will always remember that to write in Afrikaans is not a right, but a privilege bought and paid for at a price—and that it brings with it heavy responsibilities.

I think of her and how I love her. How I was brought up with what is the best and the proudest in the Afrikaner. And I wonder about the responsibility of a leader. Shouldn't he be establishing a space within which we can confront ourselves and our past? Shouldn't he bring to the table the Afrikaner's blunt honesty and fearlessness to grapple with the impossible? So that we can participate in the building of this country with self-respect and dignity? Can't he just say: "I didn't know, but I will take the responsibility. I will take responsibility for all the atrocities committed under the National Party's rule over the last fifty years. I will lay wreaths where people have been shot, I will collect money for victims, I will ask forgiveness, and I will pray. I will take the responsibility. I will take the blame."

Is truth that closely related to identity? It must be. What you believe to be true depends on who you believe yourself to be.

I look at the leader in front of me, an Afrikaner leader. And suddenly I know: I have more in common with the Vlakplaas five than with this man. Because they have walked a road, and through them some of us have walked a road. And hundreds of Afrikaners are walking this road—on their own with their own fears and shame and guilt. And some say it; most just live it. We are so utterly sorry. We are deeply ashamed and gripped with remorse. But hear us, we are from here. We will live it right—here—with you, for you.

I put my glass on a table and flee outside into Adderley Street—the polite applause for the leader's coming speech blown in my back by the southeaster.

I think of the piece that my mother wrote. How easily and naturally the story shifts from politics to language. And is this not where the heart lies? It has been stated openly that Afrikaans is the price that Afrikaners will have to pay for apartheid. Was it not a debate for years on Robben Island: What do we do with the language of the *boere?*

And I also wonder: Is it better to have a leader like Verwoerd mesmerizing a people to do the wrong thing blindly? Or is it better to have a De Klerk, doing the right thing but unable to convince himself or his people of the rightness of it, the morality of his stance, and leaving them to stumble along in guilt and despair, nearly as resentful as their victims?

At the entrance to the Truth Commission's offices further down the street, my colleague Sello and I bump into someone. It's Wilhelm Verwoerd. "Help me make sense of the five cops," I plead with the young philosophy professor.

He smiles. "I anyway wanted to give you a quote from Paul Russell: 'If truth is the main casualty in war, ambiguity is another . . .' One of the legacies of war is a habit of simple distinction, simplification, and opposition . . . which continues to do much of our thinking for us."

"*Nee man,* what does it mean?"

"It deals with war psychosis. It means that in the past we had no choice but to live by simple white or black guidelines. But we shouldn't continue being dictated to by oversimplified credos during times of peace. We must try and make space for ambiguity."

When he walks off, Sello asks: "Who is that?"

"The grandson of Dr. Verwoerd."

Sello stops. He gapes at me. His eyes widen. Then he sits down flat on the pavement—notebooks and cassettes scatter. "This man?"

"*Ja,*" I say.

"And where does he work?"

"He now works for the Truth Commission."

Sello hurls himself backward; his feet stick right out into busy Adderley Street. He shrieks with pleasure. He pummels his fists on the paving. It becomes quite a spectacle, among the hawkers underneath the statue of Jan Smuts. Sello sits up and wipes the tears from his eyes: *"Jirrre! Julle Boere."* ("Jesus! You Boers!")

I ran to the Kadett . . . someone seated on the rear left-hand seat fired three shots at me . . . a person stretching across the car shot at me . . . he pointed the gun at me. I saw his hand . . . it was a white man's hand. I can still picture the orange spark coming from the gun . . . I ran back home . . . I found my father sprawled at the drain in our courtyard with twenty-five bullets in his head. My mother was spread-eagled further away with one shot only. She didn't seem injured. There was no blood. I held her in my arms and she sighed—that was her last breath.

(Chris Ribeiro)

POLITICS

CHAPTER NINE

The Political Page
Curls over Itself

It's only when the Truth Commission's offices are filling up with more foreign accents than usual that we realize something special is happening. And make no mistake, Truth Commissions are a worldwide industry. The swarm of overseas journalists is speedily followed by flocks of demure commentators and troops of mild-mannered, bespectacled academics.

Because they are particularly interested in the victims of apartheid?

No, because for the first time politicians and political parties are making submissions before the commission. "There have been seventeen previous Truth Commissions in the world, and politicians have participated in none of them," says an American professor, squinting in the sun outside the building where the Worcester hearings are taking place. "How on earth did you do it?"

"No idea," I answer.

It is not just that one is tired of the people who jet in for a week, squeeze in an interview with Archbishop Tutu after a visit to the Kruger National Park, attend three days of hearings, endlessly pester local journalists for information and sexy quotes, and then go away to produce a thesis or a book—it is not that. It is rather because one also doesn't understand the inscrutable machinery of politics.

Sometimes I try to explain that the process was inclusive from the very beginning, from the first submissions on what the legislation should contain. That in a way, politicians in this country still feel accountable to the public. They may well lie and deceive, but to explain to "the people" has always been the way of doing things around here.

But that is so naive that silence offers its neck. Sometimes I say that politicians are opportunistic enough to realize that a political party can get more mileage out of a very public, highly moral forum than out of any number of mass rallies. Or that the richness of the victims' testimonies has moved political parties to want to tell their side of the story. I also suggest that our isolation may have played a part: people have never been exposed to this sort of process and so they don't realize that refusing to participate is an option. And then there is the groundwork done by many commissioners, the personal meetings and discussions with each party leader.

I offer all these explanations, because it sounds too arrogant to say that for the first time in the history of the world, the Big Question was resolved: how to break the hegemony of the security forces. We did it, says the chairperson of the Justice Portfolio Committee, Johnny de Lange, by individualizing amnesty applications. And it was in fact the National Party who first insisted on individual applications for indemnity before they would allow Umkhonto we Sizwe members into the country prior to the elections in 1994.

Whatever the case, the contrast between the political hearings and the others is striking. It is strange to see the commissioners among the political elite. The posters that read "The Truth Sets You Free" are suddenly drained of meaning. And so are the commissioners' rituals, gestures, tones of voice. In cavalcades, with enthusiastic audiences, the two main parties arrive. The hall smells of silk, aftershave, and testosterone. José Zalaquett's comment comes back to me: reconciliation is not possible if the two main parties do not have a secret agreement about what they see as mutually important.

Gone is the dearly bought language. Over months we've realized what an immense price of pain each person must pay just to stammer out his own story at the Truth Commission. Each word is exhaled from the heart; each syllable vibrates with a lifetime of sorrow. This is gone. Now it's the hour of those who scrum down in Parliament. The display of tongues freed into rhetoric—the signature of power. The old and new masters of foam in the ears.

The long-awaited meeting between the Truth Commission and Inkatha Freedom Party leader Mangosuthu Buthelezi late in the year could hardly have started in a more jovial manner. With a sweeping gesture and amid raucous laughter, the minister produced a framed photograph of himself and the head of his church: Archbishop Desmond Tutu. When the media have been told to leave, the archbishop sits down with Minister Buthelezi and IFP National Council member Joe Matthews . . . and prays.

Buthelezi is the last major political leader to meet the commission. And the purpose of the meeting is to secure a political submission from the party that has branded the commission an ANC witch-hunt.

After a two-hour meeting, there is a press conference. The archbishop says: The talks were full and frank.

Then, while Tutu and Boraine listen, the IFP leader slates the commission. A memo is handed to the media describing the commission as a perverted mechanism created by a centralized ANC in an effort to portray themselves as the only righteous antiapartheid force in the country. The commission is compared to the McCarthy Commission and the Spanish Inquisition. The IFP believes, according to the statement, that the combination of amnesty, compensation, and truth-finding is a recipe for great evil. People will say anything to get money and amnesty.

But Buthelezi promises to make his own submission on how the IFP was the main target of the ANC's armed struggle. The ANC, according to the memo, killed far more IFP members than the supporters of apartheid ever did.

Buthelezi's role in the Truth Commission process has been that of a spoiler at worst and a reluctant participant at best. Some sense of his role in the IFP can be gleaned from an issue of the party's own parliamentary publication.

The title is sturdy: *IFP Communicator*. But the subtitle wobbles on interminably: *The Inkatha Freedom Party National Assembly Whip's Internal Weekly Report*.

On the first page, there is some advice from Proverbs: "Whoso keepeth his tongue, keepeth his soul."

The entire middle section of the publication is devoted to a profile of Chief Mangosuthu Buthelezi. He has no fewer than five honorary doctorates in law—one each from the Universities of Zululand and Cape Town, and three from universities in America. He was made a Knight Commander of the Star of Africa by Liberia. In India he was hailed as an apostle of peace. The last award he received was in 1989—the year before the release of Nelson Mandela.

On the last page, IFP parliamentarians get their thought for the week: "When tomorrow comes, today will be gone forever. I hope I will not regret the price I paid for it."

Throughout the life of the Truth Commission, Buthelezi has been promising: if people want the country reduced to ashes, then they must subpoena him to appear before the commission.

The other leader not coming to the Truth Commission is Eugene Terre'Blanche. At the time of the local elections in 1996, the AWB stated clearly that they refused to be absorbed into one of the most bizarre democracies in the world—a democracy in which the unemployed have finally taken charge of those who work, the ineducable now rule the productive, and squatters govern the suburbs.

Despite this claim that things have changed so dramatically, a town like Ventersdorp still calls its municipal pamphlet *Die Mieliepit* (The Mealie Kernel). You still pass by two phallic pillars bidding you: *Welkom in Ventersdorp.* Just beyond that stands a giant white egg. The main thoroughfare of the town is still called Hendrik Potgieter Street. Yes, and the shops: the *Knip en Stik, Die Nes,* or even *Die Mikstok* (the Cut and Stitch, The Nest, The Forked Stick). The virile and lewd themes are continued inside the Walk Inn Hotel, where the cocktails are named "Blue Movie," *"Lang Plesier"* ("Long Pleasure")—there is even a *"Springbokkie"* and an "ANC Multi-Racial," consisting of layers of yellow, green, and black liqueur.

In the barred cage of Terre'Blanche's sunny enclosed veranda in Ventersdorp stands an *ossewa* with full harness.

The political submissions to the Truth Commission are a radical departure from its public focus until now: a shift from individual tales to the collective, from victims to the masterminds, from the powerless to those in power. Political parties have been asked to state their case and sketch the frameworks within which South Africans killed one another. Will they come?

No need to worry. Whether their politics required them to govern, to protest, to pray, or simply to make money—they are coming. At the eleventh hour, the Democratic Party realizes that an opportunity to bestride the moral high ground wrapped in the honorable cloak of the Truth Commission does not often come a party's way.

For an obedient organization like the National Party, the issue of participation must have been complicated. It was surely not without relief that the Nationalists first heard that each party would have only ten minutes to explain its role in South Africa's past. A week before the date, the party was raring to present a somewhat slender submission under the leadership of Leon Wessels (the Leader Himself was away on leave). Then the ANC withdrew. Then the date was postponed. Then the venue was changed—at the insistence of the ANC. It's no longer the small, newly painted offices of the Truth Commission, but the spacious Good Hope Centre—home of the wrestling match, the pop concert, the religious revival, and the political rally. Then more time was allowed for each submission. Now the National Party suddenly finds itself with a full day to tell how it ruled the country from 1960 onward. At the last minute, Leon Wessels is replaced by party leader F. W. de Klerk.

No one knows what to expect.

What will the parties say? Will the NP gloss over its responsibility for the past thirty years? It's been said that as fast as the shredders destroyed crucial documents, photostat machines were churning out copies. Several foot soldiers are apparently walking around with documents signed by well-known politicians. Will the party acknowledge its past?

Similarly, will the ANC, which has found it very difficult to admit to mistakes since it came to power, turn in a self-righteous performance? Will the party expose the rotten apples in its midst? Or will it protect them under the guise of collective responsibility? Will it treat disadvantage as an alibi, or will it force individuals to own up to their actions?

And what about the IFP?

They say they are still busy writing their submission, thank you, and they will come when they are finished.

But everybody expects the political submissions to see the emergence of the real debate around the Truth Commission—that of personal responsibility. Is the individual merely a puppet in the hands of politicians or appointed authorities? Or is the individual, soldier and comrade alike, ultimately responsible for his own actions and deeds? Is the phrase "I was only carrying out orders" a good enough reason for having committed murder?

The corridors and caucuses are alive with speculation on what will come out. The puppet-masters keep mum. The audience wonders which of the rulers will be clutching a Kleenex. The media installs its run-down equipment in the Good Hope Centre and tries to get hold of copies of the submissions.

F. W. de Klerk, accompanied by a large, jubilating colored contingent, accepts responsibility for some of the repressive measures undertaken by the National Party government, including the 1985 state of emergency. De Klerk admits that this may have created circumstances conducive to human rights abuses.

"There is that which was wrong with the NP past and that which was right. It is my responsibility to admit to that which was wrong." Yet his submission contains no specifics on any high-profile abuses. He says he cannot provide information on cases he does not know anything about. He cites the case of the Cradock Four. "If we had known what had happened, and who committed this crime . . . the perpetrators would have been arrested, tried, and, if found guilty, sentenced. No president can know everything which takes place under his management—not even an archbishop."

De Klerk says he sanctioned unconventional strategies, but "they never included the authorization of assassination, murder, torture, rape, assault. I've never been part of any decision taken by Cabinet, the State Security Council, or any committee authorizing the instruction of such abuses. I personally also never authorized such action."

De Klerk makes it clear that those who committed abuses had their judgment clouded by overzealousness or negligence. "It is not my intention to gloss over the many unacceptable things that occurred in the period of National Party rule. They did happen and I want to reiterate my deepest sympathy to those who suffered from it."

The ANC presents a much longer and more detailed document. It contains specifics as well as spy reports. It tells the commission more about National Party violations than did the National Party's own submission.

During the eighties, South African forces invaded three capitals and three countries in five years. In the same period, South Africa tried to assassinate two prime ministers, backed dissident groups that brought chaos to Angola and Mozambique, disrupted oil supplies to six countries, and attacked the railway routes to seven. More than 100,000 people died as a direct or indirect result of these actions, most of them from famine. More than a million people were displaced. The damage done in the region during this period amounted to nearly $62.5 billion.

The ANC provides a list of those who died in its training camps. I become aware of the absolutely still presence of Dumisane Shange, one of the journalists on my team. The ANC submission lies like a thrown weight in his hands.

"Dumi?" I ask. All around us a babble of shouts and noises. I touch him. Behind his glasses, his eyes are expressionless.

He flips open the document, pages to the back. A long list of names. His finger goes down and then stops. "This is my brother."

I read the heading: "Died in Angola."

"We never knew that," he says.

(We seize on the story like vultures and file this report: "Journalist finds the name of his brother on the ANC death list.")

The ANC's whole submission centers on the notion of a just war. Because the war was just, the battles were just. Necklacing, they say, was never part of official policy. And they avoid spelling out the chain of command that led to incidents like the Magoo's Bar bombing.

After the ANC's appearance, Deputy Chairperson Alex Boraine confirms that the Truth Commission has received more information from their submission than from any other.

The Democratic Party tells the commission about the deadly combination of unaccountability, lies, and false information that came together in Parliament to produce the building blocks of apartheid. First there was the cornerstone: the Population Registration Act. Then the rest followed:

the Group Areas Act,
the Native Labor Act,
the Black Affairs Administration Act,
the Labor Restrictions Act,
the Bantu Education Act,
the Separate Amenities Act,
the Prohibition of Mixed Marriages Act,
the Suppression of Communism Act,
the Terrorism Act,

the Riotous Assembly Act,
the Gathering and Demonstrations Act,
the Protection of Information Act,
the Publications and Control Act,
etc., etc.

Helen Suzman says: "These laws went hand in hand in Parliament with patently inaccurate and deliberately false or untruthful information. One such instance was when former Progressive Federal Party leader Van Zyl Slabbert was told in 1976 that no South African soldiers were in Angola. It turned out they were actually one hundred twenty-five kilometers outside Luanda. And then the parliamentary process was further flawed with the presence of the State Security Council. They usually got together just before a Cabinet meeting to create a decision-making momentum that dominated Cabinet. All their activities were clothed in secrecy."

Freedom Front leader Constand Viljoen always presents a dilemma. He claims to be speaking on behalf of ethnic Afrikaners? What is an "ethnic" Afrikaner? One of those who still speaks about *"kaffers"*?

"If you have to ask what an ethnic Afrikaner is, then you aren't one," Viljoen once told me. "But *afgedwaaldes* [people who go astray] like you, they wander so far off the track that they usually end up with you again."

Viljoen tries to explain the past: "When the realization sank in that black people actually wanted what we had . . . that the black liberation struggle already had links with Communism . . . for the ethnic Afrikaner, it spelt atheism and dialectical materialism. There was no turning back—we were with our backs against the wall.

"We were reminded about past atrocities in Africa and already experienced a visible decline in the quality of our lives. Yet . . . as the rich and the liberal moved to safer and more lucrative homes elsewhere on the globe, the Afrikaner braced himself to stay in Africa, to which he was indigenous. Naturally he dug in his heels. But don't blame him for not being concerned and for not being able to show sensitivity at a moment when his world was turned upside down."

The foreign media react with skepticism to De Klerk's apology. Some foreign journalists feel he has stopped short of really apologizing;

others think he was too vague in specifying what he was apologizing for.

The chairperson disagrees. "To say the words 'I'm sorry' . . . Now, you know, I know that some of the most difficult words in any language are 'I am sorry.' And because it is such a delicate business in which we are involved, let us not blow out the flickering lamp. If you had been with us on the many delegations that went to meet with Mr. De Klerk when he was still state president . . . where we were trying to say to him: 'Apartheid is evil' . . . and when you remember how he hedged around qualifying his apology—where we are now is a very significant step forward."

This is the advantage of growing old, says the archbishop, you don't put everything under the microscope. "I've learnt not to be cynical or skeptical. I find it wonderful that someone can say on a public platform what many people find difficult to say face to face."

"But didn't he say," I ask the archbishop, "the way someone would say to his wife—'I'm sorry I hit you, but, you know, you deserved it'?"

He bursts out laughing. "If he hadn't said anything, people would have said: 'How callous!' If he had not said something toward that side, we would have criticized him. He is in a no-win situation. Because even if he had . . . What did you want him to do? Grovel? Go on and say: 'Pleeease, Archbishop, I'm verrry sorry' . . . ? Then you would have said: 'Is that genuine? Isn't he putting it on?' I mean—he can't win."

Although the new South African flag flies over Parliament, Louis Botha still rears up on his horse as Statesman, Warrior, Farmer. Queen Victoria still grips her little melon next to the Senate. But the paintings inside Parliament have been removed, at last. Three of the largest paintings provide an insight into three distinct eras of our past.

In the parliamentary dining hall, there hung a massive painting of the legislature at the time of union in 1910. Those in the painting are all bearded, all white, all somber. And—of course—all male. Yet some light trickles in from a window. It took the personnel of the art museum a whole day to remove this painting from the wall, lower it to the floor, take it out of its gilded frame, roll it up into a numbered bag, and carry it off to wherever these works will be stored.

By contrast, there is no light to be seen in the painting of Hendrik Verwoerd's Cabinet, which also hung in the dining hall. No windows—

not even a crack of light. The members of the Cabinet sit in a wood-paneled room around a table. Their studied attention is focused tightly on the architect of the homeland ideology—indeed, he is explaining it to them. He is standing like a schoolteacher pointing to a large map of South Africa. His wrist may be limp, but his eyes are steely. The only conclusion to be drawn is that he is pointing out the borders of the Bantustans—the linchpin of his policy. Outside the tight circle of seated Cabinet ministers, three younger men appear—two of whom are John Vorster and P. W. Botha.

Some twenty years later, the painting of P. W. Botha's Cabinet found its way into the lobby of Parliament. It hung on the right as you entered the building, a gigantic picture painted by someone called Fleur Ferri. The gold-framed artifact, in shades of civil-service green and pure-new-woolen-suit blue, pictured the swan song of the Cabinet on July 26, 1984.

They emulate the seating arrangements at the Last Supper. Around a table. An empty table. Here and there a clean sheet of paper and a pen or two. Each body is supported by the knurled timber of a chair; each body's head appears to have been screwed on afterward. This creates a sense of disjointedness, a feeling of togetherness in deformity. They sit together, but there is no interaction. Uniform and in control. Every hair on the head is accounted for. The curtains are open, yet the windows offer no glimpse of an outside world. The only visible watch belongs to a deputy minister.

The chief apostles sit together around the table. However, P. W. Botha is not in the position of Jesus—the central area is taken up by the four crown princes: Gerrit Viljoen, Lapa Munnik, F. W. de Klerk, and Chris Heunis. De Klerk, Ferri prophesies, is the Judas. He is the only one looking directly, yet humbly, at P. W. Botha. Indeed, P.W. finds himself squeezed to the head of the table next to a limp flag, clutching a pencil, glowering in the direction of Pik Botha. Pik and Louis le Grange sit back to back. Hendrik Schoeman, pipe in hand, seems unusually sour and burdened for the Cabinet's official joker. Prophet Ferri draws him without a neck. *Vat-hom-Dawie*, his hand artistically draped over a nameless book, sits wrapped in a blond halo—if he is not the Messiah, then the former Springbok rugby captain is at least the beloved John. Magnus Malan, his profile brightly lit, lends the only touch of indulgence to the massive canvas with his golden pinkie-ring.

Barend du Plessis, behind the agriculture minister with the *bywoner* face, shows his shiny chafed kneecaps. The only minister who is happily looking off in his own direction, and whose hands are not visible above the table, is Pietie du Plessis—currently in jail for fraud.

Behind all this, in a corner, the deputies are chatting in miniature.

Chapter Ten

Reconciliation:

The Lesser of Two Evils

"This thing called reconciliation . . . if I am understanding it correctly . . . if it means this perpetrator, this man who has killed Christopher Piet, if it means he becomes human again, this man, so that I, so that all of us, get our humanity back . . . then I agree, then I support it all."

—Cynthia Ngewu, mother of Christopher Piet,
one of the Guguletu Seven

Once there were two boys, Tom and Bernard. Tom lived right opposite Bernard. One day Tom stole Bernard's bicycle and every day Bernard saw Tom cycling to school on it. After a year, Tom went up to Bernard, stretched out his hand, and said, "Let us reconcile and put the past behind us."

Bernard looked at Tom's hand. "And what about the bicycle?"

"No," said Tom, "I'm not talking about the bicycle—I'm talking about reconciliation."

Father Mxolisi Mpambani told this story during a lunch-hour panel discussion on the subject of reconciliation at the University of Cape Town, organized jointly by the Truth Commission and the Department of African Studies.

In an interview after refusing to forgive Dirk Coetzee for killing and "braaing" her son, Mrs. Kondile says: "It is easy for Mandela and Tutu to forgive . . . they lead vindicated lives. In my life, nothing, not a single thing, has changed since my son was burnt by barbarians . . . nothing. Therefore I cannot forgive."

But the word "reconciliation" is used most often by Afrikaner politicians. Although you might expect them to use it as a cover-up for their fear that they alone will be held responsible for the country's shameful past, they mainly prefer to use it as a threat: "Give us what we want, or we *won't* reconcile with a black government." They use reconciliation to dictate their demands.

The dictionary definitions of "reconciliation" have an underlay of restoration, of reestablishing things in their original state. The *Oxford* says: "to make friendly again after an estrangement; make resigned; harmonize; make compatible, able to coexist."

The Afrikaans dictionary says: *"weer tot vriendskap bring* [to restore to friendship], accept; not resist."

But in this country, there is nothing to go back to, no previous state or relationship one would wish to restore. In these stark circumstances, "reconciliation" does not even seem like the right word, but rather "conciliation."

Archbishop Desmond Tutu's reconciliation theology ties in with the classical definition of reconciliation. Academics say that reconciliation has formed an integral part of his theological thinking since 1979. But Tutu has "Africanized" the concept in such a unique way that it shows up the usual Western Christian motive for reconciling as sometimes being too far removed from the world to be of value. The Church says: "You must forgive, because God has forgiven you for killing His Son." Tutu says: "You can only be human in a humane society. If you live with hatred and revenge in your heart, you dehumanize not only yourself, but your community.

"In the African *Weltanschauung*, a person is not basically an independent, solitary entity. A person is human precisely in being enveloped in the community of other human beings, in being caught up in the bundle of life. To be . . . is to participate."

Michael Battle, an African-American Christian ethics professor in Tennessee, who has studied Tutu's unique theology, writes: "Central to Tutu's life and thought is his appeal to his society to move beyond racial distinctions as determinative of human identity. People should not kill because they are black and white, but they should rejoice in how they are created differently so that new meanings and identities are always possible . . . As Tutu's *Ubuntu* theology unfolds it gives access to a new identity for South Africans; it also appeals to ancient African concepts of the harmony between individual and community which John Mbiti concludes as: I am because we are, and since we are, therefore I am."

Although the best-known exponent of reconciliation in South Africa is President Nelson Mandela, it is interesting to look at the way in which his successor, Thabo Mbeki, views reconciliation and forgiveness.

At the end of 1996, the University of Natal presented Mbeki with an honorary doctorate at their "Reconciliation Graduation Ceremony." Initially Mbeki seemed a somewhat illogical choice to honor in this way. It also seemed—after the motivation for the distinction and Mbeki's curriculum vitae had been presented at the ceremony—that the university itself was not familiar with the reconciliatory actions its honored candidate might have undertaken. The mere bestowing of an honorary degree on an ANC leader by a former "English liberal institution" was perhaps the University of Natal's version of reconciliation. No one mentioned the major personal part Mbeki has played in some of the most effective peacemaking achievements in a province that has been racked by violence and revenge. ANC sources say that Mbeki has spent weeks and weeks in Natal, consulting and paving the way for reconciliation.

Before the ceremony, Mbeki's speech on the subject of reconciliation was distributed to the media. But when the time came, he took out a totally different set of notes about the achievements of his recent European visit, and so the speech on reconciliation was never delivered. However, it contains three illuminating paragraphs. Where for Tutu, reconciliation is the beginning of a transformative process (one must be able to transcend one's selfish inclinations before one can transform oneself and one's society), for Mbeki, reconciliation is a step that can follow only *after* total transformation has taken place.

"What are the essential building blocks for the construction of true reconciliation? . . . Replacing apartheid with democracy—real reconciliation cannot be achieved without a thorough transformation and democratization process."

And later in the speech: "The point we have sought to make this evening is that given the history of our country, true reconciliation can only take place if we succeed in our objective of social transformation. Reconciliation and transformation should be viewed as an interdependent part of one unique process of building a new society."

Mbeki is clear on what he regards as transformation. He quotes Chief Albert Luthuli: "There remains before us the building of a new land . . . a synthesis of the rich cultural strains which we have inherited . . . It will not necessarily be all black, but it will be African."

At the risk of oversimplifying, there may be a contradiction between the versions of reconciliation propagated by Mbeki and Tutu. Tutu believes that black people have access almost to a superior humanity, which enables them to do things that surpass cold logic. When a woman at the Truth Commission hearings says that she forgives the killers of her son, Tutu tells her: "You make me so proud, Mama, to be a black person like you." What the world lacks, black people have. In his view, the main thrust of reconciliation is between people of all colors—embodied in the idea of the "rainbow nation."

Mbeki, on the other hand, doesn't necessarily care what the world lacks. He spelled this out in Durban. He wants black people to work together to transform the country and the continent. He talks about an African Renaissance. He wants to show the world that black people can run a country and a continent successfully. For him reconciliation should take place among all black people with white people in peaceful coexistence.

At the panel discussion on reconciliation held at the University of Cape Town, most of the input ranges between these two positions.

"Reconciliation is already taking place on a large scale as individuals and communities invent ways and means to reconcile their lives with what has happened." Professor Pamela Reynolds of the Anthropology Department underscores Tutu's vision that in a wonderful way people are already forgiving and reconciling. The fact that no revenge attacks have taken place in the wake of revelations at the hearings means that people in their everyday lives have already weighed the costs of reconciliation and revenge.

For Abner Mofokeng reconciliation walks hand in hand with survival. As the human resources manager at Southern Life, his analysis is practical: "The South African experience has taught us that reconciled coexistence is essential for survival. Personal survival is inextricably linked to the survival of others."

Reconciliation will only take place, as far as Nozipho January-Bardill is concerned, the day whites also feel offended by racism, instead of feeling sorry for blacks. (To "feel sorry" for blacks has lately become the ultimate crime—the specialty of the bleeding-heart liberals, to use the catchphrase.)

Shirley Gunn brings the audience back to some basic questions: Who should be reconciled? Who will gain from reconciliation? What will they gain? She echoes the words of Charity Kondile: It is easy for Mandela to forgive—his life has changed; but for the woman in the shack, it is not possible.

Abner Mofokeng confronts Gunn: "It is simply not true that Mandela is not conscious of the woman in the shack. But Mandela keeps the bigger purpose, the fuller picture, in mind and because of that, in the end her children or grandchildren will benefit."

A professor from America conjures up an unexpected picture of reconciliation. "True reconciliation in America was visible when we saw on television how whites and blacks together looted a furniture shop . . . you cannot carry furniture alone and they simply worked together in self-interest."

Then a tall young student stands up at the back and goes straight to the issue that has been carefully skirted thus far: "I would like to say something about the issue of racism now surrounding the commissioners themselves. If there is one thing that irritates me, it is when the new black elite whines about racism—while in actual fact all they want is the power and the positions of the whites so that they can exercise those very same values."

Everyone avoids everyone else's eyes.

When Professor Mahmood Mamdani of Uganda, the current A. C. Jordan Professor at the university, is asked to conclude the discussion, he startles us by asking: "If truth has replaced justice in South Africa, has reconciliation then turned into an embrace of evil?"

We gasp. Words like "amnesty," "blanket amnesty," flash through my mind.

"Five years ago, if someone mentioned to me a new democracy and a genocide, I am not sure I would have fitted South Africa and Rwanda into the correct slots. What I still ask myself is whether it is not easier to live with perpetrators than with beneficiaries."

Beneficiaries? With precise language, Mamdani cuts the whole debate loose of the hazy black and white distinctions stifling most of the current thinking.

An article in the *Sunday Times* provides the perfect example of what Mamdani was trying to get away from. The article suggested that whites should pay for the wrongs of the past by means of a special tax and by giving up all their privileges. The deadlock in readers' responses to the piece was only to be expected: all the whites said, "I won't pay because I'm not guilty, I was not one of the perpetrators"; and all the blacks said, "Yeah! It's about time someone tells these whites what they ought to do."

Mamdani says: In Rwanda there are a lot of perpetrators and a few people who benefited; in South Africa there are a few perpetrators, but lots of beneficiaries. Should reconciliation take place between victims and perpetrators, or between victims and beneficiaries? The legislation guiding the commission, he says, forced it to narrow the injustice to murder and torture, and the victims to militants. Resentment could follow if the majority, who understandably expected to gain from reconciliation, are excluded.

In a review of *Reconciliation through Truth*, by Kader Asmal et al., published in the *Southern African Review of Books*, Mamdani elaborates on this point: "It becomes a problem when the history of resistance is seen as synonymous with the history of the ANC . . . then apartheid becomes reduced to a terror machine and resistance to the armed struggle." Mamdani uses the 1992 referendum as an example of how complex the issue of resistance is. At the time, the whites-only referendum, in which whites had to vote for or against the notion of power-sharing, was regarded by many South Africans as nothing more than a moment of narrow self-interest. In fact, it was a milestone, he says, the historic moment in which, for the first time, a white settler minority on the African continent reached out toward a settlement with the majority—"Without this moment, any talk of reconciliation would have been wishful thinking."

Mamdani asks whether the basis for reconciliation after the Anglo-Boer War was not redistribution to Afrikaners, rather than punishment of the English. "Were the English and Afrikaners partners in a common crime (apartheid) against humanity or was apartheid a program for massive redistribution, reparation, of today's loot in favor of yesterday's victims?"

This analogy raises the difficult question: Is the Truth and Reconciliation Commission the equivalent of the symbolic Ossewa Trek of 1938—a tool to create a particular nationalism, not a new South African identity? The story goes that Alan Paton participated in the ox-wagon trek, organized by the Broederbond to commemorate the Great Trek, because he believed it was the start of an authentic new South African-ism. But after listening to the speeches at the laying of the foundation stone for the Voortrekker Monument, Paton went back home, shaved off his *boere* beard, and said, "There was no space for me there."

Mamdani's analysis may be making space for both the seemingly contradictory formulations of reconciliation put forward by Tutu and Mbeki. Mamdani says durable reconciliation will be built only if its basis straddles both race and ethnicity. Race was meant to define the identity of the privileged; ethnicity, the identity of the oppressed. Race was urban; ethnicity, rural. So if Tutu deals with racial reconciliation and Mbeki with ethnic reconciliation, they could complement each other. And if some evil is embraced in the process—may it be the lesser of the two.

Between about eight and nine A.M. on Sunday morning, I was taken to another office in the police station. There were a lot of white men in the office. All the men were dressed in plain clothes. These men in the office pushed me backward and forward from one to the other and smacked me. I was like a soccer ball that they were playing with. All the time, they asked questions about the "necklacing" [which had taken place in George in March 1986] and the George Youth Congress. The pushing went on for about fifteen minutes . . .

On Monday afternoon at about two P.M., I was taken to Mossel Bay by Coetzee . . . Captain Van der Merwe and Kruger were present and they interrogated me about the necklacing.

I said: "Even a dog can see that you are stupids—surely you know that I wasn't there."

They got angry and one of them said, "We'll see who's a dog," and they closed the doors, the windows, and the blinds. Kruger put paper and a piece of cloth in my mouth. Van der Merwe bound my hands and eyes.

Kruger took off my jersey and my shirt and pulled me up to the desk. One of them took off my bra. They forced me to bend over the open drawer so that one of my breasts would hang in the drawer. They then slammed the drawer shut so that my breast was squashed. They did this three times to each of my breasts. Their actions caused me a lot of pain and my whole body became weak. They also pulled handfuls of hair out of my head.

They then untied my hands and left me in the office. I unbound my eyes and mouth and noticed that my nipple had split and a watery sticky substance was flowing out. I took the cloth from my mouth and dried my breasts. I kept the hair and the cloth and when I went to the toilet, I found a plastic packet and put the hair and cloth inside it. I still have this packet in my possession.

. . . After they did that to my breasts, I started having nightmares, which carried on throughout the time I was in detention. I found it difficult to sleep and would often wake up very early in the morning and then not be able to fall asleep again.

Throughout the time in detention, I felt tense and lonely. But it did not help when I was with other people, as it became difficult to be with others and to communicate with them. For example, when I was in a cell with other women I knew, I found it difficult to be with them. Being with them made me recall the times I was tortured . . .

(Ntombizanele Elsie Zingxondo, Beaufort West)

CHAPTER ELEVEN

Amnesty:

In Transit with the Ghosts

That the Truth Commission would be controversial was to be expected. Also that the most vociferous resistance would come from the perpetrators. But what could not be foreseen was the effect the commission would have on the African National Congress. From the very beginning, the ANC's reactions to the commission have been clumsy and uninformed. So uninformed, in fact, that one is often left wondering why members of the executive don't consult people like Johnny de Lange, Willie Hofmeyr, or Priscilla Jana before they make statements about the new legislation.

I secure an interview with Joe Modise, former commander of Umkhonto we Sizwe and current minister of defense. Will he be applying for amnesty? Yes, he says, because many things can happen under your command that you don't plan for. I put the story out on the news. There is an angry call from an ANC spokesperson: Modise is not applying personally for amnesty, but will form part of a collective ANC application.

"But the law doesn't allow for collective amnesty," I say to this man, who suddenly sounds a bit like Eugene Terre'Blanche, Johan van der Merwe, and Constand Viljoen on the subject of amnesty.

"Lady, who would know better what the ANC is saying—you or me?"

Shortly after this, another ANC politician tells me that amnesty is unnecessary.

"But people will sue you," I say.

"Our people will never sue us; we brought them freedom."

"Yes, but the whites will sue—people will sue Robert McBride for the Magoo's Bar bomb."

"I'll get back to you on that one."

But then decisive confusion strikes in the form of the man with the astonishing name of Bantubonke Holomisa. He begs the commission to let him testify. Although the hearings are primarily for people who have no other forums in which to tell their stories, permission is granted. And all hell breaks loose. It's not his revelations of National Party and third force involvement in violence that do the trick, nor the shoeboxes full of documents he hands over. It's his claim—later described by Dumisa Ntsebeza as an "old-news one-liner"—that public enterprises minister Stella Sigcau, back in the days when she was still a minister in the homeland government of Transkei, received a R50,000 cut of a R2 million bribe allegedly paid by Sol Kerzner to Transkei prime minister George Matanzima for gambling rights in the homeland.

The Truth Commission was initiated, promoted, and eventually set up by the ANC. It had the obvious blessing of the party—from the president down to the lowest-ranking member of Parliament. But the ANC's reaction to Holomisa's testimony is unexpected. Is he telling too much truth? Is he pulling a General Johan van der Merwe on the ANC leadership? Or is the party merely using his testimony as an excuse to dump him? Everyone knows he's a loose cannon. Holomisa is called for a disciplinary hearing. Suddenly there is tension—between a high moral position and the survival of the party in power, between morality and unity.

The ANC takes the opportunity to force its high-profile members to stick to the party line. And the party line is unity. The chairperson of the Disciplinary Committee, Kader Asmal, is tasked with providing the moral motivation for the ANC's insistence that it vet its members' submissions to the Truth Commission. Asmal says that while one is free to approach the commission in one's private capacity, one still has a moral obligation toward one's colleagues within the party. But the impression remains that unity is more important than truth.

The commission issues a statement. It finds the ANC's stance astounding. It is incredulous that a party would seek to muzzle its rank-and-file members by demanding to check their statements.

It is clear that the commission has taken on a moral life of its own and is willing to oppose even the party that gave it birth. This stance raises serious questions for both the politicians and the Truth Commissioners. When the Truth Commission says, "The truth will set us free," is the ANC adding, "The truth as determined by us"? When the commission says, "Tell your truth as you have experienced it," is the ANC adding, "The truth as approved by us"?

And then the final straw. Mpumalanga premier and legal adviser to the ANC, Mathews Phosa, says that ANC members do not have to apply for amnesty, because the war against apartheid was just. Boraine issues a statement: unjust acts can be committed within the framework of a just war, no less than just acts in an unjust war. Tutu takes the bull by the horns and announces that he will resign if the ANC grants itself amnesty. He refuses to be abused by a party that will not accept equal treatment before a Truth Commission.

There are opposing opinions on the merits of applying for amnesty. The one is that all the applicants deserve some praise—at least they had the guts to come forward. The other is that it is foolish, and for a politician fatal, to acknowledge any wrongdoing. Rather take your chances with the courts.

"A lot of these people applying for amnesty, if they were my clients, I would have advised them not to apply, simply because there is not enough evidence to convict them."

"So why do they do it?"

"I think some of them have been sweet-talked into amnesty by Tutu—morally it's the right thing to do. A lot of greedy lawyers are swarming around too, hungry for state money."

The first applications from politicians still in government come from Joe Modise and Ronnie Kasrils. The commission responds with unequivocal praise: these applications underline the fact that leaders are accountable and this will set their followers free to come forward.

But another key force driving people to apply for amnesty is the threat of impending court cases—brought either by the attorney general or by private individuals. What should one read into the fact that neither De Klerk nor Buthelezi has applied?

And then there is the question of dates.

The controversy is about two dates: the cutoff date and the amnesty deadline. The cutoff date concerns the violations themselves: deeds committed beyond this date will not be considered for amnesty. The deadline concerns the amnesty procedure: applications for amnesty will not be accepted after this date.

It's not clear why the Justice Portfolio Committee never really dealt with this matter. Right from the beginning, political and police leaders, whose cooperation was absolutely necessary for the commission to fulfill its task, were asking for the cutoff date to be extended. The committee argued about it for weeks. Then, on the morning when the date was supposed to be finalized, the matter was quickly resolved by stipulating that the cutoff date would be as the Constitution states. The date given in the Constitution is December 6, 1993.

"Why have you just left it like this?" I asked an ANC committee member at the time.

"I don't know. We'd like to move the date, because then the Shell House shooting would go away like a bad dream. But apparently Mandela himself doesn't want it changed."

Another committee member alleges that it was left open-ended so that it could later become a sort of bargaining chip for the commission.

Those who are now arguing for the cutoff to be extended say that December 6, 1993, was an arbitrary date established by the Kempton Park negotiators. Few of those who were involved in violence even knew about it. On the other hand, the inauguration of Nelson Mandela as president was a clear signal to everyone that change was under way, and this should be the new cutoff. If the date were to be moved to May 10, 1994, then the Election Day bombers and the attackers involved in the Heidelberg Tavern and St. James Church shootings would also become eligible for amnesty. But changing this date requires a constitutional amendment, and that in turn demands a two-thirds majority in a full parliamentary process.

The amnesty deadline is simpler. It can be changed by the president. What complicates things is the fact that the deadline depends to some extent on the cutoff date, and changing the one means changing the other to allow time for a new flood of applications.

Ten days before the amnesty deadline, which is on December 14, 1996, and the uncertainty surrounding the two dates is crippling the amnesty process. Both dates need to be fixed: one by Parliament, the other by the president. A meeting is scheduled for the commission and the government to discuss the deadline, but then the deputy president goes to India. The president postpones the meeting until a day before the deadline officially expires. What is more, Parliament is already in its December recess, and apparently the changing of the date in the Constitution is not even on the agenda.

The commission is battling to preserve its credibility. If the dates are not extended, if important figures in the ANC do not apply for amnesty, then the commission will limp into its second phase the following year without having achieved much more, in the end, than any of the other Truth Commissions.

Three days before the amnesty deadline. I'm sitting in one of the passages at the Truth Commission offices, studying the amnesty rulings on twelve applicants. The Amnesty Committee has made its findings public under pressure from the Truth Commission itself: desperate lawyers and advocates have been complaining to the commission that only two amnesty rulings have been made so far. As a result, legal representatives cannot fathom how the Amnesty Committee is interpreting the law and don't know how to advise their clients or prepare their cases. And the committee offers them no guidance.

As I'm writing down the names in my notebook, I hear Alex Boraine roaring down the hallway: "Bring it all to my office—I don't understand these people."

I crane my neck: Boraine never raises his voice. I grab a staff member who comes running by. "What's going on?"

"Actually, you're not supposed to be here yet. Please don't report about the amnesty rulings, we still have to add some names to the list."

I do some calculations. Of the twelve amnesty applications, seven were awarded. All seven are black ANC members. Of the five who were refused, four are white. This will not go down well among the people who are being encouraged to apply for amnesty.

When the list is eventually released, it includes the names of another four successful applicants. All four are white right-wingers.

Now where is this coming from?

When Boraine saw the initial list, I hear later, he was furious. He phoned one of the judges: "Have you not given amnesty to any white people?"

"No—well, we have . . . Where are those names? . . . They must be here somewhere."

"Then send them through," Boraine hissed.

From the beginning, it's been clear that the Amnesty Committee has decided to work closely and calmly within the framework of the law and legal procedures. For the most part, it seems as if none of the members of the committee have a real sense of the political climate or the broader political picture. They go from case to case. Sometimes one feels their attitude will be disastrous; it is totally out of touch with Thabo Mbeki's request that the Truth Commission complete its task of granting amnesty speedily and not leave the new government burdened with the mess of the past. Yet at other times, one thinks: No, hold on to the letter of the law; please hold on. In the end, when the political screws are tightened, that will be what saves you.

It is a small office with a standard-size desk. Boxes of files clutter the desk, the chairs, the table, the floor. This is where the official life of all amnesty applications begins—here on the desk of Mandisa Dukumbana. And it's two days before the deadline expires. The phone rings. Someone rushes in to ask her something. I snoop around: several brown envelopes addressed to *Die Komitee oor amnestie*. Although the preposition is wrong, the spelling of "Committee" is correct: one "m" and one "t" in Afrikaans. On the desk lies a big parcel covered in courier-post wrappings.

"The applications arrive in different ways: by post, in faxes, some are brought in by attorneys, others are sent twice to make sure. Some people bring them in personally. They're usually somewhat stiff and nervous at first, but when they see the stacks and stacks of applications, they laugh sort of helplessly, and then relax."

As the deadline approaches, the pace has picked up. Dukumbana says the number of inquiries increased first, followed by urgent requests for application forms to be faxed. She's also noticed that the inquiries are no longer being made by attorneys, but by prospective applicants themselves.

"The first thing I do is stamp the date and give it a reference number and from there put it in the database." It seems special arrangements have been made with people who phoned to say their applications won't be on time. Their names have been entered into the database and their applications will be processed the moment they arrive.

After the applications have been scanned for information by the investigative unit, they are locked away in a safe. The third safe in fact—the other two are full . . . chockablock. I shudder . . . the Amnesty Committee suddenly seems too frail, too busy with meticulous, step-by-legal-step procedures to deal with three dark safes crammed with secret confessions.

Just a few days ago, I discover, APLA, the armed wing of the Pan-Africanist Congress, paid a visit to the Truth Commission. They wanted to know: What exactly is amnesty? For how long will such an amnesty be valid?

How is it possible that they still don't know? "Nothing focuses the mind like a deadline," says Archbishop Tutu.

I add a note for the news desk: "Mandela discusses two dates tomorrow with the Truth Commission—please keep in mind that there is a DIFFERENCE between cutoff date and deadline." I get a snotty note back: "According to the dictionary, there is NO difference between cutoff date and deadline."

President Mandela graciously agrees to the extension of both dates. The new cutoff date is May 10, 1994, and the new deadline, May 10, 1997. With a sigh of relief, everyone goes on holiday.

Rumors abound that the army is orchestrating an effort to ignore the Truth Commission and avoid public hearings. At a gathering of former military personnel to discuss their approach to the commission, the infamous Colonel Jan Breytenbach cried out, "Me, apply for amnesty? *Se moer!*" ("Like hell!")

The extradition of an Australian pedophile from Jeffreys Bay a week later makes many army men sit up and take notice. What extradition agreements does South Africa have with Lesotho, Namibia, and Angola? And with Britain and France? Could the family of Dulcie September charge a suspect in Paris and ask the South African government to hand him over? The legal implications of amnesty become crucial. It is being said that amnesty means a clean slate, and nobody, not even the government, can touch you. Does this mean that you cannot be removed from a position you hold or extradited to another country? This leads to more questions. Do other countries have to honor these amnesty agreements? Or could they do as the Americans and Israelis have done elsewhere in the world, and sneak into South Africa, kidnap someone, and take them back to their own country to stand trial?

This is what worries him so much, says the legal representative of Generals Jannie Geldenhuys and Kat Liebenberg. There is a growing tendency in Africa to form war-crime tribunals heavily supported by the United Nations. What he wants to see is special legislation that will oblige the government to protect successful amnesty applicants against extradition, kidnapping, prosecution, and arrest. Then former SADF members will be able to travel overseas without a care—or go hunting in neighboring countries.

Recently, Craig Williamson, a former spy who has extensive business interests in neighboring countries, was arrested in Angola. He has been linked to the bombings responsible for the deaths of Ruth First and Jenny and Katryn Schoon, as well as an attack on ANC headquarters in London. Williamson also approaches the government to ask for guarantees that he will be protected against prosecution.

In the meantime, the hourglass keeps running.

But there is a thin line between establishing credibility and overplaying one's hand. Sunday newspaper headlines read: "TRC's gloves are off— TRC raids military base." The next day, the Truth Commission issues a statement: it was *not* a raid. Barely a day later, this front-page headline: "TRC probes internationally." And another statement follows: it was *not* a probe, it was merely a request to a Dutch organization to collect documents relating to covert operations overseas.

Are the media looking for action and goading the Truth Commission? Is the commission still trying to find its feet after shifting its focus from victims to perpetrators? Or has taking on the previous regime proved too rough a ball game?

Then the incident that caps everything. At ten o'clock one Friday, the SADF announces in a terse two-sentence statement that it is postponing its submission to the Truth Commission scheduled for the following Monday. At eleven o'clock, Alex Boraine, his voice hard with anger and conviction, announces that the hearing on Monday will go ahead. Everything has already been organized—the security, the translation, the panel. The Truth Commission will ask Minister Modise to see to it that the generals come. If they do not, they will be subpoenaed. Subpoenaed? Are they serious? What high-profile person has been subpoenaed before now? But so decisive is Boraine's tone, and so vigorous are the assenting nods of his colleague Dumisa Ntsebeza, that for a moment it seems the great test has come.

The test of power. Does the Truth Commission carry enough weight with the government to force the authorities to back them? Do Minister Modise and his deputy Kasrils have the clout to force Generals Meiring, Klopper, and Mortimer to appear on Monday? And more important, does the Truth Commission really have the teeth and the will to use them against the powers that be and the powers that were?

In the late afternoon of that same Friday, the army issues a statement that its attempts to involve former members of the Defense Force have prevented it from finishing its submission on time. Seconds later, the Truth Commission puts out a reply that is in sharp contrast to the earlier threat to issue subpoenas. It says that Monday's hearing has been canceled because there is no sinister motive behind the SADF's delay.

The Truth Commission's major task is to find the truth. But to do this, it needs hard information. And getting that might be the commission's real test of strength.

The deadline for amnesty applications expires at midnight on Saturday, May 10, 1997. Amnesty applications are still streaming in on Saturday morning, and when the offices close at midnight, the total number of applications received since the commission started its work stands at about 7,700. "My God, when we took this job on, we were told to expect about 200 applications," a member of the Amnesty Committee tells me with a shudder, "and now there are seven thousand!" Among the last-minute applications is one from Vlakplaas commander Eugene de Kock. The commission believes that about 2,500 of the applications will warrant a public hearing.

There are several surprises among the piles of papers. Piet Koornhof is seeking amnesty for the forced removal of 3 million people while he was minister of cooperation and development. With this application, says Koornhof, he wants to say all of this was wrong and he is sorry. There are also applications from Civil Cooperation Bureau operatives like Joe Verster, Staal Burger, Slang van Zyl, and Calla Botha, and this sets the cat among the pigeons. A former military commander once remarked: "Joe Verster is the military equivalent of Eugene de Kock. The day he talks, he will take everyone down with him." Then again, an eastern Cape artist wants amnesty because she feels that she didn't reflect the atrocities of apartheid in her paintings.

The ANC applications arrive shortly after lunchtime in a huge box. They are neatly arranged in large brown envelopes, and include close to 40 applications from senior ANC leaders and about 400 from MK cadres and self-defense-unit members. The high-profile ones are those of Deputy President Thabo Mbeki and Ministers Mac Maharaj and Joe Modise.

Just before midnight, six black youths walk into the Truth Commission's offices in Cape Town. They insist on filling out the forms and taking the oath. Their application simply says: "Amnesty for Apathy." They had been having a festive Saturday evening in a township bar when they started talking about the amnesty deadline and how millions of people had simply turned a blind eye to what was happening. It had been left to a few individuals to make the sacrifice for the freedom everyone enjoys today.

"And that's when we decided to ask for amnesty because we had done nothing." They went to a nearby shop, asked the owner if they could use his computer, and typed out their "Amnesty for Apathy" statement.

"But where does apathy fit into the act?" a Truth Commission official asks.

"The act says that an omission can also be a human rights violation," one of them quickly explains. "And that's what we did: we neglected to take part in the liberation struggle. So, here we stand as a small group representative of millions of apathetic people who didn't do the right thing."

With applications like this, the amnesty process has become more than what was required by law. It has become the only forum where South Africans can say: We may not have committed a human rights abuse, but we want to say that what we did—or didn't do—was wrong and that we're sorry.

Every respectable historical building has its own live-in ghost. The South African Parliament in Cape Town has several. In this labyrinth of hollow corridors, forgotten cellars, underground streams, and echoing chambers, it's not very clever to burn the midnight oil.

When the bells chime at St. George's Cathedral (where Archbishop Desmond Tutu's throne still stands), they say that Parliament swarms with ghosts. "The old parliamentarians," the workers there maintain.

"Hulle skuur-skuur so langs jou boude verby as jy by die wasbak buk." ("They squeeze past behind your bum when you're bending over the washbasin.")

One night a guard had to put away the flags. He saw a light on the second floor. From the committee room came laughter. As he walked past the open door, he saw a group of parliamentarians with wineglasses in their hands. "And by chance," he tells me, "by pure chance, I looked down toward their feet and saw that some of these guys in the woolen suits had no ankles—yes, between the polished leather shoes and the trouser legs, there was . . . nothing . . . absolutely nothing."

The more powerful the politician, it seems, the more formidable the ghost. In Parliament's new wing, the former Speaker, Louis le Grange, has no rest. He is always pacing up and down—"The footsteps of a very tall man," the cook says. The lift next to his office keeps on opening and closing by itself. And it only stops if you jump a little into the air and say: *"Laat los, Le Grange!"* ("Let go, Le Grange!")

The most famous ghost in Parliament haunts the corner office that was once used only by ministers, but is currently occupied by the SABC-TV news boss. This is the ghost of Prime Minister Louis Botha. The story goes that he committed suicide one rainy night in his office. Jan Smuts discovered the body, quickly had it moved to Botha's house, and then announced that he had died of natural causes. Botha, with deep sorrow etched in his posture and face, regularly haunts on rainy nights in that part of the Marks Building.

One night TV cameraman Pieter is working late on a current-affairs program. Because it is raining outside, he waits in his boss's office for his wife to come and fetch him. He switches on the light and then the TV. After he sits down on the sofa, he becomes aware of somebody behind the desk. "A man with his head bowed, his arms and hands held despairingly in front of him. I first made sure that it wasn't a computer or a coat or something, but it was definitely a man."

On another occasion, Pieter is on his way back to the studio to fetch a pair of glasses left behind by a TV guest. A man is waiting at the door. "The glasses are lying on the table," says the man.

"I know, thank you," Pieter says. He takes the glasses. At the front door, he asks the guards: "Who else is in the building?"

"Just you and your guest went in tonight. I'm just waiting for you, and then I'm locking up."

But do I know about the ghost of the tall Cabinet minister? The waitresses from the new wing huddle together and talk in guilty whispers. He was very tall, *nè*, and they couldn't find a coffin for him, *nè*. Go and ask his secretary, she still works here . . . The minister's wife sent an air ticket to this secretary to attend the funeral. Because the minister could do nothing without her, he took her everywhere. So this secretary flies to Johannesburg, rents a car, but on her way to the town where he's going to be buried, she passes the hearse. She stops the hearse and says that she had such a bond with the man, could she not see him one more time? Alone, where there are not many people? The driver opens the coffin—she's thinking that it doesn't seem quite long enough for the deceased—and she discovers that the poor man's legs have been sawn off at the shins and fitted in next to him with his shoes still on. *Sowaar*, go and ask her, they tell me.

I track down the shy, unmarried secretary, and struggle to formulate my insensitive question. "So did they manage to find a coffin for such a tall person?"

"It wasn't really long enough," she says after a while and stares at the floor in front of her.

"How do you know that?"

"I saw the body and he was lying crumpled up at the neck."

This is definitely not the whole story, the workers insist. Why does he haunt like that . . . floating around at night with his empty pants legs fluttering?

"Is there a Verwoerd ghost?" I ask. Hey, we have to get back to work, they tell me.

One morning I meet a cleaner in the old Assembly Hall busily cleaning the carpets. "Look at this spot," she mumbles. "This stain is where Verwoerd's blood spilled. They've gotten professionals to come and wash the carpets, but after a day or so, the stain is back again . . ."

One of the messengers explains to me why the stain is next to the bench and not in front of it. Verwoerd apparently sat down just before the start of the afternoon session, with his one arm across the bench behind him. When he was stabbed, this messenger heard him say: "No, son, what are you doing?" The blood then streamed from his chest, ran down his arm, and poured from the end of his sleeve onto the carpet.

The National Party left the large bloodstain there for months. Later it was covered by a light carpet. After months all the carpets in the hall were dry-cleaned—and a day or two later, the stain was back.

CHAPTER TWELVE

The Political Tongue

at Anchor

The ANC, under the leadership of Deputy President Thabo Mbeki, will be the first party recalled to answer the list of questions sent to them by the Truth Commission. This time there will be no opportunity to claim the moral high ground or sketch the broad frameworks. The commission has questions and it wants answers.

Mbeki's first words are: "Can we take our jackets off? It's a bit hot." A perfectly simple request carrying two messages: today you are the boss, we will ask your permission to do things; and second, we're here to work.

But the direction of certain questions catches the delegation off guard. They are clearly no longer used to being called to account in public by those with no political power. And these are not the lightweight questions of journalists looking for a headline. Maharaj, Modise, and Kasrils shuttle between questions and struggle to explain. At one point, Mbeki sounds a warning: "We should avoid the danger whereby by concentrating on these particular and exceptional acts of the liberation movement, which could be deemed as constituting gross human rights violations, we convey the impression that the struggle for liberation was itself a gross violation of human rights."

The questions posed by Truth Commission lawyer Hanif Valli are sharply focused and backed by evidence: incident, speaker or activist, date, and direct quote. They are also the kinds of questions that have long been on the lips of South Africans, whether supporters or victims of the ANC. Questions about the murder of black policemen, the violence of the self-defense units, necklacing, slogans inciting people to kill, as well as stories of torture and executions in ANC camps. And all these questions are formulated in such a way that the ANC is forced to abandon its rhetoric. When it slips into habit, the chairperson puts his foot down: "A characteristic of your evidence today was the absence of self-justification—keep it like that."

The Truth Commission has obviously been trying to provide a safety net so that political parties can look human rights violations squarely in the eye.

And, with sustained pressure, that's what the ANC does. From their multifaceted answers, you can tell that these violations have been debated thoroughly over the years. But whereas previously the issues were presented simply as dilemmas, now the deputy president, three Cabinet ministers, and a provincial premier can admit that they were wrong. It's quite a strange experience to see this high-powered delegation sitting there for two solid days trying to provide answers, to the best of their ability as politicians, while secretaries with cell phones, bodyguards, liaison officers, scurry around—these people are busy governing the country, after all. At one point, a short break must be called because Mandela is on the phone for Modise.

On the issue of self-defense units, cross-examination is incisive. How could grassroots supporters be given weapons without control being exercised?

"I think it's clear that when the thing changed in character, when we realized that people were not being issued with firearm licenses, which is how we thought the SDUs would work, but that arms were being distributed at random, we should have reviewed the situation," Ronnie Kasrils acknowledges. "It was a mistake."

The party admits to several other mistakes: that its first tribunals had fundamental flaws, that they extracted evidence under torture, that cadres were charged and sentenced without legal representation, that they waited too long before condemning necklace murders. The slogan "Kill the Boer, kill the farmer," they concede, was not a political statement and should not qualify people for amnesty. And they admit that none of their members were authorized to engage in violence against the IFP.

On the first day of the submission, Mbeki was just an ANC leader accounting for human rights abuses. But on the second day, he is the president-to-be, pleading for reconciliation. Without it, he says, the government will inherit an insoluble problem. The ANC will make a third submission, he says, this time about reconciliation, which is fundamental to the country's future.

Despite this successful session, uncomfortable questions remain. To what extent was the submission an exercise in political damage control after the party's blunders about the Truth Commission? Why was it so vague on who did what and who gave the orders? No information was given that really went beyond what is already in the public domain. The burning questions of parents whose sons died in ANC camps were not addressed at all. Some observers are also disappointed that the party did not deal openly with its role in the death squads in KwaZulu-Natal. The delegation did not really seem convinced that individuals should own up to their actions.

The National Party. A new panel of commissioners and a new cross-examiner. In the morning, with the appearance of F. W. de Klerk, there is already a buzz in the corridors.

"Today he will be taken to task," says a committee member in the media room. "An excellent set of questions was worked out around the issue of 'bad apples.' We will start at the bottom, with the ordinary cops. Are they bad apples? And then we'll work our way up to General Johan van der Merwe. Is he also a bad apple?"

Today is obviously the day.

As usual, the chairperson lays the table for the fatal encounter. He praises De Klerk for his contribution to peace in the country, he quotes from the Bible, he prays, he speaks Afrikaans, he smiles. But across the table, De Klerk seems in total control. He alone takes the oath. He alone is going to speak. Former state president P. W. Botha has refused to cooperate with the NP on its submission. No predecessors, no ministers, no generals, to escort De Klerk. His isolation from the senior leadership of the past is total.

And it becomes a battle of lawyer against lawyer. In his submission, De Klerk says that the gross human rights violations committed in the past were due to the bad judgment, overzealousness, or negligence of individual policemen. In his cross-questioning, Glenn Goosen takes up De Klerk's phrasing. It becomes a chorus: "The Cradock Four, those who were responsible—was it bad judgment, overzealousness, or negligence? The Pebco Three, those who were responsible—was it bad judgment, overzealousness, or negligence?"

"But this is ridiculous," De Klerk protests.

"Please answer my question," says Goosen.

It quickly becomes apparent that the Truth Commission will get nowhere with this line of questioning. The commission sees De Klerk as a leader come to explain the past; but in fact he is fighting for the survival of his party. The commission has not taken into account the fact that the National Party is in serious trouble; Roelf Meyer, De Klerk's second in command and the most prominent NP figure in the negotiations, has resigned just a day before the submission. De Klerk isn't there to look the past in the eye. He's there to minimize the damage and to play on the sentiments of his voters. And these are: we did not know, we are just as shocked as you are, and we feel that these people are criminals who should be punished. De Klerk states repeatedly that his whole upbringing, his entire experience of politics, allowed no room for the kinds of atrocities now coming to the surface. And, yes, then everybody, from General Johan van der Merwe, who misled him, down to the foot soldier who did the deed, is a bad apple. As he resists the line of questioning, the documents used, the assumptions made, his delegation erupts: "Shame! . . . *Sies!* . . . Witch-hunt!"

The end of the hearing is in sharp contrast to the previous day. No inspiring words, no prayer, from the chairperson, who sits deeply sunken in his chair.

I go to the cross-examiner: "What the fuck did you want him to say?"

"I wanted him to say: 'Although I didn't know about it, the fact that we never condemned these killings outright may have led people lower down in the ranks to believe it was our policy.' "

"My God, but that is not so impossible to say! Except that you allowed him only one route to get to it, and that is the route he as an embattled political leader could not afford to take."

I pack up my recorder, laptop, and cassettes. Outside on Adderley Street, someone tugs at my skirt. "Do you know Brecht's poem 'In favour of a long, broad skirt'?"

I am so distressed, so full of unformulated despair, that I cannot answer. "Come," he says. He pulls the bags off my shoulders and we get into a taxi. We drive out high above the city to Vlaeberg. "Actually, you should close your eyes now." He leads me through the rooms. "Do you want some wine?" I sob for air. At my feet is a swimming pool and above me Lion's Head so close that I feel I can touch it. Of stone and of green. He gives me wine. He ties up my hair. He washes my feet in the cool water. He feeds me thin slices of raw meat.

"Help me make sense of De Klerk."

"It's easy. The safety net they strung up for the ANC yesterday was not there today. They were out to get him. And they couldn't."

"Then why do I expect better from the commission, but not from De Klerk?"

"There you are wrong. De Klerk has just disappointed millions of people because he refuses to think of more than covering his wickets against Roelfie. De Klerk has always been like that. All the changes were made because of some small, practical reason—he has never had a vision."

"But the Truth Commission are the moral lot. If they give up on De Klerk and the Afrikaner, then how can they expect the rest of the country to live with us?"

"The Afrikaner can in no way detach himself from the past," says Constand Viljoen as leader of the last party being recalled for questioning. "But we must be allowed to make for ourselves an honorable role in the new dispensation. The Afrikaner feels disempowered, unsafe, his language is threatened, his educational structures are in pieces—in short, the Afrikaner feels flooded by the majority and he has nowhere to turn."

Viljoen also tackles the issue of a just war head-on. "For a war to be just, it must comply with four requirements: the aims must be just, the war must be fought by a recognized and accepted authority, the relationship between the means and the ends must not be disproportionate. Lastly, all other avenues of resolving the differences must be exhausted before violence becomes an option." According to Viljoen, neither the previous government nor the ANC tried out all the options available to them before they started fighting. Also, the means employed to secure ultimate ends were often out of proportion. "We all have dirty hands," he says. "Terrorism and revolutionary war are as evil as nuclear war."

The conflict of apartheid was essentially political in nature. Viljoen says that the army begged the government for years to find a political solution to the conflict, because this was the sort of war the army could not win.

Viljoen claims that General Johan van der Merwe admitted to him that agents infiltrated the AWB, but that they were never used to manipulate events. "This is difficult to believe. It is unbelievable to see how well we've planned . . . and we *can* do proper, detailed planning . . . how at that crucial moment at Kempton Park, when we were on the point of stating our case to the negotiators at Codesa—here is Eugene Terre'Blanche and the AWB with an armored car. Who arranged that car? Who decided on the exact time? To me it's just fishy. In Mmabatho, when we undertook to protect President Lucas Mangope from ANC violence, the same thing happened . . . everything was planned to the last detail and I deliberately prohibited the AWB from participating. That night everything was in place, we were deployed, disciplined, organized . . . but here they come charging across the borders in their bakkies, shooting at people and shouting racist insults. They just moved in and destroyed the whole cause and made fools of us. Is Eugene Terre'Blanche being used by the security police to destroy the right wing or to strengthen the NP's quest for concessions from the new government?"

To assimilate truth piece by piece

The commissioner spreads the photos on the table. A slope of *tamboekie* grass, a wind-blue sky, some fresh soil.

"He shows us the place . . . we dig . . . we find red topsoil mixed with black subsoil . . . we know . . . and then the spade hits something . . ."

"She was brave this one; hell, she was brave," says the grave indicator, the perpetrator, and whistles softly through his teeth. "She simply would not talk."

Next photo: the earth holding a bundle of bones. Delicately they are chiseled loose. Cigarette butts, an empty bottle. "It's hard work, digging," says the grave indicator.

A man in short sleeves puts the bones on a small piece of canvas next to the grave—building blocks. A vertebra . . . the thin flattened collarbone . . .

The skull has a bullet hole right on top.

"She must have been kneeling," says the commissioner.

Ribs. Breastbone that once held heart.

Around the pelvis is a blue plastic bag. "Oh yes," the grave indicator remembers. "We kept her naked and after ten days she made herself these panties." He sniggers: "God . . . she was brave."

The commissioner's eyes are purified in the brilliant yellow of anger. It is he who said: "Sometimes at night I wake up with a rage pounding in my breast . . . as if to wipe me out like a veld fire."

It was he who tried during the last half hour of F. W. de Klerk's political submission to pin down a connection between National Party policy and the deaths in KwaZulu-Natal. But like the Truth Commission's lawyer, like the other commissioners, he just slid like water off F.W. His head knuckled back into his shoulders, shaking in disbelief.

De Klerk and his hostile delegation leave. The room and passages are filled with rage. People swamped with fury and desperation. Dejected, the commissioners stand around. Archbishop Tutu's skin hangs dull and loose from his face. His shoulders covered in defeat. I want to go to him, to make some infantile gesture or other. To kiss his ring, to touch his dress.

When De Klerk walked out, it was as if something slipped through my fingers forever.

Speechless I stand before the archbishop. Whence will words now come? For us. We who hang quivering and ill from this soundless space of Afrikaner past? What does one say? What the hell does one do with this load of decrowned skeletons, origins, shame, and ash?

That was the day—the day the "Big Dip" began. The Day of the Undeniable Divide. One moment it was the closest, the next moment the farthest apart, that people in this country have ever been.

The National Party immediately started mobilizing on anti–Truth Commission sentiments. Those in and around the commission showed symptoms of the untenable—the impossibility of the process, the futility of the dream of reconciliation.

What we have hoped for will never be.

Some journalists want to be moved to other beats.

"We cannot leave now," says a colleague. "We must see the process through, otherwise we will be dangling in the air forever."

We ask the commission about its plans for the rest of the year. Any special occasion lined up to get rid of six solid months of perpetrator hearings, any ceremony to conclude the workings and set people free of the past? The commission is vague. It is obviously more concerned at this stage with the final report and with two vaults full of amnesty applications that the Amnesty Committee must work through at its tranquil pace.

Why do people hang in there? Has the Truth Commission become the last empire of naive righteousness and impossible dreams?

But those in and around the commission have been singed into their own versions of Vlakplaas units. We from the press can only talk to each other. We look each other up, we buy food for each other, we live each other's stories—we experience the process through a thousand eyes. Every second person in the street looks like a commissioner, every group looks like the investigative unit on its way to a breakthrough. We are on first-name terms with the guards. We all want to resign. We all yearn for another life.

At Tzaneen a young Tswana interpreter is interviewed. He holds on to the tabletop; his other hand moves restlessly in his lap. "It is difficult to interpret victim hearings," he says, "because you use the first person all the time. I have no distance when I say 'I' . . . it runs through me with 'I.' "

"Now how do you survive it?"

"I don't. After the first three months of hearings, my wife and baby left me because of my violent outbursts. The Truth Commission provided counseling and I was advised to stop. But I don't want to. This is my history, and I want to be part of it—until the end."

The end. We all wait for the end. And we assume the Truth Commission will provide this end.

"That is a disastrous attitude," says Dr. Sean Kaliski, the Valkenberg psychiatrist. "People thought that the Truth Commission would be this quick fix, this Rugby World Cup scenario, and that we would go through the process and fling our arms around each other and be blood brothers forevermore. And that is nonsense—absolute nonsense. The TRC is where the reality of this country is hitting home and hitting home very hard. And that is good. But there will be no grand release—every individual will have to devise his or her own personal method of coming to terms with what has happened."

Antipathy for the Truth Commission blasts into the open. The commission is bombarded with demands and legal threats; Parliament is besieged with Truth Commission debates; those who report on the commission are targeted with hate mail.

A columnist in the Free State writes: "Reject the Truth Commission with the disgust it deserves—on untested evidence it tries to portray the Afrikaner as the icon of all evil. Untested evidence has become the truth of the *'boerehaters.'* "

"Don't despair," says Kaliski. "The fact that a person feels compelled to say: 'These things are not true, these things are biased,' points to the first step in dealing with the Truth Commission. Previously people said nothing, now at least they are denying the information." He refers to the five stages experienced by terminally ill patients: denial, rage and isolation, bargaining, and depression, out of which acceptance will eventually surface.

"I think people are too impatient. I personally would be very concerned if, overnight, whites could integrate information that turns their whole worldview upside down. It will take decades," he says, "generations, and people will assimilate the truths of this country piece by piece."

Kaliski says that Afrikaners in particular are feeling terribly exposed. "If you personalize it, a very proud person who is publicly exposed as a scoundrel will hardly ever respond with humility and contrition, he will almost always respond with anger and outrage. The community feels exposed because they have been caught out, shown up as evil, and this is very hard to deal with."

The vocabulary around the Truth Commission has changed from phase to phase, but the word that turns up most often is "underestimate." Everything about the dynamics of the Truth Commission has been "underestimated." The only nightmare is the possibility that the commission will stumble so badly that it wipes out all its successes. Of late, "overestimate" has become a popular word. And this shortly before the commission has to pass its last two milestones. Two impossible ones: reconciliation and reparation.

And the two go hand in hand. The one cannot be without the other. If people don't get reparation, they won't forgive. If people are not forgiven, they won't offer reparation. Or rather, this was my thinking.

De Klerk was nothing more or less than a politician looking for a forum to sort out tensions in his own ranks. The single-minded strategy adopted in the questioning of De Klerk provided him with the stage he was looking for. "Don't worry," someone says, "the commission has enough evidence on De Klerk. He will eat his words." And if he eats them, and has his nose rubbed in them, what will happen then? I wonder. Will he then be forgiven? Will people assist with reparation because they feel deeply humiliated? Will white and black in small rural towns now work jointly for the benefit of those who suffered the most?

I take a Jewish colleague aside: "What kind of reparation was done by the Germans?" He provides an impressive list, ranging from pensions and free transport, to leaders kneeling at Jewish memorials. And money—money from the Federal Republic of Germany was the largest contributing factor to the full industrialization of Israel . . . I listen perplexed, thinking about the unimaginative document on reparation workshopped some months ago. They could come up with nothing more inspired than a lump sum of money. No special study fund, housing subsidy scheme, pension provision, medical assistance—just a sum of money that the government has to dish out. And if it cannot afford to do so, the commission can wash its hands and say, "It's not our fault."

I also know better than to ask my Jewish colleague whether anyone was forgiven on the basis of reparation. Is contrition in the form of reparation, then, just as futile as denial?

And suddenly it is as if an undertow is taking me out . . . out . . . and out. And behind me sinks the country of my skull like a sheet in the dark—and I hear a thin song, hooves, hedges of venom, fever, and destruction fermenting and hissing underwater. I shrink and prickle. Against. Against my blood and the heritage thereof. Will I forever be them—recognizing them as I do daily in my nostrils? Yes. And what we have done will never be undone. It doesn't matter what we do. What De Klerk does. Until the third and the fourth generation.

Famished. Parched, one waits for Constand Viljoen's party to make its submission. They form a modest group.

Viljoen speaks as if he wants to capture something, bring something back, confirm some essence of Afrikanerhood that is wholesome. I want it too—but at the same time know it not to be. When Viljoen talks about how the British took away the land of the Boers, an English-speaking journalist mutters sarcastically, "Ah, shame!"

I cannot help it, I spit like a flame: "Shut up, you! You didn't utter a word when De Klerk spoke . . . Viljoen is at least trying."

"You must be joking—this poor man is an anachronism." My anger shrivels before his Accent. And his Truth.

Viljoen was the only political leader who requested that a special Reconciliation Commission be set up in the future to deal with "the hardening of attitudes I experience daily."

After the first political submissions in August 1996, I interviewed Archbishop Tutu. "Weren't you irritated that you had to listen to four versions of South Africa's past?"

He spreads his four skinny fingers under my nose. "Four versions . . . four . . . exist of the life of Christ. Which one would you have liked to chuck out?"

I try another question. "Why did the last part of the ANC's submission sound so paranoid? As if the whole world is in a conspiracy against Thabo Mbeki."

Tutu tilts his head in surprise. "You should be the last person to ask me this. You are sitting with me daily, listening to what happened in the past. Many people are the second and third generation of being persecuted. And if you don't know the past, you will never understand today's politics."

A friend who has emigrated visits me in the office. She answers a call for me: "It's your child. He says he's writing a song about Joe Mamasela and he needs a word to rhyme with 'Vlakplaas.' " She lowers the phone. "Who is Joe Mamasela?"

A massive sigh breaks through my chest. For the first time in months—I breathe.

The absolution one has given up on, the hope for a catharsis, the ideal of reconciliation, the dream of a powerful reparation policy . . . Maybe this is all that is important—that I and my child know Vlakplaas and Mamasela. That we know what happened there.

When the Truth Commission started last year, I realized instinctively: if you cut yourself off from the process, you will wake up in a foreign country—a country that you don't know and that you will never understand.

REACTIONS

CHAPTER THIRTEEN

Blood Rains
in Every Latitude

"That moment I remember. I was called in and told: 'The South African government wants to kill you.' And I remember the indescribable solitude of the moment . . . because it was so personal . . . they didn't want to kill ANC members, but me specifically."

Father Michael Lapsley. Born in New Zealand, trained in Australia as an Anglican priest in the Society of the Sacred Mission, and then in 1973 sent to the University of Natal in South Africa.

"I was a convinced pacifist when I arrived in South Africa . . . but quickly discovered that in this country neutrality was impossible. During my ministry, I met students from several backgrounds and it was clear to me that if you were white and did nothing to change the situation, you were actually a functionary of the apartheid government.

"Although I did not then have any political affiliations, the South African government deported me. In neighboring Lesotho, I trained Anglican priests."

A friend from Lesotho: "Michael's house was open to anybody in Lesotho. For I who am from quite a closed white community, it was the first time that I met black South Africans on an equal basis . . . and we discussed and argued about everything . . . we also prayed, because Michael's house was essentially a house of prayer."

While Michael Lapsley was visiting his family in New Zealand, a group of well-trained South African soldiers made a cross-border raid into Lesotho. Phyllis Naidoo, who survived the attack, describes that night in her book *Le Rona Re Batho:* "At 1 A.M. on Thursday, 9 December 1982, Lesotho was held captive by the moon. It was a beautiful clear moonlit night as only the Maluti mountains can produce. Ironically, it was the moonlight that assisted the South African Defense Force in their killing spree. They came in helicopters, guided by searchlights, frightening off the usual night walkers . . . 42 people died that night . . ." The ANC moved Michael Lapsley, who was then a member of the organization, to Zimbabwe.

"It was a normal warm autumn day . . . April . . . when I became the focal point of all that is evil. I returned from a series of lectures in Canada. A pile of mail had accumulated on my desk, among others something with an ANC letterhead. The envelope stated that it contained theological magazines. While I was busy on the phone with someone, I started opening the manila envelope on the coffee table to my side. The first magazine was Afrikaans . . . that I put aside, I can't read Afrikaans. The second was in English. I tore off the plastic and opened the magazine . . . and that was the mechanism that detonated the bomb . . . I felt how I was being blown into the air . . . throughout it all, I never lost my consciousness . . ."

A friend from Lesotho: "I visited Michael three days after the explosion in the Harare Hospital . . . It was terrible to witness . . . his face was charred and black . . . his beard had melted into his face, which was swollen to twice its normal size . . . both his hands had been amputated, and he had to keep the stumps in the air, since anything touching them caused him insufferable pain . . . he lost his one eye . . . his eardrums were burst . . . I wanted to comfort him; I wanted to hold him . . . but there was nowhere I could touch him."

Michael Lapsley: "When I made my political choice, I often thought of death. What I never thought of was being maimed. After the explosion, I felt that it would have been better if I were dead, because now I am someone without hands and I had never . . . never before met someone without hands.

"Hands transmit love . . . tenderness . . . I endured an endless and intensely overwhelming sorrow over the loss of my hands . . . when they brought me the prosthetic hands, I started crying . . . because they were so ugly . . . Now I have these . . . and it is actually amazing what they can do . . ."

It is these stainless-steel pincers that Father Lapsley raised to take the oath before his submission to the Truth Commission: "So help me God . . ." But it is also these pincers that prevent him from wiping away his tears like other victims. When their stories cut too close, victims often bury their faces in their hands, and wipe their eyes with tissues. But how do you hold the fragile veil of a tissue in such pincers? How do you complete the simple action of blowing your nose? Several times the pincers move toward his face in a reflex action—as if he wants to cover his face with his hands—and every movement flashes the inhumanity of South Africa's past into the hall . . . hard, shiny, and sterile.

"I do not see myself as a victim, but as a survivor of apartheid . . . this is part of my triumph of returning to South Africa and living my life as meaningfully and joyfully as possible . . . I am not captured by hatred, because then they would not only have destroyed my body, but also my soul . . . Ironically, even without hands and an eye, I am much more free than the person who did this to me . . . I say to everyone who supported apartheid, 'Your freedom is waiting for you . . . but you will have to go through the whole process.'

"Someone had to type my name on the manila envelope; somebody made the bomb. I often ask the question: 'What did these people tell their children that they did that day?' However, the fact that such a sophisticated bomb found its way through the post to me, *after* 2 February 1990, *after* Mandela's release, and on the eve of important discussions between the NP and the ANC, I lay sole responsibility for that with F. W. de Klerk. De Klerk knew of the hit squads—Frederik Van Zyl Slabbert[1] himself told me that he told De Klerk about them—but De Klerk chose to do nothing about it.

"Forgive I will be able to, but then the asking of forgiveness must take place within the framework of repentance . . . but from the direction of De Klerk, not a single sound of admission has come. And I also want to know, what is a person doing now to make up for what he or she destroyed in the past?"

Archbishop Desmond Tutu: "There is always a special silence when Michael takes the Communion. First you think people are nervous that he may knock the cup over with his pincers—but then it becomes absolutely quiet . . .

"And it is as if light beams from him . . .

"And you know that you are in touch with something that will always triumph over darkness. And I give to God the glory for you, Michael, and I am thankful for you . . . because you can talk of the crucifixion and the resurrection, because it is in your body."

---

[1] Former leader of the antiapartheid Progressive Federal Party, a predecessor of the Democratic Party.

Obviously moved, Tutu stands up, followed by the whole hall, and prays while Michael Lapsley slowly sinks back into his chair.

Queenstown. On the surface, a normal platteland town among the soft, grass-covered mountains of the eastern Cape. But Queenstown holds buried the most gruesome of histories . . . something that is never talked about, never referred to. Not one of the cases that the Truth Commission listened to in Queenstown gave any indication of the unusual extent of horror in the town.

Queenstown is unique. It is known as the Necklace Capital of the World. In August 1985 the first person to be necklaced, Bill Mentoor, was killed because he ignored a consumer boycott instigated by the ANC Youth League. It is thought that thirty-nine necklace murders took place here over the next four years—more than nine a year, almost one a month . . . while in the great majority of South African towns, such a thing never happened.

Nozibele Madubedube testifies on two murders in her family. Later I run into her, crying, in one of the side rooms of the Queenstown City Hall. "The Truth Commission treated me like dirt. Commissioner Bongani Finca kept on asking: 'But didn't you know that the people were against councillors?' So? Is he saying we deserved to be necklaced?"

The big woman in the navy cardigan then tells me her story:

"My sister Lungelwa came home specially from Johannesburg for her birthday. She would have turned eighteen.

"That morning the comrades surrounded the house. They were singing: 'Let the *impimpi* die' . . . They shouted: 'If Lungelwa does not come out, the house will burn' . . . I went out with Lungelwa . . . they grabbed her . . . I cried out, but they immediately closed around her. I could not see her . . . I could only hear her cries . . .

"I ran to the police . . . They told me afterward . . . Lungelwa burnt in a different way to anyone else . . . they poured petrol over her, they put a tire around her neck . . . 'We will make you pretty,' they said, 'necklace upon necklace . . . And perfume?' And they poured petrol on the tire. They also told her to drink the petrol, for the flames to have a shiny path . . . Then they called: 'Time for sparks!' Then they threw matches . . .

"They say Lungelwa, whose hands and feet were still tied with wire, kept lying down until she caught fire and everybody had to stand away from the roaring flames. They say Lungelwa suddenly became stronger than a man . . . stronger than an animal—and she was young!—she sat up on the ground . . . her arms and legs broke loose from the wire . . . the tire around her chest she pulled off with a powerful gesture and hurled it into the hysterical crowd. 'Never, never again will you burn anyone like this!' she screamed, and ran to a sandy gully where she rolled and rolled until the flames on her body were extinguished . . .

"She died the next day in the hospital in Queenstown."

It is bitterly cold in Queenstown. The Truth Commission adjourns. I eat dinner in a badly lit café.

"Queenstown is different to other places," the waitress confirms. "There are two madhouses here, you know?" The next day, I establish that this is indeed so: Queenstown had two psychiatric sections for years. Here in the mornings, necklacer and victim sit in the sun together.

The local history teacher suspects some innate weakness in the place after a century of conflicting tensions. Queenstown was the first town founded by the English after the final victory over the Xhosa in 1847. This region is also the home of the Mfengu, the first black people ever to be proclaimed British subjects, and since early times, they have been under pressure to do away with tradition. They are also, according to Noel Mostert, the only group in the eastern Cape who refused to take up any Khoisan into their tribe.

I track down a leader of the ANC Youth League in the town. Yes, he was in Queenstown during those days, but he thinks that people are blowing this necklacing business out of proportion:

"You must remember how it was here during that time. Two Bantustans bordered on here. You could trust no one. No one. When I slept at night, two groups had to stand guard and also keep an eye on each other. I know people say the word 'necklace' originated here from Queenstown. But we heard it from other Xhosa-speaking people from Johannesburg. We called it 'tire-to-tire' . . . We had no weapons, but tires and petrol were easily obtained. It was also a way of controlling the community—and your comrades. During a necklacing, everybody observed each other carefully . . . if you burnt with less fervor than the others, then maybe you had something on your mind . . . With the advent of F. W. de Klerk, the necklace murders stopped . . . we suddenly felt things were changing.

"*Impimpis.* Spies. The police manipulated the idea of informers. They will say to you in passing: 'Just check tonight, around six . . . just check what Vuyo is doing . . . you know what, we're going to catch all of you.' And then we keep an eye on Vuyo while we're planning strategy. And, yes, every now and then he wants to know what the time is. When it's exactly six, he says he has to go. When we grab him two days later and ask him where he was the other evening, then you see how startled he is. Anyway, even if he tells you a hundred times that he visited his sister in hospital, then the fear in his eyes and the fact that the police pointed him out is enough proof to know: it's either him or me . . ."

Nozibele Madubedube: "It's not true, they targeted us because they were jealous. My parents were educated people. My father belonged to the ANC long before they were born, but because he served on the local town council, they said that he sold black people out."

The ANC youth leader: "These bourgeois councillors. They enriched themselves through the system. The lot of black people never bothered them . . . it is us, the youth, *these hooligans*, as they like to call us. It is us who through our own discipline, strategy, and actions drove this country to change during the eighties. That old Madubedube . . . two streets of families had to share three toilets when he was councillor; today he can vote, and his haughty daughter too, because of what we brought here for them."

Nozibele Madubedube: "Less than a year after my sister Lungelwa's death, the comrades also grabbed me one morning. They did exactly the same to me . . . When I swallowed the petrol, my husband fell down on the ground and screamed—sounds that I had never heard before on this earth and have never heard again . . . my children hysterically tried to pull him up from the ground . . . I felt the petrol burning in my stomach and saw the comrades' shoes dancing right in front of my eyes . . . shoes you know . . . tattered shoes . . . suddenly our neighbor stormed in amongst the crowd and she kneeled over me . . . 'To this woman you will do nothing, I know her, she is not an *impimpi* . . .'

". . . But actually I was alive, but also not. If any light flickers anywhere, I instinctively think it's fire. My whole family is . . . just partly alive . . . only parts of us have to do with one another . . . When we're driving in the car, I look at my husband and my children and I feel . . . I see them . . . and I do not see them at all . . . when I touch them, it feels as if there is a thick skin over my hands . . . especially my oldest child always seems to be afraid of me. My husband looks like an exhausted human being. In 1989 I was converted and baptized with water . . . it was so cool, this water . . . and I can honestly say, this is why I'm still functioning. This morning when I sat in front of the Truth Commission, I saw two of those who grabbed me and my sister in the hall . . . and they are still . . . *nothing* . . . only . . . now I am also nothing. My life keeps on slipping through my fingers."

Chief Anderson Joyi punctuates the names of every one of his nineteen generations of forebears with his knobkerrie on the floor:

> King Thembu begat Bomoyi,
> and Bomoyi begat Ceduma,
> and Ceduma begat Mngutu,
> and Mngutu begat Ndande,
> and Ndande begat Nxego,
> and Nxego begat Dlomo,
> and Dlomo begat Hala,
> and Hala begat Madiba,
> and Madiba begat Thato,
> and Thato begat Zondwa,
> and Zondwa begat Ndaba,
> and Ndaba begat Ngubenuca,
> and Ngubenuca begat Mtikara
> (this is the house where Matanzima comes from,
> the right-hand house),
> and Mtikara begat Gangeliswe,
> and Gangeliswe begat Dalindyebo,
> and Dalindyebo begat Jongiliswe,
> and Jongiliswe begat Sabata,
> and Sabata begat Buyelekaya,
> and this is where I begin.

The Xhosa interpreters come out of their booths. "Man! That was deep, deep Xhosa. We had to use the King James version of English to give people a real impression of how this old man is talking."

"Why do you start your testimony with your lineage?" I ask him afterward.

"Their names organize the flow of time," the interpreter explains to me. "Their names give my story a shadow. Their names put what has happened to me in perspective. Their names say I am a chief with many colors. Their names say we have the ability to endure the past . . . and the present."

This goes back to 1976. I took a train from Barberton to Komatipoort. As I alighted from the train at Kaapmuiden and we just took a few drinks, then the train arrived and we boarded for Komatipoort. Most of my friends got off at Hectorspruit. As the train arrived at Komatipoort, I was asleep . . . I'm not sure because I was drunk a bit. And then the railway police came in—they were searching the train—and they asked me, "Where are you going?" I said, "Komatipoort."

[. . .] He took me to the railway police offices . . . he said I must agree that he found me at the border. Then I said, "What are you telling me now? Why are you forcing me to say something I don't know? I can't allow that." Then he came closer to me and said I must agree and he called a black policeman to stand by the door. Then he went out and called a station commander. When they came, they said to me I am a communist. And then I said, "What is a communist?—because I don't know what a communist is." Then they said to me, "*You* are the communist; why are you having this document? This document is from Mozambique." I once visited Mozambique and I got this document, because at one stage there was a person I negotiated with to get cattle. Then they said to me no, and they took my ID and they said I must agree that they found me without an ID document. I said, "No, I can't allow that, I am a bona fide citizen of South Africa—you can't say that."

Then they changed my name. I am no longer Mahlasela Paul Mhlongo, I'm now Carlosh Tjhira . . . now I was surprised actually . . . *[audience laughter]* . . .

YASMIN SOOKA: Please . . . remember the witness is supposed to be telling the story. Whilst I will not completely say you are not allowed to laugh or to . . . be merry, I think you should allow him to speak his story and allow him some dignity.

MHLONGO: At that juncture, they said to me, "You are Carlosh—now we are giving you a new name—you are Carlosh," and they had to beat me and as they were beating me I was also defending myself. Then they took a wire, they tied it to my toe and they took a towel and they blindfolded me so I cannot see whatever is happening. I could not speak and I could not see, and they shocked me and they tied my hands at the back. And they said to me—"Do you still disagree that you are from Mozambique? That you are an alien?" And they said, "You are a *kaffer*," and then from there they tied my genital parts with that wire, and my hands were tied to the back, and they shocked me on my parts . . . And if I told them, "I am *not* from Mozambique," they were beating me, shocking me . . . I was so surprised! "I'm not from Mozambique! I'm not an alien!" "Think properly, you *kaffer*," they said . . .

The black police officer was watching as they did this to me. He said to me: "If they come back from tea now . . . if you continue to resist, they're going to put you in a bag and put some stones in the bag, and also a cat sometimes with you in the bag, and they throw you right into the river. It is not that they're only doing this to you, this is actually their thing which they normally do to each and every person. So I'm requesting you, when they come back, you must agree you are an alien." I got frightened, because I realized their aim is to kill me now.

When they came back, they started kicking me—"Are you still re-sisting?" And I said, "I come from Mozambique"—I agreed with everything they were asking. A black person came and removed the wire from my penis and they took the towel and they untied me again. I was unable to walk. My body was totally useless. I did not know whether I would ever walk again . . . This thing worries me a lot . . . the problem is, there was a woman. The woman said . . . now the woman is complaining at home that I am no longer able to perform the . . . the sexual activity. Now this is because of what they did to me.

[. . .] At the magistrate's court, we were not actually given a fair hearing. They brought us all, the whole twenty-one, and took three of us and said, "You are sentenced to six months, three months suspended." Now the interpreter that day, fortunately I happened to know the interpreter, it was Mr. John Sbiya. I said to John, "Man, tell these people I'm from Barberton . . . now they're group-ing me together with the people from Mozambique." Then this Sbiya said, "Well, I have nothing to do with you." And this worried me a lot.

Then from there they took us, they said we are sentenced, we must go to jail now . . . They put us in a truck and took us to Bar-berton. And the people of Barberton knew me very well—even the warders—and they said: "Mr. Mhlongo, where're you from, why are you a prisoner?" And there was nothing I could say . . . people were just pushing me. My belongings I had to give away because I could not carry them—it was clothes for my children which I bought for Christmastime. Now in Barberton I was working in jail, but it was not easy for my body . . .

[In jail, Mhlongo refused to work, insisting that he had done nothing wrong. His case was taken up with the Department of Home Affairs and he was released in April the following year.]

I lost everything. My house and everything that was in those four rooms. Now the reason why I came before the commission is that I now have a problem—because I'm now no longer able to perform the sexual activity to my wife. My body actually has turned to be useless. Now I don't know what to do next. I just want to find out, what can be done? Because during that apartheid era, I was labeled a terrorist and I am not a terrorist. Something should be done so that I can get a pension—that would console me and help me support my six children, who are still at school.

A man has lost his manhood—and he wants it back.

WYNAND MALAN: You spoke about the changes in your body—but you had five children after the shock treatment . . .

MHLONGO: Yes, I do have children . . . but I'll say this: I'm supporting these children and . . . I'm getting these children, and I suspect I am not the father of the children.

(Mahlasela Paul Mhlongo, testifying in Nelspruit)

My child was retrenched from Sasol. When he came back, he was waiting here at home. He stayed at home for almost two weeks. On the third week, he said to us no, he cannot remain here at home because he doesn't work. One night . . . he came home. He went to his room. He slept there.

While he was sleeping there, in the morning at half past six, there came a lot of boys and they said, "We want this boy, we are going for a meeting." The boy woke up and said, "Why such a noise here?" They said, "There is a meeting." And he said, "I don't know what the meeting is about." And they said, "It is a meeting for the comrades." They took my boy.

[. . .] They took an ax and they actually axed him on the head and he had long hair and this . . . this hair was actually inside in the wound . . . and from there he ran to another home and at that home there were two boys and they recognized him and they ran to my home. On arrival at my home, they said to me: "Stand up, Frank has been burnt to death." I asked, "What wrong has he done?" They said, "No, we don't know . . ." [crying]

I then left, I went. I just decided to run. I crossed the river and behind the other women called me and said: "Please come back; where are you going to?" I said, "No, I heard that my son has been burnt." They said, "No, come here, we saw a person running from the other direction . . . that was black with ashes." Thinking that it was my son, I went back. I took another direction and I asked him: "What happened to you, who injured you?" His whole body was burnt except the face and the nose. And he said, "I do not know. I don't know who the perpetrators of this act are." And . . . he said to me, "I don't know the people who burnt me." I said to him, "Not even one of the people who have done this to you?" And he said to me, "I will tell you tomorrow." He said, "I will tell you when I arrive in the hospital." I said to him, "Please, tell me, you said to me you know the perpetrators." He only opened his mouth like a bird and closed his mouth again and his eyes were now changing their color and . . . I cried . . .

These are the terrible things I saw with my eyes.

(Anna Silinda on the death of her son in September 1986)

I saw my younger boy coming, he's twelve years old. He said to his father there are people who are calling him. They are calling him in the passage and they want to know whether he is there or not. "Well," their father said, "I'm not going out." [The boy said:] "I want to go out and check who are the people." And when he went out, he met the people at the door. While he met them, one of them came closer and said to me, "Is your husband in?" and I said, "Yes, he's in."

My husband came out. And after he came out nothing much was said. It was a group of boys, I don't know their age, I don't know what was their aim. I saw a lot of people and confusion in my yard and some of the people had *sjamboks* with them and some had very dangerous weapons, and my husband, when he came out, he had a slasher with him. As they were just chasing him around in the yard, beating him with the sjamboks, and he fell down, and as he was falling down, he surrendered. And then when they checked him, his right ear was already damaged. After that, my boy was also present and he was around there, his sisters ran away.

Then one person came and said they must take out a tire and put it on my husband's neck . . . As they were taking two tires, he said to them: "If you want to kill me, kill me." And then he took the tire himself and then he said to them, "Do whatever you want to do to me." And the other person had a five-liter can of petrol. He poured petrol. And then they took a match and they lit it. And I took the match from him . . . And then they took the match again . . . and they gave it to him. I took it back again . . . and I took it and I threw it away. Then someone in the back threw a battery—he was actually aiming to hit me with this battery—and they gave it to me for the second time, the very same match. In the end, the same person, who was standing in front of me, took away that match and he set it alight. And they said he must be the one who actually set it alight.

. . . And then they dispersed . . . and he remained there . . . and he was burning. After that I took water, trying to pour the water on top of him . . . I could see nothing happened . . . I took some soil, and at that time, he was burning seriously . . . I scraped some soil and was pouring soil on top of him . . . my younger boy went to ask for transport somewhere . . . he went for a long time . . . by that time, I covered him with a blanket . . . We took him to the clinic, and from the clinic, we took him to the hospital. But one could see that he was tired . . . he actually did not reach the next day.

(Anna Mtimkulu on her husband's death in June 1986)

My wife and I and our three children attended church on Sunday. We drove to church in two vehicles, because I had to be there earlier. We left that evening around ten past eight. My wife and three children drove in front of me in our car. We came to the farm turnoff on the gravel road. We drove until the road splits to the house. Here, where my wife came to the fork, you could already see the lights in the house burning. All three children sat in the backseat. My young boy sat behind his mother, my baby of fifteen months lay on his sister's lap on the left—she was five years old. My wife gave the keys to my son: "Jaco, here are the keys to the house, please unlock the door for us." He stood up in the seat and leant over to take the keys. At that moment, she hit the land mine.

I, who was behind them, saw the whole event. I saw how the flames boiled out from under the car. I saw how the car shot up into the air. Right out of the road, ninety degrees, into the bush next to the road, pieces of metal, dust, earth, flew through the air. I pulled up, jumped out, crying: "God, why?" I went closer, I looked at my wife. She sat in her seat, crushed. Pieces of her feet were gone, her body was bloody, full of cuts, she moaned and asked, "Where are my legs?" My son who had stood up behind her was sitting on the backseat, head skew and unconscious. My other two children, my baby boy and girl, were fearful and just crying. His sister held him. I took these children out and loaded them into my vehicle and took them to the nearest house. [. . .]

We bent open the driver's door of the wreck. We lifted my wife out. I took off my jacket, put it on the grass, and laid her down. Then we tried lifting my son out. The front seats were pinning his legs. I asked [my neighbor] to take my wife to hospital. While he was fetching his car, I knelt next to her and said: "My wife, don't lose hope. Look up to the Lord." And I prayed for her. One is confused . . . Mr. Pretorius took her away.

Then I turned my son's feet aside and freed him from the seats and took him to hospital. My wife was taken out of the operating theater around three o'clock the next morning. They amputated her right leg under the knee. Her left leg was crushed at the ankle. They put in pins. She had several open wounds and her throat was cut open; they stitched it up, but her whole face was singed and her arms were torn.

At daylight my father and I went back to the scene of the accident. I knew a piece of my wife's leg from the shin down was still in the wreckage. We went to look if we couldn't find the limb in order to bury it. However, we could not find anything. What we did find was a piece of my son's skull in which he had a hole. On the top left. Some of his . . . brains were also on the seat. I put it in a tissue and buried it at home. Do you know how it feels . . . what it does to you? [. . .] How can you be human again after such an experience? Three days later, my wife died—20 August 1986. She never talked again.

[. . .] Sometimes I had to go to Pretoria in the middle of the week when my son got convulsion attacks. His four sisters, my father, and me had to hold him down on the bed. We learned that the morphine prescribed to him was not enough and that morphine of other patients had to be used to calm him down. I had the privilege to take him home for Christmas . . . but he did not recognize me as his father . . . he had to learn how to speak again . . . but he had lapses. Jaco died on 5 March 1987.

It was not an easy time for my daughter of five . . . that child never cried. That child still does not cry. The world can go to pieces around her, but it wouldn't matter . . .

(Johannes Roos)

It is dark when I enter the foyer of the Nelspruit Hotel. I cannot put things together. The cries of the night are in my ears; the jolly faces in the bar and the air that smells of spring—how do I integrate it?

A note waits with my room key:

This life is terrifying . . .

One could whistle through life like a starling,
or eat it like your nut cake.

But both of us know it's impossible.

—OSIP MANDELSTAM

I stare at the words.

The tight knot of my heart shivers.

A fountain falls on leaves and stone in the courtyard. It is dark where he is sitting. "Let's go and eat somewhere."

"It's going to rain," says the maître d'. "I suggest you sit inside."

"We want to sit outside," he says. We order antipasto.

"The two Annas—back to back like that. And the Anna whose son burnt to death—did you see her daughter next to her wore a piece of material with fuckin' dolphins on it—dolphins! I thought I was going off my head to see these grim faces, the description of the son's death without the word 'death' ever being mentioned, while there is this carefree space—there amongst them, there is a space where dolphins warble."

"The other Anna—have you ever seen a real NG Kerk hat at a hearing? Such a nice broad-brimmed white one made of voile . . . and she sits so alone and it's as if there's a great silence around her. And did you see she never cries . . . she just stares at the table in front of her . . . as if these stories are not the beginning or the end of something, but part of the ongoing horror of her life. How do people ever live together in the same neighborhood after such a thing has happened? Every time the comrades see her walking—and she's also tall, and so dignified— something must stir inside them."

The food is put down.

"And then there's the difference between the black victims and Johannes Roos. Full medical treatment was available immediately and the story was covered fully in all the newspapers with photographs and interviews. And still this doesn't make it any less terrible. Maybe you don't understand the Afrikaans, but he sounded really pious . . ."

"Yes, I picked it up in the translations. But why would he do such a barbarous thing like burying his son's brains at his house?"

"Just as barbarous as you, eating a whole plate of antipasto with your fingers. Why did they want to bury the leg . . . do you think they were afraid that it would be eaten by animals?"

It starts raining. The maître d' comes out. There is a table for us inside. No, we would like to sit here. We like the rain.

A Lowveld thunderstorm bursts over us—a spectacle of lightning and sound. It tears open neighborhoods—purple with jacaranda and wisteria.

"Oh, but Mr. Mhlongo. And he says it so directly: that the apartheid regime robbed him of his manhood and he wants to know what the Truth Commission can do about it. And trust the Truth Commission *manne* to understand that perfectly. And then they turn it around for him, so that he is actually looking for money for the children that are not his."

The waiter comes running out with an umbrella. Do we need anything? We order more wine.

"Two of the black journalists were sitting chatting and laughing while Roos was talking. How should one read it? I tried to work out in the beginning if I only cry when whites are testifying, but to my relief this was not so. But I have never seen a black journalist cry over any of the victims."

"So why don't you ask?"

Slowly we walk back. His hand reassuringly on the back of my neck. Soaking wet we walk—back into the oppressive night.

CHAPTER FOURTEEN

Letters on the
Acoustics of Scars

A letter from Tim

This last week has, for me, been a sort of microcosm of the whole TRC experience. On Tuesday I went out to dinner with a friend of mine at Cavendish Square. While we were having dinner, we sat next to two Afrikaner men. One was in his thirties and the other in his fifties—the topic of their conversation was the TRC. We overheard names like Georg Meiring being bandied about and, during a gap in our own conversation, I distinctly heard the younger man mention his amnesty application. I felt weird . . .

On Friday evening, I was invited to a party. Sometime during the evening, I got talking to a tall, good-looking, and well-built young Afrikaner man. After he learnt that I had been in the Defense Force, he called me into another room. He took off his shirt and showed me his chest and back—a mass of scars from a mortar bomb which narrowly missed killing him while he was on some mission. He was deeply upset. He started crying and I ended up holding him like a small child.

And on Saturday morning, I read your article in the *Mail & Guardian*. In one week—the generals, the foot soldiers, the victims, and the world outside.

Briefly my story is that in 1980 after matriculation I was called up to do my two years' national service. During my second year, I felt that I could no longer reconcile all that I believed in with the actions of the SADF in Namibia.

(I had the fortune to attend very good schools during my teenage years, schools that tried to teach the old "Mr. Chips" values of "being brave, and strong, and true, and to fill the world with love your whole life through . . .")

I deserted from the SADF and made my way to the Botswana border. I planned to go to Gaborones . . . My long-term aim was to join MK and do something against what I perceived then as an intrinsically evil system.

Being young, foolish, unprepared, and on my own, I was caught as I was about to climb over the border fence at Ramatlhabama. It was then that the nightmare began. I was handed over to the Zeerust branch of the security police, who interrogated me for about a week. I was beaten, given electric shocks, suffocated, kept naked, and repeatedly raped with a police baton. I remember very few details, except the screaming. I was nineteen years old at the time.

I was then handed over to the Walfish Bay Security Branch, where everything continued . . . It was a relief to be handed over into military custody after about two months—the military treated me far better than the police did . . .

This brings me to the point of my story.

The TRC has deeply affected my life in the short space of time that has elapsed since I first went to their offices here in Cape Town and told my story to one of the investigators.

In my own life, I think that my parents found it most difficult of all to accept what I had done and what had happened to me. They have only this year begun to talk about it—before that, it was never mentioned. I think the problem that they had was that the regime criminalized the actions I took—as law-abiding bourgeoisie, they felt torn between their loyalty to me, as their son, and the fact that I had committed a crime.

Now, with me having gone to the TRC with my story, it seems almost as if it's all right to talk about it. Slowly, things are changing. It's as if I have been freed from a prison that I've been in for eighteen years. At the same time, it's as if my family have also been freed—my brother is all of a sudden much softer, more human, more able to talk to me. The last time I saw him, he told me that he should have done more, that he should have tried harder. After watching the television documentary on Eugene de Kock, my mother came up to me, horrified: "We didn't know," she said to me. "We just didn't know."

Perhaps this is the most important role of the TRC. Not to extract confessions from F.W. and Magnus. No. They must live with their own conscience. Fuck the perpetrators. The point of the TRC is to enable healing to happen. And let it be said that here in me there is at least one person they have helped to reconcile: myself to myself.

And the silence is ending. It's as if we are waking up from a long, bad nightmare. Even the reaction in the Afrikaans press is encouraging: although I have never read a letter supporting the TRC in the Afrikaans press, there is also no questioning of the stories or the evidence. Not being able to attack the evidence, they attack the next-best thing—the commission itself. But the fact remains that we are no longer living under the tyranny of silence.

Yours sincerely,

Tim

A letter from Helena
(Translated from the Afrikaans by Angie Kapelianis)

My story begins in my late teenage years as a farm girl in the Bethlehem district of the eastern Free State.

As an eighteen-year-old, I met a young man in his twenties. He was working in a top security structure. It was the beginning of a beautiful relationship. We even spoke about marriage. A bubbly, vivacious man who beamed out wild energy. Sharply intelligent. Even if he was an Englishman, he was popular with all the *Boere* Afrikaners. And all my girlfriends envied me.

Then one day he said he was going on a "trip." We won't see each other again . . . maybe never again. I was torn to pieces. So was he.

Three years later, I moved to the old eastern Transvaal, where my circle of friends basically consisted of those in the security forces. I could never forget my first love. An extremely short marriage to someone else failed, all because I married to forget.

More than a year ago, I met my first love through a good friend. I was to learn for the first time that he had been operating overseas and that he was going to ask for amnesty.

I can't explain the pain and bitterness in me when I saw what was left of that beautiful, big strong person. Years had dug deep spoors in his face, robbed of all dignity, no one and nothing to live for. He had only one desire—that the truth must come out. Amnesty didn't matter. It was only a means to the truth. A need to clean up.

He was gruesomely plucked out of our lives at the beginning of the year. Is that the price he had to pay for what he believed in? The highest price for the truth?

After my unsuccessful marriage, I met another policeman. Not quite my first love, but an exceptional person. Very special. Someone with whom you feel safe. A well-balanced person who cares about others . . . with friends who you can count on.

Then he tells me that he and three of our friends have been promoted. "We're moving to a special unit. Now, now, my darling. We are real policemen now." We were ecstatic. We even celebrated.

He and his friends would visit regularly. They even stayed over for long periods. Suddenly, at strange times, they would become restless. Then abruptly mutter the feared word "trip," and drive off.

As a loved one, I knew no other life than that of worry, sleeplessness, anxiety about his safety and where they could be. We simply had to be satisfied with "what you don't know, can't hurt you." And all that we as loved ones knew was what we saw with our own eyes.

After about three years with the special forces, our hell began. He became very quiet. Withdrawn. Sometimes he would just press his face into his hands and shake uncontrollably. I realized he was drinking too much. Instead of resting at night, he would wander from window to window. He tried to hide his wild, consuming fear, but I saw it. In the early hours of the morning, between two and half past two, I jolt awake from his rushed breathing. Rolls this way, that side of the bed. He's pale. Ice cold in a sweltering night—sopping wet with sweat. Eyes bewildered, but dull like the dead. And the shakes. The terrible convulsions and blood-curdling shrieks of fear and pain from the bottom of his soul. Sometimes he sits motionless, just staring in front of him.

I never understood. I never knew. Never realized what was being shoved down his throat during the "trips." I just went through hell. Praying, pleading. "God, what is happening? What's wrong with him? Could he have changed so much? Is he going mad? I can't handle the man anymore!"

Today I know the answers to all my questions and heartache. I know where everything began. The background. The role of "those at the top," the "cliques," and "our vultures," who simply had to carry out their bloody orders. The churches and the community leaders.

Yes, I want to answer Antjie Samuel's question on the radio, I stand by my murderer who let me and the old White South Africa sleep peacefully, warmly, while "those at the top" were again targeting the next "permanent removal from society" for the vultures.

Yes, I have forgiven the freedom fighters for their bombs, mines, and AK-47s that they used so liberally. There were no angels. I finally understood what the struggle was really about the day the Truth Commission had its first hearing. I would have done the same had I been denied everything. If my life, that of my children and my parents, was strangled with legislation. If I had to watch how white people became dissatisfied with the best and still wanted better. And got it. I know they also have loved ones who have to suffer and struggle with their deeds. . . .

I envy and respect the people of the struggle—at least their leaders have the guts to stand by their vultures, to recognize their sacrifices. What do we have? Our leaders are too holy and innocent. And faceless. Long as our vultures were useful, tributes were dished out. Today, when the same vultures are wasted and ask only for recognition and support—are those White Afrikaners "at the top" too high and mighty, too righteously Christian and better than the rest, to acknowledge those they used?

I can understand if Mr. De Klerk says he didn't know, but, dammit, there must be a clique, there must be someone out there who is still alive and who can give a face to the "orders from above" for all the operations!

What else can this abnormal life be other than a cruel human rights violation?

Spiritual murder is a more inhuman violation than a messy, physical murder. At least a murder victim rests. The only operative is the faceless leader who plays God and decides who should be physically murdered and who should be spiritually murdered after he has done his dirty work.

I wish I had the power to make these poor wasted people whole again. I wish I could wipe the old South Africa out of everyone's past.

I end with a few lines that my wasted vulture said to me one night when I came upon him turning his gun over and over in his lap: "They can give me amnesty a thousand times. Even if God and everyone else forgives me a thousand times—I have to live with this hell. The problem is in my head, my conscience. There is only one way to be free of it. Blow my own brains out. Because that's where my hell is."

Call me:
HELENA

I am Mananki Seipei. I live in Orange Free State, Tumahole. I am Stompie Seipei's mother. Stompie was my firstborn, and we lived in a very poor family. Until Standard Two[1] I have been struggling to raise him. He met his fate in Standard Two. In 1985 the police took him. They took him to Parys police station. It was suspected that they robbed the bottlestore. Until in 1986 I saw the police coming to him in large numbers. On entering they said, "Where is Stompie?" I said to them, "He is not here." They said, "Take him out. He is here. We don't know is he a child or is he a person? Why do you let him go into politics?"

On 9 July in 1986, it was very early in the morning. Stompie was from the shop to buy bread. They met him. It was the Special Branch police. They said to me Stompie must get warm clothing, and they left with him. Stompie was detained in many prisons. He had been to Sasol, to Leeuhof, Heilbron, he went to Koppies, and he was in Potchefstroom. On 26 May in 1987, Stompie came back from Potchefstroom. On 25 June, that was the first time I saw Stompie. He left Tumahole. He was being chased by the police and he decided to run away. He went to Johannesburg because he was running away from the police. He was in Johannesburg and he came back. There was a comrade, Master Nakede, who passed away. Stompie had to come for his funeral.

And in 1988 he was arrested and he was sent to Koppies. When he went back to Koppies—he went back to Johannesburg. In 1988, on 1 December, Stompie appeared in court in connection with the burning of municipal cars. We used to call them the "green beans" at that time. Stompie went to Johannesburg. I was searching for him. I wanted to see him on 1 December. I was asking his friends, "Have you seen Stompie?" I was so afraid to go to the police because he didn't like the police at all. On 12 January 1989, there was supposed to be the next hearing for Stompie, but he never pitched up.

There was another lawyer at Parys who asked me, "Are you Stompie's mother?" I said, "Yes, I am." While listening to him, the lawyer told me that Stompie was dead. I was puzzled. Contrary to that, Stompie's friends did not tell me that he was dead, they said

---

[1] Standard 2 is roughly the equivalent of middle school, or junior high.

he was alive. As time went on, I met people and they said to me, "Are you freely moving here? Don't you know your son is dead?" I wasn't sure whether Stompie was dead or not. I was a woman fighting for the human rights. I couldn't feel anything that Stompie might be dead.

One woman told me that I should go to one of Stompie's friends and ask him, "Where is Stompie?" I went to see him and I only got his father. His father said to me, "They are all lying. Stompie is still alive." Stompie used to ride a BMX bicycle. He said to me, "He only has a small bruise on his leg." I stayed in 1989, expecting something to happen. Sometimes I would go to town, and that is where I received the news that Stompie is dead. I fell into the water, and that gave me an indication that he is dead. But nobody from the organization came to tell me the truth.

In 1989, on 30 January, two ministers from Johannesburg Methodist Church arrived. It was Bishop Peter Storey with Paul Verryn. They told me that they are seeing me in connection with Stompie. They said it was on 29 December in 1988 when Stompie was taken from the Methodist Church together with his friends. They were taken to Mrs. Winnie Mandela's house. They said to me they don't know, they are still searching for Stompie, they don't know whether is he alive or is he dead. And they told me that his friends told them that his brain was leaking. I stayed at home, expecting something to happen, but they said to me, "If the police arrive and they want to give you help about Stompie, you have to agree with them, because they are the only people who can help you."

On 13 February, the police came to me. On their arrival, they asked me—they said, "Is he Moeketse?" I said, "No, he is Moeketse." They said to me, "We will come tomorrow and fetch you so that we can go to Johannesburg."

On 14 February 1989, they took me and we went to Brixton. We went to Diepkloof Mortuary. That's where I identified Stompie. His body was decomposed, but your son is your son. I was fighting for my rights. There were signs that really indicated to me that it was Stompie. After having been killed, he was thrown into the river between New Canada and Soweto. You couldn't even identify him. I looked at Stompie because I am his mother. I had a deep look at him. I saw the first sign. I said, "I know my son. He doesn't have hair at the back." His eyes were gouged, and I said, "This is Stompie." The time Khotso House was bombed, Stompie was involved during those times. He had a scar on his eye. I looked at his nose, and he had a birthmark. I looked at his chest and I could see a scar, because he fought with another boy in Tumahole. And I looked at his left hand. It was identical to mine. I looked at his thighs. Stompie was very fit, just like his mother. I looked at his private parts, and my sister just winked her eye. His left leg is similar to mine. Underneath the left leg, there was a birthmark as well.

And they asked me, "How much does Stompie weigh?" I said, "No, the police would know that." They asked me, "Was he short or was he tall?" I said, "He was very short." But because he was thrown into the water like a dog, that's why he's stretched. They brought his clothes. I said, "I can see these clothes." There are two things that I realized as well that indicated to me, that proved to me, that it was Stompie. His white hat was there. I looked at his shoes, a new pair of running shoes. I said, "Yes, they are Stompie's." I said, "He used to wear size four."

We went back to Parys together with S. B. van der Merwe, with Richard Malambo. We went back to Tumahole. On the way, they were telling me that they don't believe it is Stompie. The next day they fetched me, they said Dr. Koornhof and Joubert indicated that it is not Stompie. I had to go back to Johannesburg. I was supposed to fight for the rights of my son. I went back to Johannesburg.

They asked me many questions. "Was Stompie suffering from anything?" I said, "Yes, he had tonsils. He had epilepsy, but when he was five years, he was healed." They said, "Did he have any problem with his eyes?" I said, "No, when he was released from Koppies Prison, he already had this problem with his eyes. He had the eye problem because he got it from the prison in Koppies." They said to me, "We don't believe it is Stompie." He was very young, he didn't have an identity document. He was fourteen years.

They said to me, "Do you think we should believe you that it is Stompie?" I said to them, "Yes, you have to." They came back and they gave me hands. They said, "He is your son. We could identify him through his fingerprints."

They said they will help me to bury Stompie. I said to them, "No, I will first speak to my family. I won't take the law into my hands, because Stompie was falling under a certain organization." We went to Parys. I told them that my family doesn't agree with their help, because you wouldn't say anything in those days because of apartheid. Even the mother of the child, you wouldn't speak anything in front of the police because you'd think that they would harass you. There was a mortuary called Bosman Mortuary. I went to that mortuary together with Sergeant Nel. I told the owner, Mr. Msipidi, that they should go and fetch Stompie from Johannesburg. They said no, they can't help me in any way because my family will help me.

On the last day, it was a Friday, the reporters came to me. They said to me, "Stompie is alive. He is in Botswana." They said Mrs. Mandela told them that Stompie is alive, he is in Botswana. I said to them, "I am not burying a zombie, I am burying my son. I know his birthmarks. I raised him from childhood. Nobody will ever tell me anything about my child."

We went to the mortuary to see him for the last time. He was decomposed, he had a bad smell. We couldn't bring him to the house. Together with my family and my father we went to see him and he was the real Stompie. But Mr. Msipidi said to us, "This is not Stompie." He said he appointed one member of his staff to take a very good look at Stompie, and he said that day there were many people from Stompie's organization. They were spreading the rumor that Stompie was an informer. I spent so many years raising Stompie. I have spent so many times talking to Stompie, and after that I was told that he was an informer.

On Saturday—the very same night—people from overseas came. They asked me, "Do you remember in 1987 when Stompie was released from prison we came to see you at 241?" I said to them, "Yes, I remember." They said, "Remember the police were just after us. They didn't want us to speak to Stompie?" I said, "Yes." They showed me a picture, a photo of Stompie, together with his friend Gili Nyatela, and they said to me, "The owner of the mortuary says the person who died is not Stompie." I said, "Those are news to me. The person that I am going to bury tomorrow is my son." We went to the church.

Something happened that really hurt me. The same person, the owner of the mortuary, said, "I took a look at this child and I discovered it was not Stompie. I called a member of my staff and he also said it is not Stompie." Reverend Mabuza stood up and he said, "I am here to bury Stompie Seipei. I don't care whether he is Stompie or not, but I am here to bury a fourteen-year-old child, Stompie." One reverend stood up and he said, "I don't know Stompie as much as he has been portrayed here. I know him. He was a very friendly person." Reverend Paul Verryn said, "I lost a very deep friend. I lost a real friend."

Saturday night I never slept. The same organization—we know that Jesus Christ was betrayed by one of his disciples. There was a rumor Saturday night that I should be happy that Stompie is alive. They toyi-toyied outside my house. Isabella Seipei stopped me from going out. Sunday morning they arrived again. They were crying. They said, "Mrs. Seipei, that is not Stompie. We were told that that person didn't have teeth." I just kept quiet. My grandmother tried to chase them, because she said to them, "Listen, if you keep on insisting that the person we buried is not Stompie, we will call the police," and they kept quiet. Monday morning another woman came and she said to me, "You buried a very wrong person." And she said, "You will receive a call on Tuesday from Botswana. Stompie will tell you that he is going to send you money." I was so desperate, and I left the woman, I went home.

COMMISSIONER: Mrs. Seipei, this story is very painful for you, and we understand that. But did you receive a death certificate of any kind for Stompie?

MRS. SEIPEI: Yes, I received a death certificate.

COMMISSIONER: Are you satisfied that you buried your own son?

MRS. SEIPEI: I am satisfied. I buried Stompie. I buried no one but Stompie.

(Mananki Seipei, mother of Stompie Seipei)

CHAPTER FIFTEEN

It Gets to All of Us—
from Tutu to Mamasela

I'm sitting opposite my child's tutor to discuss his bad math marks, when the beeper in my jacket pocket goes off. "Archbishop Tutu in hospital for cancer tests."

Everything falls away.

In my head only a flame-thin sound.

It cannot be. It dare not be.

I phone John Allen, the Truth Commission's media director and for years Tutu's right-hand man. They have decided not to keep it a secret, he says, as that would just lead to all sorts of rumors that would be hard to dispel later. Tutu will have a photo session in the hospital at twelve.

The tutor shows me how, page after page, my child escapes from his math homework into the margins with little sketches and doodles. In my thoughts, I want to press his brush-cut head against me—this tall, ungainly child of mine. But already the day reeks of mortality. The mountain, magnificently wrapped in blue earlier in the morning, now shimmers toothlessly in shock and sorrow.

What are we shuffling into?

The process is unthinkable without Tutu. Impossible. Whatever role others might play, it is Tutu who is the compass. He guides us in several ways, the most important of which is language. It is he who finds language for what is happening. And it is not the language of statements, news reports, and submissions. It is language that shoots up like fire—wrought from a vision of where we must go and from a grip on where we are now. And it is this language that drags people along with the process.

It takes me forever to choose the right flowers. I cannot find a card that seems special enough.

And I am angry. Why wasn't Tutu taken care of better? At the end of last year, I asked him in an interview: "Most of us have given up all attempts to maintain our health, our spiritual lives, and even family routines. How are you coping?"

"My training as a priest taught me to put supports and structures in place. And if your day starts off wrong, it stays skewed. What I've found is that getting up a little earlier and trying to have an hour of quiet in the presence of God, mulling over some scripture, supports me. I try to have two, three hours of quiet per day and even when I exercise, when I go on the treadmill for thirty minutes, I use that time for intercession. I try to have a map in my mind of the world and I go round the world, continent by continent—only Africa I try to do in a little more detail—and offer all of that to God."

A Dutch television director once asked me who Tutu's friends on the commission are. I couldn't think of anyone. There is cooperation and respect, but there is also some irritation: that Tutu from the beginning unambiguously mantled the commission in Christian language, that he finds it difficult to move from the strong hierarchy of the church to the democracy of the commission, that he is so popular with whites, that he so often mentions black people's wonderful ability to forgive. Those wrestling out their own agendas call Tutu the fool, the court jester, the ultimate cover-up artist.

He admitted how difficult he found it to function within the commission: "I found this year in a sense more taxing. Because I'm working in a setting with people with whom I have not always jelled. People with very different perspectives—they come from different backgrounds. Whereas in the church, say, I had a clear position and relationships with all the people with whom I worked. We formed a team more easily and naturally. Here there were those of us who thought it was important to become prima donnas—difficult for the sake of being difficult. But in general, we have gone over many hurdles, and despite what I've said, every commissioner's dedication has seen us through a rough ride."

At the hospital, a horde of journalists, cameramen, and photographers wait outside his room. With flowers in one hand, I know I have already broken the code of objective journalism.

We wait among trolleys and intercom noises and my thoughts wan-

der to the funeral of South African Communist Party leader Chris Hani.
How furiously bitter the speeches, how angry and volatile the crowd.
But Tutu got up, spoke into that crowd of thousands, and got them—
all of them—to wave their hands in the air, saying: "We are all God's
children—black and white."

"Did you plan to say that?" I once asked him.

"You see, I do believe very fervently that I'm being prayed for. Maybe
it's presumptuous, I don't know, but I think sometimes God says I
should say something—now that is something people may find it difficult to understand, but there are times when I actually don't know what
I am going to say until I've said it. This seems like a very bad way of
putting it, because it seems I'm not in control. When I got up at Chris
Hani's funeral . . . I think I have been helped to have a rapport, to in-
voke from the people what is already in there."

But I disagreed. "What you said was definitely *not* there. You were
taking an enormous risk—there were thousands of people who could
have publicly rejected you because you brought the kind of message nobody, not even I as a white, wanted to hear! When you said that word
'white,' I froze. I thought you were absolutely crazy . . . That word
could have been the spark to racial dynamite."

Tutu says: "But I mean, people pray . . . or if you want to be scientific, there is the credibility thing, that he stood up for us—'He was at
Duduza when the first necklacing happened and he stood there, he
was at funerals, he was at places when we were hurting and he was
crying with us . . . and maybe he is one of us and maybe he cares. So
when he says this, maybe he is saying something we ought to listen
to?' There are many factors at play here, but for me the most important of all is I'm not alone—I am not alone. A solitary nun in Califor-
nia once told me that she prayed for me at two o'clock in the morning.
In a scientific, materialistic, secular society, this would be described as
nonsense. For me, it brings a kind of confidence that things will be all
right."

The whole media contingent enters his private hospital room.

I cannot see him. I climb onto a visitor's chair.

There he lies. And I catch my breath. This wonderful man in whose
presence I always experience humanity at its fullest—humanity as it
was meant to be. This man who has made sense for us of the torturous
process of dealing with the truth by illuminating it with insight, humor,
and hope. And here he lies, smaller than I remember. And without his

purple robe and wooden cross—but in ordinary, rough, hospital pajamas.

He looks so worn. And gray. My whole face suddenly awash with
tears. We cannot finish what we have started without this man. The
cameras click away. Everyone is ushered out. I turn back and hold his
hands. He smiles at me: "Don't look so concerned . . . I will be okay . . .
besides, we are fighting *mos* on the side of the angels."

My cell phone rings in the dark. It's the news desk. There is a front-
page story in the *Star* about racial tension in the Truth Commission.
Could I get a story for the six o'clock news? The voice carries the accusing undertone of: Why have you missed it? I switch on the light. It's
half past five.

Who can I phone at this hour who won't kill me?

More problematic: Who can I phone who will take neither the black
nor the white side?

John Allen says: "I'll speak to you about the racial thing but only for
background, it's actually nothing serious."

Dumisa Ntsebeza laughs from his belly: "We represent South African
society and we have all kinds of tensions in the commission, we have
gender tension, age tension, racial tension, tension between staff and
commissioners, political tension—but this story, off the record, is just
the women fighting among themselves."

Despite all these denials, the story makes headlines for days. It is the
story everyone wants to hear, because it reflects the problems every
other integrated firm, group, or body is battling with. Racism among
equals. As the Truth Commission has gone along, it's become clearer
that everyone wants to find all the answers here. The commission must
point out spies in the government. The commission must dig up bodies. The commission must investigate what Big Business has done in
the past. In a way, the commission has become the voice of the people—the only place where people still have a voice, some say. And now
the commission must give leadership on racial tension.

And let it be said, the men stand together. Tutu issues an angry statement: "Newspaper reports on the alleged marginalization of black
members of the TRC have forced me into doing something which I
would rather not be doing, which is issuing a statement from my
sickbed.

"Firstly, all major decisions are taken by the full commission. Most commissioners are black. Most members of each of the three constituent committees are black. The chairpersons of each of the committees and the chief executive officer are black.

"Secondly, the suggestion from anonymous sources in the commission that it is run by a clique of white liberals is insulting to me and I take very strong umbrage. The implication is that I am almost a token chairperson who is not in control."

The Reverend Khoza Mgojo of the KwaZulu-Natal office also denies any knowledge of racism.

News reports note that the Truth Commission concluded its hearings the previous year on a high note, with amnesty applications flooding in and the amnesty cutoff and deadline dates generously extended by the government. But that the new year has been ushered in by news that the chairperson has cancer and that there is racial tension among commissioners.

The commissioners fly in for the first meeting of the year at the offices on Adderley Street. In a city lashed by a virulent southeaster, without even a bit of cricket to distract him, Archbishop Tutu lies at home. He has had a CT scan, a bone scan, and a chest X ray. No decision has been taken on the kind of treatment he needs, which may be further surgery, radiotherapy, hormone treatment, or some combination of these.

Everyone is waiting for the Truth Commission's truth on race, in the expectation that it will help ordinary mortals to resolve their own racial problems. The meeting will be a severe test. Can the commissioners hold it together without the verbal force of Tutu?

Indeed they can. During the press conference afterward, the whole racial issue is put down to "blocked channels of communication." Certain departments have now been restructured to facilitate communication between commissioners and offices. And that is that. Even as window dressing, the statement is disappointing—the moral overlay that Tutu could have provided is missing. The commission will surely have to confront racism at some stage. Perhaps a frank confession that the commissioners don't want to lose their substantial salaries and have therefore decided to stick together, come what may, would have been more relevant to South African racism than a bland statement about faulty communication?

· · ·

Tutu is back in his office. Waiting outside for an interview, I remember the very first interview I had with him at Bishop's Court. My news editor, Pippa Green, who once worked for Tutu, convinced him of the importance of radio for the Truth Commission: if you really care about the masses of people who have access only to radio, who understand only their indigenous mother tongues, then you take radio seriously. So Manelisi and I had this interview one Saturday morning. When we came in, Tutu was standing at the window, dressed in khaki shorts down to his knees, socks, and a T-shirt saying "I love reading." We sat down and began to fire away enthusiastically. He held up his hand. Let us pray. And to our utter astonishment, he mumbled a kind of prayer, clearly not intended for our ears. What kind of intimidation was this?

I also remember how he had to choose a bodyguard from a list. "I want an Anglican," he apparently said, and so a young bodyguard was chosen who never suspected that he would have to take Communion daily with the archbishop of his church.

At the farewell service the Anglican Church gave for Tutu when he retired, my eyes popped out of my head when the long, impressive procession of bishops passed me, with incense and chanting and bobbing miters, and, lo and behold, a pace behind the archbishop, solemnly in step, walks the bodyguard in a priest's cassock—his gun bulging conspicuously under his arm.

The bodyguard sat through the whole four-hour sermon, yawning shamelessly until tears were streaming down his cheeks. Even Tutu's sermon did not make a difference: "God has a tremendous sense of humor. How else could you think of a God who would choose *iemand soos hierdie ene met die yslike groot neus* [someone like this with the huge nose], with a funny name that you could make graffiti with: 'I was an Anglican until I put tu and tu together.' Or make a song out of: 'Don't mess with my tutu.' And God is smart, you can't beat God's timing. In the past, we were 'against.' Against oppression, against apartheid. Our essence was against. And we were so single-minded. But the time has come to change from the 'against' mode to the 'for' mode. Isn't God then smart to say: 'Bye-bye Tutu'?"

So many stories about this man.

A man interceding. The mayor of Johannesburg tells how police broke up a protest march one day. They grabbed one of the ministers, Tom Manthata—later a committee member of the Truth Commission—

and brutally kicked and beat him. "I could not bear it, I ran away, it was too terrible for mortal flesh. But Tutu, and I will never forget this, grabbed a policeman by the arm and angrily told him: 'It is a *human being* that you are treating like this.' "

A man praying. The war between the squatters and the *witdoeke* on the Cape Flats. Tutu organizes a meeting between the factions. When the one faction does not arrive, he refuses to get out of the car and spends hours praying there until the other group appears. "Yes, on the way to a march or a struggle funeral, in the back of the car, he usually sits bowed and praying all the way," Pippa Green tells me. "Just a mumbling human bundle. But when the door opens and he gets out among the masses of people, he is at once extraordinary and exceptional—larger, stronger, than all of us. The energy, the power, that beams from him, his voice, his charisma, make thousands upon thousands of people obey him blindly. And when he speaks he speaks for all—yet he utters the most secret sorrow of your heart."

That is why the SABC of old found it so effective to show Tutu's energetic gestures on TV, but to replace his words with somber music and sinister text.

"The illness has confirmed that one is mortal, that one is not superman, that you are not the savior of the world—and that you don't have superhuman powers."

I ask him about the things that happened in his absence of six weeks.

"I am thrilled by the new information that has come out in amnesty applications about the Pebco Three and Cradock Four—and especially Steve Biko. We've never got this information before and the country deserves to have it. This uncovering more or less justifies the existence of the commission.

"I am less than thrilled with the tiff that happened among the commissioners. People rightly must say to us: 'For goodness' sake, physician, heal thyself! What do *you* know about reconciliation?' So I am sad about that—because I believe the commission had begun to do enough to have a credibility that was becoming acceptable to a very large part of our society.

"I am very deeply distressed. But what pleased me about it—is that it backfired. People thought by using those old-style stereotypes they were going to attract support. And in the past, they may have been able to do that, but today most people just say: 'For goodness' sake, why do they *want* to be victims? Why don't they confront those people who are sidelining them?'

"But what saddens me is that we have been chosen by the nation through the president. We've been given an incredible privilege, chosen as people representative of South African society. We were chosen so that we could be an icon—demonstrating the longing that we can transcend the conflicts of the past. And say yes, that is where we come from, but it is possible for people coming from all the different backgrounds to cohere.

"If we can't, how in the name of everything that is good can we expect people who have experienced worse traumas than we have to be healed and to reconcile? We have to look at ourselves very carefully, even at this stage, and decide whether we are willing to take on this mandate, this vocation, the nation has given us."

"Pain and suffering are remarkable things—our universe is very odd. Pain gives a quality to what is happening that nothing else seems able to give. I have a time bomb inside me and I know that . . .

"Most times I think of my mother . . . you know . . . always I think of my mother . . . I think of her. I mean I will never forget, I was going to high school—and there was no money at home. My mother was a washerwoman and I went with her to her white madam. And she was going to do the washing and cleaning and she was going to get at the end of the day two shillings. And my mother collected her two shillings in the morning and gave it to me and then I walked to the station for a ticket to go to school in Westbury . . . And I always thought at the end of the day, my mother had done all that work . . . and she would get nothing . . . Ja . . . she died the year I got the Nobel Peace Prize . . . I look like her—short, with a large nose."

The National Party sends an ultimatum to the Truth Commission. Tutu must apologize unconditionally for dismissing the party's second political submission, Boraine must resign because he is biased, and the executive of the investigative unit must refrain from contact with any of their members in the future. If these demands are not met, the party will go to court. The NP believes it has proof that the commission is not abiding by its own legislation. It is supposed to make findings *after* gathering all the evidence. Yet, the NP says, both Boraine and Tutu have prejudged its submission.

"We are about reconciliation in this country," says Tutu. "A standoff is of no use to anybody and that is why I say: 'What is a court case going to prove?' If we won, who would be better off? If they won, who would benefit?"

The fact is, the National Party would benefit. A question mark would be left hanging over the Truth Commission's summary of the NP's role, contained in its final report to the president. Even though it was Tutu, weeping after the party's submission, who asked: How can De Klerk say he did not know? "I personally met with him so many times to tell him that simple people, people with no reason to lie, are talking about how white people were involved in the massacre at Boipatong."

You can't give up, I plead with Tutu in my head. If you give up, then all is lost.

And I ask: "Are you saying you need the National Party?"

"It hurts me," says Tutu, "when I think of the quiet strength and resilience and magnanimity of the victims, that there is just no response from their side. And for reconciliation we need everybody. This is a national project and everybody is important. They are important because they are from an important constituency in our country."

"Does the National Party need you?" I ask.

There is a long pause. "I don't know. We've been given a job to do and we are trying to do it to the best of our ability. I think if they want a country that is not alienated, not traumatized, not broken, not divided, then yes . . . if we are regarded as an important instrument of reconciliation . . . then they need us, yes."

It is not surprising that the NP has displayed the most resistance to the commission, Tutu says. Anyone would react this way to the uncomfortable exposure of things from the past. However, the Truth Commission cannot bow to the Nationalists' demands. "Basically, they have unreasonable demands. I think this is the point. I myself have no problem with apologizing . . . it's no skin off my nose to say I'm sorry. But I don't know what I have to apologize for. It seems such an extraordinary red herring.

"I'm deeply committed to reconciliation and I care enormously for all the people in this country . . . and would do everything within reason. And I have done extraordinary things, I mean things that make people think I'm crazy, just to say: 'We want you, we want you, we really want you, and we will not just go that extra mile, but many, *many* miles.'

"You see, we can't go to heaven alone. If I arrive there, God will ask me: 'Where is De Klerk? His path crossed yours.' And he also—God will ask him: 'Where is Tutu?' So I cried for him, I cried for De Klerk—because he spurned the opportunity to become human."

Any VIP itinerary in South Africa includes the inevitable visit to an impoverished community. This week Queen Margarethe of Denmark visited the Trauma Centre for Victims of Violence and Torture in the lower part of Woodstock. It has run for years on Danish money.

But it also seems inevitable that a royal visit should look like a spearhead of affluence and privilege thrust at the heart of poverty. First a line of brand-new red and white combis pulls up. The assembled schoolchildren wave their flags and the choirmaster lifts his hand. A lot of whiteys get out simultaneously. Who is who? But they are only the door-openers. The sliding doors of the vans empty a media flood into the street. With flashing cameras and wobbling microphones, the Danish press swoop down enthusiastically on the rows of neglected children and the unemployed of Woodstock who are lining the street to observe the occasion. A formal cavalcade of eight black Mercedes-Benzes delivers the queen and the young crown prince. Again, leaping from the cars simultaneously: exceptionally pale, plump men in even paler khaki caps, vigorously opening doors for the palest-looking, delicately smiling dignitaries from the northernmost north of the globe . . . On cue, the Masahile Choir of Khayelitsha launches into—you guessed it—our national anthem of fake unity left over from the Rugby World Cup: "Shosholoza."

The queen wears a dark-blue hat upon which a white-linen butterfly has settled. She approves everything smilingly. She says not a word. Tutu speaks, Tutu tells jokes, Tutu says we are standing on hallowed ground; Father Michael Lapsley thanks the people who came to plant the trees yesterday, who rolled down the lawn this morning, who delivered the plants keeling over in their wet sockets, who installed the lights, who painted the place out. Choirs sing. Victims tell their gruesome stories while they stumble in pain. She approves everything smilingly. Queen Margarethe says not a word.

Along with Mandela, Robben Island, and Khayelitsha, a Truth Commission hearing is a must-see. But since the hearings are held in such obscure places, a visit to Tutu is the next-best thing. Either the whole of Milnerton is paralyzed as Al Gore's security personnel cordon off the routes to Tutu's rented house in the suburb, or a ring of steel is thrown around the Adderley Street offices for a visit by Hillary Clinton.

We are in a hall full of media people waiting for a press conference. We gaze with astonishment at the journalists, who look as if they have just walked out of *The X-Files*, reporting live on Hillary Clinton's day. Everywhere you turn, there is a 100 percent made-up woman, microphone in hand, rattling off a paragraph about your country. And you recognize neither "Cantantia" nor "Speew Whinestate." If you were just a little absentminded, someone would simply grab you like a piece of seaweed and toss you in a corner. There are celebrities among them too. "Oh look! There's the son of the guy who broke the Watergate story . . . and there's Annie Leibovitz—*the* photographer in America."

We can come in now.

Stampede is an understatement. That selfsame photographer shoots her sharp elbows out like an umbrella and buggers your ribs—this is her space. I crawl in among the legs up to the front and stretch out my arm to hold the microphone up in between Tutu and Hillary Clinton. "Remove that microphone!" somebody yells. My God, I'm also just doing my job. With the lowering of the microphone, my eye falls on the shoes, ankles, and shiny, shapeless legs of Hillary Clinton here right in front of me. And at once I'm overcome by a deep depression.

I do not want to hear what she is saying. Even if she is the First Lady of the Mightiest Nation. Even if her visit destroys all distinction between symbolism and reality. Even if she gives thousands to the Truth Commission. I don't want to know.

Pumps, I think they're called. Golden pumps with little golden buckles on the heels. From the shoes bulge her feet, up into the hosiery that disappears in the straight pink skirt. Armored. And she has to be, because questions are raining down, the spotlight bright on her face. She daren't show an inch of human being. My leg goes to sleep, I shift my balance, and my eyes fall on Leah, the wife of Tutu. Leah stands on the far right of the row, turned against the crowding journalists, because she isn't looking at Hillary but straight at Tutu, standing next to her. And then I know. The press releases on his illness do not tell the full story.

. . .

Overseas visitors attending the Truth Commission hearings often express their surprise at the absence of anger in the black audience. Although the venues have been packed week after week, there hasn't been a single violent outburst or aggressive incident.

Where is the anger? *Is* there anger?

Have decades of oppression eroded black people's sense that they have a right to show anger? Or has the fact that the majority now rules defused all the rage? I try to get some answers from clinical psychologist Nomfundo Walaza.

"People make a grave mistake if they assume there is not an immense feeling of outrage among blacks. A crying person and an angry person are two sides of the same coin," she says. "But the whole structure of the Truth Commission specifically contains all anger. The catchword is 'reconciliation,' and on top of that, the chairperson is an archbishop of a religion in which forgiveness is the central theme.

"So at the witness table of the commission, it seems better to cry than to be angry and smash things up. They know that the basic premise is reconciliation and forgiveness . . . In Xhosa the word they have chosen for 'reconciliation'—as in 'Truth and Reconciliation'—is *'uxolelwano,'* which is much closer in meaning to 'forgiveness.' "

At times, says Walaza, anger is crucial for progress.

"I think black people's anger has been self-contained. And I don't say that all black people are criminals, but when people are saying crime has increased in the townships, I say it could be expected, because I'm sure it's all due to a lot of pent-up anger that has been there for a long, long time."

In the Free State, I'm usually confronted with the heart of things. I tell Walaza: "A white woman said to me, 'I don't even watch the Truth Commission on television—because all you see there is a sea of hatred.' I told her I attend most of the hearings, and that is not true. There is really no hatred."

"That is pure projection," says Walaza. "Firstly, she knows instinctively that if apartheid had been done to her, she would have hated. And secondly, whites prefer to think that they are being hated; then they don't need to change. It goes to the whole notion of saying: 'Blacks are so angry with me, there is no way I can go and live with them because they are going to kill me. And we shouldn't bring black people here because they essentially hate us.' "

During that same Free State conversation, a farmer said vehemently:

"If these things were done to me, I would hate deeply and passionately, like the Russians. I would have destroyed everything around me: the fact that they didn't just shows you that blacks are not even able to *hate* sufficiently."

There is a long silence.

"In essence we are dealing here with a definition of humanity," says Walaza. "And this remark is the clearest proof that whites with their self-centered, selfish, capitalistic character have never been able to fathom the essence of humanity.

"Besides that, I'm not sure that black people's anger has to be measured by what white people say. If white people want to say black people cannot hate sufficiently, then that is their business. I think the Soweto uprisings were proof enough what blacks can do when they are being pushed too far. But what we're probably dealing with here is people who are coming from a culture with a capitalist notion of existence in the world, where you have things for yourself and your group, the people that look like you. And the other notion that people can actually share things is totally incomprehensible to them. When whites came to the country—and I know I wasn't there—but it seemed that black people initially were happy to share things and give over . . . but that kind of sharing went wrong. This whole concept of *ubuntu* that is being bandied about all over the place, that went horribly wrong.

"What makes me angry is that whites are privatizing their feelings. If you as a black person cry, you cry alone at the hearings. If you are angry, there is no perpetrator to direct that anger against verbally—they hide in their suburbs, they hide behind their court interdicts and legal representatives. The pain of blacks is being dumped into the country more or less like a commodity article—easy to access and even easier to discard."

"But isn't the attitude of whites at least a sign of guilt?"

"Guilt is such a useless thing," she says impatiently. "Guilt immobilizes you. 'I am guilty—so what can I do?' Feelings of guilt are also open to abuse by those who suffered: 'You are guilty—so give me a thousand rand.' I prefer shame. Because when you feel shame about something, you really want to change it, because it's not comfortable to sit with shame."

"But just as whites suddenly pretend that no one supported apartheid," I say, "so it seems to me that suddenly all blacks were part of the struggle and made huge sacrifices for liberation. Shouldn't one say that every black person who is alive today also didn't do quite enough? Did all black people pay a price?" I shudder after having said this.

"All black people did pay a price," Walaza says. "What happened to your next-door neighbor and in your area affected you—you lived in a constant vibration of fear and insecurity, of being utterly deprived in all kinds of ways, of knowing you could never develop your full potential. So some paid more, others paid less, others paid differently—but every black person in this country did pay a price. On the other hand, I have problems when this price becomes a mere tool for self-aggrandizement. At the end of the day, we all have to stand up and say, 'This is what we did *not* do . . .' "

The response of whites to the Truth Commission is regularly articulated in letter columns, editorials, cartoons, in the opinions of the National Party, the Democratic Party, and the Freedom Front, and in hate mail to journalists. One of the letters in my postbox reads:

> Die vernaamste eksponent [van Boerehaat] is daardie onvergenoegde veld-prediker van die Ween-en-Verdrietkommissie Radio sonder Mense se per-soonlike Gesant en buitengewone, spesiale afgevaardigde by die WVK, Antjie Samuel.

The most important exponent of Boer-hatred is that dissatisfied bush preacher of the Crying and Lying Commission—Radio without People's personal Envoy and extraordinary, plenipotentiary delegate at the Truth Commission, Antjie Samuel.

Her dramatized versions on "Monitor" in the mornings and "Spectrum" in the afternoons (with the appropriate drumbeating or the slow tones of the funeral march or the triumphant heights of "Nkosi Sikelel' iAfrika") have the whole country in tears (or in a state of rage) about the untested evidence and accusations put before the TRC.

(Personally I never know whether to laugh or cry.)

In a voice that sounds as if she's in a crypt.

Shame, the poor confused child. And she comes from such a good home.

Foeitog, die arme verwarde kind. En sy kom uit so 'n goeie huis.

. . .

The reactions of white South Africans to the revelations of the Truth Commission can be divided into two main groups, says psychiatrist Dr. Sean Kaliski. There are those who refuse point-blank to take any responsibility and are always advancing reasons why the commission should be rejected and regarded as a costly waste of money. And then there are those who feel deeply involved and moved, but also powerless to deal with the enormity of the situation.

"People in the group refusing to have anything to do with the commission see themselves as pedestrians, as mere passersby," says Kaliski. "They didn't know what was happening, and even if they did, they had no power to change it. Research shows that on the emotional graph this is the group that has changed least since the first democratic elections. It includes those white English-speakers who feel that the atrocities of the past are solely the baggage of the Afrikaner. But the vast majority of this detached group are, of course, Afrikaners themselves." They call the commission the *Lieg en Bieg Kommissie*, they feel unfairly treated, and they deny everything. "Untested evidence" is their buzzword.

As an outsider, Kaliski sees it as the task of Afrikaner leaders to guide their communities in dealing with the commission and redefining Afrikanerhood.

But what happens when the leaders are also still in the denial phase?

"Then you're in big trouble. You have to find other leaders . . . you have to find people who stand up and say: 'Look, that is not how we are, *this* is how we are.' Because personally I think the Afrikaners are great survivors and they will find people who can interpret these revelations for them."

But there is the other group, also made up of Afrikaners and white English-speakers, who have followed and supported the Truth Commission from the beginning. They do not switch off when the Truth Commission is mentioned, they follow the hearings on Radio 2000, they turn up as solitary white figures at the hearings, they send letters with prayers and support for the commission—study groups, women's groups, individuals. They are going through something totally different: emotional and mental fatigue, a depression that flares into irrational outbursts.

"It's my impression that inadequate preparation was made before the TRC started its work," says Kaliski, "to investigate ways in which people could integrate all the information that would be revealed . . . and that is why we're unable to cope with what is coming out. And worst of all, I think, is that we are not using the truths we are confronted with to effect any reconciliation.

"One will have to come to terms with the past in one's own personal way," he says. "If you live in this country, if you want your children to have a future, you will have to devise a method for yourself."

Another silent voice is that of the Afrikaans churches. Although some Dutch Reformed Church elements visibly take part in the process now and then, few people know whether or how the church and its members—once described as "the National Party at prayer"—are participating in the search for truth and reconciliation.

Professor Piet Meiring, a committee member of the commission, was invited to observe the annual ceremony welcoming new students to the Stellenbosch Theological Seminary.

The ceremony started with anecdotes about the seminary back in 1937, interwoven with the names of theologians Koot Vorster—the man who called the Afrikaans writers of the sixties "'n spul vuil spuite," a bunch of dirty squirts—Kosie Gericke, and the like. This is usually a red-letter day for the dominees of the western Cape. They come from all over; they kuier with old friends. They packed the hall last year, when the theme under discussion happened to be "Was Jonah in the Whale?" This year, with the focus on the Truth Commission, the hall was barely half full—and that included a row of first-year students in compulsory attendance. The opening was performed by Dr. Fritz Gaum. His text was "I am the Truth and the Light" . . . and in his prayer, he confirmed: "We know the Truth, because we know the Lord."

Then it was the turn of Meiring—a professor in missionary science. "I asked a visiting Rwandan what the role of the Church in their massacres was—a country where eighty-five percent of the population is Christian and where a million people lost their lives. He didn't like my question. The Church was part of the problem. Their hands were covered with blood . . . the priests, the nuns—their hands were red with blood."

The reaction of the white Afrikaans churches to the Truth Commission has been subdued, to put it kindly, says Piet Meiring. He often has to contact the ministers of amnesty applicants, and the body language of most dominees shows that they want nothing to do with the commission. Why? They're afraid of a witch-hunt, the professor says; they're afraid the Truth Commission will increase the desire for revenge. They think the findings will not be objective and they say: "Confession and forgiveness is a religious act; how can it be done in a secular way?"

No one can escape the process, says Meiring, and the churches ought to be doing much more than anybody else. The Church has a prophetic responsibility. It must admit and confess its guilt. Guilt? Who then is guilty? Meiring spells out the categories of guilt: criminal, political, moral, and metaphysical. But the Church also has a pastoral responsibility. It must support amnesty applicants; it must support the victims in that area, that town; it must assist the whole community as it wrestles with truth and reconciliation. Meiring says the Afrikaner in particular has been traumatized by the process. Like the psychiatrist Kaliski, Meiring refers to the phases described by the psychologist Elisabeth Kübler-Ross in her work on terminal illness and death:

"The first phase is that of denial: as the truth is put on the table, people deny it. The second phase is that of anger—with God, with the new government, with those who are doing this to you. The third phase is that of bargaining with God, and that is what some people are already doing—those bargaining for amnesty. The fourth phase is a deep depression, and that is the most important phase because it opens up the door of acceptance."

An aged professor emeritus by the name of Koekjan de Villiers stands up: "My time is short," he says. "And I who have lived in the paradise time of apartheid, I am begging you young men—do something, put the whole history of my Church at the feet of the Truth Commission—before it ends its work and before the millennium is upon us."

Ou Antjie Somers,

Geniet jy nog die aanklagte en Swartsmeerdery van die Afrikaners? Is jy nog by jou man of het jy nou 'n hotnot, 'n mede wapendraer in jou stryd teen die Nasionale Party waarvan jou pa so 'n getroue ondersteuner is/was?

K.K.K.

[Old Antjie Somers,

Are you still enjoying the accusations and besmirching of the Afrikaner? Are you still with your husband or have you found your-

self a Hottentot, a weapon-bearer in your struggle against the National Party of which your father is/was such a loyal supporter?

K.K.K.]

A provisional document on the proposed reparation and rehabilitation
policy of the Truth Commission is to be discussed at a workshop. The
media are allowed to attend.

The Reparation and Rehabilitation Committee could make or break
the Truth Commission. It will help little if the transgressors walk away
with amnesty, but the victims, who bear the appalling costs of human
rights abuses, experience no restitution. No gesture of recognition or
compensation.

When the legislation was first explained to the commissioners, so
it's been said, some of them started crying when they realized the perpetrators did not have to show remorse for their deeds. One may well
ask why no one objected to the fact that the person who gets amnesty
is freed immediately, whereas the victim has to wait for the commission
to complete its investigation, draft the report and the policy, submit the
policy to Parliament, and see whether the government applies it. In the
interim, victims are dying for want of the necessities of life.

Over time, a certain skepticism has built up about the vision and
ability of the Reparation and Rehabilitation Committee. When it became apparent that the racial conflict had actually started in this committee, no one was surprised. The workshop to discuss the proposed
policy is thus attended with great interest.

The committee's first suggestion is that of urgent interim relief. This
is already being applied on a small scale, although it has not yet been
officially approved by the government. It means that victims can ask for
up to a thousand rand (about $170) to access medical services. The sec-
ond suggestion is that by the end of the commission's term every
victim should get monetary compensation from the government—a
substantial amount, says the document, enough to make a qualitative
difference to their lives. "This would not be asking too much," says
Archbishop Tutu, who attends the opening session of the workshop.
"Given what the country has gained, this is peanuts."

Apart from suggestions for a monument here and a clinic there, this
is the sum total of a year's thinking. We look at each other.

Then a whole discussion erupts on who exactly the victims are.

There are clear-cut guidelines for primary victims: you are a primary victim if your rights were violated directly, if the hurt was done directly to you. But the category of secondary victims is fuzzy: if a man was killed, who gets the monetary compensation? His mother? His wife and his children? And if he had other children by other women? It also seems that not all those who have testified are necessarily victims. The investigative unit must first corroborate your story before you will be classified as a victim. Did this really happen to you? But then someone testifying about the death of a neighbor's child cannot be a victim. Or imagine the following situation, someone says: A is an organizer in the struggle—he leads the marches, he is hunted, he cannot go to school. One day B, who has never participated in the struggle, sends her child to buy some fish. The child gets killed. Now B is a victim, while A finds himself without an education or a job. And what about the shysters rushing to swindle victims out of their money?

While the discussion is in full swing, we file stories about the main suggestions. To condense this kind of policy-planning document into accessible hard copy is difficult. Two of us work on the stories—we listen to our tapes, compare notes, juggle with words, argue about the right weight of every sentence. We write it. We check it. We send it.

After the lunch break, a furious commissioner comes up to us. "How can you say that the Truth Commission is going to give only a thousand rand to every victim? It's not true!"

"We didn't say that. We wrote that victims can ask for a thousand rand to access medical services."

"Well, that is not what I've just heard over the radio."

We are unconcerned. Even quite cheeky.

Later I hear a newcomer ask: "How can Tutu say this compensation is peanuts? He is criticizing your policy before it has even been discussed."

"But he never said that . . ."

"That's what the radio said."

Around six o'clock, we go back to the SABC offices to file our stories for the next morning. We look into the computerized bulletin system and see our stories . . . changed. "By God, look here 'The Truth Commission is planning to give victims a thousand rand.' And two sentences later it says 'to access medical services.' "

"Look at this one: 'Archbishop Desmond Tutu says the compensation for victims is peanuts.' Full stop."

I am furious—I am *livid*—that our copy is being treated so shabbily, so unprofessionally, as if we started doing this job yesterday. I make a printout of the stories and go to the bulletin editor. I put the stories down in front of her.

"Who gives you the right to change our copy—so that it's incorrect—without the decency to at least consult us?"

She reads through them. She reads the originals.

"But it isn't incorrect. We've just changed the angle and we are allowed to do that."

"It's not the angle I'm talking about. I'm talking about a major mistake. Surely if you say, 'Victims will get a thousand rand . . .' that's quite different from 'Victims will get a thousand rand to access urgent medical services'!"

"But we've got that in—only a bit later—so the context is exactly the same."

I start shivering. My tongue paralyzed in a fucking second language. I grab her arm.

"You are an intelligent woman. Your news bulletins have told thousands of victims they will all get a measly thousand rand. That is wrong. That could cause a riot. And we look like fools not understanding what's going on. We don't just shake hard copy out of our sleeves, you know. We don't just happen to say something like this and not like that. We think about it; we debate about it. What the hell is wrong with you?"

"I really don't see what you're on about . . ."

I feel faint. My eyes fasten on her pale-blue polka-dot blouse—the white button at her brown wrist. I hear the sudden quiet suspense in the news room. I feel powerless and exploited and unable to formulate my grievance convincingly.

"*Jissis*, I refuse to discuss this any further," I hiss in her face. "We have been filing good solid hard copy to you for more than a year, and I demand respect from this fucking desk." Punctuated with my fist on wood.

I walk back to my desk, smoke two cigarettes, and then call the members of the Reparation and Rehabilitation Committee to apologize about the report.

The next day, I find several nameless letters on my desk: "Good for you! You told her to her face. We never thought you had it in you."

Someone else comes up to me: "I heard you threw all your toys out of the cot yesterday. Nice, man. It's time she gets some real competition."

A note: "We will testify for you if necessary"—and a list of names.

Until someone tells me: the bulletin editor has asked that I be called for a disciplinary hearing. The charges are insubordination and assault. I feel myself blushing. Then cringing in utter embarrassment. "What is the Afrikaans for 'assault'?" I ask.

"*Aanranding,* as in hitting her. She says you hit her in front of her whole staff."

I gape like an ape. It can't be. This is not happening. It can't be true!

"But I didn't hit her."

"She says you did and she has witnesses."

"Well, I also have witnesses."

But after I've thought it through, I realize that when it comes down to it, there is probably not that much difference between grabbing an arm and *hitting* an arm. But I will die. I will absolutely die if I have to talk about this before any committee.

"Other people want us to describe the incident over and over, because no one has ever heard you even raising your voice, never mind shouting, shaking, hitting, and demanding."

God, what is happening to me?

I phone home. I cry. My husband sounds far away. "Resign and come back—we miss you."

My news editor says: "Fight back."

But are these the kinds of things one fights for?

The dispute is settled after a long discussion in the boss's office. I apologize. She withdraws the charges.

I am deeply, completely embarrassed.

We lie on our backs in the autumn. The leaves sift like coals from the burning trees. Your voice smells of bark.

"Come with me . . ."

The flaming season plunges into us. And it lies heavily on my arms—this late inopportune lust to abandon what is seen to be my life.

People involved with the Truth Commission are "breaking down," packing up, or freaking out. There are complaints that our reporting over the radio is becoming too opinionated. So a workshop is organized for the radio team. For two days, we will be discussing how to keep your anger out of a story, and someone will come and "debrief" us. Whatever it turns out to be, I suspect some of us really need it.

We descend on an unsuspecting guest house. And if any doubt existed about the abnormal effects of covering the Truth Commission, that evening dispels it with hard evidence. At once we become our own little hit squad. We talk contemptuously and drink destructively. Some people park themselves behind the bar counter for the evening. Others tell stories in front of the fireplace—Truth Commission stories. What happened to this one or that one, acting out the mannerisms of commissioners and judges, mimicking victims until we roll on the floor with laughter. Everybody speaks as if they've been in solitary confinement for months. In the end, no one is listening to anyone else, but everyone keeps on talking.

The next morning, the psychologist arrives. We all sit nervously around the table. He begins. What physical symptoms have manifested themselves recently?

We answer: neck ache, backache, ulcers, rashes, lack of appetite, tiredness, insomnia.

Right. So how do we feel? He says we each have to answer individually.

Mondli says: "I am not affected, because I grew up with these things. My sister's house was burnt, Bheki Mlangeni was one of my best friends. So, I mean this is nothing new. Usually I laugh at testimonies. I listen but I don't feel pain."

The same story is repeated by all the black journalists—they are actually fine. The commission's work doesn't affect them because they grew up with human rights abuses all around them.

Angie and I start crying silently, and so copiously that we are out of action for the rest of the session. Our colored colleague jumps up and runs out. Someone goes after him, but he only returns much later with red and swollen eyes. Our white male colleague sits motionless: "I'm not okay, but I knew what I was in for—so now I take it."

The psychologist shuffles his papers together. "I am not suggesting that you *are* affected—I'm merely asking a question. Are the black journalists in this group telling me that they have a special capacity to handle pain? Everyone always talks about how well black people are coping in this country after centuries of oppression. Are you coping? Are you saying that God has given black people this stunning special capacity to deal with suffering? What has changed in your behavior—and it may have nothing to do with the commission—but what has changed this past year? I want to know."

And with these words, he cracks open what has been a mystery—the feelings of black journalists about the Truth Commission.

Mondli sighs. "There is something that has never happened before— I hit my children with a belt the other day."

Makhaya: "Something very strange happened to me. During our current affairs program, I got Joe Mamasela on the line and I asked him: 'How on earth can you expect people to forgive you?' And he said, 'You don't have the right to ask this question, Mrs. Hashe is the one to ask that.' Now Mrs. Hashe was with me in the studio. I turned to her and said, 'Mrs. Hashe, will you ask him?' And she began to cry . . . but right from the heart, she cried. And then something strange happened to me. I also started to cry. I haven't cried since I was a child. I pulled the producer in to take over the show and I went to the bathroom and cried and cried. Then I washed my face and thought: if my father knew about this, he would be very disappointed."

Thabo: "I also grew up with the notion that if you don't cry, if you bear it out, it will make you a better man. I didn't even cry at my father's funeral. But the other day at the funeral of my best friend, I broke down and cried. Afterward I said to my wife: 'I'm getting soft.' "

Sello: "I'm a religious person, so I have found my inner peace of mind. I am fine. Because I know where to go when I am upset. It was only when I watched *Prime Evil*, I felt this spark of hatred. It was quick, but it was very severe. And I was surprised at it. But then I settled down and became peaceful again."

Patrick: "I used to be a *bok* for parties. But that has totally disappeared. I don't belong there, yet I cannot stand being by myself. But what upset me very much—the other day my wife put a bowl of porridge in front of me and when I took the first spoonful, it burnt me, it was too hot. When I came to my senses, I was standing with the bowl in my hand ready to throw it on the floor or at her. And I don't want to become abusive."

"Do you talk at home about the hearings?"

We all shake our heads; we don't talk.

On the board, the psychologist draws an iceberg, with its tip sticking out above the water. This tip, he says, is the part of themselves people show to the world—friendship, integrity, compassion, love, honesty, and so on. Hidden from the eye are the other things: hatred, dishonesty, anger . . . But normally within the iceberg, there is continuous movement between these two spaces: as a person, you easily access anger and show it, then you become yourself again. "The moment you experience something traumatic, then the ice packs in between these two spaces and you can no longer access anger, hatred, jealousy. Every traumatic experience packs the ice thicker. But your body is not stupid—your body knows. And the cooped-up emotions manifest in physical symptoms."

"Would you say that the archbishop's cancer is a symptom of his suppressed anger?"

"My! Are we sharp in this group," says the psychologist. He shrugs his shoulders. "I won't comment on that, but I can tell you that most of the commissioners are experiencing harrowing physical illnesses."

He explains that we have to drill holes in those ice layers, and that crying is one way of doing it. We also have to prevent other layers from forming by debriefing ourselves after every hearing. And that means you sit by yourself for five minutes and say: "How do I *feel* about it?" This is especially important for journalists, who have to report with the head and not the heart. We should also talk to one another.

And then he draws two parallel tracks on the board. "This is the Truth Commission track and this is your personal relationship track. Instinctively, you do not want the Truth Commission one to 'contaminate' the personal one—you want your friends, your family, your beloved, to stay pure, to be protected from what you are experiencing. You find it impossible anyway to convey the totality of the impact to anyone. Most people become totally withdrawn from their families. But to stay sane, you create on this Truth Commission track a substitute for your personal life. You re-create your personal relationships in the commission—you find a father, a mother, a sister, a beloved, a son. Which is fine in itself, so long as you remember that the one track is coming to an end in eight months' time."

"Where does violence fit into all of this?" I ask, tasting blood on my lip.

"I find that white journalists are carrying a lot of guilt. Have you asked yourself why more Afrikaner journalists are covering the Truth Commission than any other group? To compensate for this guilt, white journalists tend to put more into their involvement with the commission. But it takes its toll.

"The more you empathize with the victim, the more you become the victim; you display the same kinds of symptoms—helplessness, word-lessness, anxiety, desperation. But for some people, it is so unbearable being a victim that they become a perpetrator instead. You get rid of the pain by putting it into someone else, you become violent and make someone else your own victim. So be very aware of that."

"Hey, Antjie, but this is not quite what happened at the workshop," says Patrick.

"Yes, I know, it's a new story that I constructed from all the other in-formation I picked up over the months about people's reactions and psychologists' advice. I'm not reporting or keeping minutes. I'm telling. If I have to say every time that so-and-so said this, and then at another time so-and-so said that, it gets boring. I cut and paste the upper layer, in order to get the second layer told, which is actually the story I want to tell. I change some people's names when I think they might be an-noyed or might not understand the distortions."

"But then you're not busy with the truth!"

"I am busy with the truth . . . *my* truth. Of course, it's quilted to-gether from hundreds of stories that we've experienced or heard about in the past two years. Seen from my perspective, shaped by my state of mind at the time and now also by the audience I'm telling the story to. In every story, there is hearsay, there is a grouping together of things that didn't necessarily happen together, there are assumptions, there are exaggerations to bring home the enormities of situations, there is downplaying to confirm innocence. And all of this together makes up the whole country's truth. So also the lies. And the stories that date from earlier times."

The second narrative has been heard. For two years, South Africans have been listening to the voices of amnesty-seekers. Some sound sin-cere, some insincere, some sound pathetic, some opportunistic. Many simply lie.

A voice that has not been heard yet is that of the best-known black violator of human rights, the man whose name has cropped up more of-ten than anyone else's at amnesty hearings—Joe Mamasela. The only image South Africans have of this Vlakplaas *askari* comes from the video footage shot by journalist Jacques Pauw: the heavy black face with thick lips and thick glasses relating cold-blooded killings as if in slow motion.

So it's not without trepidation that I'm waiting with Radio Lesedi's current affairs anchor, Sophie Mokoena, in front of the SABC building, for Joe Mamasela. Sophie presents the Truth Commission slot in Sesotho on Friday evenings and has built up contact with Mamasela over the months. He trusts her unconditionally. But he said that we have to wait outside in front of the building, so that he can see whether it's really just the two of us, and that the one with Sophie is indeed only a woman. We stand around uncomfortably. My cell phone rings. Yes, it has been ascertained that we are who we say we are, but we have to go to the Carlton Hotel and wait in the foyer. We take a car, struggle to find parking in the city center, and walk into the fancy hotel. Sophie sits where she can observe the revolving door. I fiddle to get my recorder working perfectly—this is the last moment for flat batteries or a faulty cassette. I wonder how I will manage to interview the man in the lobby without passersby hearing the words "Vlakplaas," "Dirk Coetzee," and "Mxenge."

"There he is," says Sophie.

Outside the entrance, several men are walking around. "Which one?"

"The one standing with his back to us, looking up the street."

Sophie gets up. I want to tell her to be careful, but she's already making her graceful way over to the door. The man turns around and I am certain that Sophie is mistaken. He is not wearing glasses, does not have a heavy face or a large head—he looks like a thousand others. But his face breaks into a smile when Sophie extends her hand. He glances over his shoulder once more and then enters the hotel. He comes up to me with outstretched arms. "I've heard so much about you!"

God, what can I say . . . Yes, the same here? An honor to meet you?

"I would never have recognized you. Where are your glasses?"

He laughs. "I never wear them in public places. Please find us a private corner somewhere. I can't be interviewed here."

We can go up to the third floor, where there are sofas down the hall, they tell me at the information counter. While he is busy on his minuscule cell phone, I get a chance to study him. He is wearing a dark-green silk suit, a freshly ironed shirt, an unobtrusive tie, gold jewelry, and the kind of shoes with just the toe caps made of patent leather. After each question I ask, he flatteringly comments on its quality before answering in a continuous flow of words. The pauses in between sentences are shorter than those between words.

When were you born?

"Good. I was born in Soweto in 1953 on 2 June, I'm the last of six children."

What kind of person was your mother?

"Thank you for asking that one. A very Christian woman, very loving, she was nurturing us as mothers do, but unfortunately because of the political circumstances in the country she had to leave us at a very tender age and go and stay in a domestic suburb. And we will see her maybe once every six months when she has accumulated enough money to come back home and provide for the family."

Who looked after you?

"Like all black families, we had an extended family, we lived all of us with our grandmother—it was four or five families together."

How many brothers and sisters?

"This is an interesting question. In our four-roomed house—we had to share it—we were about sixteen. There was absolute chaos, no privacy, there was nothing. And the worst part of that was even the house itself was turned into a shebeen to augment the income.

Mamasela says he reconciled with his God in 1992 and is now part of the International Fellowship of Christ. He attends church in Hatfield and as a cell leader in the Rhema church, he converts many people.

"That is the only time I am alone is when I decide to have a quiet time with the Lord. When I feel that there are burdens, there are problems that I cannot solve with my own human intelligence, then I say to the Lord: 'Take full control of the situation.' "

Mamasela's voice is disturbingly familiar. While he's talking to us, a few meters away, a waiter stops dead in his tracks. Slowly he turns around and stares expressionlessly at Mamasela.

Until he left school in Standard 9, Mamasela fought his own battles:

"I had to rely on my physical fitness. I stayed at Tladi location and I attended school at Western Central Jabavu, Morris Isaacson. I had to travel through various townships to reach my school and during those times, each and every township had its own gangsters—in Tladi it was maScotch, in Moletsane it was maHazel, if you go to Molapo, it was another type of gangster—and because I was harassed every day by gangsters, I joined karate and I excelled in karate and I defended myself, my peer groups, my friends, and my immediate relations . . . I survived, unlike all my brothers and sisters, who died of apartheid-related diseases like asthma, tuberculosis—my elder brother Stanley died of polio . . ."

At school Mamasela was involved in student politics. After the student riots of 1976, he became secretary-general of the South African Students' Organization at his school.

"I became a student activist at a very young age. There was this brilliant young man, Donald Mashigo, from Turfloop University, who gave me the SASO books of the late Steve Biko, where he used to write under the nom de guerre of Frank Talk. And I used to like that. One of the quotes is still in my head; when he talked about the Hegelian theory of dialectic materialism, he said: 'Since the problem is white, we need a very strong black force to counterbalance the state.' Mamasela agreed."

Just after school, he got married to Nombi Dube. "We were both very young. As I was starting to work, she fell pregnant and I felt duty-bound and honor-bound to marry her. We had a son, Sizwe, and my job took me out of my home for several months . . . She was very young and she had to go out and fool around. And when I came back, I heard these reports and I thought it would be better for both of us if I grant a divorce."

In Jacques Pauw's book on the death squads, *In the Heart of the Whore*, Mamasela's biography reads as follows: "Mamasela became a police informant in 1979 while in jail awaiting trial for housebreaking and theft. He was released shortly after a security policeman visited him and persuaded him to 'combat terrorism.' He infiltrated the ANC in Botswana, undergoing intelligence training with them. In the winter of 1981, his cover was blown and he was kidnapped and taken to an ANC base in Botswana. A fellow police informer was allegedly tortured and killed, but Mamasela escaped and joined the Vlakplaas unit."

But according to Mamasela, things happened differently. He tells a story of treachery and a solitary fight on all fronts.

Mamasela claims he joined the ANC in Botswana in 1977, having been recruited by Snuki Zikalala, now a television journalist. He received training in intelligence and became leader of his own cell. But after 1981 things turned against him. One night he was arrested by security police—sixteen carloads of them. He says he was assaulted until there was blood on the walls; he was tortured, given electric shocks, and interrogated. "The information I was confronted with could only have come from my commander Sipho Makopo. After forty-eight hours, I broke . . .

"I merely confirmed what the police knew. Just like my President Mandela. He confirmed in court about the Rivonia Trial, but because he was a leader it is fine; when Mamasela does the same thing under duress, it's called selling out. It's double standards!"

He was recruited by a Major Kruger to become an *askari*. "They don't recruit anyone—you must have a particular knowledge and intelligence." Mamasela says he had no choice but to join—he was a mere child of nineteen up against the brutal might of the apartheid state. But the sums in my head tell me that in the early eighties Mamasela was nearly thirty.

"You could have preferred to go to jail," I say. "Robben Island . . ."

Mamasela snorts: "Don't think everybody on Robben Island was holy. They were never put before a choice, they were simply sent. What is more, the comrades who went to Robben Island, not all of them were genuine . . . we recruited some of them and they infiltrated on Robben Island, so not all of them are Jesus Christs, not all of them are Moses as they claim."

Sometimes he wishes that he had the power of Samson to bring down the castle of the ANC, says Mamasela. But the only thing he hopes for now is that his children and his people will know the truth about him.

"I am happy because the majority of the black people today, even those who were against me, are beginning to get back their senses and ask intelligent questions, and they don't get answers."

Later I ask one of the *Sowetan*'s journalists: "What is Mamasela saying here?"

"*Jong*, you whites have not even begun to understand what lies behind black politics. You jive on Madiba Magic and you analyze ANC politicians, but what lies behind all that you do not have a clue about. A single example," he says graciously. "All of us know that the main income of the ANC for the struggle inside the country came from gunrunning and drugs. Do you think those networks have disappeared? And likewise the third force was busy with gunrunning and drugs. Do you think *those* networks have disappeared? Why wouldn't they rather combine? Do you think it's coincidental that Mandela's daughter is caught with a friend's stolen car? If a politician wasn't in prison or in exile for a long time, you must study him carefully. We just smile when we hear that the Truth Commission is satisfied with the ANC's submission, we shake our heads over you white journalists who always think you have the big scandals out in the open . . ."

Children? Yes, says Mamasela, he has two sons and a daughter by his second wife. So, while the marriages of the Vlakplaas Five—Cronje and Hechter and the rest—have almost all been destroyed, Joe Mamasela and Dirk Coetzee have their beloved families intact. Two men apparently in control of their pasts. Mamasela says his wife is involved in the top structures of the Gauteng Ministry of Health and is currently doing her Ph.D. in social welfare. She understands me, he says. "I informed my children in 1993 that I was coming out with the truth about my deeds. But it is difficult . . . They actually become concerned when my face appears on television like last Sunday, you know; out of the blue my face was there and my child came back to me and said, 'Daddy, there's your picture . . .' and even my eldest child, they can see that there is a concerted effort by certain self-appointed legal gurus within the SABC who are trying to besmirch my name . . ."

But didn't you do anything wrong? we press him.

"I had to fight for my own survival. I was a political hostage, I was a dog of war."

Joe Mamasela says he saw how the *askaris* around him turned into wrecks. But he who doesn't smoke, doesn't drink, or have any addiction of any kind had to find some way to stay sane. A dossier was the answer, he decided. He would compile a dossier about Vlakplaas and one day he would buy his credibility back with the information he'd gathered. According to Mamasela, this dossier is the real truth about Vlakplaas and the security police, and it's now in the hands of the attorney general.

At this very point, a strange thing happens. Mamasela's cell phone, lying on the coffee table next to my tape recorder, starts to ring. On the little window, the word "Winnie" flashes. He looks at me, throws his hands in the air: "What can I do? I have to answer . . ."

He presses a button: "Hello, Mama . . ." and then he gets up and goes to finish the conversation around the corner. Across from me, So-phie's eyes are wide. "Maybe it's not her," I whisper.

But Sophie fervently shakes her head. "Mamasela is big friends with Winnie—it is said that he will one day clear her name."

Sophie relates how she often puts Mamasela on air in her current af-fairs program and opens the phone lines so that people can phone in. And they accuse him of all that is evil—and then he says: "*Bua!* Speak! Insult me, curse me, spit it out. Then I feel better. Then I become whole."

That evening when I transcribe the interview, I hear how my voice changes within the first few minutes, how even my most critical ques-tions sound like I'm sucking up. He says good-bye to us with a great bear-hug. "Only the best for SABC Radio."

But how do you kill a person and live a normal life the next day?

Humor, says Mamasela to our astonishment. "I used humor a lot to cure me and my fellow *askaris*. You know we will joke about the bad things . . . even when *askaris* were taken one by one to be killed by their own commanders like Coetzee or De Kock, we'll say: Who's going to be the next one? 'Hey!' you will say. 'Jeff, you are getting fatter, I think they are going to choose you next time.' "

According to his colleagues, Mamasela was a unique *askari*—the cleanest of them all at Vlakplaas. Paul van Vuuren told Judge Wilson: Mamasela had a talent for killing. If you wanted it quick and clean, you sent Mamasela—he had the talent.

"Mamasela is *moerse* intelligent—that's all I can tell you. That guy is more than clever," says Paul van Vuuren. "But we cannot figure out what his game is now—it will not be out of stupidity that he doesn't apply for amnesty. But to us it seems that he is overplaying his hand."

Mamasela laughs: "I will tell you one thing: I managed to fool Paul van Vuuren. Not only Paul van Vuuren—I managed to fool the upper echelons of the South African security police, which is not an easy thing to achieve, particularly when you are black and an *askari*. I managed to fool them with the curative power of humor. Because I insulted myself, I used to call myself a *"kaffer"* and they loved it, that—'this one, we have turned him so hard that he is one of us.' I used to say, '*Ek is 'n Boer.*' '*Wat? Jissis!*' '*As my Boere sê, "Maak hulle dood"*'—*dan maak ek hulle dood.*' ['I am a Boer.' 'What? Jesus!' 'If my Boers say, "Kill them"—then I kill them.'] Because I wanted them, I wanted them to believe me, to love me, to make me one of them . . ."

All to get information for the dossier, he says.

Now Sophie and I confront him: People say in the old days you betrayed your own people for money, now you are betraying your colleagues—again for money, because the attorney general apparently pays you a handsome retainer to be a state witness.

Mamasela explodes: "I did not choose to kill black people for money. When I was betrayed by the ANC and sold out on a silver platter to this brutal regime—I was never promised money, I was fighting for my life. I was a prisoner of war who was abused against his will, against his convictions—anybody who says Mamasela killed for money . . . I would be a multimillionaire today . . . judging by the forty-plus people that we killed."

He acknowledges he has a high lifestyle. His children are at the best schools, he takes his family on luxury holidays—but that's because he built up businesses in Swaziland over the years. But he has lost all of that, he adds, and that is why the attorney general pays him.

Why doesn't he ask for amnesty?

"I will never go to the TRC to humiliate myself in front of them. I will not give the politicians the honor of humiliating Mamasela after what they have done to Mamasela—both black and white.

"Furthermore. It will be stupid of me, it will be a foolhardy exercise for me to ask for amnesty, because one of the main ingredients of amnesty is that whatever you did, you killed for political reasons. I had no political reason to kill black people."

The similarities between Mamasela and his peer Dirk Coetzee are evident. Especially around the mouth—which always gives away other tensions. Dirk Coetzee's mouth is often set in a smiling grimace, while thin threads of spittle cling to the dry teeth. Right through the interview, Mamasela's upper lip had an uncontrollable quiver. Both are deadly, charmingly persuasive. Both talk incessantly. Both are able to rattle off names, details, dates, quotes, and impressive words. Both claim they were usually onlookers at murder scenes. Both refer to themselves in the third person. Both killed on behalf of whites. Both say they were betrayed by their own colleagues. But despite these similarities, one is black and the other white. The black one has apparently been forgiven by the family of Griffiths Mxenge. The white one not.

CHAPTER SIXTEEN

Truth Is a Woman

They asked me if I knew why I was arrested, I said no. They said it was because I'm Poqo.[1] I denied any knowledge of Poqo. They said they would show me. They made me stand like an aeroplane on my toes. They beat me all over. I fell. They kicked me severely. They tortured me for three days . . . Pus came from my ear. I could not urinate. I felt dizzy. They kept on calling me Poqo. They said I should die, as I cannot live with white people. In Cape Town, I was sentenced for a year and six months.

Let me start by giving my story.

In 1968, Wednesday 24 at 4 A.M., I had a three-year-old child on my lap, and I was trying to light the stove, as it was a chilly day, when I heard a knock on the window. The police entered with heavy coats and asked for the owner . . . My wife gave me some overalls and a coat. I put on my socks in a disorderly manner . . . I saw they were very severe . . . They pushed me into the van. I saw Mr. Menena in the van. He didn't know why he was there . . . There were many of us at the police station. The yard was full. We come from a small town, we all knew each other. They told us to keep quiet. They divided us into groups and drove us to Beaufort West. The whites were very happy. I kept talking to myself wondering what was wrong. Later Mr. Makulani joined me. We shared a cell. He told me we were accused of being Poqo. Then they took us, and I hoped I was going home . . . *[cries]*

TUTU: Even if this is tough, we go on . . .

MHLATSI: My wife was pregnant and it was her time to deliver. But we

---
[1] The military wing of the Pan-Africanist Congress (PAC).

were taken back to Oudtshoorn and beaten. There were twenty-three of us. Then we were taken to Victoria West—others got in. The allegations were that we would poison the dam and disconnect the electricity of Victoria West and we were said to be an army and we would then take over the whole town. It was not true. We were in jail in Pollsmoor. My wife sent me a letter—she told me of the birth of a son . . .

The judge asked me if I was Alphius. I said, "I am Alwinus." I took out my ID book and letter and the judge said: "You are Alphius." There was an argument. I was discharged a year later. In May 1969, I came back to Victoria West. At home I found the house disorderly. My children were thin, my wife was working for Mr. Van Drieten, a farm owner. She had never worked before. She earned four rand [sixty-five cents] a month. I saw my baby boy and I was looking at my baby—he ran away from me crying. But he got used to me. They are now grown men.

Willie Menena was a Methodist and he and his two brothers accused me. One could make a story out of this. I hated Willie Menena for five years. I wanted to stab him to death because he had hurt me and implicated me in that Poqo meeting.

In 1972 I was with the children in King William's Town . . . and there was Willie Menena in a showroom for cars. My child saw him. I asked the child for a knife—I opened it and put it in my pocket. Then I went up close to him. "This is God's work. Here he is: Willie Menena." Then a white man asked me if I wanted a car. I said no. Willie Menena saw me—a person who is guilty will always spot you. I greeted him: "How are you?" I asked him to go out with me. He had difficulty in talking. I was surprised. I could see that he had been through a lot of suffering—it showed on his face. I asked him: "Do your people know you are like this?" I asked about his other brothers.

He said he was suffering from high blood pressure and pains in the hip, and that his son was beating him. I called my wife and my son that was born while I was in detention. I said: "Willie, here are your children"—because we have the same clan name. "There are your children. You can see you are old."

He said: "Are you still going on?"

I asked my wife to give him one pound so that this man could eat. He never went home. He went to the hospital. It was the end of his life.

I drove the car. He was standing there. This man who tried to drown me. He waved. I waved back, I kept on waving. That was the last time I saw him. The hatred faded away.

We cannot do bad things to others. We have children to bring up.

(Alwinus Mhlatsi, Beaufort West)

Does truth have a gender?

"Rats would come into my cell at night to eat the soiled pads. They would try to get between my legs when I sleep."

"As women speak, they speak for us who are too cowardly to speak.

"They speak for us who are too owned by pain to speak.

"Because always, always in anger and frustration, men use women's bodies as a terrain of struggle—as a battleground," says Thenjiwe Mthintso, chairperson of the Gender Commission, in her opening speech at the special women's hearings held by the Truth Commission in Gauteng. "Behind every woman's encounter with the Security Branch and the police lurked the possibility of sexual abuse and rape." Some activists say they sometimes didn't know which was worse—the actual assault or dealing with the constant fear in the confined and isolated space of a cell. "When they interrogated, they usually started by reducing your role as an activist. They weighted you according to their own concepts of womanhood.

"And they said you are in custody because you are not the right kind of woman—you are irresponsible, you are a whore, you are fat and ugly, or single and thirty and you are looking for a man.

"And when whatever you stood for was reduced to prostitution, unpaid prostitution, the license for sexual abuse was created. Then things happened that could not happen to a man. Your sexuality was used to strip away your dignity, to undermine your sense of self." You had to ask for toiletries like deodorant, soap, and sanitary towels. You had to strip in front of a whole range of policemen making remarks about your body. Women had to do star-jumps naked, breasts flying, Fallopian tubes were flooded with water until they burst; rats were pushed into vaginas . . . "Women have been made to stand the whole day with blood flowing down and drying on their legs. Did they gain strength from looking at their blood? From asking you to drink your own blood?" asks

Mthintso. It is only when men in prisons are forced by sodomy to behave like women that they realize how it is to live with a constant awareness of your body and how it can be abused and ridiculed.

Mthintso says a man who didn't break under torture was respected by the police. "There was a sense of respect, where the torturers would even say: 'He is a man.' But a woman's refusal to bow down would unleash the wrath of the torturers. Because in their own discourse a woman, a black *meid,* a *kaffermeid* at that, had no right to have the strength to withstand them."

Banning orders for women were also handled differently. "Women were constantly peeped at and preyed on. They wanted to prove that you were a whore. Someone whose inclusion in the liberation struggle was simply to service the men. To tell you, 'You are not a revolutionary, you are a black bitch on heat.' "

She concludes: "While writing this speech, I realized how unready I am to talk about my experience in South African jails and ANC camps abroad. Even now, despite the general terms in which I have chosen to speak, I feel exposed and distraught."

We were running through the shacks, only to find out the *boers* were also going through these shacks after us. I turned back alone, I was trying to find other comrades. I couldn't see them. I could feel the tear gas coming through my eyes and I—I went to the toilet to hide. And I thought that here I am going to get injured, because I can't see the others. When I got out of this toilet, I saw one *boer,* only to find that he also saw me. He shot at me.

ADV. NTSEBEZA: Where did he shoot you?

MS. TSOBILEYO: He shot me on my left arm—leg—then I fell, then he shot me . . . the underpart of my body. They took me into a house where I was bleeding so heavily that the basin they used to collect my blood was full. The doctor who phoned for the ambulance had problems, because the ambulance was not allowed to come in—to come to Crossroads.

ADV. NTSEBEZA: Let's go back to the scene of where you were shot. Did you two see each other at the same time, you and this white policeman?

MS. TSOBILEYO: Yes, we saw each other at the same time, he was wearing a blue uniform. And he shot at me.

ADV. NTSEBEZA: Could you please show the archbishop and the

commission your scar on your leg. That isn't the only place where you got injured, is it?

MS. TSOBILEYO: No.

ADV. NTSEBEZA: Some of the bullets are still in your body.

MS. TSOBILEYO: Yes, I have several bullets in my body, some are still in my leg, some are somewhere in my body, some under—underneath. Some of the bullets are in my vagina.

ADV. NTSEBEZA: Obviously those bullets didn't just fly on their own to where they are now.

MS. TSOBILEYO: These bullets were—these were the first bullets that were shot at me. He shot directly there.

(Nomatise Evelyn Tsobileyo)

When I got into one of the offices, I found that there was a huge crowd of the police and soldiers and a commotion. I was taken into one of the offices that was full of policemen and I was informed that one of them was a karate man. I asked: "What is going on?" And one of them said: "*Ja*, we've got you!" I took a seat and I was shivering. I've never seen such a big crowd of white persons. One of them asked me: "Where were you last night?" I said I was at home. Then he started shouting at me that I was a liar. I insisted that I was at home. While I was still responding to one of the questions, the other one said I am *spoggerig*.

They kept on interrogating me for hours. "Who burnt the municipality's bar?" They were so rude toward me and I was getting tired of answering all these questions, so I kept quiet.

One young boy, he was a student, slapped me slightly on the cheek. He said: "Speak, you bitch!" I just kept on staring at him. He grabbed me by the throat and then slapped me hard on the face. And then we fought. It was an exchange of blows and I was very angry because he was just as old as my children. The others were ridiculing me: they said I was "John Tate" and "Gerrie Coetzee"—the boxers. At the end, I could see they were also embarrassed, because some of the black detectives came in and my shirt was in tatters, and then all of them said: "Are you fighting back, you *kaffer*?"

Late that night, I was alone in a cell. I heard two men communicating outside. One of them called my name. They took me outside and I was ordered to board this Hippo. They started driving the

Hippo away, over the bridge to Rawsonville. I was alone in the back of the Hippo. It was pitch-dark outside. They alighted from the Hippo and took me out. One of them said to me, "Can you see what you have put yourself in?" And then they asked me, "When did you last sleep with a man?" I was so embarrassed by this question. And I felt so humiliated. I informed them that I have nobody, I don't have a partner. And they asked, "Who do you stay with?" I said with my family. The other thing they asked is how do I feel when I am having intercourse with a man. This was too much for me because they were repeating it time and again, asking me the same question. Asking me what do I like with the size of a penis or what do I enjoy most. So the other one was putting his hand inside me through the vagina. I was crying because I was afraid, because the soldiers are very notorious with rape. This one continued putting his finger right through me—he kept on penetrating—and I was asking for forgiveness and I was asking them, "What have I done? I'm old enough to be your mother. Why are you treating me like this?" This was very, very embarrassing. Then one of them—I think God just came inside him—and the other one said: "Let her go," and they took me back to the police station and locked me up . . .

I was detained for a long time.

When I was released, my house was burnt down—one of my children died in the fire. The community ridiculed and ostracized me because they said I was giving information to the police.

(Yvonne Khutwane, Worcester)

There has been concern that so few women activists have come to testify before the Truth Commission. They have their reasons. "The day I became involved in the struggle . . . I made a choice and I fully understood the consequences of it. To run to the commission now just doesn't seem right." In an effort to draw in the experiences of women activists and get a fuller picture of the past, the commission creates special forums. At a hearing on prisons, Greta Appelgren, who drove the getaway car for Robert McBride when he planted the Magoo's Bar bomb, testifies. She is now known as Zakrah Nakardien:

"What bothered me were the rats. They were the size of cats and they were in the passage all the time. While I was eating, three of them would watch me. I took my clothes to block their access, but they ripped all that and came in, crawling up, until one night they reached my neck . . . I screamed the place down and they found me in a corner eating my T-shirt. This is how berserk I was.

"Isolation for seven months taught me something. No human being can live alone. I felt I was going deeper and deeper into the ground. It felt as if all the cells were like coffins full of dead people.

"I had to accept that I was damaged. That part of my soul was eaten away by maggots and I will never be whole again."

"A group of six guys and myself in Sebokeng decided to form an organization to keep the senior comrades busy all the time. We rape women who need to be disciplined. Those who behave like snobs. They think they know better than most of us. And when we struggle, they simply don't want to join us."

A seemingly simple question like "What is rape?" can derail a whole discussion. South African law defines rape as occurring only between a man and a woman and involving the penetration of the penis into the vagina. Acts of forced oral or anal sex and penetration by foreign objects are not considered rape. But the Truth Commission has to establish whether one can rape with a political motive and whether the raping of nonpolitical women to keep the comrades busy is indeed a political act. The Geneva Convention regards rape as a crime of war and prosecutions for rape in Bosnia have begun only because of its link to ethnic cleansing.

The Truth Commission might recommend that rapists should not be granted amnesty. But why would a rapist testify if he knows he won't get amnesty? Then again, few women have testified about rape, and fewer, if any, have named the rapists. So why would a rapist apply for amnesty at all? There seems to be a bizarre collusion between the rapist and the raped. Although rumors abound about rape, all these mutterings are trapped behind closed doors. Apparently high-profile women, among them Cabinet ministers, parliamentarians, and businesswomen, were raped and sexually abused under the previous dispensation—and not only by the regime, but by their own comrades in the townships and liberation camps. But no one will utter an audible word about it.

The silence is locked into loss and cultural differences, says clinical psychologist Nomfundo Walaza. "Women who have been raped know that if they talk about it now in public, they will lose something again— privacy, maybe respect. If you knew that a particular minister had been raped, what would go through your mind when you saw her on television? Another deterrent is that some of the rapists hold high political positions today—so if you spoke out you would not only undermine the new government you fought for, but destroy your own possibilities of a future. There is also a culture of not discussing these things with your own family."

"When they raped me, I was already torn and injured by electric shocks," testifies Thandi Shezi. "I hurt deep inside. I could tell nobody. My mother is sitting here—she is hearing it for the first time. I'm suffering from a womb that feels as if it's jumping. I'm frigid. I'm cold. When I get involved with a man, I get scared. I didn't tell a single soul about it. I don't want them to pity me. I don't want them to call me names."

Men don't use the word "rape" when they testify. They talk about being sodomized, or about iron rods being inserted into them. In so doing, they make rape a women's issue. By denying their own sexual subjugation to male brutality, they form a brotherhood with rapists that conspires against their own wives, mothers, and daughters, say some of those who testify.

There is a lot of ambiguity surrounding sexual torture, says Sheila Meintjes. It is not difficult to understand why. "There is a hypothesis that the sexual torture of men is to induce sexual passivity and to abolish political power and potency, while the torture of women is the activation of sexuality. There is a lot of anger about women—because women do not have the authority, but often they have a lot of power."

The picture of Rita Mazibuko in her brown dress, beige cardigan, and neatly knotted *kopdoek* is in stark contrast with her story of rape, torture, and rejection. And neither she nor the Truth Commission is prepared for the storm that follows her testimony.

Mazibuko underwent military training in Angola and Mozambique, and was then placed in Swaziland to work out routes for cadres moving in and out of the country. When nine of these cadres were shot, suspicion fell on her. The fact that she had R35,000 (about $5,800) in her bank account was proof enough for the ANC that she worked for the apartheid regime. In reality, Mazibuko says, she earned the money by sewing and selling tracksuits. Accused of being a spy, she was taken to Tanzania and Zambia, and kept in a hole for six months—sleeping on pieces of cardboard.

"On the day I was taken out of that hole, they said I should go and wash. The clothes I was wearing at the time was the same dress for about six months—when I tried to take off the clothes, they were in tatters. When I washed my hair, it fell out; my skin was greasy because I didn't wash for three months."

Two comrades, Jacob and Mtungwa, ordered her to pick one of them. She needed a man to take up her case, they said. Some comrades said she was guilty; others disagreed. They kept on torturing her.

"I refused to have sex with them. Then they tortured me between two chairs. I fell on the ground. They were kicking me across my face, they treated me like a donkey . . . They pushed a pipe with a condom in and out of my vagina. While they did it, they asked how it felt. When I did not respond, it was put deeper and deeper—to satisfy me, they said . . . After being assaulted, I was bleeding from my mouth and nose, but still I was hanged, left dangling from a tree—they wanted to kill me that day. I was made to wear overalls so that if I messed myself up, they wouldn't catch sight of my mess. When they brought me down, they said: 'This dog is dead.' "

Afterward, Mazibuko wrote to comrade Mathews Phosa, because she had once shared a house with him and cooked for him. He spoke to a senator about her case, but the assaults continued: "At Sun City prison, someone called Desmond raped me nine times. Nine times. He is quite a young man—he was twenty-nine at the time. And I saw myself as his mother. Comrade Mashego was staying at Swaziland—when I met him, he raped me until I approached the authorities. And then Tebogo, who was also very young, he raped me and cut my genitals—he cut me through from number one to number two. And then he put me in a certain room, he tied my legs apart. He tied my neck and then poured Dettol [an antiseptic] over my genitals."

ANC members sold her house and furniture in Swaziland for R20,000 (about $3,300). "It's now Comrade Mike who sleeps in my bed and uses my dressing table," she says. When she finally returned from exile, she bumped into Jacob Zuma. He lent her money to report her case to Shell House. But one of her former rapists took her from Shell House to Boksburg, where he again raped her for the whole night in a house with a "For Sale" sign in front of it. "He warned me that I would not get away. That he would kill me if I talk."

Mazibuko tells the commission that she doesn't have a cent to her name. She borrowed the clothes she has on. To crown it all, two weeks after she gave a written statement to the Truth Commission, she received a phone call from Mpumalanga premier Mathews Phosa, warning her not to testify—because then he would be obliged to defend ANC members against her claims.

"I fell in love with the late Chris Hani and gave birth to his son Simphiwe. Hani showed this boy to his family but not to his wife. I gave the son to my sister-in-law to avoid a divorce from my husband." On Mazibuko's confidential written statement, the name of Simphiwe is underlined—a plea for extra reparation? I wonder.

It is strange testimony. Is this woman with the good-natured face, who speaks of rape as if it is water, who emphasizes the youth of her rapists, nothing more than a prostitute? And is her sexual history perhaps the reason why Phosa says afterward that he has never heard of Rita Mazibuko or "Mumsy Khuswayo"—her code name in the ANC?

When she leaves the witness table, she pulls her cardigan closed and folds her arms protectively over her body. As if she already knows that a mighty provincial premier is going to discredit her evidence repeatedly in public and threaten to take her to court. As if she knows no one will stand up for her. The Truth Commission does not utter a single word in Mazibuko's defense. Not one of the commissioners, not one of the feminists agitating for women's rights, stands up and says: "We respect the right of Rita Mazibuko to tell the truth as she sees it, just as we respect the right of Mathews Phosa to tell the truth as he sees it. But we expect him to do the same."

"And the next thing, he came back and he beat me right across the room into the wall and he kept on beating me right into the wall and I felt myself going down . . . And I just found myself lying there on the floor and being completely, completely terrified. At that stage, a man came in, and he said to the man, 'Just rape her, just rape her,' and this man came up to me and he—he didn't actually rape me, but he . . . the threat of it was—I felt I was going to die at that point.

"I hadn't slept for days. And they gave me some food . . . And he said he was going away, but he was coming back again. And I started seeing . . . all my veins in my hands dilating. And my arms, my veins in my hands and my arms, and I . . . I felt pains across my chest and suddenly I started feeling like . . . all my insides were going to come out . . . And I said to them, 'I am going to get sick . . .' And the one guy ran to the toilet to take me; the other guy ran to the phone and he said, 'It's starting.' Now at that point, I didn't think anything of it [that she was being poisoned], I was just seeing all my veins dilating, it looked like worms—it looked like worms coming out of my hands. It was all standing up. I thought my blood vessels were going to burst and I just felt these pains across my chest . . . Then Captain Du Plessis came back and he said: 'Zubeida, you know, you are never going to make it, you're going to have a heart attack, you're going to die.'

"They said, 'Zubeida, if you don't cooperate with us and tell us . . . then we are going to detain your father.' And I thought they were just trying to trick me again. But then in the course of the morning, they made a phone call and they called me to the phone . . . and it was my father on the phone . . . I was shattered at that point. I just felt that it's fine if they involve me, but why involve my family? And so after they put the phone down, I signed the statement . . . And the effect of it all was that it completely humiliated me, it completely made me feel like I was worthless, that I had gone against everything that I stood for, that I believed in, and that I had been too weak to withstand the pressure . . ."

After her first arrest and torture, Jaffer decided to become a full-time ANC activist. "Because of the trauma of it all, I think there wasn't a day that went by that I didn't think we had to do something about bringing the system to an end. It totally consumed me, I couldn't think of anything else . . ."

She was arrested a second time and held in custody with her husband. Lieutenant Frans Mostert then threatened the pregnant Jaffer with a chemical he had prepared for her: "We are going to burn the baby from your body, if you don't give us information."

"Now this was a real threat to me because of the drug experience during my first detention. I knew that they could do it . . . and so I sat there in the cell not knowing what to do. Eventually I decided not to give them any information because I felt that I didn't want my child to grow up with that burden on her, because I felt that . . . if she is brought into this world thinking that her mother gave information so that she could live, that is a heavy burden for a child to carry. So I think that that unborn baby inside of me made it possible for me to be strong enough not to give in to their threats."

(Zubeida Jaffer)

. . .

"When I look around, I marvel at how we battle to be normal—and no one knows how shattered we are inside . . .

"I shared my first detention spell in the Old Fort with Winnie Madikizela-Mandela, Fatima Meer, and Joyce Seroke. This was a powerful group. The wardresses called Winnie by her name and she had such amazing strength. She taught us to stand up for our rights and dictate our terms. We discovered that black female prisoners were not allowed to wear panties. We changed that. We also heard children screaming at night and demanded that these children be released."

Human relationships can be forged under the most deprived circumstances. People can cherish one another, survive, and foster the kind of humanity that overcomes divisions. "Hardened criminals—murderers in the next cell—taught me how to use the toilet as a telephone to chat with them, how to smuggle in pen and paper. I never saw their faces. I don't know where to find Chillies and Nandi today, but they only gave me warmth.

"When I was rearrested at Vrede in the Free State, I was detained at Phoenix. After a week, I demanded to see the security police. The wardress asked me: 'How dare you call the security police? Don't you know they will kill you? You're much better off here . . .' But that Saturday afternoon they came. Two of them. They were drunk. The one said: 'Yes, Deborah! So you say you are ready.'

"They handcuffed me to a big iron ball. I stood there the whole night while they were having a braai outside. By Sunday they asked me to write a history of myself. They kept on tearing the paper. My legs were swelling, and I began to get delirious. On Tuesday they started beating me up, they strangled me with a towel—I collapsed. When I came to, I was lying on the floor and I was all wet—they must have poured water over me. This Roy Otto threw a pack of sanitary pads at me. When I went to the bathroom, I realized that I was menstruating and I wondered how he knew that.

"The cell was swarming with lice. The blankets were caked and smelt of urine . . . I was screaming and shouting and had severe asthma attacks. But I was lucky along the line. Because an Afrikaner came, Taljaard, I'll never forget his name. He said he thought I was mad. I told him I was a political prisoner. He listened carefully and smuggled an asthma spray and some tablets in and helped me hide it behind the toilet. Every day Roy Otto came in and said, 'We don't have to kill you, you are going to die naturally of asthma.'

"I used to envy the common-law prisoners for their easy interaction. The wardresses were scared of us—they were told we were terrorists. So they just opened the door and kicked our food in. The food was clogged with ants. But then one silly day, this wardress, Botha, when she walked past, I grabbed her through the bars. I would have liked to strike up a relationship with her, I would have loved to talk to a woman about any woman's thing. But she refused to treat me like a human being. So I grabbed her hair and I bashed her head against the bars. I let her have it. She was by herself and she screamed and screamed. I bashed her because I wanted to be charged, just to talk to somebody. But the funny thing was, the magistrate came to ask whether I needed anything and he brought me a Bible the next day from his home.

"For some strange reason, I've overcome my asthma, to this day. I don't know why. Eventually my family was allowed to visit me. My sister and my dad came. I cried that day. The only reason was that I hugged somebody, I saw some real people . . . Joyce Seroke sent me pajamas and slippers, Judy made an egg mixture for my scalp because all my hair fell out, Ellen Kuzwayo sent me oil to nourish my skin . . .

"In the Middelburg prison, another thing happened. There were two wardresses, Kara Botha and Maryna Harmse—they were meant to be the meanest of the mean. But they jumped back every time they opened my cell—so I walked around with impunity. One day I was exercising in the yard and I saw one of them, Maryna, talking to her boyfriend at the gate. And she was crying. When she opened my cell that afternoon, her eyes were red. I asked her, 'Why are you crying?' She said: '*Dis nie jou besigheid nie. Los my uit.*' ['It's none of your business. Leave me alone.'] I told her I was not going to leave the cell until she tells me. I said to her, 'I heard your boyfriend saying that he is going to Katima Mulilo and you will not see him for a long time. Who is he going to fight there? You see, you are in the same position as me. He is going to die at the border and it's my brothers and sisters who will kill him. Maryna, why do you allow that?' And she cried and she opened up and we talked."

The Truth Commission venue is silent. No one wants to interrupt this story of the power of women to care, endlessly. The moment surpasses all horror and abuse.

(Deborah Matshoba)

.   .   .

I don't seem to have an identity that belongs to me. I'm either Zeph Mothopeng's daughter or Mike Masote's wife. But I feel I am me. That is why I am here. I am Sheila Masote. And I have here a summary of what I was stripped of.

I was born into a happy family—my father and mother both teachers. They stayed in the best place—Orlando West, where you'd find the elite, the Mandelas, the Sisulus, the Matthews, the Masekelas . . . bear with me . . . I cry a lot . . . sometimes it's anger . . . This was a beautiful place. My father was a cultural man—he was the first chairperson of the Johannesburg Bantu Music Festival that brought forth the Eisteddfods, Dorkay House. All of this happened. My mother is a singer with a wonderful coloratura voice—where do I get these terms from? I'm highly cultured . . . I make no apologies, I am . . . I married a highly cultured man—the only man, the only black, in Africa who holds a licentiate in violin teaching. He established the first black orchestra. I know what I'm talking about—but all of this has crumbled . . . I had a family that was home and togetherness. That was destroyed. I couldn't realize any dream. As a young girl, I lost role models because at the time, in the sixties, that was when everybody left—the Mphahleles, the Malebos, the Mjis. The frequent imprisonment of my father destroyed us, the imprisonment of my mother and later of myself and my husband. This communal living—we could play next door, my mother could go to work, and she knew her children would be safe. We left our key at the third house from us—no one came to steal anything. All this crumbled because of the system and the Security Branch. My father and mother were dismissed as teachers because of their political involvement. My brother went into exile. There was loneliness. My father in and out, in and out, of prison. My other brother turned into an alcoholic. He became violent. I saw my mother crying. She lost her energy. It was PAC policy that women should stay at home and should not participate. And the husbands did not share much. I used to go for ballet with ribbons in my hair—I was a pretty little thing in a tutu—the only daughter in a well-off family. We read, we talked politics. I'm not saying all of this to brag, but to tell you what cultured, educated, intellectual society existed in Orlando West. Then people were arrested, others went into exile—this whole world crumbled. Our home became cold and needy. I and my mother—for me there was a real war against my mother. We were so clumsy with each other. Mam Mothopeng—the wife of the PAC president. I wanted to go to a ballroom party. I didn't wear a bra because I had beautiful breasts. And she was angry. I felt so unloved by her. I was abused by stick, by mouth, by neglect. I now understand why she was like that. She was always alone. She had to take decisions every day and she didn't know whether they were right or wrong. Can you imagine that? How vulnerable she must have felt? But she was breaking the very family she was trying to protect.

And I took that with me into my own family. I bashed my son. I almost killed my son. Today he is in Switzerland—he is a fine cellist at the Yehudi Menuhin school. But his sister at the age of eight saw him go up, he was about six, trying to hang himself in a tree because I used to bash him so much. I sent him to the shop. I spit on the floor. "You must be back before the spit dries!" My son would run. My boy would run . . . I'm sorry I cry, bear with me . . . And then I worry. He is too short, they wouldn't see him at the counter. Maybe someone kidnaps him. Maybe he dies. And when he comes back, I take the *sjambok*—I would beat him, I would beat him, I would beat him—until the neighbors jump over the fence and stop me. And this son of mine, this one so close to my heart, I hear him say to his friends: "I don't know suffering."

(Sheila Masote)

In the mid-eighties, at the height of the struggle for liberation, youths danced in the streets, singing:

Informers, we will kill you. *Hayi! Hayi!*
Witches, we will burn you. *Hayi! Hayi!*
Those who do abortions, we will kill you. *Hayi! Hayi!*
Mrs. Botha is sterile—she gives birth to rats. *Hayi! Hayi!*
Mrs. Mandela is fertile—she gives birth to comrades. *Hayi! Hayi!*

'We even flew a little'

It's raining. It's raining in Mdantsane, like it hasn't rained in years. Outside the sports center, stormwater washes sewage down deep grooves in the ground. It's raining hard on the zinc roof. Water slashes down the windows. But right from the start, it's very clear: the women of Mdantsane, who have packed the hall, have come to tell their stories.

The Truth Commission has come full circle in East London. It started here: the first hearings on human rights violations were held in the city hall of East London. Now, fifteen months later, it is ending here: the last day of the last hearing in the eastern Cape is held in the township just outside East London. Mdantsane, the second biggest township in the country, is selected for a hearing dedicated to women's testimonies.

"They said they were putting me with other women in an ablution block without a roof. They said I will be abused by the other women and I will have to live among excreta. They threw me among these women, who stared at me because I was well dressed. I had a fur coat on. 'The lice will eat the fur from your body,' the police said, 'because you are a terrorist witch.' But the women sustained me. They talked to me. We sang. After a week, they took me again for interrogation. They tripped me. They jumped on my body. They took me by my belt, they lifted me and then banged me on the floor—and I was not so ugly then. I had beautiful hair. They grabbed the hair and lifted me by my hair. They put a bag over my head and poured water over it so I couldn't breathe."

Nosipho Marxewu: "They strangled me, they pulled down my head-scarf—they pulled it down my neck and one pulled from the left and the other from the right. I lost all strength. I urinated on myself. I was pregnant at the time. They said I must tell the truth."

In the first row of chairs sit the victims, looking anxious and uncomfortable at the prospect of testifying in front of so many people. Some of them have babies on their laps.

"After six months, I had infection. I couldn't urinate because of the electric shocks. I lost my appetite. I threw the food in the toilet. When I flushed it, no water came out. I smelt something. When I opened the taps, I smelt gas. I felt dizzy. My throat was very dry. I tried to drink water from the loo. When I came to my child on the bed, I saw he didn't wake up. I started screaming. I took the child to the bars and tried to push it through the bars. It was all foggy. Just my screams. I knew they wanted to kill me and my child."

And then the power shuts down for the umpteenth time this week in Mdantsane. Nothing works—not the lights, not the microphones, not the equipment in the interpreters' booths. The hearings adjourn. It's half past eleven in the morning, yet it is dusky in the hall. No one can go anywhere.

It pours and pours. Everyone waits. The women sing: *"Mali Bongwe."* They sing: "No one can destroy us—we are made from a dangerous metal."

In another corner, the men attending the hearings come together and tell stories and jokes. The Truth Commissioners stand or sit around with their cell phones. Almost as if they're hoping the women will leave. No one organizes food. No one can say when the power will be sorted out. Whether the hearing will go ahead. People are getting tired. A woman stands up and takes a bowl of peppermints off the victims' table and shares them out. Another woman takes a jug of water off the same table. She also shares it. Someone takes the box of Kleenex to the lavatory, where the toilet paper has long since run out. The only light in the gloom is the big candle that remains lit for the victims. No one leaves the center. By half past two, the singing stops. The joking stops. Everyone sits down. The women of Mdantsane sit—their arms folded resolutely across their chests. Frantic calls are made from commission cell phones.

At about four o'clock, a light-green Golf Chico roars up to the center, leaving a spectacular spray of mud behind it. In the trunk is a knee-high generator. Its best years are clearly far behind it. The technical staff climb in—it is fuses, torches, sockets. Under his breath, one technician asks the other: "When does a married man stop masturbating?"

"I don't know, when?"

"When he is divorced." With this he pushes a button and there we have it! The solid pumping of an engine.

"They forced us out of the bus. They let us lie down on our stomachs. They trampled on us. They trampled mostly on me, because I was pregnant. They said women are breeding the enemy."

"I heard these men speaking in Zulu: 'Let's kill these dogs of Mandela.' She jumped over the fence of our backyard. She was wearing pink cloth. They disemboweled her—she was eight months pregnant."

"This burning ball on the dining-room floor, I see it was my daughter . . ."

" 'Mommy, they shot me . . .' I saw the biceps hanging from her arm."

Nomkephu Ntsatha: "They took a wet sack and put it over my face. They suffocated me. While they were doing that, my child was crawling on the floor. They gave her a toilet bag to play with. They slapped me. They sat on my stomach. They took my baby's blanket and stifled my face."

It is dark when the last woman finishes testifying. Some of the commissioners have already left to catch their planes. The cold of the wet night is seeping up through the cement floor. The women of Mdantsane slowly get up. They fold their blankets, they smile, they congratulate one another . . . no rain, no power failure, no men, could silence their stories today.

I'm visiting a friend in town. In their backyard lives a maid. "Doesn't she miss her children?" I ask, thinking of the large families on the farm.

"Maids don't feel like other people about their children. They like to be rid of them. Anyway, Alina likes me now."

On a previous visit. "Why doesn't she have a heater?"

"Maids don't get cold like white people."

The reason she stinks I already know from the farm, where water is rolled along to the houses in big drums—they don't like washing.

A myth is a unit of imagination that makes it possible for a human being to accommodate two worlds. It reconciles the contradictions of these two worlds in a workable fashion and holds open the way between them. The two worlds are the inner and the outer world.

Myth makes it possible to live with what you cannot endure.

And if the myth has been learned well, it becomes a word—a single word that switches on the whole system of comforting delusions.

Like the word *"meid."*

"I cannot take the crying in front of the commission any longer," says a farmer from the Northern Province. "If I see a black woman crying, then I remember two Afrikaans expressions from my youth: 'to cry like a *meid*' and 'to be as scared as a *meid*.' What do I do with this? The most despicable behavior, cowardice and loss of control, we have equated with the actions of a black woman. Now the commission just reinforces the stereotype."

In the big Afrikaans dictionary, you will find words like *"kafferbees,"* *"kafferwaatlemoen,"* *"kafferkombers"*—and each time the word is used derogatorily: *kafferbees*—low-quality cattle; *kafferwaatlemoen*—tasteless melon; *kafferkombers*—cheap type of blanket. There are also words like *"kaffersleg"* and *"kafferlui,"* indicating the intensive form. "Very useless" is *"kaffersleg."* "Very lazy" is *"kafferlui."*

Like the word *"kaffermeid."*

The function of a myth is to provide a logical model capable of overcoming a contradiction. The myth proves that things have always been like this, that things will never change.

CHAPTER SEVENTEEN

Then Burst the Mighty Heart

Testimony of three Guguletu mothers before the Truth and Reconciliation Commission, day 2, April 23, 1996

I am Cynthia Ngewu . . . Where I come from is Alice, but I got married in Transkei in Khombo location. I have four children; the fourth one is the one who was shot by the *boers*. I have six grandchildren. I now live with my husband here in Guguletu.

In 1986, on 3 March—it was a Monday if I am not mistaken—the comrades were asking about Christopher Piet, who is my son. They told me that some children had been shot at Marais. So I went to the police station, and I asked the police about the shot people. "I just want to find out about my child, I want to find out if my child is one of the shot children."

So they said, "We don't know, we'll check the books, we don't have a list of shot children. You must go to the mortuary at Salt River."

I immediately went to Salt River mortuary. There they asked me, "Will you be able to identify him?" I told them, "Yes, I will." They said, "Go on then."

I saw the trolley which was next to the door. The trolley had him in it. So I identified him. They asked, "Are you sure?" I said, "Yes." I saw that he had a wound, a wound shot on his head, and there was blood coming from his ears. I told everybody, "Yes, I identified my son, he is also one of the Guguletu Seven"—the seven of us, myself and these women next to me.

I told everybody else. I said to my kids, "Let's watch all this on TV, because we don't really know what happened, maybe they will have it in the story on TV." While we were still watching the seven o'clock or six o'clock news, I saw my child. I actually saw them dragging him, there was a rope around his waist, they were dragging him with the van. I said, "Switch off the TV, I've seen what I wanted to see. Just switch it off."

During that time, when all this happened, I was too weak. What I—what I knew was that I didn't want to see any white man in front of me, because I was—I was full of hatred at that time, because of the way my son was killed.

He had many bullet wounds on his body. After the postmortem, the doctors told me that he had twenty-five bullet wounds.

I remember the funeral on 15 March. There were many people. I remember the *boers* didn't want all this to happen. I even remember that some of the people didn't manage to come over, they were told to turn back. The stadium that we were holding this whole funeral in was surrounded by the *boers*—that was in NY49.

Everything went well, because nobody was taking any notice of these *boers*. We decided to ignore them, the only thing that we were concentrating on was the funeral . . . I think . . . even when I am just alone, I am thinking to myself . . . Was there any survivor out of all of these killings? And why did the *boers* kill everyone? Couldn't they just warn them, or even shoot them in their legs just to save their lives?

Didn't these *boers* have any feelings at all? Why did they just kill everyone, absolutely everyone? Not leaving even one to give witness. Now nobody knows the real, real story.

(Cynthia Ngewu)

I am Eunice Thembiso Miya. I have five children; the fifth one is Jabulani, he is the one who passed away on 3 March 1986. I am from Bloemfontein.

On this day, 3 March 1986, I was working in the offices in town. I had to leave my house at half past four in the morning—rushing for a quarter-to-five train, rushing for six o'clock at work.

It was usual for my son to go through the back kitchen from where he slept. But on that morning, just before I left, he knocked and I opened for him. Now it was quarter past or twenty past four. When he came in, he ate bread and cold water. He said, "Mama, please give me two rand."

I said to him, "I only have five rand, I'll be short if I give you two, because I want to buy a weekly ticket." But because I wanted him to get a job, I gave him the two rand.

He said thank you. Then he said, "Mommy, I want to come with you to the station."

I said, "No, you are not to do that. I've been going to work at this time of the morning every year, but you've never accompanied me. It's all right, you don't have to come with me."

But he insisted . . .

Now, by that time, I was becoming suspicious. "Don't do this—don't shock me like this," I said to him. "Look, turn back, I don't want you to come with me."

But he insisted, and he accompanied me up to NY59. He wanted to still go on with me, but I told him, "No, turn back."

That was actually the last time I saw him.

I got into the train at quarter to five, got to work. I was working two shifts: two hours in the offices, then from there I would go to char, just to have more pocket money, because the money that I was getting from the offices was too little.

I worked as usual, I continued working, but around half past ten, my boss, Ms. Van Horvet—I can't remember the actual station of the radio where we listened to all this—she came to me and she said, "Eunice."

I looked at her and said, "Madam?"

She said: "I just heard from the news that there are Russians in Guguletu who have been killed. They are from Russia." And then she said, "Is your son involved in politics?"

I said, "No, I don't have any son involved in politics."

So, well, I just continued working. Around two o'clock in the afternoon, it was time for me to go home. I did my usual shopping. Then I went home with the train. We switched on the TV for the news, it's my daughter who did that—her name is Thombisodwa who switched on the TV . . .

The music started for the news. Then in the news I was told that these seven children were killed by the guerrillas from Russia. And one of the children was shown on TV who had a gun on his chest. He was facing upward. And now we could see another one, the second one, only to find that it's my son Jabulani.

We were arguing, myself and my daughter. She said, "It's him." I said, "No, it can't be him, I just saw him this morning, it can't be him. I can—I can still remember what he wore this morning. He had navy pants and a green jacket and a warm—and a warm woolen hat." I prayed, I said, "Oh, Lord . . . I wish—I wish this news could just rewind . . . Why is it just him? . . . Why were the others not shown, why is it just him?"

I was told it was just a hand grenade that did this to him, that was next to him. That's the time I collapsed . . . I don't know what happened after that . . .

What makes me cry now is that these policemen, they were treating people like animals, that's what makes me cry right now. But even a dog, you don't kill it like that. You even think that the owner of this dog loves it. Even an ant, a small ant, you think you have feelings even for an ant. But now our own children, they were not even taken as ants. If I say they were treated like dogs, that's not how it happened, I am actually honoring them. They were treated like ants.

(Eunice Miya)

Now these men at the mortuary, one of them said he would accompany me. When we got there, when they opened the door, I felt this cold breeze, that's when I lost consciousness. Then they took me to some place that I didn't know, they gave me some pills, and they asked me, "Do you still want to go back there?"

I said, "Yes, I do." So I went and I saw Zabonke.

When I looked at him, his body, I couldn't see his body. I didn't want to look at his body. One of his eyes was out, there was just blood all over. He was swollen, his whole head was swollen. I could only identify his legs, because they were just thrown all over the place. One of his eyes was out. His whole head was swollen.

What I can only remember now are his feet, I could only identify his feet, that's how I could see it was my son. They asked, "Are you satisfied?" I said, "Yes, I am."

And in the morning, in the morning we were told: "These children should be buried now because, after all, these seven dogs have been dead for a long time."

After his funeral, I was so miserable. I had nowhere to go. I live in a shack, it was very difficult. Something told me to go and pick up coals, it was on a Thursday. I was knocked down by a rock, this big rock hit me on my waist. I tried to move so that I could get some air. It was eleven in the morning at that time, but they could only get me out of that rock around five in the afternoon.

When I woke up, I felt like I was just getting out of bed. And there was a continuous cry that I could hear. It felt like I was going down—down—down. When I looked, I was wet—wet—wet—I was wet all over the place. I asked for water. They said, "No, we don't have water." I said—I was talking to one of the women who was with me—I said, "Please—please urinate on a plate so that I can drink." She did and I then regained consciousness, I woke up.

When I was awake, they put me into a van and I was taken to hospital. The doctors said to me I must just go away, I must go back under those rocks where I was before, I am no one—I am nothing, what is ANC, what is ANC . . .

(Ms. Konile)

UNWINDING

CHAPTER EIGHTEEN

The Shepherd and the
Landscape of My Bones

The hearings in the Northern Province take place in the prefab halls of the showgrounds at Louis Trichardt, Messina, and Tzaneen. At some of these venues, the media sit outside on the veranda, the thick vine of cables from the audiovisual and translating equipment drawn through an open window. The testimonies reek of witch-burnings, zombies, and Bantustan brutalities.

In Louis Trichardt, a fleet of vehicles from the provincial traffic police escort the Truth Commissioners the two kilometers from their hotel to the venue. They roll through the empty streets of the town—even the main intersection with the national road is no more than a four-way stop. At the showgrounds, there is a massive contingent of 122 policemen and soldiers. "We overestimated the turnout," says the captain. For most of the day, between ten and twenty police vehicles sit parked under the trees. A helicopter also pays a visit to see "how things are developing."

By late morning, a cricket match commences on the field next to the hall. And it is clear that the more things change on this side of the Soutpansberg, the more they stay the same. While the commission listens to testimony of human rights violations, cheerful white families with their Tupperware, sun hats, and small-town familiarity spend the day picnicking on the grass outside. Caught between the field and the hall, we in the media sit listening to bitter crying and choked words, interspersed with cheering and applause from an enthusiastic cricket crowd. The division carries through to the policemen patrolling the showgrounds. The white policemen loll about, watching cricket, while their black colleagues stand solemnly in the doorways of the hall listening to the testimony.

Perhaps the oldest person ever to testify before the commission is William Matidza, born in 1895. Bolt upright, with a white goatee, he walks onstage without assistance. He is here, he says, not because the police arrested him from time to time for political reasons. Not because he was already eighty the last time he was detained. But because all his things have been confiscated. He doesn't care about the house and the furniture and the livestock, these losses he can deal with—but it's his trees. He wants his trees back . . . He wants reparation for *that*. The commissioners explain somewhat uncomfortably that they don't really have the power, that they can only submit suggestions to the president, that it will take time. "Doesn't matter," says Matidza. "I know waiting."

Oudtshoorn.

You could say that Oudtshoorn is a town like most other rural towns, where high unemployment causes the tensions between colored and black, between white, colored, and black, to simmer just below the surface. A deeply divided town like most others. Or you could say that Oudtshoorn is special. Despite all the divisions, it has a history of people who were doers, who raised themselves up from financial depression, who made something out of nothing, who built mountain passes, organized festivals, and, in their day, took on the apartheid regime. That is why, during the visit of the Reparation and Rehabilitation Committee, the proceedings suddenly come to life when suggestions must be made on how the town should address its past.

The black and colored groups look each other in the eye and speak frankly: "The colored women are full of talk, but they never do anything for the community."

"*Ja*, but we got tired of arriving at meetings Sunday after Sunday and finding no one there."

"Division is part of Oudtshoorn . . . like ostriches . . . so let's rather look ahead."

A very old lady says: "Those without forgiveness in their hearts were born yesterday: me, I forgive everybody."

"We will make gardening tools out of old spears," Dominee Gerald de Klerk says. "I went personally to all the other ministers and asked them to join us, but during all those years of struggle, only one of them came to a meeting. And when he heard we were talking about justice, he said: 'No, unfortunately I did not come here for justice, but for the gospel.'"

The undertow of each contribution at the Oudtshoorn hearings is the obvious longing for the one group of people who aren't there. The white group. The only group in this town—as in all the others—who hope the commission will pass them by. How will a town become whole when one group is so apathetic? The man selling medicinal herbs in the street laughs cheerfully: "A town that was first called Hartebeesrivier, then Velskoendorp, then Polkadorp, then Knikspoordorp, and then Kannaland will surely not struggle long with change."

A big fire burns in the fireplace. My husband sits in a steamy bath. I soap my hands and wash him limb by limb—slowly, gently, caressingly.

"I will never forgive you—you have destroyed everything," his voice breaks into the towel that I hold out for him.

What do I say? Do I quote definitions? "Narrative understanding is our most primitive form of explanation. We make sense of things by fitting them into stories. When events fall into a pattern we can describe in a way that is satisfying as narrative, then we think that we have some grasp of why they occurred. Nations tell stories of their past in terms of which they try to shape their futures."

"Stop talking crap," he says. I stop.

I have no framework in which to address him. I have no words for why something so right is so wrong. Definitions leak like sieves. "The act of forgiveness involves a refusal to blame . . . Though an essential element of all personal relationships, the importance of forgiveness is not much reflected in contemporary ethical theory."

"I need to know everything. I need detail. I need to churn it over and over in my mind until it stops hurting and humiliating me. I need to have language for it in order to pack it neatly away. I want the truth. Who, where, when, and how."

The word "truth" is explained by different theories: the correspondence theory, the coherence theory, the deflationary theory, the pragmatic theory, the redundancy theory, the semantic theory, double truth, logical truth, and the subjective theory of subjective truth. Pragmatic truth theorists say the truth has no cognitive value—that we literally should not care whether our beliefs or stories are true or false, but rather whether they enable us to achieve happiness and well-being. There is a connection between what is true and what is useful. Some people say that this conflation of truth with utility is pernicious, because the ethics of belief require us to pursue the truth with honesty even if its consequences should prove detrimental to our material well-being.

"It is precisely this ideological mumble-jumble that makes cruel deeds like this possible. And you want amnesty from me, I must not hold it against you, I must forgive you, we must leave the past behind . . . Well, two can play that game. So let's have a hearing. You can confess and I will call that man and he can say whether you are telling the truth. And I want to sit in the front row like Limpho Hani and whisper to my children: 'The motherfucker!' "

"That's been my point all along. It is useless to talk about truth. My whole telling of what happened will be driven forward, determined, trimmed, slanted, by my desire not to hurt you, to entice you back, to protect your honor, and to convince you to exonerate me."

"Rubbish. There is always a basic truth: you cheated on me. Why? Where? How? From when to when—all of that is negotiable with the things I already know. So the more I know, the more you will confess. What truth I don't know, you will never tell me. More pertinent: when I know the full truth, will I be able to share a space with you?"

The maximum security prison in Pretoria was the head office for hangings—it was a place designed for death . . . Its sole purpose was to imprison persons condemned to death, to clothe them, feed them, and keep them whole until they were killed.

Elaborate mechanisms were put in place to ensure that [they] would not kill themselves. Lights were kept on twenty-four hours a day, prisoners wore no belts, and after the suicide of Frikkie Muller, who gouged his wrists with a shoe nail on the day before his execution, all the condemned wore soft shoes.

Those without hope for appeal or clemency turned to religion and myth—the strongest myth being that no one on death row was hanged—you were dropped beneath the floorboards into a great cavern that was the South African mint. There, for the rest of your life, you made money. You would never be allowed out because then you would be able to tell everyone the secret of money-making. This myth was sustained by the fact that no one ever met anybody who officially made money or saw the bodies of those people who were hanged.

On the night before the execution was to take place, the prison service would give each of the condemned prisoners a bang-up meal with a whole, deboned chicken to eat, as was the tradition inherited from Britain, where you were given the last supper, and four rand to buy something from the prison tuckshop. The whole night before the hanging, there was singing. People would sing other people to their death.

The following morning, they were visited by the prison chaplain at about six A.M. and they prayed with him for about half an hour. Seven were hanged at a time. During the period looked into by the Truth Commission, twenty-five hundred people were hanged in the country—a hundred people each year. Ninety-five percent of those hanged were black—one hundred percent of those who sentenced them were white. By 1989 there were eighty people on death row in Pretoria for politically related offenses. In that year, in what came to be known as "the Christmas rush," twenty-one people were executed during the third week of December—seven on Tuesday, seven on Wednesday, and seven on Thursday.

The heart surgeon Professor Chris Barnard describes the hanging as follows: "Put a rope round a man's neck, tie the knot next to his ear, fasten his wrists behind his back and drop him a distance of just less than two meters. If you haven't botched it by miscalculating, you'll achieve several things at once: The man's spinal cord will rupture at the point where it enters the skull, electrochemical discharges will send his limbs flailing in a grotesque dance, eyes and tongue will start from the facial apertures under the assault of the rope and his bowel and bladder may simultaneously void themselves to soil the legs and drip on to the floor—unless you are an efficient hangman who has thoughtfully fitted your subject with a nappy or rubber pants."

(Paula McBride)

"Later on we stopped making use of young guys. You became so familiar with your work . . . it basically became addictive. You always wanted to be present. When they were hanged that day, you wanted to be there. Later you became aggressive about small things, you started abusing alcohol. It's not the kind of job you could discuss with anybody. You could not tell your family that you hung people, you kept it to yourself." (Prison warder J. S. Steinberg)

"They put me in a trench. They instructed some prisoners to cover me up, to bury me alive with only my face open. Then Kleynhans urinated in my mouth. There were four Kleynhanse on the island. They told me: '*Nee, my Poqo—ons gaan jou nie doodmaak nie, die kruiwa gaan jou doodmaak.*' ['No, my Poqo—we won't kill you, the wheelbarrow will kill you.'] You want to govern the country, but you can't even govern a spade." (Johnson Mlambo)

"The first blow that landed, landed right in the middle of my buttock. It cut my buttock down the middle. I felt the pain, but I just held my mouth and I held on. Their attitude was that this is Robben Island, and no prisoners leave this island alive. Unfortunately, we were the first three coolies to be on the island and the warders would say: '*Waar's daai koelies?*' ['Where are those coolies?'] And they'd pull us and give us a bad time . . . they'd call us *koelies, kaffers, boesmans,* terrorists, you name it . . . And I heard the warder shouting: '*Kak hom uit! Kak hom uit!*' ['Shit him out!'] . . . All of a sudden, I found someone pushing a finger right up my rectum. And this was one of the most humiliating things that ever happened to me. And I heard the warder saying: 'Oh, he's still a virgin . . .' " (Indres Naidoo)

"The ANC kept us in freight containers. No ventilation. When it's cold, it's cold. When it's hot, it's hot. No food, no water. 'Quatro' means number four. A hell of a place. A place where if they give you bread, you think it's cake. The whole cell have to share a cup of water." (Diliza Mtembu)

"On Robben Island, they lined us up, the political prisoners. Then they called the criminal prisoners and invited them: 'Take your pick.' This sodomizing happened to us." (Johnson Mlambo)

I come here on behalf of my family. I come here to express the feeling of betrayal by compatriots and comrades. I come here to express our disappointment and the way we feel cheated of a dear little brother, a brilliant young man. I come here to talk about the hypocrisy that's taking place in our country.

There is one thing that is messing up our country—the lack of sincerity. It is the lack of recognizing other people's contribution if they don't belong to your camp, if they don't belong to your tribe, if they don't belong to your race.

We are still victims of fragmentation.

We have achieved very little.

I have said, I have walked, I have contributed, I have met people inside, outside, the country. I have risked my neck, my life, and yet I am the one to sit here—who does not know what happened to his brother. And it pains me when I hear the rhetoric of shallow honor and integrity of disclosure. Yet underneath, it is vilification, vilifying those who can't speak for themselves. They are called rapists, murderers, mutineers.

I want to ask for the true records of those trials in Quatro camp. I want somebody to come and tell me what my younger brother actually did that he deserved to be shot like an animal—to be put down after being so brutally disfigured that his best friends could not recognize him. I want that comrade of mine to come up and be honest and tell a little lie at least to the family—a little white lie. Say, "We shot him accidentally when we were practicing," and we will be satisfied.

Why do you cheat me of my brother's bones?

Why do you think our contribution is worth nothing?

Why do you think we ran and volunteered to risk our lives calling for your own return home, for justice, supporting you in your call to be treated under the Geneva Convention? And you couldn't even treat your own that way.

Just say the truth, come back and tell us. We have been tested. We can forgive. We can reconcile. Yet we are also capable of forming third forces to hit back. But that is not what we want.

I looked for my brother very quietly and silently. I knew what was happening in the country. I was on Robben Island and I saw what was happening—where people were just destroyed out of sheer rumor, sheer suspicion, that you could be labeled anything and you could die the next day. That made me quiet. It took me more than ten years to find anything . . . the young chappie resembles me, we look alike, but suddenly no one remembers this Seremane. Suddenly no one has a record to show what kind of trial he faced in Quatro. Was he defended?

Where is the accountability?

The system in a way resembled accountability. Because when they were finished with me, they threw me on the lap of my people and said, "There is your rubbish." And my people can't even come and dump my brother's bones and say, "We are through with those bones." I can ask for my court records and find them. But my movement can't offer me even a piece of paper on how they conducted the trial [of my brother].

Questions have to be answered, because without the questions, the weaker ones are going to go back and do it again.

And my family are saying: "Hey, Boet Joe, you are going to pay a price again. You are going to disturb even this government. *Tlogela batu bane*—they'll victimize you." And I saw I had to make the same decision again that I made when I faced the system—if it is for the truth that I must die, so let it be.

(Joe Seremane)

Bram Fischer

Communist and Afrikaner. Reason enough to be singled out for extra humiliation in prison. Then add the fact that this son of a prominent, staunch Afrikaner family had successfully defended ANC members, including Nelson Mandela, in the Rivonia Trial. It was thanks to Bram Fischer that the death penalty was not imposed, people said at the time. Such things were not forgotten by his jailers.

"There seemed to be a very determined effort to humiliate and undermine Bram. The man in charge of the section, called Du Preez, seemed to take particular delight in humiliating him. He cut Bram's hair short. He made Bram wear clothes that were far too big for him. He made Bram wash toilets on his knees with a rag . . . endlessly."

The two calm-voiced daughters of Bram Fischer testify before the Truth Commission.

The day after the Rivonia Trial ended, Fischer and his wife, Mollie, drove down to Cape Town to be with their daughter on her twenty-first birthday. Not far from Kroonstad, at Koolspruit, a cow wandered into the road, just as a motorcycle was approaching from the other side. Fischer swerved and lost control of the vehicle. "By an extraordinary chance in the middle of the Free State—normally no water at all—in the middle of the winter, there was a river that had a huge, deep pool and the car sank into the pool." Mollie was drowned.

The government wanted Fischer's blood, and soon after the accident, he was arrested—but he had already been granted a visa for a Privy Council case in London. Everyone expected that he would skip bail and stay in England. But he came back. "It was important for Bram to say that, as an Afrikaner, he would never leave the country of his birth," says his daughter Ruth. "This land is ours just as it's everyone's who were born here, he used to say."

The case of Fischer and twelve others charged under the Suppression of Communism Act continued through December of 1964, until it was adjourned for ten days on January 15, 1965. It became clear that he was going to be convicted. Before the end of January, he disappeared and went underground. He left a letter to his daughter Ruth and another to his legal counsel. In the latter, he stated:

"I have not taken this step lightly. As you will no doubt understand, I have experienced great conflict between my desire to stay with my fellow accused and, on the other hand, to try and continue the political work I believe to be essential. My decision was made only because I believe that it is the duty of every true opponent of this government to remain in this country and to oppose its monstrous policy of apartheid with every means in its power. That is what I shall do as long as I can."

After months of living underground as Mr. Black, Bram was caught on November 11, 1965. One of the many stories about his arrest is that a security policeman, who had worked on Bram for years, was walking in the street one day when he recognized a familiar gait. His heart skipped a beat. Only one man walked that way. He fell in next to the man with the disguised face and said: "Good day, Abraham Fischer."

Fischer was charged under the Sabotage and the Suppression of Communism Acts. In a four-and-a-half-hour speech from the dock, he concluded his case with the words of Paul Kruger: "With confidence we lay our case before the whole world. Whether we win or whether we die, freedom will rise in Africa, like the sun from the morning clouds." Found guilty on fifteen charges, he was sentenced to life imprisonment. When the verdict was read, his counsel seemed more distressed than he. He smiled at his three children, Ruth, Ilse, and Paul, in the gallery and raised his fist in a salute. Then he was led away to prison. It was 1966.

In 1971, Fischer's only son, Paul, died of cystic fibrosis. "My brother was . . . twenty-three and just finishing his honors in economics at the University of Cape Town. He fell ill and died within six weeks."

Fischer's brother broke the news to him. His fellow prisoner, Hugh Lewin, describes the scene in his book *Bandiet:*

> They wouldn't give permission for a contact visit. They wouldn't let brother meet brother, at a time like that, in one of the offices. That would threaten the security of the State. They stood, two on one side of the partition with Bram and at least two on the other side with Bram's brother.
>
> Paul died this morning.
>
> They couldn't touch each other.
>
> Bram came out of the box-room just as we were being locked up for the night. There was no chance to talk to any of us. He was locked up as usual—alone, in his cell for the next fourteen hours, alone. Fourteen hours, through the usual prison night, alone with the news of his son's death. They refused him permission to attend the funeral.

Fischer had a prostatectomy in July 1974. The surgeon suspected cancer and asked for more tests to be done.

A quarter of a century later, the daughters of Bram Fischer read the litany of their father's last days into the record of the Truth Commission. The facts were written down at the time by another fellow prisoner, Denis Goldberg, and smuggled out of prison in the spine of a book.

"September 1974: Bram saw doctor because of acute pain in hip. Bram not examined, but given analgesics and physiotherapy. After two weeks therapist referred Bram back to doctor who suggested X rays and orthopedic opinion. Nothing however was done. The pain was so severe that Bram needed crutches to walk. Still not sent for X rays.

October: Dr Groenewald did send Bram for X rays.

Late October: Bram saw an orthopedic surgeon who warned that the neck of the femur was very fragile and that a fall could be dangerous.

6 November: Bram fell while struggling into the shower with crutches.

7 November: Bram asked to see a doctor, who did not come.

8 November: Bram asked to see a doctor, but the medical orderly said it was impossible to get a doctor and he did not do so.

9 November: Bram in great pain. Medical orderly provided analgesics.

12 November: Dr Brand says there is no fracture. Bram in great pain.

15 November: Nine days after the fall. Bram again saw Dr Brand. An X ray was at last done and radiographer identified fracture of neck femur.

16 November: Bram seen by specialist who confirmed fracture and advised hospitalization.

19 November: Thirteen days after the fall and four days after fracture diagnosed Bram eventually admitted to HF Verwoerd hospital.

4 December: Bram returned to prison. His fellow prisoners found him alone in wheelchair, confused and unable to speak.

For forty-eight hours I, on my own request, nursed Bram in his cell. He was feverish, and unable to speak or to do the simplest things. Had to pick him up to put him on toilet. Throughout this time he was in great pain, but not seen by a doctor.

6 December: Bram readmitted to hospital where cerebral secondaries were diagnosed."

Now, for the first time, the prison authorities notified the family that he was ill. Ruth flew to Cape Town to plead her father's cause to the minister of justice, Jimmy Kruger. But she was informed by General Hendrik van den Bergh that even though it was clear Bram was dying, he was too great a danger to the state to be released.

After Bram Fischer had spent four months in the hospital in Pretoria, the authorities, although they still refused to release him from imprisonment, agreed to transfer him to the home of his brother Paul in Bloemfontein. Bram Fischer died there on May 8, 1975, at 7 A.M. The prison authorities were informed and arrived within thirty minutes. They stipulated that the family could keep the body for a funeral, provided it was held in Bloemfontein within a week, and that in the event of a cremation, his ashes would have to be returned to the Department of Prisons. Twenty years later, in response to a question in the new democratic Parliament, we were told that his ashes had been scattered by prison officials, in a place of their choice, about a year after his death.

After their testimony before the Truth Commission, I see people embracing Ruth and Ilse as if they are delicate, special creatures. I ask for an interview. These two, who are of Afrikaner blood, have reawakened the pain always flapping somewhere inside me whenever the name of Bram Fischer is mentioned. He was so much braver than the rest of us; he paid so much more; he did so much more; his life seems to have touched the lives of so many people—even after his death. And yet so little is known about him. His daughters speak English.

How did your father connect being an Afrikaner to his politics?

"Bram's earliest memories were of how he and his mother were taking food to General Christiaan de Wet in jail and how his father defended them as rebels. And he saw his commitment to change as a natural progression from Afrikaner nationalism, which is where he started. That was the family history—the Boer War and the rebellion and Oupa drove an ambulance in support of the rebels—it was a whole antiimperial struggle. And Bram saw it as a continuation of the struggle, just extending it beyond the Afrikaner to include all people. In fact, when Bram was arrested the first time in 1946 and phoned his mother in his gentlemanly way, she said: 'Never mind, my dear, we've been here before.' And that was the kind of history of struggle that he came from. I once asked Ouma how she felt about the fact that her son was so different from her and she just said: 'Family is more important than anything else.' "

Unlike many children of activists who try to keep the memory of their parents alive, or react with anger to the hurt their parents' politics have caused them, the Fischer sisters have always remained in the background. But last year, they were invited to the Communist Party's seventy-fifth anniversary celebrations—a memorial lecture about Bram Fischer, presented at the Bloemfontein school where he matriculated.

"It was held at Grey College and it was absolutely wonderful. We were shown to our seats by boys in those very distinctive Grey College blazers—*swart* and *wit* boys! Ruth and I were ushered onto the platform and Ruth was sitting on a chair which was labeled 'P. U. Fischer'—who was our grandfather. And on the rolls of honor, there was Bram's name; and Oupa Abraham—who was our *oupa-grootjie*—his name was also there. It was a bitterly cold night, but all these people had come. The head of Grey made a wonderful speech about the class of 1923 and what happened to them all. And Terror Lekota made a wonderful speech and Ruth made a speech and Bram would so much have enjoyed it—the fact that the Communist Party and Grey College and Afrikanerdom were at last coming together in this kind of celebration."

But how do you live with so many deaths? No sooner has the question left my lips than I regret the prying of it. To my surprise, both of them laugh.

"Switch off the machine." Which I do.

"You drink! At times you drink." And they both laugh again.

"We're not bitter," says Ilse.

"You know, right up until today—Albertina Sisulu says to us, 'You are my daughters.' And she means it. Our lives have been unbelievably enriched through the involvement of our parents in the struggle."

During the second part of the Truth Commission's life span, its work has unexpectedly taken a new and chilling direction. And now this image keeps hanging in the mind: the discolored bones being packed out, one by one, next to the fresh mound of earth. At last the commission has enough evidence that missing activists were interrogated, tortured, killed, and buried on farms all over the country, says the head of the investigative unit, Dumisa Ntsebeza.

In the beginning, the only farm we knew about was Vlakplaas. Then it came to light that similar farms existed in the old Natal, the Transvaal, the Orange Free State, and the eastern Cape. Ntsebeza identifies three kinds of farms. "Firstly, there were farms used solely as bases for *askaris*. Secondly, there were farms where people were interrogated, tortured, and killed. And thirdly, there were farms that were not rented but simply used as dumping grounds for bodies.

"What emerges is a clear pattern with its roots in the theaters of war in our neighboring countries. Well-known Rhodesian activists disappeared in the areas where the Selous Scouts were active. The first disappearances on a regular basis in South Africa happened shortly after the independence of Zimbabwe. And the commission has evidence that not only the police, but also the South African Defense Force, was involved in these farms. People were picked up around the borders, then killed and buried, because no hostages were to be taken. No bodies were to be made available for defiant funerals."

But Dirk Coetzee has described how bodies were burnt or blown to pieces with explosives. Why would the Security Branch bury a body in a grave on a remote farm?

"Because they never thought the day of the Truth Commission would come," says Ntsebeza, "or maybe the burning of bodies was revolting even to them. But I suspect the real reason was a practical one. It takes up to eight hours to burn a body and often they probably just didn't have the time."

Ntsebeza believes there must have been a policy on these killings. He says it's hard to accept that farms spread across the country were run and used in exactly the same way without there being some clear and accepted policy about it.

The revelations present a huge problem, according to Ntsebeza. The commission never imagined that it would be responsible for exhuming bodies. "I think our wildest guess was that we would have to look for a few bodies thrown down mine shafts, but I for one never thought we would be disinterring bones. There is no budget for it. We're battling with the financial director to figure out what sort of line item the grisly fact of exhumations should be."

When Eugene Terre'Blanche said, "This country is drenched with blood"—he didn't know how right he was.

Pietersburg.

In the middle of the town, in the middle of the garden, beside the lake, you will find the world's only bronze *boere-orkes*. The band, which looks more like a symposium of underachieving academics than a group of jolly musicians, stands embedded in Afrikaner codes. A sculpture garden. Our garden. Let us go walking there.

God rules. And God does not perish; he is made of bronze. He rules over the earth and over the land. He paves our paths in concentric circles; he plants indigenous trees with Afrikaans names.

God is a God of animals—from the herd of bronze giraffes at the entrance over there to the bronze pelicans and bronze blue cranes. A fish-eagle unfurls its claws next to this metaphysical thought on a plaque: "And then he caught the fish." God is not a snob. He lets his sun shine on the humble donkey too, ruttishly cocking its bronze hind hoof. The plaque: "For the donkey—carrier of gold into this area from 1871–1892."

God is also the God of the spaces above the earth: a Sabre 358 in camouflage livery soars over the granite monolith erected in memory of the members of Regiment Christiaan Beyers who lost their lives on the Angolan border in 1976.

Rest in peace. *Pro patria*.

Behold! The garden is filled with God's prophets. They appear in flights of bronze—head-and-shoulders for the lesser lights, full-length for those with whom the *volk* was on first-name terms. And for the chosen few: a grassy slope, stone steps, and a ladder of animals.

Past a full-length Tom Naude—"Patriarch of Parliament"—to a distant corner. With her back against the hedge, glowering, the only bronze woman in the garden: Lien Grimm. This bust was donated by her two daughters. The inscription—"First and *Only* Female Mayor of Pietersburg"—confirms our worst suspicions: God rules over women too.

Staggering backward in the saddle, gun clenched under his arm, full beard waving, sits the man after whom Pietersburg was named: General Piet Joubert. Next to the voluptuous horse with its veined, bulging neck, stormy hooves, and flaring nostrils stands a woman with her arm raised. According to the plaque, this is Hendrina Joubert, wife of the general, who on the morning of the battle at Majuba "first spotted the Redcoats and pointed them out to him." That the honor for the victory should fall to her is not a possibility—Hendrina has already departed the flesh. With a flat bun of hair, a long hawkish nose, skeletal limbs, a prophetic cloak over her shoulders, Hendrina has little to do with earthly matters. She accompanies the general on his campaigns for one reason only: her eyes are better than his.

Now all paths wind downward.

All paths lead to the Bronze Band beside the lake. Five musicians in a pyramidal group wait soundlessly with their instruments. They are performing on the town square of the "Bastion of the North." Make no mistake, they may be playing *boeremusiek*, but they are intellectuals fighting for our European heritage.

On a low wall sits the banjo player—in a loose shirt and flowing curls, and a mustache filched from the inimitable Johann Strauss of Vienna. He keeps time with the toe of a polished bronze homemade shoe. Opposite him stands a boy with his guitar across his thigh, in leg-of-mutton sleeves from the time of Henry VIII.

Europe, Africa. There, here. The band represents the triumph of civilization.

As for this one, he may be only a concertina player, but he is deep. He transforms the innermost heavings of his nation's soul into polka. His concertina is held head high; his ear is turned toward the instrument, finely tuned to it. There can be no doubt—it is a young Pik Botha in a neckerchief.

Towering over Pik . . . the bass player (the plaque says it's a *cello*). Dignified, staring at the ground, his body solemn beside the big instrument—which might just as well have been a cannon or a horse—stands General Koos de la Rey.[1]

The most important instrument—the violin—completes the pyramid. The violin player's body is sexless, his buttocks clenched, his bowing arm raised. Verwoerd with a fiddle under his chin. But no sound swells from the bronze sound box—the bow has long since been broken off by vandals. He smiles impassively, empty-handed.

Cover your eyes!

It simply cannot be that so much unbridled symbolism could find expression in bronze! But it is. Slightly behind the band, in bronze of a garish red, a massive crocodile rears up on three legs. It twists its head around to snap viciously at its own tail.

Just lately, the king of Kwela, Lemmy Special Mabaso, has been honored with a bronze statue in the garden of Pietersburg. The famous pennywhistler is the first black man to be honored in this way by the town. His statue stands beside the *boere-orkes,* as if they just might invite him to join in on the next number.

"I am sure this Boereorkes does not mind sharing the garden with me. My wildest dreams have been exceeded—we are all brothers and sisters and at last we all stand together!" *(Die Burger,* 1997)

"This brings us to the end. Not only of the public hearing in Ladybrand, but also of the last hearing for victims that will ever be held in this country. It brings to an end a unique experiment in South Africa's history. And it brings to a close one of the most far-reaching steps that this new government has taken to acknowledge the loss, the pain and suffering, of thousands of victims of this country's political past." The words of Commissioner Richard Lyster, in his closing address at Ladybrand.

How could anything resembling brutality possibly have happened in this town with the golden sandstone glow? With the late afternoon sun pleasant as an amber coat against the stone cliffs? Over the plains of grass frosted to blond and brown and rust?

---

[1] A hero of the South African War between the Boers and the British (1899–1902), De la Rey is regarded as a kind of Boer prophet because of his forecasts and visions of the Afrikaner in the twentieth century.

"Over these past fifteen months, we've been taken by victims like yourselves into the very heart of darkness—into the most cruel and lonely corners of the human temperament. We remember the testimony of a man who worked as a cook on a ship, who came back from sea to find that his wife and two children had been murdered, had been hacked to death and their bodies thrown into a pit toilet."

The last hearing on human rights abuses takes place in the sandstone town hall in the middle of Ladybrand. Right across from the farmers' co-op. While the farmers park their bakkies, load up implements, seed, and fertilizer, the venue is packed from wall to wall with Basothos. "This is a very pure Sotho that you can hear in this area," says interpreter Lebohang Matibela. "That means I cannot just use slang, but I have to produce my best Sotho."

What happens when the Truth Commission descends on such a small town? Obviously, inquiries are made beforehand to see whether the commission would be welcome. Whether people of all races would be welcome. And somebody from the town is usually contracted to do the catering—tea, sandwiches, and lunch for the victims. "This is the first time that I cater in a white establishment," says a black man in a suit. He delivers the food in large porcelain plates, packed into the back of his combi. In another town, a rosy woman with a large floral apron says: "Our politics are right-wing, but money is money and we have to live."

In Ladybrand, the commission's personnel are staying at a guest house run by English speakers. When I ask advice about accommodation in *Heila se Modes,* the owner says: "Rather go and sleep on a farm, my dear. This town is infested with Tutu's arse-kissers—it's the 'Black Circuit against the Boers' all over again."

Because of the atmosphere of hostility in smaller towns, real or imagined, the entire Truth Commission fraternity usually ends up in the same restaurant or bar. In the event of a brawl or an eviction, there will at least be eyewitnesses and support—and they've been needed more than once. At the bar, a brotherly hand on your shoulder and a friendly face leaning over to say: "Haven't seen you in here before—what are you doing in this town?" An answer including "the Truth Commission" has often been a spark into gunpowder. Some have been insulted; others have had drinks thrown in their faces. Black members of the contingent have been refused service or chased out into the street. In small towns, we usually send in a white "spy" first, to check how many overweight men are sitting at the counter, how many are drinking brandy and Coke and talking about rugby.

The first night in Ladybrand, we all sit together in the town's over-crowded Italian restaurant. And we talk about the testimony of Mrs. Makhutu of Bothaville. The town of Bothaville in the northern Free State was once called the richest place in South Africa—or rather, it had more wealth per square meter than anywhere else. The rich English mealie farmers who earned the town this distinction were also the first to build special houses for their workers and supply them with electricity. "Just wait," farmers in other parts of the country said. "These Bothaville types will get what's coming to them. They are creating aspirations that will never be fulfilled." So no one was surprised when the first school riots in the Free State broke out in Bothaville. "These are the children who grew up with water and electricity," the argument went, "and now that they're in high school, they can see their lives are going nowhere." One of the children involved in the riots was Eliot Makhutu. His mother came all the way from Bothaville to testify. Her pink, crocheted skullcap, and her face and hands shiny with years and years of manual labor, re-mind me how in South Africa's first democratic elections a number of women were found to have no fingerprints—their hands had been worked into smooth blanks. In a deep bass voice, she tells us that she cannot understand what happened to her last-born.

"I said, 'Who are you?' And they said, 'We are the police. Open up.' And I opened the door. They came in and they said, 'Where is Marumo?' That is Eliot. I said to them, 'He is present, but he is asleep.' They said, 'Where?' I showed them the room where he was sleeping. When they got into that bedroom where he was sleeping, they switched on the light . . . There were many in number. They were in their uniforms. They had batons, they had *sjamboks*, black in color, and they had their firearms. They pulled off the blanket. They threw it away. They said, 'Stand up, get dressed.' Eliot just . . . laughed. He stood up and he dressed. I said to them, 'Can he please put on his shoes?' And he did put on his shoes. They didn't allow him even to take his jacket. They went away with him.

"On the day of the trial, the lawyers came late. Eliot was together with the rest of the detainees. The lawyers were speaking on their behalf. They were discharged. When Eliot was released, he was not the Eliot I knew. He was mentally disturbed. He was insane. He was laughing all by himself. He would sit wherever he liked. That is my problem. I've taken him to many doctors. I even took him to Hillbrow Hospital. He brought a letter back. He is just a human being. I do not have anything left."

This letter, says a commissioner, states that Eliot is a schizophrenic. And that complicates the case. The commission must corroborate each and every statement made at the hearings. It must establish that a violation did indeed take place, where it took place, and how. Then the commission can classify persons or groups as victims. A classified victim will be able to claim reparation. In Eliot's case, it might be argued that his schizophrenia was under control, but that the shock of his arrest caused it to erupt. Or it might be argued that he was schizophrenic anyway and so does not deserve compensation. In other words, the violation of a schizophrenic's human rights is not really a violation. Then again, one could argue that as a schizophrenic he already gets a disability grant and that is enough . . .

"None of which allows you to blot the face of Mama Mokhutu, in her pink cap, from your mind's eye."

As if a suction pump has been switched on, all the other people in the restaurant get up and leave. Only we remain. A biting frosty air streams into the room. "Rugby—quarter past six on M-Net," says the waiter.

The next morning, on my way to town, I take a detour through the countryside. As far as the eye can reach, there is *rooigras*. I stop. I once wrote: "I adore *Themeda Triandra* the way other people adore God."

I want to lie down. I want to embrace. I want to sing the shiny silk stems upward. I want to ride the rust-brown seeds, the rustling frost-white growth around ankles. Grass, red grass, bareback against the flanks.

This is my landscape. The marrow of my bones. The plains. The sweeping veld. The honey-blond sandstone stone. This I love. This is what I'm made of.

And so I remain in the unexplainable wondrous ambuscade of grass and light, cloud and warm stone.

As I stand half immersed in the grass crackling with grasshoppers and sand, the voices from the town hall come drifting on the first winds blowing from the Malutis—the voices, all the voices, of the land.

The land belongs to the voices of those who live in it. My own bleak voice among them.

The Free State landscape lies at the feet at last of the stories of saffron and amber, angel hair and barbs, dew and hay and hurt.

The Shepherd's Tale

LEKOTSE: My family was affected since that day.
The woman who has testified before me
      is a picture of my wife.
She cannot walk.
She goes for treatment.
I also go for treatment at Botshabelo Hospital.
I took my *last* tablet this morning.

Now my life was affected since that day.
It was at night . . .

ILAN LAX: I want to know about your children first.

LEKOTSE: I have ten children, two have passed away . . . now—

on the day of this assault
I was with three children at home
      and the grandchildren—
      five in number and they go to school—
      some of my grandchildren belong to my son
      who is mentally disturbed.
The last-born has a pair of twins.
Their father is also mentally disturbed.

LAX: Just try not to speak directly into the microphone . . . they
are very sensitive and will pick up your voice very nicely. Which of
these children are still living with you and your wife?

LEKOTSE: I am staying with Thomas Lekotse, my son, he is now
the breadwinner and he is also taking care of the one that I just said
is mentally disturbed.

LAX: Can you tell us about the incident that happened? Was it in
May 1993?

LEKOTSE: Maybe you're right—you know my problem is,
I was a shepherd.

I cannot write
and I forget all these days, but I still . . .

Can I repeat what I said earlier on about the harassment?

Now listen very carefully,
because I'm telling you the story now.

On that day
it was at night,
a person arrived and he knocked.
When I answered, the door just opened
    and I said, "Who's knocking so terribly?"
He answered, he said: "Police."

And I said,
"What police are knocking on my door this way?"

He forced his way through with many policemen.
The door was already down.
Three policemen were black and the rest were white
    and they referred to us as *kaffers*.
Many of them were white.
They were together with big dogs—
    two in number.

They said every door of the house should be opened.
They pulled clothes from the wardrobes.
I said, "When a jackal gets into the sheep
it does not do this—
please unpack neatly and pack them back neatly."

They did not provide an answer.
They pushed us outside.
I fell on my shoulder: *kaboem!*

I asked them, "What do you want?"
but they never provided an answer.

They pushed us outside.
It was terribly cold on that day.
The children were woken up.
I said to them, "Will you provide me with the money
        to take these children to the doctor?"
They did not answer.

I said to them,
"Please, the policemen are not supposed to behave this way."
I said, "When a policeman goes to a farm
        he stops first at the farmer's house.
        If the farmer doesn't allow them entry,
        they leave.
Now where do you get the permission from
        to come into my house
        and break the doors—
is this the way you conduct your affairs?'

When I looked thoroughly,
the door was not just kicked,
it was even broken down with their gun butts.

Even to this day the doors are still broken.

My children took pity on me this year,
they bought a new door and a new frame
and we had to get another person to come and fix the door.

At sunrise life began to be easier.
They wanted to cut open the wardrobes that were locked.
And I said to them,
"How dare you cut open these doors?"

I said to my children,
"Prepare tea,
prepare coffee for these people,
they are hungry."

I asked them,
"Can I offer you beer,
can I offer you drink,
can I offer you *boerewors*?
Are you hungry?"
I said, "These people are hungry.
I have to provide them with food."

I said to them,
"You are not policemen,
    you are just *boers*."
One of them pushed me outside—
that is where I fell on my shoulder and hurt myself.

I was not supposed to speak that way, I admit,
but because I was hurt and disturbed that day
I spoke wrong words.
I said, "I know you policemen are thieves.
You want to take us all outside so that you can implicate us.
I know.
You're going to leave behind diamonds and *dagga*
and you're going to drop them behind and implicate us."

I said, "You bloody policemen."
That's what I said on that day,
because I was hurt.

[audience laughs]

LAX: Please . . .

LEKOTSE: I ended up saying to them: "Look here,
my whole family is standing outside.

It's cold.

I want you to kill all of us now.
I'll be very glad if you kill us all."

They were . . . you know,
it's a pity I don't have a stepladder.
I will take you to my home to investigate . . .

I asked the policemen, "What do you want?"
They did not provide an answer.
I told them:
"I don't have diamonds.
I don't have *dagga*.
What do you want?"
No answer was given.

I said to them, "You want to leave after breaking my doors?
When are you going to come back and fix them?"
They said, "APLA will fix them up."
I asked them: "What is APLA?"
No answer was given.
I don't even know what APLA is,
I am expecting APLA even today to come and fix my door.

Now it was just about sunrise.
My son Thomas said, "No, go and search in my garage."
They said, "Where is the garage?"
He said, "Wait, I have to get a key."
And he said, "You must be very careful—
    don't scratch my car."
They went into the garage with their dogs—
    these were fierce-looking dogs.
After searching the garage, he said,
"You are not yet finished.
I've got another place where you can search.
I have a four-roomed house.
Go and search.
I also have a supermarket.
Go and search it too
because you don't seem to get what you want."
And they left with him.

Now at sunrise they were still at home.
They arrested him for the whole month . . .

There were three *kaffers*
    just like myself,
the rest were white.
They had many vans.
The vans were lining the whole road . . .

    LAX: Was your son Thomas connected to APLA[2] or the PAC?

    LEKOTSE: Yes, sir.

    LAX: Was he charged with anything?

    LEKOTSE: I do not know whether they attended a court case. You
know—

an uneducated person is just down.
You cannot follow anything.
Just like the whites referred to us as dull donkeys.

I do not know many things.

    LAX: He would have told you if he went to court, wouldn't he?

    LEKOTSE: Can I give you an answer on that?

[long pause]

I taught these children,
but because I provided them with education,
    the whites used to say we have short hair
    and our brains and minds are just as short.
Now these children do not tell us anything.
They just go on their own,

---

[2] Azanian People's Liberation Army, an armed wing of the Pan-Africanist Congress.

you just see things happening—
they don't provide you with any information.

[audience laughs]

LAX: You indicate that you injured your shoulder. Did you sustain any other injuries?

LEKOTSE: I was not injured anywhere else—

since that day
that the jackals came into my house to bite us,
I cannot even carry a spade to do gardening.
Otherwise I'm not sick,
it's just the usual sickness of old age.

LAX: In your statement, you mentioned you were injured in your ribs? I'm just helping you to remember.

LEKOTSE: Are you not aware that
the shoulder is related
to the *ribs,*
sir?

LAX: Did you or your son ever make a case against the police?

LEKOTSE: We never took any initiative to report this matter to the police, because

how can you report policemen to policemen?
They were going to attack us.
That is why I said to them,
"Kill us all
so that there is no trouble thereafter.

It is much better to die—
all of us."

It was even going to be easy for the government to bury us—
   they were going to bury us in just one grave.
It could have been much better.

If one of these policemen is around here,
I'll be happy if one of them comes to the stage

and kills me immediately . . .

During the lunch break, I walk over to the co-op with my tape recorder and approach a farmer getting out of his four-wheel drive. "Sir, how do you feel about the Truth Commission's visit to Ladybrand?"

He stops in his tracks. He looks me up and down, while his lip curls in disgust. "The SABC and the Truth Commission. *Fôkôf!*" he explodes with such venom that passersby look in our direction.

"*Fôkôf! Fôkôf!*" he screams as he storms into the co-op.

I find myself on the pavement, my blood thick with humiliation. God, has nothing—nothing!—changed?

"Again and again," says Richard Lyster, "we've heard evidence of people who have suffered the most shocking experiences, standing up confidently and powerfully relating those stories of their past. And we've heard them ask the commission not just to recognize them, but also to recognize the thousands of other people who have also suffered. We've seen these people also caring and nurturing other people and helping them. We have been moved by that."

The proceedings are concluded with the anthem. I stand, caught unaware by the Sesotho version and the knowledge that I am white, that I have to reacquaint myself with this land, that my language carries violence as a voice, that I can do nothing about it, that after so many years I still feel uneasy with what is mine, with what is me. The woman next to me looks surprised when I sing the Free State version of "Nkosi." She smiles, holds her head close to mine, and shifts to the alto part. The song leader opens the melody to us. The sopranos envelop; the bass voices support. And I wonder: God. Does He hear us? Does He know what our hearts are yearning for? That we all just want to be human— some with more color, some with less, but all with air and sun. And I wade into song—in a language that is not mine, in a tongue I do not know. It is fragrant inside the song, and among the keynotes of sorrow and suffering, there are soft silences where we who belong to this landscape, all of us, can come to rest.

Sometimes the times we live in overflow with light.

The shepherd's narrative, given above in the exact words in which he spoke it, describes the experience of one night at the hands of the security police. "My family was affected since that day," the first line of his testimony reads. Although he starts off describing the poor health of his wife and himself, this is not why he remembers the incident. He remembers it, as the subsequent story makes clear, because that was the day when his entire life's philosophy, his perception of the world and his own place in it, was destroyed. Without this perception, his life is not possible; in a sense, he is already dead. He repeats: "Now my life was affected since that day."

At the beginning, Ilan Lax of the Truth Commission interrupts the story repeatedly. The leader of testimony has two tasks: to steer the testimony in a direction that will yield enough facts of use to the commission, and to let the testimony unfold as spontaneously as possible, so that there can be healing and renewed self-respect. The leader of testimony therefore always encourages the witness to begin on a highly personal note—usually with the family.

This technique makes the shepherd impatient. When he is asked how many children he has, he answers: "I have ten children . . . now—/on the day of this assault . . ." But he still tries to accommodate Lax's needs by weaving details about his children into the story—marked by the word "two": two of his children are dead, two of them are mentally disturbed, there are twins among his grandchildren.

The tension of the moment and Lax's interventions cause the shepherd to speak too close to the microphone, and he is asked to speak more softly. Lax uses three longish sentences, with a pause in between, to break the tense rhythm of the narrator, to create an interval of calm, before he formally asks him to relate the incident. But then Lax indicates where he should start: at the date.

This throws the narrator off course again. Surely the precise date on which your life was destroyed is irrelevant? It could have been any day; the important thing is that it happened. But he's not quite sure. "Maybe you're right . . ." he muses. And, of course, being a shepherd and therefore unable to write, he cannot remember dates. But he is a hardened survivor, and he rightly gets firm with Lax: "Now listen very carefully,/because I'm telling you the story *now*."

He starts with a contradiction: "On that day/it was at night." And this introduces the ambiguity, the tension between two poles, the difficult equilibrium that is maintained throughout the story, not only in the facts of the testimony but in the symbols used: day and night, white and black, life and death, educated and illiterate.

Lekotse describes how his family's personal, private space is brutally invaded by the police. They knock "so terribly," they literally break the door out of the frame; they storm into the house with dogs; they insult the occupants; they wrench open the closets and throw their belongings on the floor. Lekotse, as head of the family, tries to take an honorable stand against these assaults, but every honorable action on his part is negated. He asks who is knocking so terribly—and the door is broken down. He asks them to replace the contents of the wardrobes neatly—and they are chased out into the cold night. Even a jackal, says Lekotse, when it gets in among the sheep, does not behave like this.

To appreciate the power of the image, we must bear in mind the kind of predator the jackal is. He's a quiet, neat, gourmet hunter. He calculatedly corners a few sheep, singles one out, and then sinks his teeth into the artery high in the neck. When the sheep has bled to death, the jackal will first eat the spleen and the liver and then the hind legs. If there are lambs, he'll kill one or two and devour nothing but the fourth stomach. And the jackal can do all this almost silently—he doesn't even have to chase the sheep to tire them out. Unlike the dog. A dog in among the sheep, biting to left and right, causes a tremendous cacophony of barking and bleating. And if a dog kills, it won't eat.

They were worse than jackals, says Lekotse. And since the jackal is the shepherd's greatest enemy, a threat to the flock night and day, he means that the security police exceeded his worst expectations of evil. As a shepherd, he often had to measure up against the sly jackal—but against this opponent he was at a loss. Notice that at the end of the narrative Lekotse returns to the comparison—"the jackals came into my house"—as if he cannot find another image.

With the entry of the police into the shepherd's space, a second leitmotiv is introduced: "They did not provide an answer." Lekotse asks several times: "What do you want?" When they refuse to answer, he plagues them with further questions. Will you give me money to take my children to the doctor if they become ill from this cold? Who gave you permission to visit my home? Is this the way you conduct your affairs? How dare you cut open my wardrobes? Do you want beer, drink, *boerewors*? Are you hungry? Do you want to implicate us by planting *dagga* and diamonds? When are you going to fix my doors? Who is APLA?

This kind of questioning is the foundation of all philosophy. How do I understand the world around me? What is right and just in this world? The fact that none of his questions are answered explains why the day affects him so deeply: his ability to understand the world around him is taken away. He is plunged into a mythological darkness, where no explanation suffices, where no answer is given. The withholding of information goes further later on, when his own children keep things from him—because they are educated and he is not, he says.

In a desperate attempt to understand the behavior of others, Lekotse imaginatively transplants himself into several other positions. The farmer. How could a farmer give permission for this kind of action? The police. They must be hungry if they are carrying on like this—and he offers them food and drink. A little later, he imagines that they are going to plant diamonds and *dagga* in his house. What makes his story all the more poignant is the fact that he can imagine himself in the other characters' positions, but no one seems able to empathize with his own.

His empathy, his ability to think himself into other positions, goes beyond the night he is describing. It even includes the people from the Truth Commission. Perhaps, he is thinking, they are struggling to understand fully the destruction that was sown in his house. "It's a pity I don't have a stepladder./I will take you to my home to investigate . . ."

These two sentences form a poetic and imaginative climax in the story. Lekotse knows he cannot insist that the commission visit his house: but if only he had a ladder that he could set up, perhaps they could see his hut from the top of it, with its newly mended door. It is a yearning to be understood, to give the people in front of him a perspective on the impossible. A ladder would give the Truth Commission insight; it would raise his story from one plane to another, from the unreal to the real, from incomprehension to full understanding.

Lekotse refers to himself at the end of the story as a *kaffer* and a dull donkey. And he names those who have reduced him to this unworthy role: the whites, the police, the farmer, his children. Without his self-respect, he cannot live, and he cannot make life grow. "Since that day/that the jackals came into my house to bite us,/I cannot even carry

a spade to do gardening." The destruction of his whole sense of co-
herency is thrown into relief by the behavior of his own children, who
manage to run circles around the police, and even taunt them.

Lekotse's interaction with the Truth Commission strengthens his
frustration about the lack of communication. At the end, Lax asks him
two questions. He answers both with counterquestions in which his
dejection about the incomprehension of the Truth Commission comes
to the surface.

In your statement, you mentioned that you were injured in your ribs,
Lax says. Now you say it's your shoulder?

Lekotse, who has slaughtered many a sheep in his lifetime, responds
by asking: "Are you not aware that/the shoulder is related/to the
ribs,/sir?"

Then Lax asks whether the incident was ever reported to the police.

Again Lekotse responds by asking: "How can you report policemen
to policemen?"

And then comes his request: "That is why I said to them,/'Kill us
all/so that there is no trouble thereafter.' " It would have been cheaper,
he says, to bury them all in one grave. And he ends his narrative by re-
calling the day/night that changed his life forever, with this repeated
request: "If one of these policemen is around here,/I'll be happy if one
of them comes to the stage/and kills me immediately . . ."

The full tragedy of his final request becomes apparent in the light of
some remarks on the African narrative made by the Zulu poet Mazisi
Kunene in an unpublished interview with Colleen Scott, an American
academic: "When the first white men came . . . the elders went to those
men and said: 'Tell us about your world.' There isn't one world, there
are many worlds . . . in the African system, there is diversity. The ideal
is diversity, not symmetry."

This notion of diversity echoes in Lekotse's urgent need to understand, to have access to, to be informed about, the world of the intrud-
ers and their thinking. He does not naturally ignore or resist the police.
His instincts are to give them access to the fullness of his world, and he
expects to gain access to their world in return.

Lekotse constantly makes use of archetypes that support the theme
of access to diversity. As a shepherd, he is the leader and protector of
his flock and family. He leads them to nourishment and safety: he is
therefore the pathfinder to worlds that may enrich his group.

A door closes off a space, but it also opens into it. Both these meanings are present in Lekotse's story. The policemen's intention is not just to invade his private space, but to damage the access to it in such a way that it will never be a private space again. Although the police penetrate his world, they refuse him access to theirs, and even to their intentions, which would help him to redefine his own space. They will not even tell him what they are looking for. (Note that the police, the jackals, burst into the house with dogs. Jackals are creatures on the move between night and day, life and death; dogs are bound to one place, the faithful guardians of unbreachable borders.)

From the safe shelter that the shepherd has created for his family, they are driven out to where it is so cold and inhospitable that the best place for his flock becomes the grave.

Kunene says: "You can't kill once, it is said you must kill twice. In other words, after you've killed, you must recognize that the one you've killed is also yourself. He is also a son, a father, a brother."

Lekotse is left standing outside his shattered house, bewildered, never again able to judge the world around him or enjoy it, to discover other worlds or share in them. His worth as a father, a brother, a son, has been negated; he has been treated as a *kaffer* and a donkey, and so he is already nothing. Now he asks for the deed begun that night to be fulfilled. His physical death must be added to his spiritual death. He must be killed twice. He'd be happy, he says, if someone would kill him immediately.

"It is quite interesting to sit in that booth. You're aware that you are becoming an actor, but you know people will say afterward: 'Lebohang, you were really smoking—what was going on?' And you didn't even realize that you were acting—you know, you are just looking at the victim as he is speaking and unconsciously you end up throwing up your hands as he throws his, you end up nodding your head when he nods . . . But it becomes very difficult to interpret when they are crying, then they speak in installments. He says something, then he keeps quiet and he starts again . . . you have to bring the pieces together." (Lebohang Matibela, interpreter of the Shepherd's Tale)

Water Holes

The island inherits the last light as we disembark from the ferry. Down into a colonial story, with black schoolboys carrying our bags all along the beach. Against the old slave quarters, the sea spends itself. Our shoes sink into the beach-sand streets. The roofs lisp milk, and rosy villa walls flake and stain like European skin. In the remains of the excesses of former exploiters, the island's inhabitants live.

A poetry festival on Goreé—the slave island just off the coast of Senegal.

We embrace the day and swim out into the bay's silvery haze. In the square, the trees forge blood. We meet the other poets. Somewhere in the shimmering, a folk-music group is practicing. There is raw honey from Casamance, cloth and jewelery from the Tuareg. We sit with two poets from Holland. A prickly one with scars and a sweaty one with a white undercoat and countless pairs of sunglasses. We eat out of the baskets. Cream of tartar and hibiscus juice. Youngsters doze on the sand next to the beached fishing boats. You just cast down a rag wherever you are and doze off. "Who's making all that noise?"

"Those drunken poets at the hotel," someone mumbles.

It is the day of the performance. The Dutch poet with the many glasses sits sweating beneath the woven screens. The hotelier scurries around him, yelling at his waiters—the poet is waiting for his suit. He refuses to perform without his suit. His white-linen suit was sent by *chaloupe* to the mainland to be dry-cleaned in Dakar. The hotelier is trying to repair the telephone connection. The sun is magnesium silver. The poet with the many glasses says that if his suit doesn't arrive, he will not get up from his chair again.

In the meantime, several groups perform. A dancing bird from Mali. His toes stabbing like knives into the sand. Here is a camel with an oryx mask—over his body hang mats woven from rope and dune air. A puppet show. From one character's shining robes shoots an inch-long, blood-red penis—the ornate children fall on to the sand with laughter. A great big condom is pulled over the penis. The late afternoon sun smells of bark and aubergines, of spearmint and fried fish. The poet remains in his chair.

Eventually, a joyful boy comes running down the beach with the suit in a brown paper bag, folded like an offering of atonement in his arms. Soon the poet appears, resplendent. He is wearing a different pair of glasses and his shoes are shining. "Art Tatum is God," he says, and walks over to the stage, where, since early that day, the musicians have been warming their drumskins at a big open fire.

The poetry begins. The poets from West Africa are first. They use

French. After the first few lines, the poet with the many glasses starts moaning: "Rubbish! Clichés! Nothing but clichés about blood and land." He gets up irritatedly and walks over to the fires, where the masks and dancers throw writhing shadows against the walls of the square.

The next day there is a workshop. Two Senegalese poets are there and also a Berber—he wears a light-purply-blue robe, has a dark skin and blond hair, and his poetry (which we heard the night before) is interspersed with cries and the sounds of sandstorms and horses. Breyten Breytenbach, who organized the festival, translates back and forth in French and English.

I am uncomfortable with how easily Europeans write off our continent—never as "different to," only as "less than." I ask Breyten to translate: "In my culture you are a good poet if you can say old things in a new way. We have been saying 'I love you, but you don't notice me' for centuries. The 'newer' the way you say it, the better poet you are. In the culture of Senegal, what makes you a good poet?" The Dutch smoke quietly. The Senegalese poet speaks and Breyten translates: "In my culture, you don't just become a poet. You have to apply first. And the older poets come together and your ancestry is studied and your ability tested. And if you are chosen, you take up an apprenticeship with the chief poet. And he teaches you the nation's poetry. And your people's poetry is your people's lyrical soul, their history. And you may *not* say it in a new way, you may *not* change it, because then you forge what has happened. You change history. If you are talented enough, you may add your own piece later and maybe change something small here and there . . . And the chief poet can tell you exactly what part has been changed or added in by which poet at what time. The more accurately you preserve the poetry, the better you perform, the better poet you are."

The attention shifts to the nomadic poet. "In my culture, the task of the poet is to remember the watering places—the metrical feet of the water holes. The survival of the whole group depends on whether you can find the water holes in the desert. You must remember them in such a way that other groups are none the wiser. The group will never cast you out or see you as mad—but the day you betray the position of the water holes to someone else, that is the day they will leave the poet behind in the dunes."

CHAPTER NINETEEN

A Tragedy of Errors

Snow has a smell

"There is a deal between the ANC and the Truth Commission, we accept that. What we're trying to figure out is how far the deal stretches." The man opposite me bristles with energetic efficiency. Embarrassed, I look out of the window, where it is snowing as I've only ever seen it snow in movies. This man, a citizen of the country my ancestor Johannes Christoffel Krog left in 1776, has made an appointment to ask me informal questions about the South African Truth Commission.

A deal?

Of course there must be a deal! How stupidly naive of me never to have thought of it before. My mind reels in an effort to find a new position—but it keeps getting stuck on one man.

"Deals may have been made with certain groupings or individuals, but a deal with the whole Truth Commission?—that is simply impossible. Someone like Archbishop Tutu would never willingly destroy a lifetime of standing up to the harshest possible oppression, give up a lifetime of sacrifice for what is right, in exchange for some or other improper political deal. It doesn't make sense strategically or psychologically. Tutu—and this goes for some of the other commissioners too—is the kind of person who would actually prefer to resign dramatically and use the opportunity to spell out why. The man is dying . . . he has nothing to lose except his impeccable integrity."

The man nods his head. "But does Tutu know what is going on in his commission? Does he know . . ."—he touches his glasses and I realize for the first time that there are no reflections in them, the lenses absorb everything—". . . does he know it is said that three investigators were seconded to the Truth Commission from ANC intelligence? Does he know that people say your new government has taken over the chemical weapons program from the old regime just as it is and probably the nuclear program as well? Does he know it is also claimed that this information is in the hands of his investigative unit, and will he demand that it become part of the final report?"

I don't know how to respond. He hands me a small, earless bowl of heavenly coffee. I wet my lips with it, and then I say:

"I am not an investigative journalist. I find the whole idea of scoops and the breaking of stories slightly ridiculous, if not pathetic. Headlines make me cringe. So how do I report on this, what should my role be?"

He doesn't hesitate: "It is to report in such a way that you strengthen the hand of those who have *not* made deals, who have the same priorities as you. Do not always look at the Truth Commission as a whole, but focus on what is in it that makes it worthwhile to all of us."

Suddenly I want to go home. I have nothing to say to his "all of us." In a moment, he has made the snow vanish and I am gazing out on the familiar landscape of my country—but from behind glass. He wants me to deal with the Truth Commission as if from the heart of a different life.

At Charles de Gaulle, I bump into a comrade I haven't seen for years. We check in for the South African flight, joking about how we no longer have to sweat it through customs, with our communist tracts hidden in the bottom of the suitcase. He explains to me about foie gras and truffles and helps me choose a bottle of champagne for my husband. At the bookstall, a magazine with Winnie Mandela on its front cover and a loud headline: "Fugitive speaks out on murder of child activist."

My old comrade has seen the BBC documentary in which Katiza Cebekhulu implicated Winnie in the murder of Stompie Seipei. He tells me about it as we find a seat in the departure lounge. But he also knows more, he says. He knows that Nelson Mandela tried to discuss the Stompie issue with Winnie, tried to talk sense into her head about her handling of the matter. But she would not listen to reason, and he believes she became so angry that she physically attacked Mandela. "The woman is demented," he says. "Do you think the hearing will reveal that Mandela himself was responsible for the cover-up?"

My blood turns to ice water. "If he was responsible for a cover-up, I don't want to hear about it." It slips out before I can think. My friend looks puzzled.

"I mean, the so-called litmus test we used to talk about—what would you do with information implicating the highest authorities in the dirty work?—this is it. I was full of moral indignation when they were interviewing prospective commissioners and some of them said they'd treat such revelations differently. But here I am! It's my choice now! And I'll tell you this: if Mandela did something wrong, I *don't* want to hear about it. Something, *something*, has got to survive out of all of this."

He laughs: "You whiteys—we can never just talk to you. We talk a bit, then we have to educate for a long time, then talk a bit again . . . You are not the Truth Commission, the decision won't be yours. But tell me something else: Will someone like Joe Modise, as the last commander of MK, also have a public amnesty hearing?"

"Of course! He's applied, and all gross violations have to be heard in public. There might be quite an interesting time ahead with all the ANC people asking for amnesty—it will do a lot to dispel the feeling that the commission has targeted whites."

"I am torn," he says. "One part of me feels that the ANC shouldn't appear at the commission at all. We were fighting a just war . . . Then another part of me thinks of my brother, who was killed after he joined MK. The story we have is that he was part of a group based in Mozambique who decided that they couldn't tolerate the gross mismanagement, arrogance, and downright abuse of a certain MK commander any longer. God knows what they were planning to do. Whatever it was, we've heard that this commander got wind of it and asked the Mozambican army to get rid of them. One morning at dawn, they were surrounded and wiped out."

"Will you come to his hearing and tell your story?"

"My uncle is the head of our family, and he was given a large sum of money. We will not talk. What would it achieve?"

We sit there, the two of us—with our confused South African moralities. When our flight is called, he gets up with a sigh. "It doesn't get easier to live an honorable life in our country."

A day after my return from Europe at the end of October, Glenn Goosen, the director of the Truth Commission's investigative unit, resigns. A Sunday paper carries the story that his resignation came after accusations of racism. The next day, the Truth Commission issues a statement saying that Ntsebeza and Goosen disagreed about the restructuring of the unit and that the resignation had nothing to do with any racial incident. The following Sunday, the same newspaper tells its readers that it now has the *real* reason for the resignation: Goosen claims he was hampered in his investigation into claims that Ntsebeza's car was used in the attack on the Heidelberg Tavern.

The fat is in the fire. It is Sunday evening. My colleagues at the radio, busy preparing for the next morning's current affairs show, are on the line: What are you doing on this Ntsebeza thing? I phone John Allen, who sounds as fed up with putting out fires on a Sunday as I am with following the smoke. The commission stands by the statement it made last week. Perhaps I should phone Goosen, I say. Goosen doesn't want his number given out, Allen says, but he'll call him and ask him to call me. Goosen doesn't get back to me. Phone Boraine, John Allen advises.

Why? I wonder. Would he be ready to confirm the corridor gossip of the past week? My work at Parliament has taught me one thing: you cannot rely on what is whispered in the corridors, but you can certainly judge by the amount of whispering being done when there's tension in the Halls of Power. I ask around: Did Goosen hand in a report to the Truth Commission? One liaison officer says no, the other says yes . . . but he's not sure. Maybe this is what the man who made the snow disappear was trying to tell me. Strengthen the hand of those who keep their eye on the ball.

I file this report: "Every commissioner has a past—most of them a political past. It has happened twice now that cases have been put before the Amnesty Committee in which Commissioner Chris de Jager was involved. On both occasions, before the case started, De Jager made a public statement recusing himself."

What I don't say is that this is precisely the reason some of us felt the commissioners should *not* represent constituencies but principles—chiefly the principle of human rights. Then there would be no space for pressure and blackmail. "But people will never accept the commission unless they feel it represents them," I was told by those who know.

My report continues: "Earlier this year, the media carried a story alleging that a white Audi belonging to the head of the investigative unit was involved in the Heidelberg Tavern attack. Dr. Alex Boraine issued a statement saying that the matter was being looked at by Ntsebeza's second in command, Glenn Goosen. He also stated that he and the chairperson had satisfied themselves that no irregularities had occurred.

"The commission was clearly in a dilemma at that stage. Ntsebeza was indispensable to the Truth Commission process. It was said at the time of his appointment that he represented the Pan-Africanist Congress and Black Consciousness constituencies. Maybe that is why Ntsebeza was not immediately temporarily removed from his position as investigative head until the report had been completed. Why Ntsebeza himself did not decide to step down temporarily is also unclear.

"Ntsebeza has brilliantly honed a profile for himself in the past eighteen months—not an easy thing to do alongside a dynamic, dramatic chair and a busy deputy chair. (Few commissioners have managed it—ask those who still get stopped at the door for their entry permits because no one knows who they are.)

"Ntsebeza's not stepping down created a neat time bomb for the Truth Commission: a man has to investigate his own boss. It is common knowledge that the man and his boss are not seeing eye to eye. The white man is dispensable; his black boss is crucial. The white man has been accused of bungling the cross-examination of F. W. de Klerk and the other generals, while his boss is the man, apart from Desmond Tutu, who gains the most credibility for the Truth Commission in important black quarters.

"Now it seems from media reports that a report has indeed been completed and handed to Tutu. No press statement, no information to the public, no transparency. And suddenly Goosen resigns. What else can outsiders conclude but that it must have something to do with this particular report? On Friday we heard that Ntsebeza has been notified under Section Nineteen that he may be implicated in this week's hearings. We hear that a lawyer will represent his interests. And yet it is the very people working under him who have to establish whether he is guilty or not.

"Haven't we heard of this kind of investigating before? Doesn't it smell like the past? Are we witnessing a cover-up? And, of course: What else is being covered up?"

While this report is being broadcast, I am on my way to the amnesty hearing of the three APLA cadres who attacked the Heidelberg Tavern. On my car radio, I hear that Alex Boraine has phoned the station demanding to be put on air so that he can respond to my outrageous claims. Stammering with anger, he slashes my report to ribbons. "I am quite staggered actually that she didn't ask me the questions directly, instead of necessitating me to phone the SABC to ask for equal time. It borders on the ridiculous. I think it is a scurrilous report. It is inaccurate and probably based on corridor gossip."

At the hearing, I meet up with the radio team. This is the first time I've seen them since I got back from overseas and I am shocked by their obvious physical decline. Although we as a team have just won a nationally respected journalism prize for our work on the Truth Commission, their eyes have a desperate look and their talk has degenerated into a kind of raging, shot through with curses. I hear that a fight broke out one night between two of them, in some desolate little town after a hearing, and they came down to breakfast the next morning with bruised and swollen faces.

Shortly after the hearing starts, some Truth Commission staffers pitch up with stacks of photostats: the original statement implicating Ntsebeza, the one made later to the Truth Commission, the investigating officer's report, Glenn Goosen's report, the different statements of the Truth Commission, the whole tutti. Transparency at last—to a T.

Throughout the day, as we're working, journalists keep coming up to me and patting me encouragingly on the shoulder. Instinct tells me the reason for this kindly behavior lies in the word "scurrilous." I don't have a clue what it means. Arriving home after eleven that night, I look it up in the Afrikaans-English dictionary. "Scurrilous" means: *laag, gemeen, vuil, plat, grof*; grossly or obscenely abusive, coarse buffoonery. And I explode. I am so angry that I cannot function. Bloody Alex Boraine! Am I not his ally? I calm down. Perhaps more than any other commissioner, Boraine's personal life has been beset by traumatic family tragedies since he took on this task, including a vicious criminal assault on his daughter and the illness of his youngest son. Then I think: No, he would not dare react like this to any of the male journalists covering the commission. But I'm supposed to be supportive and nothing else.

The next day, I hear that Tutu is even angrier about the report than Boraine and that there is talk of lodging an official complaint with the board of the SABC. At the office, I find a letter on my desk. Boraine is demanding, if not an apology, then at least a very good explanation.

. . .

On the second-to-last day of 1993, just before midnight, six APLA cadres entered a tavern in the Cape Town suburb of Observatory and opened fire on the patrons. Several people were wounded and four killed. The dead were the owner of the restaurant next door, Jose Cerqueira, and three female students, Bernadette Langford, Rolande Palm, and Lindy-Anne Fourie. The first two girls were colored; the third was white. These were the final days of negotiations, and South Africa's first democratic elections were just four months away.

The white and colored victims of the Heidelberg Tavern massacre, some of them in wheelchairs, seem ablaze with anger and neglect. They sit in the rows just behind their attackers, who are slumped nonchalantly. The rest of the hall is filled with aggressive young PAC supporters. The air is thick with the potential for confrontation. To one side a concerned-looking Dumisa Ntsebeza sits with his lawyer.

I interview a psychologist who specializes in grief. And an amnesty hearing that was supposed to be about a lot of other things suddenly flares into focus around a single issue: the violent death of a child.

The effect of a violent death on a family seldom receives attention. As South Africans listen to the voices of parents, brothers, and sisters relating the loss of a family member, the unsaid, sometimes the unsuspected, is seldom taken into account.

ROLAND PALM (father of Rolande Palm): On realizing it was gunfire, I immediately stretched over the table, pulled my daughter, and said, "Get down." In that motion, I fell onto the bench and rolled onto the floor. My daughter dropped with her head to the table and her back was exposed. A hail of bullets was directed at us and a bottle and other things on the table fell to the floor.

As I tried to look up from under the table to see who is shooting, I noticed my daughter reaching the floor slowly. In the same instant, I noticed two other girls to my right fly out of their seats.

The next instant, I saw this torchlike object which knocked the side panel in the passage and rolled over to where we were. I screamed, "It's a grenade, stay down!" . . .

Immediately I noticed a trickle of blood on her shoulder as she was lying face down. I pressed her to the ground and counted to ten waiting for this explosion. Nothing happened. I turned her over and she just slumped in my arms.

I lifted my daughter up, felt for her pulse, but my hand just sunk in her neck. I laid her down on her back, tried to close her eyes, but they would not close. This is when the realization really hit me that she was dead.

After a natural death, the family can begin the process of mourning. After a death brought about by violence, political violence, the justice and police system usually disrupt the rituals of grieving. The violent death of a child usually lacks a sense of closure.

ROLAND PALM: I immediately made my way home to tell my wife. I was blinded by the shock and tears. I passed a police van on the corner of Observatory and Lower Main Road, outside the chemist . . .

A few days later, the investigating officer, Des Segal, came to my house to take a statement. In the course of making my statement, I told him of the yellow police van I saw parked next to the tavern when I ran outside. I said I felt relieved to know the police were so quickly on the scene. Segal told me I must have been drunk, as there was no such thing as a police van standing there. I insisted he take it down in his statement and he did. At the court case, they didn't use me. Segal told my wife that the suspects would walk because I was drunk that night and that the police could not possibly have been on the scene.

The irony of her death is that she was not a white person, who, according to APLA, were the legitimate targets of their death squads. I cannot begin to describe the rage I feel and have felt for the past years at her senseless killing. You simply ended Rolande's life as if she was a worthless piece of rubbish. You say you did so to liberate Azania. I say to you you did it for your own selfish and criminal purposes.

I have lost two children to the system. My son to the apartheid system of justice and my daughter at the hands of killers that the system seems to protect.

The parents of a murdered child wonder what the last thoughts, terrors, despairs, were in their child's mind. What he or she might have become one

*day. The murder of a child violates the natural order, destroying the parents'
stake in the future.*

JEANETTE FOURIE (mother of Lindy-Anne Fourie): Her black
friends called her Lindiwe and they were as important to her as her
white friends. Lindiwe could have been your friend. You did your
own cause immeasurable harm by killing her . . . she was a gentle
person. She taught me how subtly embedded my racism was—in
the most hidden-away fibers of myself . . . As a medical person, I
had to go straight back into the wards of Groote Schuur to treat
your colleague who had been shot . . . and I needed to do that without showing any bitterness that you have killed my child . . . God
gave me that grace . . . I came here hoping to hear the truth about
who the people in high command were who organized the whole
dastardly affair. I am not convinced that that truth has come out . . .
and until it does come out, I am not happy that you can just disappear into the woodwork . . .

*Although the killer should be blamed for the death, the families of victims
are often plagued by their own guilt. A sudden death may also leave all sorts
of issues between the victim and the family unresolved. Siblings feel guilty
that they survived. Parents are torn by self-doubt. Aren't parents supposed
to keep their children safe from harm at any cost?*

ROLAND PALM: The pain of losing my son was compounded a
million times by the death of my daughter. I felt responsible and
guilty for both of them. I have lived with that for the past four years.

My personality has changed. I have not been able, despite extensive therapy and counseling, to shed the anger, rage, guilt, feelings
of revenge and helpless desperation, at the system that allows murderers to escape punishment.

JOHANN FOURIE (father of Lindy-Anne Fourie): *"Ag, Pappe, moenie worry nie* [Oh, Daddy, don't worry]—we'll be all right."

These are the last words exchanged between me and Lindy-Anne
at around six-thirty on the evening of December 30, 1993.

As Lindy's father, responsible for her existence, I accepted the responsibility of raising and caring for her to the best of my ability . . .
when our children become adults, and more than equal to their par-

ents, that is when the battles all seem worth it and many of life's mysteries seem to fall into place . . . about our offspring . . . but I and my wife, Jeanette, have been robbed. Robbed of our own flesh and blood. Robbed of the most natural form of happiness that humans can experience—the love of our own daughter . . . No longer do we hear the voice on the telephone say, "Howdy, Pops, how are the brother and the Mater?" No longer do I see her wild flowing hair as she races past us with her favorite dog in hot pursuit. You see, sir, we were ordinary people, doing our ordinary work, in our own ordinary and uncomplicated manner . . . So why did she have to die so young and by such violent means?

Research proves that the stresses of losing a child are responsible for an extremely high rate of divorce among grieving parents. Research also shows that men and women grieve differently and that the differences and discrepancies often create resentment.

JOHANN FOURIE: My wife has told you her grief. She has preferred to talk directly to the killers. My grief is different. I talk to you, Mr. Chairman, as the person who decides on their amnesty.

ROLAND PALM: Suffice to say, my marriage has suffered irreparable harm. My wife suffers from extreme anxiety and nervous tension. We are both on constant medication.

BENJAMIN BRAUDE: I feel as if I have become a "monster," I feel distant from my family and am unable to guide them as leader of the household. My life seems to be a constant seesaw. I feel as if my manhood has been taken away from me. My wife and I do not share our marital bed any longer and our sex life has become nonexistent.

Events that once brought families together, such as birthdays and holidays, become reminders of loss. The internalized grief felt by parents may bring about a variety of serious illnesses. Some parents of murdered victims soon follow them to the grave.

JEANETTE FOURIE: The reason that I am here, have been here through this week and particularly today, which is very important to me, is to tell you that on that day, the day you killed my child, you ripped my heart out. Lindiwe was one of the most precious people—but I am biased, because she was my daughter—this country could have produced. I resent being called a victim. I have a choice in the matter. I am a survivor. Lindy was a victim, she had no choice. I just had major surgery which I trace as a direct result of the stress and trauma that resulted after the Heidelberg incident. It has been demonstrated that cancer of the colon results from tremendous stress. First my heart was ripped out and now half of my gut. I am happy that you are well . . . I hoped that emotionally and psychologically you could be well . . . You could not tell us here how you felt, which indicates to me that possibly you have been trained not to feel. I can see that that would be important in a killing machine . . . I have no objection to amnesty for you . . . Thank you for being able to look me in the eye . . . and for hearing my story.

The severest loss is that sense of invulnerability that allows you to lead a normal life—to go out, to drive a car, to let your children visit others—this is totally destroyed. The unnatural death of a child brings an existential despair—you feel scared, alone, and incapacitated.

BENJAMIN BRAUDE: A month after the shooting, my life had fallen to pieces. I withdrew totally from the day-to-day activities of life . . . I began to drink alcohol heavily, suffered from insomnia and a lack of concentration on things going on around me . . . After the incident, I applied for a job at the Crab Shack Restaurant in Milnerton. During my first shift, deliveries were being made to the restaurant via the back entrance. I was unaware of the delivery and when I saw the black gentleman walking into the back entrance, I thought it was a possible attack. I broke out in a cold sweat and had a panic attack, resulting in the fact that I broke down and was unable to continue working at the restaurant. The realization as to how quickly one's life could be taken became a real nightmare for me . . . I seldom feel as if I will be able to be a normal person again.

The grief about a child killed in violence is a grief unlike any other, says the psychologist.

But no one has much time to concentrate on the victims. Speculation is raging about the possible involvement of Commissioner Dumisa

Ntsebeza in the Heidelberg Tavern attack and the implications this has for the Truth Commission. Should he apply for amnesty? Should he resign? Would the commission accept a late amnesty application from one of its own commissioners?

All three of the men seeking amnesty for the Heidelberg Tavern attack deny that they ever used a white car to transport weapons or that they are familiar with Ntsebeza.

Then Bennet Sibaya, a gardener from Kenilworth, shuffles to his seat, his hands clasped in front of his chest. He has been under the witness protection program for the past week. While the legal arguments are presented, and even while he himself testifies, Sibaya never once raises his eyes. He sits with his head sunk into his body and has to be asked repeatedly to speak more slowly. When he is instructed to look up, his mouth strains and his eyes stare wildly into the room.

Sibaya says he was in Guguletu, looking for the house of a girlfriend, when he saw five men taking firearms bundled up in a blue overall from one car and loading them into the trunk of a white Audi. The men were working very stealthily, and he became convinced they were plotting to kill somebody. When the car's brake lights went on, he memorized the registration number. After the men had driven off, he saw a piece of paper in the street. He picked it up and saw that it had directions on it, including the words "Hartleyvale Stadium" and "Heidelberg." He decided to report the matter to the police. But at the Guguletu police station, the map was torn up, and Sibaya was told to go home and sleep it off. In any case, the police apparently said to him, Heidelberg is not here in Cape Town, it's an up-country town.

During the lunch break, a group of us discuss Sibaya's testimony. The way he spoke about the registration number—XA 12848—was interesting. He expressed it like this: "XA twelve, eight-four-eight." Somehow that had a ring of authenticity to it. The other convincing moment was the situation at the police station: the night before New Year's Eve, white policemen stationed in a black area . . . who would want to hear a story about guns being transported? It would just mean follow-up work over New Year, in an area you'd rather not venture into, with everyone full of the holiday spirit. And there is indeed a town called Heidelberg a few hundred kilometers away.

Then it's time for the cross-examination. And Ntsebeza's lawyer, Christine Qunta, climbs into Sibaya in a way that leaves most of us speechless. She is elegantly dressed, impeccably prepared, and utterly single-minded. None of the three amnesty applicants—the killers, the real murderers—took such a battering, and Sibaya is only a witness. Qunta hammers him with harsh questions and sarcastic remarks. She addresses him in sophisticated English, ridicules his answers, listens to his Xhosa on the earphones and corrects the interpreters, points out inconsistencies. Those of us who've been schooled for two years now in the ethics of the Truth Commission—trust the victim, believe the poorest of the poor, treat the simple and illiterate with the tenderest respect—are dumbfounded. Through the commission, we have come to accept that poor people seldom have reason to lie, whereas the well-dressed rich often have every reason you can think of. After a fierce bout of cross-examination, one of the staff members of the commission collapses into a chair in the media room: "It is sickening, it is absolutely sickening . . ." But then it hits home: if this is the only way to clear his name, it's an indication of how desperate Ntsebeza's situation must be. Qunta insists on a swift decision on allegations she describes as "a huge thumb-suck," because not only is Ntsebeza's reputation at stake, but the credibility of the entire Truth Commission.

In her cross-examination, Qunta focuses on the discrepancies between the statement Sibaya made to the police four days after the incident and the one he made to the Truth Commission. For instance: Was the white Audi parked on the northern side of the NY113 facing the NY115 or was it on the NY129? This particular question takes nearly an hour, by which point everyone—except Qunta—is totally confused. In the end, Sibaya acknowledges that he thought the car was on the NY113, but when he was taken there by the police the next day, he realized it was actually the NY129. Why does the girlfriend he mentioned in his statement say she doesn't know him? She's embarrassed now, he answers, because I picked her up in a shebeen. How can he remember the registration number of the car, but he can't remember his own ID number? Why is his statement to the police in English, when he now says he only speaks Xhosa? How could an illiterate person who left school in Standard 2 read the words "Hartleyvale Stadium" and "Heidelberg" on a piece of paper in the dark? But Sibaya sticks to his story. Now and then, he remarks darkly: "Truth and lies can never lie on the same table."

And the money in his bank account? His former boss left him his house when he went back to Germany, Sibaya says, and now he rents the place out. Qunta laughs and shakes her head.

Passionate discussions erupt in the media room, the passages, the Truth Commission offices: the whites think Ntsebeza is involved; the blacks think he has been set up. None of us has the resources of an investigative unit. Yet we are expected to gather from Goosen's flimsy report and Sibaya's peculiar testimony what is really going on. And there is no space to argue in—it has become a matter of race. The little bit of healing, the trust, the unity, that have been built up over two years have been wiped out in one day. Meanwhile, the request for an apology is still lying on my desk.

But the worst is yet to come, when the hearing continues the next day. Sibaya is asked whether he can identify the man he saw behind the wheel of the white Audi that night. Sibaya points to one of the Amnesty Committee members, Ntsiki Sandi. People laugh. "He looks like him," smiles Sibaya, nodding his head. Then he gets up, in his crumpled, faded shirt and down-at-heel shoes, and walks around the room. Some distance from Ntsebeza, he stops and wags his finger—"It's him."

No words can capture the expression on Dumisa Ntsebeza's face. It is a mixture of mortification, amazement, and a strained attempt at indifference. An excited babble reverberates through the room; every journalist knows this is drama at its best.

"When he pointed me out," Ntsebeza tells me afterward, "I felt as bad as I usually feel when I lose a case I've been defending, when I know my client has done nothing, but he gets convicted anyway. I knew (a) that Sibaya was putting on an act, and (b) that I was innocent—but I was going to lose, because the whole world would focus on the *drama* of him pointing me out and the whole world would see a likelihood of my involvement."

An indication of how fatal the incident might prove to be is that both Tutu and Boraine, who are abroad, are asked to come home.

The amnesty hearing finishes late on Friday afternoon with the testimony of one of the victims, Quentin Cornelius. We hear him . . . and we don't.

QUENTIN CORNELIUS: Lindy-Anne, whom I met in Venda, and her father came to fetch me from Stilbaai to celebrate New Year with them . . .

I dived to try and get myself under the closest table . . . the bullet went through my side and hit my spine, fracturing my spinal column in nine different places. My friend Lindy was not so lucky. She died from four bullets that penetrated her chest from behind. Bernadette Langford, who sat opposite me, was also killed.

I have mixed feelings regarding this application. Since 30 December 1993, my life has never been the same . . . for obvious reasons—being in a wheelchair . . . it is, however, very difficult when you have root nerve pain every single day of your life to such an extent that you do not know how to cope with it anymore. When you have lost a kidney and various parts of your intestines and have constant bladder and other infections. You end up in hospital twice a year. When your healthy and strong legs have been taken away from you . . . I'd like to have each of the perpetrators look me in the eye and choose whether they wouldn't mind having a rifle stuck in their spine and having a trigger being pulled on them in cold blood, fracturing their spine—leaving them emotionally and physically scarred and disabled as I have been . . . Would they rather stay in jail and serve their sentences for the crime they committed or would they prefer swapping places with me in my wheelchair. I know what I would choose . . .

I peer at the applicants for a sign of remorse, a sign of contact, a sign that they *hear*, that they understand pain, that they wish things were different . . . They seem impassive at best and proudly arrogant at worst. I scold myself—how do I know? I cannot read the body codes of black people. It is as simple as that. When I interview Boraine or any of the white commissioners, I *know* when they cannot tell me the truth, when they're battling to formulate something in a neutral, harmless way. I know it from the way their eyes change color, the slight flush, a looseness in the cheeks, the flatness of the voice, the movement of the head. But when I interview the black commissioners, I am at a loss. They can tell me anything and I will believe it. But that's not quite true, I argue with myself. I know Tutu is struggling to tell me something when he starts with "ah-ah-ahm . . ." All these ah-ahms have to be cut out for broadcast—so when I have a huge pile of recording tape on the floor afterward, I know it was a difficult interview for Tutu.

I also know how black victims misinterpret the expression and intonation of Dirk Coetzee. "He laughs," says Charity Kondile, "when he tells how he braaied my son." But I can see it's a grimace. I can see that his mouth is dry and his head has a barely perceptible tremble—he is either on medication or suffering from posttraumatic stress. But the Kondiles see a man with an arrogant smile on his face.

Will things in this country always break up in color? Will I always be a prisoner of my past with no normal vices and virtues—always with this kind of instinctive, guilty obsequiousness?

Pippa Green, one of the best journalists in the country, is waiting in my office. She has made some phone calls this morning. Bennet Sibaya does not own a house in Kenilworth. Not only does he have thousands in the bank, but he recently tried to buy a duplex flat in Claremont, and showed a bank document indicating an investment of over R200,000. He is a compulsive gambler and is often dropped off at the betting shops by white men in a combi.

"But how come the investigative unit could not find that out in three months?"

"Maybe it didn't want to?"

"Why wasn't it forced to find out more?"

"Maybe people had already made up their minds about Ntsebeza's involvement," she says.

"Well, the final report by Goosen says two things: they find Sibaya to be a plausible witness, but they nevertheless recommend an independent investigation."

"So why did Tutu and Boraine decide not to follow that up or at least release it to the press so that we could do some checking?"

I draw up my shoulders.

Monday brings a most unusual media briefing, in the wake of a crisis meeting of the full commission. Apart from the usual journalists, the room suddenly fills up with Truth Commission staff as Dumisa Ntsebeza takes a seat opposite the chairperson and his deputy.

During the crisis meeting earlier that morning, we learn, Ntsebeza left the room so that discussions about the Sibaya incident could be open and frank. And they were precisely that, says Alex Boraine. The commission has decided to ask for an independent inquiry into Sibaya's evidence by a person with impeccable credentials and to ask Ntsebeza to recuse himself from any cases involving APLA cadres.

The chairperson takes all the blame on himself. "I should really have followed my normal gut-level instincts in this case—and that is what we have been doing all along, playing open cards. I should have—and I didn't—I should have informed my fellow commissioners as soon as this became clear, I should have said to the media, you know, there is this allegation against Dumisa, and, as I felt, we should have gone for an independent investigation straightaway. In justification, one could point out that all these facts were available to the police from 1994—they've done nothing about it. When Dumisa was appointed commissioner, he had a security clearance and nothing was made of this. What is more, why would amnesty applicants prefer to lie and maybe lose their amnesties to protect him?"

Now for another announcement. Bennet Sibaya is sitting in the archbishop's office at this very moment.

It is absolutely quiet. Most of the journalists stop taking notes, but don't look up.

Yes, Sibaya has confessed that he was coached to lie. In January 1994, after being caught poaching crayfish in Bantry Bay, he was tortured and ordered to implicate Ntsebeza. Now he has been stricken by his conscience. Apparently Sibaya spent the weekend looking everywhere for the archbishop—he even turned up at Bishop's Court, his previous home. Finally he contacted the commission's offices. Sibaya told the archbishop that after he falsely identified Ntsebeza the burden of guilt became too big to carry. He had already decided to tell the truth when he testified, he said, but when he arrived at the hearing, he saw mostly whites—and no matter how hard he looked, he couldn't see the archbishop's purple robe. For him, the Truth Commission is the archbishop. Because he couldn't quite find his bearings in this sea of white faces, he thought it safer to stick to his original story until he could speak to Tutu. But the next day, he still did not see him. So he deliberately pointed out the wrong person, Ntsiki Sandi, hoping to make it clear that he was lying. But he was pressured to look again.

Now Sibaya wants to apologize to Ntsebeza in public and he wants his apology published widely.

No one says a word. I draw curly figures on my notebook.

Sibaya comes in. He is wearing a striped shirt, a flowery tie, and a navy double-breasted jacket. He clumsily embraces Ntsebeza. Enemies tried to divide them, he says, but now they are brothers.

I do an interview with the chairperson. "I am so sad," he sighs. "I am so sad, whatever the facts—you are just aware of the deceit, the underhandedness, and you feel defiled. I'm also appalled at the way the media handled this. You never investigated Sibaya . . . On the other hand, I'm glad you badgered us to the point where we ended up with this meeting and this particular decision."

As I walk back, I realize this was the first interview I've had with Tutu that he didn't preface with his usual prayer. I feel iced out, isolated in my questioning.

I sit down at my desk and write to Boraine and Tutu: "I have thought about your anger, comments, and request for a long time—questioning my motives, procedures, instincts, sources, and style. And as the week dragged on, I was sick in my heart . . . And I kept on trying to work out to what extent I personally was responsible for what happened." I set out my fears about whether the Truth Commission indeed has a system that will push all the information to the surface. I conclude: "But maybe I went about it in the wrong way. For that I say without reservation: I am absolutely and very sorry. I never meant to cast doubt on the integrity of either of you. I hope this in some way helps, because I am missing you both."

Something has shifted and I'm filled with loss.

Judge Richard Goldstone, appointed by President Nelson Mandela to investigate the Sibaya incident, finds that all the accusations against Dumisa Ntsebeza were false. "The negative consequences of the decision to allow members of the investigative unit to investigate their immediate superior are manifest. This decision has ultimately resulted in tremendous tension, dislocation, and controversy within the TRC."

I am suddenly sick and tired of the Truth Commission. The commissioners have become smug, self-righteous, morally arrogant, and bloated with self-importance. Corridor gossip flourishes. This one is vain. That one is lazy. So-and-so is sleeping with somebody-or-other. This lot get angry when they're not the focus of media attention. That lot are fishing for high-profile jobs in government. Those who have not given up their former jobs—as they promised to do—are always abroad. In the afternoons, one by one, the big, thick German cars slide out of the parking garage.

And the women! They have never managed to subvert the developing stereotype of the commission: women as victims, men as fighters and leaders. They never take the lead in a considered, directed way. At hearings they easily become sentimental or moralistic. They're either fighting among themselves or reveling in the role of the supportive little woman.

While the *manne* are busy with the Big Politics, the voices of the victims have been packed away safely on computer files somewhere. The perpetrators have been dispensed with. Reparation and reconciliation are "women's issues."

The last victim hearings finished more than five months ago, and the focus has been lost. No more the voices, like a leaking tap in the back of your mind, to remind you what this commission is all about. On television, you see the commissioners filing up the street to lay charges, or holding press conferences, or meeting dignitaries—but you don't see them listening to ordinary people anymore. For me, the Truth Commission microphone with its little red light was the ultimate symbol of the whole process: here the marginalized voice speaks to the public ear; the unspeakable is spoken—and translated; the personal story brought from the innermost depths of the individual binds us anew to the collective. What has happened to that? Has it all become politics?

I remember the words of José Zalaquett: the shorter the life span of a Truth Commission, the better its chances of success.

The following conversation, and those in the final two chapters, are based on *Het Loon van de Schuld*, by Ian Buruma; *Guilt and Shame*, edited by Herbert Morris; *Imagination, Fiction, Myth*, by Johan Degenaar; and *After the Catastrophe*, by Carl Jung.

Death is a master from Africa—his eyes are blue

wir trinken dich abends und morgens wir trinken und trinken
der Tod ist ein Meister aus Deutschland sein Augen ist blau

we drink you evening and morning we drink and drink, death is a master from Germany his eyes are blue, he will strike you with a lead bullet he will strike you with precision, a man lives in the house your golden hair Margarete, he sets his hounds on us he gives us a grave in the sky, he plays with the serpents and dreams death is a master from Germany, your golden hair Margarete, your ashy hair Shulamith

. . .

The way you say "ash." The way you say "drink." How a single letter can rip my heart to water. You close the book of twentieth-century German verse and I know that I love you.

"Every educated German knows the line: *'Der Tod ist ein Meister aus Deutschland,'* " you explain. "After the Second World War, it was said in Germany: it is barbaric to write a poem after Auschwitz. Yet Paul Celan wrote this indescribably beautiful Fugue of Death. The reception of the poem was ambivalent. Isn't the poem too lyrical? Just a bit too beautiful? Is the horror not too accessible? In the end, Celan himself felt this ambivalence and asked anthologists to remove the poem from their books."

"That is precisely why I say that maybe writers in South Africa should shut up for a while. That one has no right to appropriate a story paid for with a lifetime of pain and destruction. Words come more easily for writers, perhaps. So let the domain rather belong to those who literally paid blood for every faltering word they utter before the Truth Commission."

"This kind of *over*respectfulness, awe—it happened in Germany. In the fifties and sixties, writers didn't even call the Nazis by name—they called them 'buffalo-eaters'—the men in leather coats."

"The thing is, Germany has produced some of the best writers ever. We in this country have failed in a sense—the things told here surpass the wildest imaginings of any writer. Nowhere in our literature do you find captured the extent of the pathos, the pain, the horror, the voices of this country. Shouldn't we give up our privileged position and let the space belong to those who deserve it?"

"Are you saying this because you yourself can't find a form for dealing with your past?"

"No. I was speaking to Ariel Dorfman about this when he visited South Africa. The Truth Commission in Chile was held behind closed doors—so the stories were not told in public. Yet he writes these stories. I wanted to know—isn't it sacrilege to *pretend* you know? My experience tells me that there is no way you can begin to imagine the language, the rhythm, the imagery, of the original stories. I often write pieces down from memory, and when I check the original tape, it is always, but *always,* much better than my own effort. Dorfman answered that a lot of the stories were already known among the oppressed. 'That might be so,' I said, 'but the heightened atmosphere of the public telling usually brings the best aspects of the story and its teller together. The story told on the Truth Commission platform is usually much more powerful than the one told afterward for the television camera or the tape recorder.' Then Dorfman said his work is a sort of mixture—some of it is what he's heard, and some he makes up. So I asked, 'But isn't that a sacrilege—to use someone else's story, a story that has cost him his life?' He looked at me, and then he said: 'Do you want the awful truth? How else would it get out? How else would the story be told?' "

"I'll tell you how . . . The reluctance of German literature to look Auschwitz in the face, the refusal to deal with it except in school text-books, museums, and memorials, is precisely this fear of sacrilege you're talking about. As if any attempt to give a body to the unname-able is to trivialize its holy character. It's all well and good to listen to victims in court cases, the argument goes, but artists should keep their grubby hands off the stories. German artists could not find a *form* in which to deal with Auschwitz. They refused to take possession of their own history. So the inevitable happened. Hollywood took it away from them. A soap opera laid claim to the statistic, the metaphor, the ab-straction, that was Auschwitz."

You lock your office. Outside, the campus lies deserted in the throat of the late afternoon sky. Our conversation becomes part of the big South African tongue of consciousness groping down toward a broken tooth.

I say: "Was apartheid the product of some horrific shortcoming in Afrikaner culture? Could one find the key to this in Afrikaner songs and literature, in beer and *braaivleis*? How do I live with the fact that all the words used to humiliate, all the orders given to kill, belonged to the language of my heart? At the hearings, many of the victims faithfully re-produced these parts of their stories in Afrikaans as proof of the bloody fingerprints upon them."

"Jung talks about inferiority. Do you know about that?"

"All I know is that my grandfather wanted to send my mother to Rhodes University so that she could learn to speak English 'better than an Englishman'—and that my mother refused. She told him she doesn't *need* to speak English better than an Englishman. But why do you ask about inferiority? Do you think Afrikaners are suffering from it?"

"According to Jung, inferiority leads to a hysterical dissociation of the personality, which consists essentially in, as he puts it, wanting to jump

over one's shadow, and looking for everything dark, inferior, and cul-
pable not in oneself but in others. That is why the hysteric always
complains of being surrounded by inferior mischief-makers, a crowd of
submen who should be exterminated so that the Superman can live at
his high level of perfection. All men are dangerous if their leaders have
unlimited power."

"It feels to me that if you look at the past *only* from the viewpoint of
the victim, or the viewpoint of the perpetrator, the ultimate consequence is hatred . . ."

"Are you grieving?"

"How can I? What have I lost? Why do I feel I am gaining all the
time? One does not grieve for apartheid. Should I grieve for a phantom
fatherland perhaps? I think ultimately I feel I don't have the *right* to
grieve for the dead—I should rather take responsibility for the oppressors."

We drive out over the dark plains.

The South African Truth Commission has one unique feature—the special hearings into the role of the media, the health sector, the judiciary,
and big business in South Africa's apartheid past. Although the hearings generally fail to expose individual culprits—they have either resigned or moved sideways, and the latest black employees arrive to take
the rap—the mere fact of making a submission usually creates some
turmoil in these structures. In some of the media houses, journalists
have publicly taken a different stand to their bosses; in some businesses, there have been endless debates and angry words.

The business hearings provide a touch of surrealism. In the posh foyer
of the Carlton Hotel in downtown Johannesburg, where not so long ago
I sat waiting for Joe Mamasela, the Truth Commissioners look somewhat forlorn. Tutu's purple robe is a vivid splash of anachronism. When
he opens the meeting with a prayer, most of the businessmen look
around, wide-eyed and nonplussed.

And yet. The breathtakingly wealthy, the Captains of Industry, like
Nicky Oppenheimer and Johan Rupert, the bosses of mighty organiza-
tions, like Julian Ogilvie-Thompson and Bobby Godsell, sit opposite the
Truth Commission just as hundreds of others have sat before them.
Free to be questioned and held accountable like ordinary mortals. Cre-
ating the impression that no one is above the law—not even the rich.

The tone of the hearings is set by Professor Sampie Terblanche, with his flailing limbs, snow-white hair, and wonderful, horrible Free State English accent.

"The hissstory of a hunnndred years of rrracial capitalism enrrriched whites *unnndeseeervedly.*" He says that by the end of the last century, black farmers were producing more maize than white farmers, which is why they did not want to work on white farms or in the mines. But they were eventually driven off the fields they had plowed by the Glen Grey Act of 1894 and the Land Act of 1913. Black farmers were turned into a reservoir of cheap labor for business.

He spells out the exploitation: The wages of black workers did not increase at all between 1910 and 1970. In fact, their wages in 1972 were even lower than they had been in 1911. And yet during this period, the gold price rose by 45 percent and the wages of white workers doubled.

In 1970, Terblanche says, the system of racial capitalism changed once again, from favoritism, to patronage, to protection. Under P. W. Botha, an abnormal cooperation developed between the securocratic state and business. Business did not destroy apartheid, says Terblanche. It actually strengthened Botha's government and helped create a neo-apartheid.

This is the first time that the idea of the beneficiary—as opposed to the perpetrator—has surfaced in full force. Did businesses *benefit* from apartheid?

Of course we didn't, say prominent white business leaders. In fact, apartheid prevented us from realizing our potential.

Lot Ndlovu of the Black Management Forum disagrees. Low wages, bad housing, and appalling working conditions increased the profit margins of white business, he says. There was no place for blacks in power structures until Durban workers marched against their bosses in 1973. Then business woke up and quickly began appointing black people into certain supervisory and management positions. "But they were just used by and large as a buffer—as messengers, as conduits, to go out and tell the workers what the bosses were saying and try and placate the workers. Alternatively to create the impression that there was progress."

But business insists that it did not benefit from apartheid. Johan Rupert says Rembrandt was started by Afrikaners and sustained by Afrikaners long before the Afrikaner had financial clout. Rembrandt has treated its shareholders well; it is treating its workers well. There is a

staff turnover of less than 2 percent. The company pays its floor sweepers more than the government pays math teachers! Rembrandt is also
treating the taxman well, Rupert smiles, to the tune of R10 billion over
the last couple of years. Maybe not enough was done to oppose
apartheid, but the fact that Rembrandt is still inside the country says
something.

It's left to the Afrikaanse Handelsinstituut to bring clarity to the
debate about benefit. When business compares itself to business
abroad, it feels deprived. Apartheid prevented the majority of South
Africans from becoming a substantial buying and economic force, and
so business feels that the system hampered its development and
profits. Bosses like Rupert have provided statistics on how their overseas branches fare better, despite facing stiffer competition. But we
shouldn't be comparing ourselves with our international counterparts,
says Theo van Wyk. We should compare ourselves with black business—and then we will realize just how much we've benefited.

When Julian Ogilvie-Thompson starts reading Anglo-American's
submission in his Victorian accent, someone in the media room calls
out: "For that accent alone, you should apply for amnesty." Ogilvie-
Thompson is at pains to point out that Anglo had no contact with the
National Party. In the thirteen years that John Vorster was prime minister, the firm spoke to him only once—and that was when Vorster
asked permission to exhume the bodies of some Ossewabrandwag
members from a mine. It is highly unusual, he says, for the biggest con-
glomerate in a country to have no contact with its rulers.

The Afrikaner businessmen quote the poet N. P. van Wyk Louw. "O
wye en droewe land," says Professor Sampie Terblanche. "O wide and
woeful land."

"I believe in loyal resistance," says Johan Rupert. Van Wyk Louw's lo-
jale verset.

"Read Charles Dickens," says Ogilvie-Thompson.

"All the bosses that oppressed us are here," a worker recites, "I feel
their hair against my shoulders."

"Forgive us for Steve Biko," says Rupert.

"Prof. Terblanche is a member of the Flat Earth Society," says Nigel
Bruce. "We English have never been advantaged by apartheid."

It is striking how drastically the tenor of the submissions changes over
the three days of the hearings. On the first day, Barlow Rand and the

Chamber of Mines get people's backs up with their insistence that they never benefited from apartheid. They rattle off pages of resolutions, statements, and newspaper articles to prove that they have always fought boldly against apartheid.

"So wonderful," says Sam Shilowa, general secretary of the Congress of South African Trade Unions, "everybody in the country was a revolutionary!"

But from day one, representatives of Anglo-American and other big companies are listening carefully from the back rows. It doesn't take them long to figure out that insistent pleas of innocence do not look too good on the eight o'clock news. By the third day, all are admitting that they benefited, and saying how sorry they are, how much more they're going to do to set things right.

Most companies try to put together a delegation including a white, a black, and if possible a woman. The Land Bank is the most blatant. They present two submissions: a left-wing one delivered by a black man, and a right-wing one delivered by an Afrikaner. In between them sits their boss, Helena Dolny, the widow of SACP hero Joe Slovo.[1]

Mist has gathered on our faces. I sense my hair escaping into sleep and water.

This is to be the last day.

Late that night, I wake up. Your head lies toppled away from me as if falling into shards of moonlight at the edge of the bed. Your heavy arm on my breast like a dark plowshare.

In silence we drive to the airport. I think of your feet licking themselves in the sun. You pile my luggage on a trolley.

"You don't have to do this, you know," you say. Your voice has lost all that I know.

I turn and walk alone toward the sliding doors. When they open, I look back. You are standing with your arms folded like breastwork. Like stone. Like an angry stump. Inside the building, my chest heaves into a spasm of pain.

---

[1] Former general secretary of the South African Communist Party, and long "Public Enemy No. 1" of the South African government.

CHAPTER TWENTY

Mother Faces the Nation

Never mind the official title—A Human Rights Violation Hearing into the Activities of the Mandela United Football Club[1]—it's called "the Winnie hearing." As a South African media event, it is compared to the release of Nelson Mandela from prison in 1990. The international news desks say: Provided that Saddam Hussein isn't bombed in the next few days, the Winnie hearing will be the biggest news story on the globe this week. It is the last week of November 1997.

The statistics are frightening. More than 200 journalists from sixteen countries, more than twenty foreign television crews and 100 news agencies from around the world, have been accredited by the Truth Commission. Apart from visual and audio feeds, these journalists need telephone lines, modems for laptops, translation from African languages, information: Who is testifying? Who is the lawyer? What case does that relate to? How do you pronounce this surname?

When the director of the Truth Commission's media department is taken to see the venue chosen by the Johannesburg office, he apparently blows his top—an ordinary low-cost recreation center with thin walls, small rooms, low ceilings, and cheap finishes. The demands of the hearing are much more complex than merely accommodating the media.

---

[1] Winnie Madikizela-Mandela took young men, mostly homeless boys regarded by government as the "lost youth," into her house. In order to win international funding, the group was turned into a soccer club with a coach and tracksuits; the members, who also served Madikizela-Mandela and her family as bodyguards, soon turned into a vigilante gang, sowing terror and destruction in the area.

Thirty-four witnesses are to testify—some for Winnie, some against. All need space to consult privately with their lawyers. They need privacy to cry and be debriefed by trauma counselors. They need space to get angry at the accused without the accused watching them. Madikizela-Mandela needs her own consulting room big enough to accommodate her bodyguards, her family, and her legal team. Since there are rumors even before the hearing starts that she is intimidating witnesses, it is essential that she doesn't come into contact with any of them at the venue. Some of those set to testify are in jail—they need a room with special security arrangements. The commissioners themselves need space to talk, rest, discuss strategy. One, in particular, needs space to pray (Tutu has been praying constantly during the tea breaks and taking longer rests than usual after his recent cancer treatment). The lawyers need space to protect their independence, so that not even a whisper of conspiracy is possible.

And all of them have to be fed.

An unprepossessing recreation center in the lower-middle-class suburb of Mayfair, Johannesburg, is destined to handle all of this.

Why is it that a woman, a black woman from a long-isolated country, creates such an unprecedented media frenzy? Is it because Winnie Madikizela-Mandela answers to the archetype Black and Beautiful? Or because she answers to the stereotype Black and Evil?

A few days after the much publicized divorce of the Mandelas, a crowd of angry youths marched down an avenue in Durban. Although they were protesting about the lack of educational reform, one of their placards read: "We don't want Nelson Mandela the Saint! We want Nelson Mandela the Revolutionary." On the same day, a group of women welcomed Winnie Mandela at a Women's Day rally in Pietermaritzburg. The song they sang said: "Winnie and Nelson—the world has parted you, but for us you are two sides of the same coin. You fulfill us. We can't have one without the other!"

There is a vast gallery of perceptions about Winnie Madikizela-Mandela.

Picture One: In Parliament she is a backbencher. She seldom speaks. Outside Parliament, at the wrought-iron gates, a hawker sells key rings bearing the image of her face. Incongruous: the woman and the legend that feed off each other.

Picture Two: As a politician, she has an exceptional grasp of the popular mood, and she plays to different constituencies in very different ways. At home she appeals to groups who feel the system somehow doesn't work for them. On American television, she plays to the black diaspora—she is the mother figure, the regal symbol of solidarity with the homeland, the long-lost mythology of what it was to be African. Media experts say she's like a chameleon, moving across boundaries in quite an extraordinary way. And her honor depends on public acknowledgment.

Picture Three: Much of Winnie's power is nonverbal. She doesn't need to shout *"Amandla!"* She just has to raise her fist. She lives in iconic images—the haunting footage of her sensual, liberated beauty set off against the dusty, desolate, corrugated-iron township of Brandfort. When she stands, she always stands triumphantly alone. When she sits, she sits alone and the air is filled with conspiracy and fear.

Picture Four: She has committed the gravest sin—she let people down. It is easier to forgive a murder than a betrayal. She was a tireless fighter—through trials and banishments, she kept Mandela's name on the map—and that gives her a great deal of credit on the political balance sheet. But it comes at a price: when you are this popular, this revered, you are expected to be like Caesar's wife.

Picture Five: Winnie is also trashy tabloid. She lusts after men and they after her. She shops, she buys diamonds and drips with them on occasion, she eliminates dispensable subjects—she's a dangerous and rowdy warlord strutting around among the glum democrats. She refuses to become part of parochial pleasantness. She refuses to serve the masters. She refuses to make the world safe for democracy.

Picture Six: Winnie is pre- and postfeminist. It is through her that we instinctively understand Helen of Troy, MaNthatisi . . . Among the enemies of MaNthatisi, who ruled the Tlokwa as regent of her minor son Sekonyela, rumors circulated that she was a grotesque giantess with one eye in the middle of her forehead, who suckled her warriors before battle and sent swarms of bees before them. In contrast to this horrible image, among her own followers, she was known affectionately as Mosadinyana—the Little Woman . . . But perhaps the character of Lady Macbeth encapsulates the diverse elements of Winnie's personality most aptly—vaulting ambition, a capacity for ruthless conspiracy, abuse of devotion, the smell of blood that will not leave her hands, the persistent ghosts.

Picture Seven: Winnie's dilemma is essentially also that of the African National Congress. Like the ANC, she has accumulated an enormous amount of political credit. Like the ANC, she is asking us to treat her differently. But the world is not here to admire a defiant, unrepentant black woman; the world has come to watch us burn a witch.

The name of Winnie Madikizela-Mandela has come up at several hearings on human rights violations. Parents testified before the Truth Commission about the disappearance of their children while in contact with the Mandela household. As a result, she was subpoenaed for a hearing behind closed doors. There she demanded a public hearing to clear her name before the elections for president and deputy president of the ANC.

The hearing held in Mayfair is an unusual one. As she does not want amnesty from the commission, she needn't tell the truth.

Will she come? Won't she simply send her lawyers?

Cameras are lined up. Shouting. Jostling. Everybody is called outside while the hall is checked by sniffer dogs.

"If she's clever, she'll come, and just sit and listen," someone says. "By the end of it, we'll all feel so sorry for her, she'll be okay."

"No, man, if she's *really* clever, she'll ask to speak and tell it all. Spill every last bean. Then she'll definitely be our next *president,* never mind deputy president."

Her arrival is swamped by the media. We South Africans, unused to fighting our way to the front, don't even catch a glimpse. "Don't worry," says an American journalist who overhears my complaints, "she's not arriving for you, she's arriving for the Afro-American audience. She's already given more than ten hours of interview time to us. Her constituency is out there." I recall how she's ignored several requests for a radio interview. Isn't she interested in talking to those she claims as her constituency—the poor who cannot read, who don't own television sets?

On the monitor in the media room, we watch the grand entrance. She is tall. She towers. And it seems incomprehensible that this woman in the prim suit and three strings of pearls, with her bevy of beautiful daughters and well-dressed bodyguards, is embroiled in so many unsavory stories.

The hearing has barely started when a bodyguard carries in a big cooler and sets it between mother and daughters. It is hot in the glare of the camera lights. As the temperature rises, as the legal arguments heat up, Madikizela-Mandela keeps her cool with ice and mineral water.

That her mere presence is intimidating is clear from the start. The victims find it difficult to look at her. The commissioners seldom turn their gaze in her direction. The cameras move from her exquisite face, her diamanté-studded sunglasses, her throngs of delicate bangles and rings, to the faces of the victims—engraved with hardship, pain, poverty. Is this a clash between the black poor and the black elite?

Outside the hall, a group of followers from the ANC Women's League are chanting support. They are all old and wrinkled and poor. "Winnie didn't kill alone!" they shout. "Winnie had a mandate from us to kill!" I switch off my tape recorder. I don't want to hear it. I don't want to broadcast it. I don't want to live in a country where women mandate one another to murder. This hearing will test us beyond ourselves. I know.

The next day, four big engines are pumping away next to the building. Massive pipes, shiny as tinfoil, feed cool streams of instant air into the hall.

Phumlile Dlamini was three months pregnant by one of Madikizela-Mandela's lovers. "Winnie didn't like that. She came to our house and spoke to my mother and said she will bring me back. My mother said, 'Please bring my child back . . . do not kill her . . .' She, Winnie, hit me first. Then she told the Football Club: 'See what you can do with this one.' They then all assaulted me. I wanted to lay a charge, but my brother said the football team will burn our house. People were scared to air their views. They loved Winnie and trusted Winnie as the Mother of the Community. After all that, I changed my mind . . . I didn't want to hear people refer to her as the Mother of the Nation."

The mother of Siboniso Shabalala agrees. She also talks of fear.

"Has Madikizela-Mandela ever threatened you?"

"Yes, I saw her scaring other people—I am scared of her even now."

"My hands are not dripping with the blood of the African children," says one-time friend Xoliswa Falati, her eyes darting all over the room. "I've never compromised her. I went to prison for her and she was so much ungrateful. She dehumanizes a person. She reduces a person to nothing. She regards herself as a demigod . . . as a superbeing . . .

"I never knew that Mrs. Mandela was taking these hard drinks. She is aggressive when she's taking that." This is the only explanation ventured for why Madikizela-Mandela's behavior changed so much during the last part of the 1980s. And it comes from the woman suspected of having supplied Madikizela-Mandela with cocaine.

"Sorry, *sisi,*" says Archbishop Desmond Tutu. "Just answer the questions, do not make a circus out of the hearing."

"I am bottled up. I'm like a bottle of champagne all the time," Falati fumes. "Now I have to explode . . ." Winnie shakes her head, laughs, and indicates with a circular movement of her hand that Falati is crazy. "She's busy indicating that I am mad. She's pointing at me that I'm crazy . . . You can laugh if you want, but *you* don't sleep at night."

Another of Winnie's lovers objects to Falati's testimony. Falati says dismissively: "Oh, you are a Xhosa, typical of a Xhosa, that's why you are denying everything. All Xhosas are lying like that, you are a real Xhosa. And Winnie is a Xhosa as well."

But why did she protect Winnie and give false evidence in court about the killing of Stompie? "That was our culture, to protect our leaders. I was scared, I had seen how people were brutally beaten. She gives you orders, you don't have to reply." Falati ends with a poetic flourish: "Yours is not to reason why. Yours is to do and die."

"Do you hate Winnie Mandela?" asks the lawyer.

"No," says Falati.

"Are you saying you love her?"

And the bewildered face is fraught with conflict. "I don't know," she whispers.

"The kidnapping and murder of Stompie Seipei are important beyond the normal horror we should feel. Because at one level they have been common-law crimes, but they are also about the ruthless abuse of power—they resemble far too closely the abuses of apartheid itself." The words of Methodist bishop Peter Storey.

As the hearing continues, the death of Stompie becomes the symbol of what went wrong in the Mandela household in 1989. Stompie, a fourteen-year-old child activist, and three other young adult males were kidnapped from the Methodist manse in Soweto by members of the Mandela United Football Club. The reasons given: they had to be protected from the alleged sexual abuse of the Reverend (now Bishop) Paul Verryn, and Stompie was believed to be an informer.

Storey captures the essence of the case. "The truth about Stompie's death has been trimmed to suit political interests. To dispel this suffocating fog of silence and lies is very important for the future of this country. This week for the first time, there is a probing beneath the surface of the skin of South Africa's shame. The primary cancer will always be and has always been apartheid. But secondary infections have touched many of apartheid's opponents and eroded their knowledge of good and evil. And one of the tragedies of life is, it's possible to become that which we hate most—a ruthless abuse of power and a latitude that allow our deeds to resemble the abuses we fought against.

"Beyond its normal horror, Stompie's death wasn't merely a political tragedy, it was also a moral tragedy. It has done things to people . . . we need not only to be liberated in this country, but we need to become human."

In a dress of brown chintz, Stompie Seipei's mother sits in the audience with her four-year-old daughter on her lap. With translation equipment plugged into her ears, Mrs. Seipei misses nothing. Her eyes are alert with concentration.

Forensic pathologist Dr. Patricia Klepp describes the body: "Stompie Seipei's body had lain in the heat for five days before it was discovered and was infested with maggots. The corpse had been that of a small boy, four and a half feet tall. The brain had turned to liquid, the skin slipping off the bones. Blood had poured out of his throat from two penetrating wounds on the right side, each the size of a blade roughly 1.6 centimeters long, caused by a dagger-type blade. His lungs had collapsed. There was blood in his stomach. He was bruised all over."

The body was found on January 6, 1989. A day later, Kenny Kgase, one of the other youths kidnapped and held at Madikizela-Mandela's house, escaped and told people how Stompie had been singled out for brutal assaults. On January 16, the other two youths, Thabiso Mono and Pelo Mekgwe, were released into the hands of Dr. Nthato Motlana—a "victory" achieved at last under growing pressure from Nelson Mandela in jail and ANC leader Oliver Tambo in exile.

The two senior ANC leaders intervened after damning reports from the Mandela Crisis Committee reached them. This committee had been formed some months before Stompie's death, after the Mandela house was burnt down by angry youths. The community, by then sick and tired of the Football Club's reign of terror, apparently simply looked on as the fire spread. To prevent a full-scale clash between the club and the community, a Crisis Committee was formed, made up of church and community leaders, under the chairmanship of the highly respected Reverend Frank Chikane. In January 1989, their mandate came to include the abduction of the four youths.

Jerry Richardson, Madikizela-Mandela's football coach: "The first thing that I did to Stompie was to hold him on both sides . . . throw him up in the air, and let him fall freely onto the ground. And Mommy was sitting and watching us. He was tortured so severely that at one stage I could see that he would ultimately die. We kicked him like a ball."

Thabiso Mono, one of those abducted: "Jerry Richardson said: 'Bring a chair for Mommy.' She questioned us why we allow a white priest to sleep with us . . . she start hitting us with fists and then the whole group joined."

Katiza Cebekhulu: "Mrs. Mandela sjambokked Stompie. She said, 'Why does he sleep with a white man?' "

John Morgan, Madikizela-Mandela's driver: "The day after the assault, I found Stompie in a deformed state. His face was as round as a football. And I tried to help him drink some coffee, and feed him bread, as he was not in a position to help himself." Morgan says he later found Stompie in a pool of blood flowing from his neck.

That was the same day the Crisis Committee visited Madikizela-Mandela and demanded the release of the boys.

"Did you demand to see the boys?"

"No."

"Why not?"

"That was not part of our brief."

The neutral, carefully chosen words come from the lips of the Reverend Frank Chikane. And I cannot but remember his interview as a prospective Truth Commissioner and how he reacted to the litmus test: What would you do if you came across information implicating the highest authorities in a violation? How impressively Chikane had answered then: "All information needs to be treated in the same way . . . otherwise we create a new injustice as bad as the previous one."

The failure of the Crisis Committee to deal effectively with the situation is described by Storey: "I realized that there were two things running here. There is an attempt to find out the truth of Stompie and possibly still save his life. On the other hand, there was a political agenda here—the Crisis Committee was involved in damage control."

According to Richardson, the assault on Stompie went too far for him to be released. That night, after the Crisis Committee left, a decision was made to kill him. Early the next morning, all the boys living in the backyard were called into the house to sing freedom songs to a depressed Madikizela-Mandela. While they were busy, Richardson dragged the weak and disorientated Stompie to a vehicle. He was taken to some open veld, made to lie on his back, and then slaughtered like a goat with garden shears. "Not a cut movement like slicing bread, but a stabbing movement."

"I loved her with all my heart," says Richardson. "I would have done anything for her. When other people got into a lift with us, I wondered why they got inside the same lift. Because I did not want anyone to touch Mommy and I was worried that they might touch Mommy. Only myself could touch Mommy—not anyone else. I loved her."

At the hearing, he carries a soft leather soccer ball ("This protects me . . . it has *muti*") and a pillowcase with these words written on it in Koki: "Now it's Jerry versus Winnie."

Ten days after the abduction, the other two boys were released. "There was a hostage situation," says Storey. "She was in charge of negotiations from the side of the Mandela house. She was the one who was deciding what was to happen. She was the one who was making decisions when, how, and under what conditions the youths were to be released. She was aware of everything that happened in her house."

The Crisis Committee saw the wounds on the youngsters, who insisted that they had fallen from trees and hurt themselves. "We didn't believe this, but if we had removed them ourselves from the Mandela home, we could have been charged with kidnapping," says Sydney Mufamadi of the Crisis Committee.

News of Stompie's abduction and death was kept from the community. It became known only when the *Weekly Mail* broke the story on January 20. The Mandela Crisis Committee tried to block the reports, because it was afraid they would harm the progress of negotiations with Mandela in jail.

Isn't there also another reason? asks Dumisa Ntsebeza: "All those people engaged in trying to resolve the conflict felt compromised by the fact that Winnie Mandela was a powerful political figure in her own right. And also the wife of one of the most revered leaders in the country. This fact even influences our ability to find the truth now—because here, today, even ourselves are hesitant to put this to you."

For the past eight years, as Bishop Storey puts it, it has not been possible to mention Paul Verryn in this country without conjuring up the idea of sodomy, rape, or sexual abuse. And Storey makes another point: "Everybody keeps talking about youths, or children—*one* was a child, the others were adults, and *everybody* has withdrawn their claims of sodomy except one . . ."

Paul Verryn speaks. "Mrs. Mandela, really my feelings about you have taken me in many directions. I long for our reconciliation. I have been profoundly, profoundly affected by some of the things that you have said about me, that have hurt me and cut me to the quick. I have had to struggle to come to some place of learning, to forgive, even if you do not want forgiveness or even think that I deserve to offer that to you. I struggle to find a way in which we can be reconciled, for the sake of this nation and for the people that I believe God loves so deeply."

A bizarre space evolves from the evidence. A house that had become the centrifugal force behind seemingly opposing attitudes. The house of the liberation movement's most revered political lineage and the house of lowly informers. The house where destabilized youngsters were both protected and killed. The house of famous, regal personalities and the house of a particular kind of gangster personality— brutal, insecure, inclined to pathological lying. Oddly enough, many of the thugs were rural, Zulu-speaking boys. Winnie Mandela was called "Mommy." Her second in command, Xoliswa Falati, was called "MaXtra Strong." Her followers were named "Shakes," "Killer," "Sponge," and "Guyboy." Her house was called "Parliament" and she had a special chair no one else dared sit in. People were assaulted in the "Fish Oil Room," and the shack at the back where the abducted were kept was called "Lusaka."

Two key areas in the Mandela home keep cropping up: the Jacuzzi and Zinzi Mandela's bedroom. The body of Stompie Seipei was seen lying near the Jacuzzi. Some discussions took place in the empty Jacuzzi. And Cebekhulu finally alleges that he saw Winnie Madikizela-Mandela in the vicinity of the Jacuzzi lifting a shiny object and plunging it twice into a body believed to be that of Stompie Seipei.

But it is the bedroom of the young Zinzi Mandela that seems to have been the springboard for pleasure and guerrilla planning. Not only did the team gather there socially, but one member tells the commission that he received a crash course on the dismantling of an AK-47 in Zinzi's bedroom. Guns were stashed in her cupboard. "Winnie is a brave woman. She is capable of everything and Zinzi takes after her mother," says a former Football Club member. "She is not only beautiful, she is capable of anything." Two of Zinzi Mandela's four children are believed to have been fathered by members of the Mandela United Football Club.

The point of resemblance between the mores of a street-corner society and those of the political aristocracy is this: both are contemptuous of legality. The political aristocracy claim the right to honor by tradition, which makes them the leaders of society and therefore "a law unto themselves." Street-corner society also claims to be a law unto itself, not because it is above the law, but because it is outside it.

Baroness Emma Harriet Nicholson presents South Africans with the unacceptable face of colonialism. On a BBC documentary screened in October 1997, she promised to confront South Africans with Katiza Cebekhulu's evidence about the Stompie Seipei case so that "they can decide what they want to do with it." In exchange for bringing us Cebekhulu, she demanded an air ticket, witness protection, a suspension of his warrant of arrest, legal representation, and permission to accompany him and testify. Granted. Now here she sits next to Cebekhulu, behind their lawyer, with a saintly smile on her face. She has allowed no journalist to come near him. "You all want to make money out of him," she snapped.

She testifies that as a champion of human rights, she came to hear that a South African was being held in a Zambian jail. She found that she could get Cebekhulu out of jail, but no country would accept him: neither the United Kingdom, nor Denmark, nor Sweden, nor America, nor Canada, nor any of the frontline states. And the reason: it would be too expensive to guarantee his safety, because he had offended "a part" of the ANC.

After her testimony, she calls Stompie's mother outside and, in full view of the media rooms, sets about convincing Mrs. Seipei to lay charges against Madikizela-Mandela.

"We're working toward reconciliation in this country," a journalist tells Nicholson, "and that's why we use a reconciliatory mechanism like the Truth Commission."

"The court needs to deal with murder," she sniffs, "and I want to be Mrs. Seipei's voice."

Thanks to the media hype surrounding the book *Katiza's Journey,* in which Cebekhulu tells his story, he was initially regarded as quite an important witness against Madikizela-Mandela. Especially as he was the only person who had implicated her directly in the execution of a murder. But the book proves to be a major problem. South Africans quickly discover factual errors in it. At the time Cebekhulu is dealing with, the ANC offices were not in Shell House but on Sauer Street. So his whole account of a meeting with Winnie on the eleventh floor of Shell House, and how she forced him to flee the country, is suddenly suspect. His floor plan of Madikizela-Mandela's house is incorrect. His affidavit has an indignant tone not usually heard in South African statements: the wives of political leaders, it suggests, should lead humble lives.

"This sounds more like Nicholson than Cebekhulu. Or is it now the BBC's Bridgeland that I'm dealing with? Who am I cross-examining?" cries Madikizela-Mandela's exasperated lawyer, Ishmael Semenya. "Is everything in the book true?"

"No," says Cebekhulu, "only the parts attributed to me—except the Shell House episode."

"None of the people present at the assault of Stompie implicate Winnie the way you do. Although most of them have turned against her. Why?"

"They are scared of that woman," ventures Cebekhulu.

"Isn't it that you were so desperate in the Zambian jail that you decided to exaggerate what you saw in order to get out of there?"

"Cebekhulu used me as his scribe," says the baroness, who has a hearing problem and relies largely on lipreading.

The ventriloquists surrounding Cebekhulu see to it that his evidence feels as shaky as everything else we've heard so far.

. . .

It's "pooh-pooh" here and "I really don't know" there. For four days, Winnie Madikizela-Mandela has watched powerful men bend over backward to avoid saying anything bad about her. And it's become clear: those who didn't have the courage to stand up to her in the past still don't have it today.

It is already dark outside when two former United Democratic Front leaders take the stand: Murphy Morobe and Azhar Cachalia.

By mid-1985, virtually the entire UDF leadership had either been detained or was on trial, says Cachalia. About 5,000 people had been detained in one year alone. Thousands of destabilized and leaderless youths saw themselves as the soldiers of the struggle. But they soon became gangs, roaming the streets and meting out their own version of justice.

"They became personal fiefdoms and small power bases using extreme forms of punishment. And it is in this climate that Mrs. Mandela created her own personal vigilante gang. I think my initial response when hearing about the Football Club was that it was inappropriate to use the revered Mandela name in this way. Surely there were other ways that Mrs. Mandela could assist youths? Soon disturbing reports of criminal activities by the Football Club emerged.

"Perhaps the most sickening case involved the abduction by the club of two youths accused of being informers. On one of them, the letter 'M' was sliced into his chest with a penknife and the words 'Viva ANC' carved down his thigh. Battery acid was then poured over the open wounds." It was said that Mandela herself oversaw this operation; but a Football Club member testifies that Zinzi Mandela did the actual lettering with molten plastic.

No wonder the pupils of the Daliwonga High School set the Mandela home on fire. By early 1989, says Cachalia, certain objective facts had emerged: four males, including one child—Stompie—had been forcibly removed from the Methodist manse to the Mandela house; they had been viciously beaten and kept against their will; one of the youths, Kenny Kgase, escaped and reported his ordeal; Stompie's body had been positively identified and all attempts to secure Winnie Madikizela-Mandela's cooperation had failed—not even Nelson Mandela and Oliver Tambo could win her over; Paul Verryn had been framed; the Crisis Committee had been ineffective; and the community had reached boiling point.

"And let me explain part of that boiling point," says Cachalia. "We were fighting against the brutalization of our youth in jails. And now this happens in the Mandela house."

In a bold and highly moral step, the UDF leadership decided at the beginning of 1989 to distance itself publicly from Winnie Mandela. One of those leaders was the organization's spokesperson, Murphy Morobe. He had grown up on Winnie Mandela's street, and would often stop by at the Mandela house on his way home from school. On Robben Island, he had heard Nelson Mandela debate the cult of leadership—how an unquestioned leader easily abuses power.

"And in all of this, I was a living soul," says Murphy Morobe. "Apart from the moral repugnance with which some of us recoiled from the activities of what people in the township generally regarded as 'Winnie's Boys,' one of our major concerns at a political level was the extent to which the activities of these boys were beginning to distract everyone from our urgent and primary task of fighting the regime."

This decision to distance himself had "a profound influence on me as an individual—on my relationship with Madikizela-Mandela . . . and had an effect on my relationship with many others inside and outside the movement.

"The point I'm making in conclusion is that I got involved in this because I believe these were issues of principle . . . and for me it was important that my organization, my movement, begin to face them up front."

No one is quite sure whether the standing ovation in the hall is for the sheer moral courage of these two men, or whether it is in recognition of the enormous price one pays for moral courage in this country. Once upon a time, they were prominent leaders of the UDF. In the new dispensation, they are nothing more than the backroom boys for politicians who still remember. Murphy Morobe is chairperson of the Finance and Fiscal Commission, while Azhar Cachalia heads the Safety and Security Secretariat.

Testimony of Nicodemus Sono, the father of Lolo Sono

I last saw my son in the company of Winnie Madikizela-Mandela—he was bleeding, bruised, shaking, crying. I begged her to leave Lolo with me. "The movement will deal with this dog," she told me before driving away in her blue and white combi . . . I haven't seen him again. I failed Lolo.

Thereafter the worst came . . . My eldest daughter was looking for a job, she was in Langlaagte Station. She saw a man exactly as her brother. She stood there, she was trapped, she was crying, and another lady . . . asked her, "What is wrong?" She said, "That man looks like my brother who disappeared in 1989." The lady spoke to the gentleman and asked him what his name was. He said he was somebody, he was a Zulu, he had taken out his ID to reassure Gail that—"I am not your brother Lolo." My child was lost, she was crying. When she came home, she couldn't speak, she couldn't eat.

We are still not at ease. I am having nightmares, dreams, sometimes I hear knocks on the door, thinking it is Lolo. When I am sleeping, I can see him flying from the sky, coming home, saying that—"Mom, I am back home." Then I will open my arms and try to hug him, and say, "Welcome home." I am pleading with Mrs. Mandela today, in front of the world, that—"Please, Mrs. Mandela, please, give us our son back."

MRS. WINNIE MADIKIZELA-MANDELA: The logic defies me. Why would I assault a boy and take him back to his father and then kill him? Why? And why is Mr. Sono jumping on the bandwagon to accuse me of the most heinous of deeds?

During the struggle, when comrades criticized Winnie Madikizela-Mandela's outrageous behavior, a specific line of argument always surfaced: "Look at Albertina Sisulu. She's been harassed just as much. She has suffered just as much. Yet she's never put a foot wrong." It's for that very reason that Albertina Sisulu's testimony before the Truth Commission is in many ways a tough test of her mettle. She is such a respected veteran of the struggle that no matter what she says, she will surely be believed—especially in the course of a hearing that is suffocating in lies, evasions, intimidation, and fear.

Sisulu—the wife of one of Nelson Mandela's oldest friends, Walter Sisulu—worked as a nurse for the Soweto doctor Abubaker Asvat. She was at work on the day he was gunned down in his surgery, just a few days after the discovery of Stompie Seipei's body. Earlier in the hearing, there has been testimony on how Madikizela-Mandela asked Asvat to treat Stompie after the assault. He refused, saying the child should be taken to a hospital. There was also evidence that Madikizela-Mandela took Katiza Cebekhulu to Asvat, demanding that he examine him for proof that he had been sodomized by Paul Verryn. This too Asvat refused to do, and referred Cebekhulu to a specialist.

Sisulu describes the day two unknown men killed Asvat.

"I heard the doctor's voice calling a patient by name and heard the examining-room door click, as this was a security door which could only be unlocked by pressing a button from the inside. I do not know what happened there—but as there was silence after the click, I assumed the doctor was busy with the patient. After about ten minutes, I heard something that sounded like a gunshot . . . I shouted, 'Abu!' I thought that perhaps he might be doing something. No response. I heard a second shot similar to the first one. This time there was also a scream by Dr. Asvat . . . I recognized his voice.

"Abubaker Asvat was like my son," says Albertina Sisulu. Yet the week before the Winnie hearing, rumors were doing the rounds that she was agonizing over her appearance at the Truth Commission. And that the ANC had sent her a lawyer.

Sisulu denies having seen Winnie Madikizela-Mandela and Katiza Cebekhulu at Asvat's surgery.

"Are you aware of any argument on the day Asvat was killed between Asvat and Madikizela-Mandela in his surgery?"

Sisulu: "If Mrs. Mandela has gone to see him, she wouldn't go to my admission room because that's where I was always . . ."

But wouldn't she have heard the click of the security door—just as she did when Asvat's killers entered the consulting room?

There is another discrepancy. Madikizela-Mandela has always claimed that she was in Brandfort when Stompie Seipei was assaulted. In a BBC documentary on Asvat's death, made at the beginning of 1997, Sisulu identified her own handwriting on a medical card that proves that Madikizela-Mandela is lying. Now, at the Mayfair hearing, she denies that the handwriting is hers.

Dumisa Ntsebeza suggests an explanation: "Can it be that you are trying your very best to say as little as possible about your comrade and colleague and as little as possible that may incriminate and implicate her . . . is it possible that it's because she is your comrade? And the

Mandelas and the Sisulus come a very long way both from the male side and the female side? And is it because of that reason that you wouldn't like to be the one who should be identified in South Africa's history as having dared to speak out about your comrade in terms that seem to suggest that she was involved in the death of Dr. Asvat?"

It is difficult to gauge who looks more distressed—Albertina Sisulu or her ashen-haired husband in the audience. Instead of answering Ntsebeza, she goes on at length about her contribution to the struggle—as if to say: "Did I not do enough?"

"So even as I am shielding Mrs. Mandela, I am not here to tell lies. I tell exactly what I know and what I have seen . . . Dr. Asvat was my child. If he had anything to do with the Mandelas and he had told me, I would have stopped him and he would not be dead . . ."

By the time she gets to this, she is covering her face with her hand.

Afterward someone sees Madikizela-Mandela trying to embrace Albertina Sisulu, who apparently rebuffs her with: *"Hayi, suka wena."* ("Go away!")

Sisulu returns to the witness stand on the last day of the hearing and it's proven that it was in fact not her handwriting on the medical card. But the fact remains that not a word of reproach for Madikizela-Mandela has left her lips. Whatever she still knows, she has become part of a gallery of lives that Winnie Mandela has, if not destroyed, then profoundly changed: Mananki Seipei, Nicodemus Sono, Phumlile Dlamini, the Asvats, Nomsa Shabalala, Paul Verryn, Azhar Cachalia, and Murphy Morobe.

The hearings are not yet over, but the toll is high.

John Allen calls me aside. "A whole lot of amnesties have been granted, but they will be released in Cape Town. I don't know why the Amnesty Committee has decided to release them in the middle of the Winnie hearing—all the journalists familiar with the process are up here in Joburg. But if radio could get the bunch out on air, it would help."

I look at the list. All the important ANC names: Thabo Mbeki, former MK commander Joe Modise, Mac Maharaj . . . thirty-seven of them in total.

"Does this mean that there won't be any public hearings for them?"

"Yes."

Outside, cars and trucks are passing in a smoky stream; hidden under a leather jacket to keep out the noise, Angie is filing a report for the news. I write the story on the laptop. Something is not right, I say over and over again. Something is not right.

To the right of the commissioners, a phalanx of mostly white lawyers—representing victims and perpetrators—is building up. "I represent the family of Lolo Sono," says the lawyer, pronouncing it "Loulou Sounou." Tutu shakes his head: "Lô-lô Sô-nô." When the next lawyer talks about Dr. Asvat, and another wants to put a question to Mrs. Mazikidela-Mandela, the chairperson simply throws his hands in the air.

But when the lawyer of the Chili family pronounces the surname like the spice, Tutu stops the proceedings: "*Agge nee boetie, nou't ek genoeg gehad* [No, man, now I've had enough] . . . it's x!ili."

"I am sorry, sir," the lawyer says neatly and confidently, "it is not possible for me to pronounce that sound."

"If you take their money, you respect their surname—put your tongue behind your teeth: x!ili."

We all wait in despair—is this the time or the place? But hark!"I represent the . . . x! . . . x!-ili family."

Tutu smiles benevolently.

In these hearings, the Truth Commission is focusing on three particular cases: the disappearance of Lolo Sono, the death of Stompie Seipei, and the death of Dr. Abubaker Asvat. The cases have a lot in common. On the one hand, they're all linked to Winnie Madikizela-Mandela . . . on the other, they involve the same three investigating policemen and a history of missing documents, defective investigations, and unusual conduct. As members of the murder and robbery squad at the Protea police station, Henk Hesslinga, Fred Dempsey, and H. T. Moodley investigated the three cases. In all three, things went wrong with the particular evidence linking Madikizela-Mandela to the murder.

The Lolo Sono case. The driver of the combi, Michael Siyakamela, makes a statement confirming that the severely assaulted Sono was sitting in the vehicle with Madikizela-Mandela when they talked to his pleading father. That statement gets lost. The Truth Commission tracks down Siyakamela, who is initially willing to give a new statement but later refuses, saying that "Mommy has contacted him."

The Stompie Seipei case. A police informer makes a statement that Winnie was involved in the assault on Stompie. His statement is removed by the security police, who say they are also investigating the matter. The informer is later blown to pieces by Vlakplaas commander Eugene de Kock. It also emerges that Hesslinga was once a member of Koevoet, the notorious police unit, and a colleague of De Kock.

The Asvat case. The two killers are arrested, but they are convicted for robbery only. In their statement, they admit that they stole R120. The Asvat family has maintained for years that not a single cent was removed from the surgery. The killers now say they were tortured into admitting to the robbery. They also say they were tortured at every point where they said something to implicate Madikizela-Mandela.

The question hanging in the air is whether Madikizela-Mandela herself worked with the police. It is clear that there was close contact between the Mandela household and the local police. She probably thought she was running them, while they probably thought the boot was on the other foot. But there was also a broader contact between the judicial system and the politicians, who knew how things stood in the first tentative negotiations with Nelson Mandela in Victor Verster Prison. At the time, some attorney generals refused to prosecute her.

The price for the negotiations was the embrace of violation and abuse—a moral ambiguity that suited the Afrikaner bureaucracy perfectly in its last decaying years.

Winnie Madikizela-Mandela denies every single allegation of human rights abuses made against her. In her response, she alternates between the words "ludicrous" and "ridiculous." She uses the words so often that relatives of the victims sitting in the audience begin to anticipate her answers with their own sneering versions of "ridiculous" and "ludicrous."

"So Mr. Ikaneng, Mr. Mekgwe, Mr. Mono, Mr. Dempsey, Mr. Kgase, Mr. Morgan, Mr. Richardson, Miss Falati, have all conspired to lie and implicate you? Is that what I'm understanding you to mean?"

"They have lied, sir." . . . "You are not suggesting, for God's sake, that I would be responsible for the actions of those youths . . . they led their lives and I led mine . . . I couldn't be held responsible for that." . . . "I am not playing around and I will *not* allow you to talk to me like that." . . . "It was not a violation of human rights that *my* car was used to drive *my* daughter around on *my* business." . . . "Why would I do that?" . . . "Azhar Cachalia is part of the Indian cabal—I learnt later they call Murphy Morobe 'Murphy Patel'—they were all part of the Indian cabal." . . . "I have given you my answer, if you don't like it, it's too bad." . . . "I was, am, and will always be the head of the household. All my life, I've been head of that family—I delegate nothing to anyone." . . . "I am an ordinary human being—they did things to me that is not acceptable. While many sat comfortably in their houses, we fought a just war."

In the middle of the flow of denials, a bodyguard carries in two huge bouquets of white and red flowers and puts them down near Winnie's table.

My brain is splitting into a headache. I have never been this depressed at a Truth Commission hearing. It's like reporting on a third-rate movie—this miasma of scandal, arrogance, ambition, lies, and unbridled gangsterism. This hearing is about my country, I am thinking. And whether there is space for all of us. And the conditions for this space.

I also have a distinct feeling that for now this hearing has nothing to do with me, with whites. Blacks are deciding among themselves what they regard as right and wrong. They are making that decision here, today. Either a black person may kill because of apartheid—or none of us may kill, no matter the reason. This hearing has little to do with the past. It has everything to do with the future.

The thought is unbearable in this confined space packed with journalists. I extricate myself from the web of cables and go outside for air. On the pavement, a man is selling little white plates with faces on them: Nelson Mandela, Thabo Mbeki, Joe Slovo, and Winnie Mandela—all in the same row. I flinch from the ardent sun and turn back.

Where to?

I cannot live in a space where the face of Nelson Mandela or Joe Slovo is interchangeable with that of Winnie Madikizela-Mandela.

"We are struggling to establish a different dispensation characterized by a new morality, integrity. Truthfulness. Accountability."

I stop in my tracks. It is Tutu. He's speaking. I burst past the guards and run upstairs. I see him sitting at the commissioner's table—grayer than in my thoughts, and more shrunken than I have ever seen him. But like a blade, he cuts through the sordid layers of lies and pretenses, dressed up for the past two weeks in an armor of legal terms.

"Some of us were devastated and also found it exhilarating what had happened at this hearing. Devastated by the performances from eminent leaders of the struggle—the moral ineptitude that emanated from them was unexpected and shattering. But there were also the splendid exceptions who stood out in stark contrast.

"We need to demonstrate qualitatively that this new dispensation is different morally. We need to stand up to be counted for goodness, for truth, for compassion, and not kowtow to the powerful.

"I acknowledge Madikizela-Mandela's role in the history of our struggle. And yet one used to say that something went wrong . . . horribly, badly *wrong . . . what,* I don't know. And all of us can only say: 'There but for the grace of God go I.'

"But something went wrong . . .

"Many, *many* love you.

"Many, *many* say you should have been where you ought to be. The first lady of the country.

"I speak to you as someone who loves you very deeply . . . I want you to stand up and say: 'There are things that went wrong . . .' There are people out there who want to embrace you. I still embrace you"—and Tutu folds his arms in front of him as if embracing her—"because I love you. I love you very deeply. There are many out there who would have wanted to do so. If you were able to bring yourself to be able to say: 'Something went wrong . . .' and say, 'I'm sorry, I'm sorry for my part in what went wrong . . .' I beg you, I beg you . . . I beg you, please . . . You are a great person. And you don't know how your greatness would be enhanced if you were to say, 'I'm sorry . . . things went wrong. Forgive me.' " And for the first time, Tutu looks directly at her. His voice has fallen to a whisper. "I beg you."

Time freezes. Tutu has risked . . .

everything.

I hear my blood slushing in my veins.

It leaps, suddenly, in me—up.

It bursts through my skin.

Ah, the commission! The deepest heart of my heart. Heart that can only come from this soil—brave—with its teeth firmly in the jugular of the only truth that matters. And that heart is black. I belong to that blinding black African heart. My throat bloats up in tears—my pen falls to the floor, I blubber behind my hand, my glasses fog up—for one brief, shimmering moment, this country, this country, is also truly mine.

The heart is on its feet.

From far away, I hear Winnie Mandela: "I am saying it is true: things went horribly wrong and we were aware that there were factors that led to that. For that I am deeply sorry."

But she didn't mean it! Outside the hall, angry victims are giving interviews to the media. The journalists are angry too. She didn't mean it! She simply aped the words Tutu put in her mouth—she aped it for the benefit of international media coverage!

I cuddle the commission to my breast. I am elated. I am so proud for all of us—Winnie Madikizela-Mandela has bent a knee to that heart. In public, she *had* to admit to the fundamental heart of this country. She had to. She danced to that blessed pulse.

"You're so naive," says a colleague who can hardly hide his anger. "Tutu has just provided her with a respectable platform for faking sweet words to further her populist political career. She's walking away from this as the only winner."

"You are so wrong."

We are rolling up cables and packing away equipment. I want to hold everything. I want to lay myself down over this place of us all.

"The essence of this hearing was the collision of two cultures alive in the black community. The culture of responsibility, human virtue, and guilt, and the culture of clan honor and shame."

He rolls his eyes in his skull. I push him down on a chair.

"Honor becomes the code, the atmosphere breathed by any close-knit group—a group *outside* the powerful group—whether it's based on clan loyalties, or ethnicity, or color. Winnie is the monarch of the people for whom the new system does not work. She symbolizes their collective honor. She personifies their aspirations and their right to status. She has to cling to that honor. If she admits to wrongdoing, she dishonors them all."

"So why do you expect ANC ministers to admit to wrongdoing, but not her?"

"Because the principle of democracy is virtue. It affirms the equality and dignity of all people, their rights and duties regardless of their status. Winnie's ethos of honor is fundamentally opposed to this. It toes the honor line. It establishes two opposing sets of rules: one for the kinsmen and one for strangers. That is why she holds the government accountable for lack of delivery to the poor—but she doesn't feel accountable for killing the same people. She and her group live according to their own rules and the result is a permanent ambivalence: a kind of self-deceit wrapped up in self-interest. In the meantime, their consciousness is obsessed with honor. And in the field of honor, might is right."

"So where's the collision?"

"Tutu instinctively latched on to her operative principle of honor and challenged her on her own turf. He left the calls for moral accountability behind. He honed in on her honor. He told her: 'You are a great person, you should have been our first lady—you deserve that *honor*. You will be even greater if you admit that things went wrong.' And by begging her publicly, he said to her: 'I honor you as my equal.' And in the culture of honor, you are answerable for your honor only to your social equals. She dared not refuse. She had to take it."

"So where is the victory for morality?"

"By admitting that things went wrong, she herself wiped out her whole culture of honor. As of today, her followers will have to say: 'She killed for us, but she herself said things went wrong.' A space was created for the first time for both her and her followers to admit in an honorable way that things went wrong. Dare one ask for more?"

"So thanks to the duality of honor, the killer becomes the chief and the tyrant the minister." He sneers and clicks his bags shut.

"But the killer and the tyrant for the first time contained in the same frame as the rest of us! Isn't that some kind of beginning?"

CHAPTER TWENTY-ONE

Beloved Country
of Grief and Grace

"We should be harder on Winnie than on Magnus Malan or P. W. Botha, because she stood for more. She is supposed to be one of us—someone with principles," says a colleague. It is midnight in Melville and we're talking about evil. He is working on a television documentary on the subject.

"Do you believe in evil?" he asks me.

"The mere fact that you use the word 'believe' means you see it as something that's not concrete."

"Of course," he says.

"There's no 'of course' about it. When I think of Hitler, it is as if total evil is a fact. It is touchable. When I touch him, I touch evil. And kitsch and evil are in perfect symbiosis in Hitler. But that is too easy, I think . . . besides, it's a male thing, this obsession with evil."

He laughs. "This is getting interesting. Why is it male?"

"For starters, all the journalists zooming in on the perpetrators are male—the smell of male bonding, male culture, misguided bravery— the machismo fascinates men. With women it's different, and I think it has to do with giving birth. You have children, they all come out of you—yet one is a wonderful person, the other a *stront*. But you know that deep down in him, he also has something good."

"But let's go back a bit—why is it too easy to decide that Hitler is evil?"

"Because you deny him his humanity . . ."

"He has forfeited his right to humanity!"

"By refusing to acknowledge that he is human like yourself, you are

saying that you are not capable of what he did. So you can relax. And I
say you *are* capable of it."

"But if you refrain from judging him, you kill off the awareness that
you should avoid certain ideologies, certain people, because they represent evil . . . that you should have *nothing* to do with them."

I put my wineglass in front of him and a pin from my jacket.

"Are these evil? Every morsel, every molecule, is being struck by perfection and imperfection—there is not a single atom that you can pin-
point and say: 'This is absolute evil and this is absolute good.' Good
and evil are never absolute. Every good is imperfect in its own way and
every evil has an underlying potential to be good."

"Are you denying there are people with the charisma, the intelligence, the power, to manipulate a whole population into doing evil?
What then would you say is the difference between Mandela and Verwoerd? Between Winnie and P.W. or Winnie and Tutu?"

"The odd one out is Tutu—he is not a politician. But the real difference, I would say, lies in what some people describe as a culture of
shame and a culture of guilt. The essence of shame is the honor of a
group, the essence of guilt is the responsibility of the individual toward
a specific morality. Verwoerd formulated a policy to build and protect
the honor of his people—white Afrikaners should be proud of who they
are."

"Wait-wait-wait . . . tell me about this distinction between 'shame'
and 'guilt.' "

"It was used to explain the difference between the way the Japanese
and the Germans dealt with the aftermath of the Second World War.
The Japanese had a culture of shame—under an emperor, a God-given
ruler. The Germans had a culture of guilt. The usual catchy definitions
are things like: People feel *guilty* when they violate the rights of others.
They feel *shame* when they fail themselves, when they fail their group.
Guilt is linked to violation; shame is linked to failure. Shame requires
an audience. Guilt does not. And shame is more overwhelming and
more isolating than guilt."

"So where does honor fit in?"

"The basis of shame is honor. Honor functions when the image a
person has of himself is indistinguishable from that presented to him
by other people. The ethos of honor is opposed to a morality that affirms the equality in dignity of all people and consequently the equality of their rights and duties. In a society in which honor is the keystone

of the values, any choice other than that imposed by the code of honor is unthinkable, and it is at the moment of choice that the pressure of the group is at its strongest."

I suddenly remember a photograph of Hitler I once saw in a magazine. He is surrounded by children, and one girl is offering him a flower. The admiration on their fine, pure faces. And I remember sitting on my father's shoulders next to the main road from Johannesburg, waiting to see Verwoerd passing by on his way to Cape Town. When he saw the cars outside Kroonstad, he stop ped. I remember he touched my arm. I also remember how we only bought at Afrikaner shops—even if it was more expensive. How the Afrikaner shop owners gave bursaries to poor Afrikaners.

"Honor became Verwoerd's driving force. To protect the honor of the Afrikaner, anything was permissible—even the most dishonorable policy. And the dishonor of the leader is the dishonor of the group. That is why the knife in Verwoerd's heart was regarded as a knife in the Afrikaner's heart. That is why P.W. says he will divide Afrikaners if he appears before the Truth Commission—he is embedded in honor and shame. And it's why Botha and Afrikaners like him do not feel guilty because they have done something wrong—they feel ashamed because they have been caught out."

"*Ja. Lekker*. The Truth Commission concurs with the universal view that the Afrikaner is guilty. We have betrayed civilization and its values. We have brought shame and disgrace upon our heads . . . And the world doesn't care whether it's Van der Merwe or Van der Berg. So, where were we . . . Winnie, I can see, definitely functions in a culture of shame. But Mandela?"

"I'm not sure whether it's possible for any politician to function in a culture of guilt. The politician's dream is to have millions of obedient, unquestioning followers. So he has to mobilize. And here's one of the differences between Mandela and Mbeki. Mandela knows the value of mobilizing on morality—it works well in the Western world and with whites. Play on their guilt by being impossibly forgiving. Mbeki, on the other hand, mobilizes blacks on the basis of honor—the honor of blacks in Africa. But both of them find it difficult to fire a minister or a media liaison officer for misbehavior or mismanagement. Maybe this is the basis of transformation from a liberation movement to a government: to move from a culture of guilt to one of shame."

Someone walking past recognizes my companion from his television reporting and shouts: "Fuck off, you with your Truth Commission bull-shit and Afrikaner-bashing!"

"How do you deal with this? Does it make you angry or sad?"

"In the beginning, it would give me a kick—I am not one of them! Now I want to grab this fool by the neck and hiss: 'The fatherland ceases to be a fatherland when its soul is destroyed. Can't you see that we have to stay true to the highest demands made on us by the best of our ancestors, not by the idols of the false tradition of Afrikaner na-tionalism?' " He laughs. "But this is not my kind of language."

"And what do our ancestors tell us?"

He grins. "Commando tactics—small mobile groups, changing direc-tion very quickly—the only principle is personal survival."

"See, the culture of honor . . . maybe the moment the word 'verraaier' or 'traitor' surfaces, you know that what is being defended is no longer a universal morality but honor."

"Okay. So the Truth Commission itself is obviously a culture of guilt making a huge entrance into an arena ruled for decades by different cul-tures of shame."

"Although in its origins and in its behavior—until it started talking to the NP—the ANC was based on a culture of individual responsibil-ity, with the virtues of consultation, human rights, and so forth. But they seem to find it increasingly difficult to stick to it."

"Maybe that is the reason why so much hope is invested in the Truth Commission, why so much publicity has been generated around it. Peo-ple realize instinctively this is the last, the very last opportunity for the majority of people to break into a culture of guilt and individual re-sponsibility. If the majority can do that, then the politicians will never again have such a stranglehold over this country."

I change tack: "But what about ubuntu—a person is a person through other persons—doesn't that safeguard the culture of honor? Through the honor of others, you are honored. Won't that discourage you from standing up against your group when they do wrong?"

"Well, Tutu has gone a long way toward redefining the concept of ubuntu. Maybe the more interesting question is: If the definition of 'us,' of 'the South African group,' of 'African,' were to be changed to the ex-tent that it now included you, wouldn't you then move happily into the culture of honor and shame? Isn't that why you so quickly apologized to Tutu and Boraine about the Ntsebeza affair?"

I am taken aback.

He goes on: "When the commission decided to investigate itself, to keep information away from the media—it appropriated a culture of shame within its broader culture of guilt. If Dumisa Ntsebeza is dishonored, then the whole commission is dishonored, then the process will fail. You dared to criticize. Then you were told in so many words by Alex Boraine that you wished to destroy the commission, that for the greater good you had to accept certain things. What happened afterward proved you right—and yet you apologized. Because you want to be included in their circle—the circle of guilt."

There's nothing I can say. Except perhaps that since the victim hearings ended, the commission has become too loud—too many egos, too many squabbles, too much politics.

litany

here along the long white shadow
where I thought where I thought I'd leave the litany of locust
of locust and death I'll always hear the litany of sound

here along the long white shadow
where I grab luster grab honor that once was luster and white
the truth I've heard and how to molest it

that I travel I travel along the corn and chaff of my past
that my past crawls forth on its deadly knees without once looking
    up
that I claw on my knees claw to that place

that light place that does not want to dim
here along the long white shadow of mortal and molested truth
we buried many we buried without shroud or ritual

many we buried and from the graves it sprouts
the shadow sprouts of luster, burdock, and wheat the locusts of
    sound
here along the long white shadow

and my past sits so well in its teeth all along
its teeth sit well in the shadow of sulphur and lime it's time
the time of assassin and shame and tin

I keep slipping slipping out of truth
while next to me along the long white shadow walks the shudder
that I was walks the long white shudder of ash

set me I who keep slipping in the long white shadow
out of time out of random and lies I want slipping from the
    shudder
along the emptiness of litany and shadow

set me set me from revenge and loss
from ruins set me from the long white scar the lichen and ash set
    me free
into remorse oh my hand my hand grabs the sheet like a throat

Cringing on the banks of the Rubicon of Truth

"The Priest and the Politician." "The Crunch between the Crocodile
and the Commission." "The Tail Is Testing the Truth." The possibilities
are endless and we use them all.

Die Groot Krokodil is the only former political leader of any note
who has not put in an appearance before the Truth Commission. When
the party he once led made its political submission under the leadership
of F. W. de Klerk, P. W. Botha refused to cooperate with his successor—
the man who cleverly ousted him.

Archbishop Tutu personally went to the Wilderness to speak to
Botha. Yes, he abides by the law. Yes, he is prepared to answer questions.

But a long list was sent to you at the end of 1996. Where are the answers?

No, the old man needs a lawyer.

Tutu personally asks the office of President Nelson Mandela to pay
the fees for a lawyer. As stipulated in state contracts, the state is responsible for footing any bills covering legal actions that flow from an
office once held. So the president's office will have to pay for P. W.
Botha's lawyer.

Not one lawyer, a team of lawyers—because a vast amount of research is needed to answer the questions.

Okay, a team then.

Where are the answers?

No, the lawyers are battling to access certain documents.

Tutu personally asks the minister of justice to allow Botha's legal team access to all documentation.

Where are the answers?

No, Botha is suffering from ill health. He had to have a hip operation.

Where are the answers?

It is June. Botha's wife, Tannie Elize, dies unexpectedly. Tutu personally attends the funeral. Tutu is crazy, the angry commissioners say.

Spring, and a hearing is held on the workings of Botha's brainchild, the State Security Council. Botha is subpoenaed to appear. He cannot come, he is ill.

Where are the answers?

Patience, patience—but the man is eighty-two and not in good health.

Apparently even an old man's fancy turns to thoughts of love. The newspapers publish photographs of a toothy P.W. lovingly kissed by a blonde woman with *skattige ogies*. In her younger days, she was a meter maid. She is half his age. She owns a guest house. He wants to sell his own house for more than 2 million and buy a place on the beach.

In the setting sun, the old crocodile stretches his jaws in a tirade against the Truth Commission.

"I will not appear before the Truth Commission. I don't perform in circuses." . . . "I won't allow myself to be threatened. The Truth Commission is tearing Afrikaners apart." . . . "I am not asking for amnesty. I never authorized murders. I will not apologize for the fight against a Marxist revolutionary onslaught."

Desmond Tutu: "I have to say that I am very deeply saddened, because we have gone out of our way to give him the kind of treatment given to nobody else . . . we have taken account of his ill health, his age, and the fact that he was state president."

P. W. Botha: "I'm not a fool. I made many mistakes, but I ask God on my knees for the light to come. An Afrikaner doesn't go on his knees before people, he does it before God."

Alex Boraine: "We are constantly told about Botha's health problems. But when we hear that he's entered into a new relationship with someone half his age and has enough energy to launch vicious attacks on the Truth Commission, we have to ask ourselves—how ill is he?"

Desmond Tutu: "At his wife's funeral, a black radio reporter came up to me, stuck a microphone in my face, and said: 'Explain, you, to my black listeners, what you are doing here.' "

Botha is subpoenaed a second time. He doesn't turn up. Tutu and Boraine march to the attorney general's office to lay a charge of contempt of court. The attorney general finds that the subpoena is invalid—the time has not been filled in.

During the business hearings, we learned of a letter written to P. W. Botha by the Afrikaner business magnate Anton Rupert (father of Johan) in January 1986, after Botha apparently stated that it was better "to be poor than to yield." Rupert wrote: "I am appealing to you personally. Reaffirm your rejection of apartheid. It is crucifying us; it is destroying our language; it is degrading a once heroic nation into the lepers of the world. Remove the burden of the curse of a transgression against mankind from the backs of our children and grandchildren . . . Should you fail in this God-given task, then one day we shall surely end up with a Nuremberg."

But Die Groot Krokodil ruled supreme.

At some point in the eighties, a group of academics went to see P. W. Botha to tell him that things could not go on as they were. After listening to all of them, Botha stood up and said: "My dear professors— you can come here with all your clever arguments and academic learning, but I, P. W. Botha, govern from a guts feeling."

"It's that 's' that made me leave the National Party," one of them said afterward.

Friday, December 19, 1997, has been set aside by the Truth Commission for the testimony of former state president P. W. Botha. The questions put to him will be based largely on the 2,000 pages of answers he has supplied in response to the commission's written questions. This pile of papers, loaded on a small luggage trolley, was delivered to the Truth Commission's offices by his lawyer two weeks earlier. By now Botha's refusal to appear before the Truth Commission has become a symbol: he represents the unrepentant white rulers of yesterday, ensconced in so much financial and political privilege that nothing in their lives has changed.

I'm preparing a radio preview, and so I ask for a recording of Botha's voice from the sound archives. Of all things, they send me his Rubicon speech. The speech all of us hoped would turn the country around. For days before, there were rumors that P.W. was going to make some major announcements. It was 1985.

I lift the following sound clip: "I believe we are today crossing the Rubicon, Mr. Chairman. In South Africa, there can be no turning back. I have a manifesto for the future of our country and we must engage in positive action in the months and years that lie ahead . . ."

And I remember Pik Botha's testimony before the commission about this very speech: "I wrote the Rubicon part of Mr. Botha's speech. He kept the Rubicon line, but removed everything I put before it—the unbanning of the ANC and the release of Nelson Mandela."

This speech, afterward described as the biggest anticlimax in South Africa's history, plunged the country into a political and financial crisis. Although Botha professed to be crossing the Rubicon of reform, outside his speech-bubble, vicious oppression continued unabated. Precisely how vicious, South Africans learned in the months of Truth Commission hearings devoted to the mid-eighties.

I file this report: "Today Botha stands before a Rubicon of a different kind.

"Some feel: leave him alone. The spectacle of a doddering old geriatric being hauled before the Truth Commission just a block away from the Parliament where he once ruled the roost will do South Africa's image of rainbows and 'Shosholoza'[1] no good.

"But those who've listened to the victims' testimonies and the perpetrators' amnesty hearings will know that in the mid-1980s, when P. W. Botha was at the peak of his power, apartheid rule acquired its coldest, its most brutal and murderous edge.

"It was also in the eighties that it dawned on the government that the law could no longer be used to suppress the surging quest for freedom. New laws, bannings, detentions—all seemed powerless to stop the uprising of the majority.

---

[1] "Shosholoza" is a song that captured the minds and hearts of South Africans during the World Rugby Cup won by South Africa in 1996—the first time after the 1994 election that people felt truly united.

"Thus the eighties became the time where new centers of control received information, took decisions, and gave instructions. Laws were no longer needed. They functioned outside the law. The taxpayer paid for the era of hit squads, vigilantes, disinformation campaigns, cross-border raids, chemical warfare, and states of emergency.

"Now people would like to see the man who engineered these systems cross the Wilderness Rubicon. They want him to step outside his luxurious surroundings, which are protected at our expense, to come with his legal team, paid for by our money, and make a gesture of accountability to the South African Truth Commission."

Solzhenitsyn's words, quoted by Kader Asmal long before the Truth Commission was established, come back to me again: "By not dealing with past human rights violations, we are not simply protecting the perpetrators' trivial old age; we are thereby ripping the foundations of justice from beneath new generations."

Botha is subpoenaed a third time. Again he ignores it. Now the Truth Commission lays criminal charges with Frank Kahn, the attorney general of the western Cape, and a summons is issued for Botha to appear in court. We don't expect him to tell the truth, but we would at least like him to feel the new South Africa where it hurts most: on his skin. What a delight it is to learn that a black magistrate, Victor Lugaju, will preside over Botha's case in the regional court in George.

A triumph for affirmative action! Thanks to this new government's policy of appointing people from formerly disadvantaged communities, we have the right man in the right place at the right time.

From the airport in George, Botha's former constituency, we drive to the Wilderness in search of Die Groot Krokodil's lair. It is the day before his appearance in court. It doesn't take Patrick and me long to identify the house: crowds of photographers, a camera slung over each shoulder, waiting. The silvery-pink Mercedes outside the door belongs to the fiancée, they tell us. Botha's relationship with Reinet te Water Naude, thirty-five years his junior, has been making headlines for months. Just six months or so after Tannie Elize died, Mrs. Te Water Naude appeared on the scene. "I am a Christian and Mrs. Naude is a Christian," Botha told an Afrikaans Sunday newspaper, "and as Christians we love each other. It is written like this in the Bible . . . what will become of this relationship I will find out on my knees."

The sun is setting in rose and honey over the luscious splendor of the Wilderness. The photographers are waiting for the arrival of former defense force generals Constand Viljoen, Jannie Geldenhuys, and Magnus Malan. We wait with them.

I pick up the tourist brochure on the dashboard. It seems that one of the great attractions of the area is a visit to a crocodile farm. *In ancient Egypt crocodiles were worshipped as gods. A whole city called Crocodilopolis was built in their honor. Their priests put gold bracelets on their arms, and fed them on cakes and honey in a sacred lake.* Apparently the old crocodiles get to lie on the soft grass, while the younger ones have to make do with the sloping banks.

I look at the huge house and suddenly become aware of a slit of light at the big sliding doors—and there he is . . . the old man himself. All I see is the silhouette of his big right ear. He is staring at us. The dusk is quiet, with only the far-off sound of cars on the highway. I call the others, but as my hand moves, he closes the curtains—so swiftly that I think I've imagined him.

At the ANC office in town, members are putting up posters on a wall. "Botha's Charge Sheet," one of them reads: "Vlakplaas Death Unit—Botha guilty . . . Victoria Mxenge—Botha guilty . . . Steve Biko—Botha guilty. From Total Onslaught to Final Onslaught. From the Forced Removals of Lawaaikamp to Forced Appearance in Court." (Lawaaikamp is a squatter area in George.)

The local pubs are full of media people. Originally the acting magistrate of George, Elna Grobler, decided that only two people from the media would be allowed inside the sixty-seat courtroom. An outcry followed. Okay, six. Then the photographers threatened to disrupt proceedings: P.W.'s appearance will be their front-page stories—they simply have to get the material. And the story is the precise moment when the former state president appears before a black man in an ordinary regional court. If they aren't given access to that very moment, they will simply have to force their way in. The police phone Mrs. Grobler, Mrs. Grobler phones Botha, Botha phones his lawyer Ernst Penzhorn, and an agreement is reached. Botha will use a side entrance and walk past a gallery of cameras. The media undertake to abide by the law and not make any recordings of the proceedings. When the appearance is over, Botha will turn around in the dock and allow the media to photograph him for five minutes. Everyone is happy.

The next day, Botha has the whole circus to himself.

To the right of the court, cordoned off with barbed wire, ANC pro-
testers are toyi-toying and singing: "Botha is not a man, Botha is a boy."
To the left, a dozen *ooms* with long socks and open-neck shirts are waving an old South African flag. Right in front of the building, from the
back of a bakkie, a black man is singing his heart out to the accompa-
niment of loud canned music: "The people need the Loooord." Over-
head a helicopter hovers and all around us the police are organizing.

I am one of the chosen six allowed into the courtroom. In the front
row sits Botha's daughter who lives in George, Elanza Maritz. "My favorite car—a Ford Elanza," whispers television journalist Max du Preez.
He is bristling with mischief.

The generals sit in the second row. "Who are the other two?" asks
Max.

"Isn't it Lapa Munnik and Greyling Wentzel?"

"No," Max assures me kindly, "both of them are dead."

But in the end, it turns out to be those two politicians—Munnik,
who looks like a car salesman, and Wentzel, the one with the *bywoner*
face, sitting next to the short black mayor of George and a group calling themselves Die Afrikaanse Kultuurvereniging van Outenikwaland
(The Afrikaans Cultural Society of Outeniqualand).

Botha enters with his petite blonde . . . "plover" is the word that
comes to mind, on his arm. *A plover pecks off the leeches and bits of food
that get stuck between the crocodile's teeth,* says the brochure.

Botha knows his turf. He takes a seat not in, but next to, the dock.
He turns around often and smiles a somewhat rattling crown-toothed
smile at Mrs. Te Water Naude in the family bench. She smiles back with
pious intimacy.

The magistrate enters. Everybody stands. The proceedings begin.

After the first few sentences, Lugaju calls a halt. Will they continue
in English, please, he does not understand Afrikaans. Some people suck
in their breath. Do they want a court interpreter? No, the lawyers prefer to speak in Afrikaans and then translate it themselves.

Before you can turn around, the magistrate has postponed the case
for a month.

The racket from the rest of the media, waiting outside for their five-
minute shoot, grows even louder. Then the doors open with a flood. I
run to put my microphone with the others on the speaker's desk. People climb up on the court furniture, cameras roll, some are already
shouting their first questions. The police yell at us to stay back. It is un-

believably hot inside the court. Botha flings the microphones off the desk in one sweep: "Take this away!" We shout that we need sound. The police cut us off. Then above the clamor, I hear His Master's Voice. "Stop! Sowing! Havoc!" he shouts. "If you don't behave yourself, I won't address you!" He storms out. We calm down and everyone gets equipment in order. He comes back.

"Life is full of irony." His upper lip curls with pleasure. "Half a century ago in this court, I was sworn in as the member of Parliament for George. And here I am today . . ."

Squashed in under the desk, Patrick and I glance at each other. All of us are sweating profusely, but Botha is enjoying himself. He thumps his finger on the desk. "I believe in God, I believe in Jesus, I believe in the Holy Ghost, and I pray that they as a unit take control of this country and this world!" God, what is this man saying? The man who masterminded the death units! "I told Mandela to his face, yes, I've met him three times, I've treated him like a gentleman in jail, I told him: 'Anarchy and the forces of communism and socialism will destroy you.'" We've heard this before.

"I am sick and tired of the hollow parrot-cry of 'Apartheid!' I've said many times that the word 'Apartheid' means good-neighborliness . . ." Some journalist laughs.

He swings around, tail thrashing. "Who's laughing?"

Everyone is *tjoepstil.*

A crocodile's teeth come out easily, but when one falls out, another grows in its place straightaway, says the brochure. *A tooth can be renewed 45 times.*

"I honor the soldiers, I honor the police of the past! I salute them!"

His eyes are enlarged by his glasses into two dark dead blots. He relishes the attention. He cocks his head, his face is flushed, his hand trembles—until he heaves it into the familiar threatening forefinger.

"The tiger in the Afrikaner is awakened!" he cries.

"Did you know that there are no tigers in Africa?" Max du Preez asks sweetly.

Stung and furious, Botha turns on him, shaking his finger. "Yes, and if there was—*You* won't be one of them!" he yells.

"Aits, maar die oubaas sê dit mooi!" laughs Max. ("My, but the old boss put that beautifully!")

The lawyers try to usher Botha out. That was the last question, they say. "I am enjoying myself." Botha grins and rubs his soft white paws.

"Are you not going to apologize?" I ask.

"For what?" he snaps.

"For the cross-border raids," I answer, "for the death squads, for the—"

He cuts in: "If you'll shut up, I will answer you! I don't apologize . . . I *pray* for them."

He looks straight into my eyes. And for a split second, I look back into the flat, mud-colored surfaces of his eyes, grotesquely enlarged by his glasses. And I know that this man, who has had Mandela offering to accompany him to the Truth Commission, who has had Tutu begging him to assist the commission, who has had the world's media chasing after him . . . is *dom*. He is not senile, or old, or suffering from the effects of a stroke: he is a fool. And we have been governed by this stupidity for decades.

I try to find a pathway in my thoughts to him. A link. An Afrikaner connection. No. I can still find common ground with those who are battling to deal with a dramatically changed order, with our part in the past—but with this swaggering fool, there is nothing.

When Botha is finally led away, I get up and start walking. Out, just out.

Fresh air hits my face at the same time as this uplifting thought: he doesn't govern, thank God; the crawling, trotting, occasionally gliding crocodile, pushing itself along with its arrogant tail, does not *govern* anymore.

A few days before December 16, Reconciliation Day, I get a beeper message: "Commissioner Mary Burton to launch Book of Reconciliation." Wonderful! I think, and rush over to interview her. I have long felt that the Truth Commission, and more specifically the Reparation and Rehabilitation Committee, have failed to mobilize the feelings of helpless guilt in the former oppressors. After the first few weeks of hearings, something as simple as a Sunday collection for the victims in churches around the country would have involved thousands of people in a liberating ritual of some kind.

Now at last something is happening. Books will be kept at the commission's offices in various centers, and ordinary people will be able to sign them as a personal gesture of their commitment to reconciliation. There will even be an electronic version on the Internet. I decide at once to take my whole family to sign on Reconciliation Day, with the idea of transforming the Blood River ritual of my personal history into a new ritual of reconciliation and responsibility.

Will Tutu or Boraine or Ntsebeza participate in the launching of the Book of Reconciliation? No, they are all busy, but they're right behind the initiative. In fact, the whole commission thinks it's a wonderful idea. So, can people sign the book on Reconciliation Day? No, we can't expect the staff to work on a public holiday.

When you report on the workings of Parliament, you realize quite quickly: if a parliamentary committee consists only of women, no one—not even the political parties themselves—will take it seriously. And no reputable male journalist will report on it. The last time I looked at the Book of Reconciliation in Cape Town, it had been signed by seven people. Another forty-five had signed on the Internet.

Most beloved state of heart—I return again and again

We travel up-country for our yearly Free State Christmas and I'm surprised how far one can see. How vast, how desperately beautiful, this country is. And the strength with which it just stays itself. My eyes lick the horizons clean. We take turns driving, and the closer we get to the Free State, the lighter we all become.

We wind our way slowly through my hometown, through streets thronged with shoppers. The Christmas rush has become completely black. The road takes us past the *plotte*, where houses stand empty and broken-down, wires hang loose, and weeds flourish. I remember my mother telling me that the township authorities had bought the land for informal settlements. From afar I see the eucalyptus trees of my youth, then the poplars and willows, and then, spangled by the midday light, the sandstone house like a honeycomb.

"What the . . . !" My husband stops. On the gate is a huge notice: "If you set foot on this farm without a specific appointment, expect to be met by an armed response." It appears in Afrikaans and Sesotho as well.

Jerked out of our memories, we are all wide awake. Surely this has nothing to do with us? Very slowly we drive up the gravel road to the yard. The lush thicket of trees around the house looks different . . . the undergrowth and low-hanging branches have been cut open to shoulder height. We understand—now no one can hide near the house.

But they are all sitting outside and we tumble into the embrace of warmth and jokes and memories. We are all there. My brother Hendrik cuts three watermelons. Afterward we swim in the big cement dam behind the orchard while the sun sets in a splendor of clouds. The noises of the yard become more distinct—the milking of cows, the tractors being put away, then the sounds of frogs and birds rising like moisture from the vlei.

That evening my elder brother Andries explains. Do not go for walks before eight in the morning or after five in the afternoon. Close the gates so that the three dogs can circle the house at night. Do not go out to any car that stops in the yard. Of the nineteen farmers murdered these past months, two were in this area.

We lie deep in the family double bed in the guest room. My children are sleeping all over the place in makeshift beds. In the night, I am awakened by thunder. I open the shutter and stand entranced by the storm—my nostrils filled with the blessed smell of wet earth and stone. This is the place that first wakened me for words and it still does—after all these years, these many other voices.

Early the next morning, I go looking for coffee in my mother's kitchen.

"*Julle Kapenaars* have brought us rain." My father is pleased.

I see my mother coming back from the chicken run with her two youngest grandchildren, each swinging a basket of eggs. She seems frail, but the scene is so peaceful, we are so lucky, so privileged . . . But whereas this privilege used to upset me in the past, now I can hold it against a truth that we are all aware of. No longer an unaware privilege, but one that we know the price and mortality of.

On Christmas Day, we go to the service in the *moederkerk* in the center of town. Next to the big church, the statue of Voortrekker leader Sarel Cilliers is still at its post—Cilliers atop a cannon, his hand raised to take the oath of Blood River: "God, if You help us to overpower the blacks, we will keep this day, December 16, holy forever."

After the service, we drive back to the farm. Just before the turnoff, Andries speeds past us in his bakkie with his lights flashing. We slow down. When he is in front, we drive on to the farm in convoy. I see the barrel of a rifle next to him, and my sister-in-law Bettie takes out her handgun. At the house, we all wait in the cars.

"The first thing you check is whether the dogs are moving around naturally," Bettie says.

But soon everybody is engrossed in preparing the Christmas meal: the ham is being carved, the turkey falls in delicate white slices spiced with tarragon and thyme—outside the children play cricket, the cousins from the farm teach the others *marabaraba* . . . the younger girls lay the table and fold festive serviettes.

I go out to the bakkie to help Andries carry in the cooler with the beer. A car draws up in the yard. Without a word, the children stop playing and move closer to the house. My brother puts down the cooler. His body has become taut and vigilant. His daughter Sumien runs into the house and appears in a minute with the gun. A black man gets out.

"Go into the house," Andries orders us. It is quiet inside. We try to hear. Then Andries's familiar chuckle and his fluent Sesotho. It is a man who grew up with my father; he has come to wish him Merry Christmas.

"How do you survive this?" I ask.

"It is difficult, especially for Ma and Pa. She said the other day land is the essence of the Afrikaner, because land brings freedom. Now this piece of land that Great-great-grandfather Delport bought with golden pounds . . ."

"*Ja, ja*, so many pounds, it broke the table," I add.

"Ma said she cannot cope with the fact that this farm, this lifelong haven, this place that has always been the safest place we know, has turned into an island under threat. That when a car comes up the gravel road, we don't know whether it's carrying friends or killers."

He sighs.

"But to a certain extent, I suppose this is more real. This is more in step with the country than the paradise of our youth. What we had could not last . . . the question is, will *this* last?"

On a tractor tube, we drift down the river. Like a small brooch of bodies, my husband and I lie entwined on the soft flow of low velvet river-water. Cicadas lisp; there is the tender rumbling of river doves, the willows with their limp green whips, the green reeds where finches hang like gems. Above it the white banks and the sky. Slowly we bob and spin.

I've written about this farm obsessively. No other season can heal my words. I don't speak of it. I call no planets hither. My being is weak with it, hangs on to it—yet it can no longer come from me. I trail my hand in the water. My husband kisses my neck. "You always return me . . ."

he whispers, and the wrinkles in his voice are motionless, "and I never recover from you."

My bones catch fire. I grab his slippery wrist. My skin will never forget him, my first love. I am with him, as I am with my own blood I am with him, my blood-beloved.

"You lot from the city who talk to politicians and read newspapers . . . what do you say—when should we leave the country?"

We're standing around the fire, where chops and wors are sizzling. My sisters-in-law unwrap garlic bread and open tinfoil with buttery patats and potatoes.

"If you wanted to leave, you should have left already. Now it's too late."

"No, seriously," Hendrik says. "When do you know the moment has come for you to load your bakkie and leave? And my second question is, where to?"

I ask the obvious question. "Why do you want to leave?"

"Because this is no longer my country."

"How can you say that! Look where we are today and how it is . . ."

"Would you die for this country? If a war broke out tomorrow, would you go? Would you send your sons to defend this country?"

The yelling of the children playing by the water is suddenly among us.

"No, I wouldn't . . ."

"There, see—it's not your country either."

"Wait, let me finish . . . I really do feel this is my country, but I think that no one, no country, no politician, has the right to ask anyone to die for them. They can make claims on my life, I'll make sacrifices in that, but my death is my own."

"Then you don't really love this country. Do you think any Englishman or American would refuse to defend their country? And why is that? Because they feel it's theirs. I will only fight for my wife and my children and this farm."

"Americans are prepared to fight for their country because they have a lot to lose," says my levelheaded husband. "You don't want to fight because you feel nothing is yours—you only want to defend the things that are closest to you."

Andries opens a beer. "I want to talk about the Truth Commission— because I keep on thinking maybe I don't understand what's going on.

But to me it looks like a bargain. The politicians discussed it and amnesty was accepted as a concession to us. Now let me ask you: Why did I only hear about the commission after the first hearings were held? Why did no politician bother to explain to us: 'We are negotiating this thing called amnesty; this is how it will work and this is what we will score'?"

"I was personally involved in organizing a workshop in Stellenbosch on the possibility of a Truth Commission—this was a few months after the election. Politicians and *dominees* and reporters were invited, but they didn't come. *Die Burger,* which could have reached Afrikaans-speakers in the Cape, refused to cover the event. Later I reported on the drafting of the legislation, and the NP politicians had only one strategy—to try and score political points by accusing the ANC of one-sidedness. Petty grandstanding suited them better than actually explaining to their voters what it was all about."

I have a question of my own. "These killings of farmers—do you agree with Mandela that it is a third force?"

"For sure. If you'd been in the army like the two of us, you'd know that the violent actions of the right wing and black criminals are always amateurish. The police usually catch them pretty quickly. I mean, Walus shoots Chris Hani and he's caught half an hour later with the gun still in his car. That would never happen to an army-trained soldier. And these people killing farmers are professional—they are swift, they are accurate, and they never kill so many people in one area that it becomes impossible for others to go on living there. I also think the killings are linked to the armed robberies. Come kill some farmers for pleasure and rob a bank for your salary in between."

"When will you leave?" I ask.

"I cannot leave. I'm too old, I'm over forty. I've lived here all my life. Where would I go? But what I will do is fight. There is no way my children, my wife, or Ma and Pa will be harmed or gunned down and I'll just stand and cry on television. That day I will fight. And let me tell you—the country's full of well-trained soldiers, thousands and thousands of men who've been in the army. It would take less than three months to put together a solid structure for effective underground violence. And when someone says the *boere* are *sus en so,* we'll take him out—neatly."

"So when will that day arrive?"

"When we don't have anything to lose."

"But shouldn't you be putting your energies into building the country?"

"They don't want our energies. They want to build the country themselves. And that's fair enough. You know, I've never heard a white man say, 'It's a pity they took my job away.' What they say is: 'It's a pity the black man who took my place can't do the job.' I don't want them to say they'll keep our schools white, or they'll protect our language, or we can keep our jobs. I don't want that. I want them to realize that we can be of help or of use or whatever."

"And when they accuse you of racism, when they hold you responsible for all this killing and destruction—don't you think it's unfair?"

"No! They're right—I was a racist. I wanted everything for myself. I wanted the best. I did terrible things to get it and to keep it. Now it's their turn."

"Surely you at least want them to treat you better than you treated them?"

"No! I just wish they would want exactly what I wanted—the best. For themselves. Then they'd realize that we can help them to get it."

Down to my last skin

The first Sunday of the New Year and the commission is on the front page: "TRC set to be torn apart over ANC amnesties." The amnesties granted to senior ANC leaders by the Amnesty Committee in November last year are still causing conflict. The newspaper says there are two factions: one group under Dumisa Ntsebeza feels the Amnesty Committee's decision should be accepted; the other under Alex Boraine feels the matter should be taken on review. This tension—the report goes on—will come to a head during a two-day retreat on Robben Island, which the commissioners will undertake this very Sunday.

I remember a press conference shortly before Christmas, where Tutu said that the commission was in two minds about the matter. Can the commission take one of its own committees to court? And what will the consequences be if it is left to the National Party to take the commission to court instead? Since the Winnie hearing, the ANC amnesties have been in the spotlight constantly. The decision produced outrage in Afrikaner quarters. General Constand Viljoen wanted to know whether he could apply for amnesty for violations that might appear on other amnesty applications. "As chief of the army, I armed thousands of young men every year. I don't know what some of them did. Can't I apply in general terms for that?" Viljoen was told that he could not. "It's not our fault that the ANC received better legal advice than Viljoen," said the Truth Commission. When the ANC amnesties were made known in the same week in which P. W. Botha was subpoenaed, one of the two Afrikaners on the commission resigned. "I am just a token," Chris de Jager said afterward. "A token with no power."

At that same press conference, I asked Tutu: "Don't you feel conned by the ANC amnesty? As a reporter, I personally made a big hullabaloo about the fact that the ANC was prepared to take responsibility—'Look, here's a huge box full of applications, all the top leaders have applied. While the National Party won't admit to a thing . . .' And now they come with these amnesty applications, which are vague at best and misleading at worst. It's a sham. Don't you—you who have threatened to resign if they don't apply—don't you feel cheated by them?"

"No," Tutu said without hesitation. "The ANC made a solid political submission confessing to a lot of important things. People who've been victimized by the ANC—many of them—have testified right from the beginning. You must remember one thing, this is a moral universe—the truth will always out. If there are ANC people who lied, the truth will catch up with them."

And now this story of a split. What if it's true? What if they are already at loggerheads? What if other commissioners resign? Now would be just the right time to do it—you've spent two years building up a profile, you've been banking a judge's salary . . . get out now and you won't be held responsible for everything that goes wrong from here on. The idea sickens me. Was it a racial conflict again? But my thoughts keep butting up against the man in the dress. Tutu has years of experience . . . but is he up to it?

Ever since he returned from America after his cancer treatment, he's seemed very rhetorical. When confronted with anything, he keeps saying: "God is good, God is good." You want to say: "That's not enough from you—sometimes God alone is not enough." Has he lost faith in the commission? Is he too ill? Is he disappointed in the commissioners? If the commission can't make it work, what hope does the country have?

On Tuesday, the media sail out to Robben Island for a press conference. Despite the crowd of blistering pink tourists, one does not travel that distance untouched. The cliché that is Table Mountain stands breath-lessly in blue; the sea is a quiet, glaucous heaving. And you think of the countless soul-destroying crossings made in this boat, the *Susan Kruger*. Named after the wife of Justice Minister Jimmy Kruger, himself en-shrined in infamy for remarking that the death of Steve Biko left him cold. As the boat slips out of the harbor, I think of Biko and how his story is the only famous one that has not been put before the Truth Commission. Because his family chose to take the commission to the Constitutional Court, we never got to hear about the last time they saw him, how they remember him, how his children cope without him, liv-ing in his gigantic shadow.

"We were not allowed to sit on the boat, to see people," says an ex-convict. "We were taken below, there was a little trap door where they kept the tires—we were kept there in the belly of the boat—so when the sea was rough, you'd feel it—many of us got sick. And you don't see a thing."

A bus takes us to the part of the island where the retreat was held. From afar I peer out to try and pick up whether any animosity is visi-ble. But the commissioners are sitting outside in the sun, drinking, talking. And they look so relaxed in soft summery clothing and sandals that I hardly recognize some of them.

It took them less than half an hour to come to the following decision, Tutu says: the commission will ask the High Court for a declaratory or-der on the ANC amnesties. And will then act accordingly. And that is that. If this is a crisis, says Tutu, then give me more. "But it seems there is a perverse desire in some quarters that this commission must fail. I want to say to them: 'A lot more hinges on the success of this commis-sion than you may think, maybe even the very continuation of our newly won democracy.'

"If anyone had told me in 1996 that we would become the kind of group that we have become in 1998—united, although we differ—I would not have believed it. Because things were often quite bad . . . you came away from commission meetings feeling chewed up. I think that overall if we—as diverse as we have been, diverse in gender, faith, race, age—if we could jell as a group, then there is great hope for our coun-try."

"What made the group jell?"

"In part, I would say it is the experiences we have gone through together, even if they were awful . . . But coming to this island was a special experience—the history of this place, the ghosts who are moving around here. Robben Island has always been a place of reconciliation. And we said we wanted to be open to God—I think God surprised us. It was actually a fun time—drinking, singing, dancing, eating. We ourselves were surprised that it could be so beautiful . . . And we just knew: our freedom will last, because it was so costly."

I do a Q and A with a radio station, standing on a low stone wall so that I can pick up the cell phone signal, looking back to the continent. There is a rawness in my chest. It is mine. I belong to that continent. My gaze, my eyes, are one with the thousands of others that have looked back over the centuries toward Africa. Ours. Mine. Yes, I would die for this. It slips out, like a smooth holy sound. And I realize that it is the commission alone that has brought me to these moments of fierce belonging.

When I am away from these people, I falter, I lose faith. I do not want to let go of them.

The commissioners travel back with us on the boat. I pick them out one by one, as they sit with the wind and sea spray in their faces. I want to remember them like this.

"Was it really that easy to come to the decision?" I ask one of them.

"Yes," she says. "Tutu has a way of making it possible, of transcending a particular problem, of taking it to a level where we all just naturally meet." I look at him in the bow of the boat, joking with his sailor cap over his eyes. Because of him.

The Truth Commission was supposed to end in the middle of December 1997, but its life span kept being extended, and as I write this now, it is due to hand in its final report by the end of July 1998. But the latest news is that even this might no longer be possible. By opting to take the slow, laborious route of full legal proceedings for amnesty, the Amnesty Committee has admitted that it will not finish the amnesties in time for the final report. So the final report will *not* be final. An addendum will be added after six months. "Six months!" one of the commissioners sighs. "It's more likely to be two years. From the beginning, it was a mistake that the Amnesty Committee was not fully rooted in the commission. I would go so far as to say that even its autonomy was a big mistake. An unfinished report after more than two years, thousands of amnesties unraveling toward the millennium, a controversial decision on the ANC leaders . . . *en ons sit met die gebakte pere.*" (". . . and we're left holding the baby.")

Some journalists move on to new beats; others prefer to stay. I take up the post of parliamentary editor for radio in Cape Town.

In a wild arch of air, I rock with the commissioners in the boat back to the mainland. I am filled with an indescribable tenderness toward this commission. With all its mistakes, its arrogance, its racism, its sanctimony, its incompetence, the lying, the failure to get an interim reparation policy off the ground after two years, the showing off—with all of this—it has been so brave, so naively brave, in the winds of deceit, rancor, and hate. Against a flood crashing with the weight of a brutalizing past onto new usurping politics, the commission has kept alive the idea of a common humanity. Painstakingly it has chiseled a way beyond racism and made space for all of our voices. For all its failures, it carries a flame of hope that makes me proud to be from here, of here.

But I want to put it more simply. I want this hand of mine to write it. For us all; all voices, all victims:

because of you
this country no longer lies
between us but within

it breathes becalmed
after being wounded
in its wondrous throat

in the cradle of my skull
it sings, it ignites
my tongue, my inner ear, the cavity of heart
shudders toward the outline
    new in soft intimate clicks and gutturals

of my soul the retina learns to expand
daily because by a thousand stories
I was scorched

a new skin.

I am changed forever. I want to say:
    forgive me
    forgive me
    forgive me

You whom I have wronged, please
take me

with you.

Epilogue

Few of us remember exactly what happened on the day that Archbishop Desmond Tutu placed the five thick volumes of the Truth Commission's final report in the hands of a grim-looking President Nelson Mandela. It was a fragile moment, but what brought the precariousness home were the two speeches. Our president and his prophet are famous for diverging from their written speeches. Both of them, that day, read their speeches sentence for sentence, comma by comma. As if each of them instinctively knew that feelings were so volatile that overstepping the invisible line would blow it all up.

It was only when the two of them were dancing after the formalities (Mandela like a boxer, upright, punching the air to joyous choral sound; Tutu like a township urchin, his head bowed, arms flailing around his knees) that we started to breathe more freely; not because the process was over, not because it had ended as dramatically as it had begun, but because of the remarkable consistency of the Truth and Reconciliation Commission. A huge pitchfork, it had repeatedly thrown the country into the air—and, without fail, the same people fell as corn and the same people were blown as chaff by the wind. And after three years one thought that perhaps people would act differently, that chaff had possibly become corn. But no—to our great relief, despite F. W. de Klerk and the ANC's last-minute attempts to influence the release of the report, the two moral giants of our country, as always before and despite immense pressure, were still, unequivocally, corn.

While this was happening, a journalist received a call on her cellular phone from an Afrikaner perpetrator. He had appeared before the

Amnesty Committee for a number of vicious killings. "I was able to take everything up until now," he breathed bitterly, "but the fact that F. W. de Klerk insisted that the pathetic half-page about him be cut from the report makes me want to vomit. Here we sit for months in the greatest shame, rejected and despised by everybody . . . and the bastard has problems with a few fucking lines—because he is scared of a Pinochet being done on him while he is gallivanting overseas with his Greek mistress."

We heard afterward that the report had already been printed when the TRC received the court order to temporarily remove its final finding on former President F. W. de Klerk. A TRC official rushed down to the printers where the first copies were being packed into a van to be transported to Pretoria. Half an hour later, people were sitting all around the printer's works, blotting out in black ink half of page 225 and a sentence on page 226—carefully placing pieces of paper on both sides of the censored pages to prevent smudging.

The report was to be handed to President Nelson Mandela on October 29, 1998—a date scheduled long in advance to suit the busy president and the commissioners compelled to fly in from abroad for the ceremony. The commission completed most of its work by the end of June 1998, leaving only the judicially trapped Amnesty Committee to slog it out with hundreds of cases still to be heard.

The journalists covering the Truth Commission were all invited to a special farewell cocktail party. Because the TRC ordinarily never paid for any alcohol, this function was a sensitive and rather unusual exception. We arrived from all over. Like the truth commissioners, all of us were battling to establish what was popularly called "life after the Truth Commission." On the escalator into the hotel in Pretoria my cellular phone rang. A colleague from the Johannesburg newsroom had just returned from an unscheduled and certainly unexpected media briefing by the ANC. A high-powered ANC delegation at the press conference announced that it was trying to obtain an interdict to prevent the TRC from making its report public on the following day. The reason given was that the party had tried in vain to secure a meeting with the commission to discuss the findings on the ANC contained in the final report. As he asks me to get comment from Tutu, I see John Allen unloading luggage from a car boot and Tutu hurriedly going up another escalator.

"Can you comment?" Allen shakes his head and replies, "Not until we've seen the actual papers." In the foyer journalists are already frantic in every corner, on the phone to their bosses. Facts begin to filter through. The ANC was sent a list of findings on the party that were to be published in the TRC's final report and was given a deadline to respond. It apparently failed to do so. In the end the organization contacted the TRC and asked for a postponement to another date. It was agreed upon, but the ANC again failed to meet the deadline. The ANC stated in its interdict application that the attitude of some of the commissioners was arrogant and confusing. As journalists speculated aloud that the offending commissioner had to be Dumisa Ntsebeza, we were informed that the interdict application would be heard later that evening or early the next morning. In a courtroom usually reserved for divorce hearings at the Cape Town High Court.

What to do now? The venue for the presentation ceremony is prepared, equipment installed, victims, choirs, and guests already ensconced in hotels nearby. Journalists are supposed to be in a secure "lockup" at six o'clock the next morning in order to wade through the final report and to start filing comprehensive news reports the moment Mandela has the report in hand, scheduled for around two o'clock in the afternoon. Some commissioners arrive and seem equally dumbfounded about the latest developments.

We all wait for Tutu. He is deeply upset, we hear, and was at one stage in tears in his room. The initially cozy atmosphere of the cocktail room suddenly becomes dingy and depressing. "They say we criminalized the struggle," says one of the commissioners. "Are they saying that to necklace someone was part of our struggle for freedom? Who is criminalizing the struggle here?" Another says: "It actually doesn't matter what happens now—the ANC has killed it for me—these past few days I felt something die in me."

Tutu and his wife, Leah, come in. He speaks, but like a depressed person. "This commission has always been more than just people," he says. We hear and we wait. Calls go to and fro during the night. At four o'clock the current affairs shows phone: where is the story? At six all of us stand bleary-eyed and desperately tired—still empty-handed—at the lockup venue. It is a beautiful spring Pretoria day, jacaranda blossoms fleecing the streets. The court will sit at 7:00 A.M.; then we hear it is to be at eight. Tutu, Yasmin Zooka, and Dumisa Ntsebeza eventually arrive after a night of negotiations with lawyers. We will fight them, they say. If the oppressed have become the oppressor I will fight them, says

Tutu. Words for which he will never be forgiven. But they look flabby, tired—worn out by politics within and outside the commission.

We stand around. Some listen to the radio. One station has opened its switchboard for people to give their opinion on the air about the ANC interdict. The lines are clogged—one black caller after another says: I vote ANC, but they have made a mistake, we demand to see that report. At the same time, in the radio studio, black academics claim to have no problems with the ANC's position. The ANC has fought a just war and therefore could not have committed gross human-rights violations.

We wait on. The TRC cannot give us the final report in case the court grants the interdict. If we wait any longer, there is scant chance that we will be able to read more than the three-page summary we are told exists. Depressed, we sit around in the heat and do listless Q and A interviews with radio stations. Alex Boraine arrives. While he is being interviewed, a journalist on a cellular phone shouts: "It's been turned down! The court has refused the interdict." "A victory!" laughs Boraine. We lurch into overdrive, but when the five bound volumes of the final report, nearly too heavy to carry, are put in front of us, most of the journalists there start to laugh. Two hours left before the ceremony. Read here, and then, overwhelmed by the paper mountain, grab something else—until most settled down to read what we could of the findings in the final volume.

Emerging eventually from the lockup to move to the hall where the actual ceremony will take place, we hear that Mandela was, apparently, not consulted by the ANC on its decision to apply for an interdict. In the hall, the commissioners sit dispersed in one area of the vast space. They are clearly divided, uncomfortable. Later we heard that the very last Truth Commission meeting was bitter and acrimonious—some felt that the ANC's simple wish to have discussions had to be accommodated, while others felt that this would set a precedent, forcing the commission to have discussions with every other party and individual. The unity of the TRC was gone—some commissioners were already in government posts, others building careers on their TRC experiences. Both Tutu and Boraine were teaching at American universities.

It was decided to put the issue to the vote. Fifteen commissioners were left after two had resigned from the TRC some time before. The outcome was seven for and seven against discussions with the ANC—forcing Tutu to cast the decisive vote. It must have been a difficult

meeting. Some commissioners who had supported the ANC throughout their lives voted against the party, opposed the very people they had
fought alongside, shoulder to shoulder. We heard that Tutu was in a total depression on the day of the ceremony and tried to secure a meeting
with Mandela. "He went in there small and timid and downcast—when
he came out, he was a different person—laughing, walking tall," someone told me. Of all of these events, we knew nothing. But we could
sense, strongly, division and an unraveling of power

The politicians start arriving—Ministers Dullah Omar, Kader Asmal,
Joe Modise, Jay Naidoo, and Alfred Nzo—also with an air of uncertainty. Thabo Mbeki should be here, but he sends word that his wife
will attend on his behalf. She doesn't turn up. Mandela and his companion Graca Machel sit stiff and stern on the stage. Tutu and Leah sit
holding hands and staring at the table in front of them.

Then the victims enter. A cross-section has been invited to attend the
ceremony: black and white, rich and poor, male and female—among them
there was no division. They have all come and take their seats between the
commissioners and staff on the one hand and the politicians on the other.

Everybody stands up.

Tutu speaks: "Many will be upset by this report. Some have sought
to discredit this preemptively. Even if they were to succeed, what
is that to the point? It won't change the fact that they killed Stanza
Bopape, they bombed Khotso House, they tortured their own people in their camps in Tanzania, in Angola, they necklaced people—that
is what the perpetrators told us. It is not an invention by the
commission."

Mandela speaks: "I therefore take this opportunity to say that I accept the report as it is, with all its imperfections, as an aid that the TRC
has given us to help reconcile and build our nation." Mandela is a solid
party man. For him to take a stance differing from his party must have
been exceptionally difficult.

It was a very significant moment: the politician and his prophet embracing each other while the clouds of political resentment toward the
whole Truth Commission process finally closed behind them in irritation and anger.

so much hurt for truth
so much destruction
so little left for survival

where does one go from here?
voices slung
in anger
over the solid cold length of our past
how long does it take
for a voice
to reach another
in this country held bleeding between us?

The TRC's final report consists of five substantial volumes. The first of these deals with methodology, concepts and principles, legal challenges, and the commission's mandate. This volume also contains the financial, managerial, and operational reports of the TRC. The second volume gives an overview of the history of the state's activities, inside and outside South Africa, and of the liberation movements. Both of these volumes contain a directory of organizational structures and the names of those who held office, as well as an account of the Special Investigations unit of the TRC. The third volume deals with the human rights abuses in every province and regional political conflict. Volume IV accounts for the special institutional hearings into the role of business, churches, media, prisons, and compulsory military service. The final volume contains a list of names of those classified by the TRC as victims of human rights violations, analyzes the context in which such abuses are made possible, and includes a reparation policy, findings, and recommendations to prevent future abuses. It includes, too, a minority position by Commissioner Wynand Malan.

The report reads fluently and is interspersed with fascinating bits of testimony. It is formidable in what it manages to pull together. For example, all the apartheid legislation ever passed—by name, intention, area, and date of passing—is catalogued. Apartheid's many commissions of inquiry are listed. Some of the contentious issues are well argued and full cognizance is taken of the most current thinking around each of them—when the report's findings differ from currently accepted norms, it provides ample examples of testimony to justify the TRC's interpretation. The report was also made available on the Internet, and most newspapers carried abridged versions of all five volumes in special inserts.

But the "taste" was gone. The ANC's request for an interdict dominated the news and overshadowed the content of the report. It was quite clear that the party could not have read the final report when it decided to go to court. The report does not treat the liberation movements in the same manner that it deals with the apartheid government. One particularly well-argued section, based on the latest human rights thinking, states that both the ANC and PAC fought a "just war," but the report makes a definite distinction between a "just war" and "unjust means."

The TRC gives its final media briefing in Pretoria on the following day. Again, only a few commissioners turn up. "We failed the victims," they say. "Our biggest regret is that we failed the victims—here we are, three years down the line, and the victims still don't have anything." They recommend that future commissions ensure that they have the powers and the means to implement some form of reparation swiftly and without government involvement or possible sanction to impede the process.

Tutu asks for his own peculiar forgiveness: "Sometimes one was arrogant in the attitude towards the NG Kerk [the predominantly Afrikaans Dutch Reformed Church]—why didn't you condemn them openly and then they would say no, we speak behind closed doors. And then Mandela comes to power, I am sitting at a meal with him and I tell him about some of the things I don't like and I say to myself: Aha, Tutu! Here you are sitting behind closed doors . . . and I would want to say I am sorry for having commended the gospel of grace many times ungraciously." He reiterates: "I did not struggle in order to remove one set of those who thought they were tin gods to replace it with others who are tempted to think that they are."

Responding to a question on the problems that the ANC has with the report, Alex Boraine says: "Very early on in our discussion with the ANC we referred to international instruments of human rights in which the ANC themselves had participated—they helped to write them—and they agreed with us that within a just cause parties should take moral and political responsibility for gross human rights violations."

I interview Yasmin Zooka afterward—of all the commissioners, she and Dumisa Ntsebeza (despite unsavory talk about the latter's sexual behavior) have gone furthest in formulating a fearless stance. She says: "It is critical to put people on the commission who are governed by their moral conscience and a fierce independence of spirit. I think that it is in the last six months of the commission that we have been called upon to go back to the inner core of ourselves."

Several reasons have been put forward for the ANC wanting the report changed. One was that they really did not read the whole report—even after its publication—and reacted prematurely. But their strong criticism in the court papers and at their media briefing revealed real irritation, anger, and a resentment that must have had its origins much further back.

Another reason often postulated is that the TRC report is particularly damning about the Inkatha Freedom Party. The ANC is regularly in negotiations with the IFP to form an alliance of some kind, and it would not do to have one's prospective new partner besmirched by its alliance with the bloody hands of the previous government. Such criticism by the TRC was, it is said, unwelcome at this stage. It is also suggested that the ANC does not wish to let go of the rhetoric of apartheid—they need the dictum that all that is white is bad and all that is black is good. A more intelligent reading is that Mbeki was in a bind: to realize his dream of African renaissance, he needs to instill pride in blacks as a black African people. He needs to isolate blacks from whites in an effort to restore pride and confidence in themselves as blacks— and as blacks in Africa. On the other hand, he needs to restore the moral fiber in a country wrecked by criminal violence. His efforts to do both sometimes lead to contradictions.

None of these reasons works completely for me. Part of me feels that this was, for once, an unpremeditated reaction by the ANC—an angry, clumsy cry from the heart. There was obviously division within the ANC itself on the report—yet no one could voice it. Only after reading an article by journalist Michael Ignatieff could I grasp the possible underpinning of the ANC's response to the final report of the TRC: "Aggressors have their own defence against truth, but so do victims. People who believe themselves to be victims of aggression have an understandable incapacity to believe that they also committed atrocities. Myths of innocence and victimhood are a powerful obstacle in the way of confronting unwelcome facts." According to Ignatieff, truth commissions can and do change the frame of public discourse and public memory. "But they cannot be judged a failure because they fail to change behaviour and institutions. This is not their function."

One wants to understand this country. One wants to live an informed life here to the benefit of all South Africans. So one continues to listen closely. But it is difficult to make sense of our daily diet of contradictory codes. How do you interpret them into your own small life? The first parliamentary debate on reconciliation, months before the release of the final report, was filled with these contradictions and raised many such questions.

ANC President Thabo Mbeki chose this occasion to deliver his famous "two nation" speech. South Africa, as he sees it, is a country of two nations—a rich white nation and a poor black nation. For him, reconciliation is not between perpetrators (of all colors) and victims (of all colors) but between the beneficiaries (the whites) and the exploited (the blacks). How does one, he asked, weld these two nations that coexist in South Africa into one? "The first requirement," he said, "is that we must accept that it will take time to create the material base for nation-building and reconciliation."

Mbeki then asked whether people in the country behave as if their main priority is reconciliation. "My own answer to this question," he says, "would be a definite no." The reasons he gave for his conclusion were that many white-owned corporations are still not registered for tax purposes; they demand more money, complain about affirmative action, did not apply for amnesty, and resist, generally, the transformation of our society. All of this keeps "us away from achieving this goal (of national unity and reconciliation) and is producing a rage among milllions of people."

Ostensibly, it seems true. There is a general rage among blacks (according to Mbeki) and whites (according to Constand Viljoen), and it does begin to seem as if people might tear at each other's throats. But for some reason it is not these two nations that are at each other, not white and black, but Zulus killing each other in the KwaZulu-Natal Midlands or "coloureds" on the Cape Flats; or criminals, of all colors, killing apparently innocent people, of all colors. Is it mere coincidence that the groups who were most reluctant to participate in the TRC process are experiencing intense internal turmoil?

Currently, South Africans seem to be further apart than before. But this is a sign of reconciliation, say the experts in reconciliation!

But the response of Afrikaner leadership to the TRC has a final consequence. I remember attending a speech by Tutu to the press gallery in Parliament, in which he pleaded with Afrikaners to accept and offer the hand of reconciliation. He was, quite literally, quivering, sweat running down his face, his mouth distorted, his eyes angry and full of tears. The journalists present, mainly English and black, watched impassively.

I grew heavy with desperation. What does one do with this anguish of Tutu? This need for an appropriate response from Afrikaners? How does one define "appropriate"? Despite everything, Afrikaner churches, Afrikaner businesspeople, and a group of Afrikaner journalists did ask for forgiveness—mainly Afrikaners appeared before the Amnesty Committee. What more does Tutu want? Is it something as insignificant as an apology from a senile P. W. Botha? Is it more? An Afrikaner Million March? Is it more than money? Is it to give the land back? What word, what embrace will unburden us all?

Shortly before the handing over of the final report, I interviewed the German government on its reparation of Holocaust victims. More than a hundred billion dollars was given to Jews outside of the country, making Germany a prominent redistributor of wealth. Its money changed Israel into an industrialized state. I also interviewed the head of the Jewish community in Berlin. "How can you possibly suggest that this is enough for what they did?" Dead weight in my arms. Why try?

But as the months after the final report go by, I slowly realize something else. The failure of Afrikaner leadership to admit that something is owed has not only left the Afrikaner community trapped in anger and guilt, but it has, somewhat deviously, deprived the oppressed from the opportunity to say, clearly: this is what you owe.

We of the white nation try to work out the conditions for our remaining here. We are here for better or worse. We want to be here, but we have to accept that we can no longer stay here on our terms. Therefore I prick up my ears and try to hear what the new conditions for my existence are. Taxes. Mbeki mentioned that—the transfer of resources. Is that it? Is he saying: your money will do, but please dear God, spare us your meager little white souls?

We are being told who we are, what we have done wrong, but not what we owe. Why this vagueness?

"I cannot believe my ears when I hear that whites still want to know what they should do," says clinical psychologist Nomfundo Walaza, interviewed before the Truth Commission debate in Parliament.

"I really don't know," I tell her. "The struggle taught me to listen. In the eighties I thought I could contribute my writing skills, my access to power and the media, for the struggle, but it was soon clear that was not what was needed—what the struggle wanted at that stage was my minibus and my fax machine. I don't want to fall into that trap again—assuming that I know what black people want. Do you only want us to ask forgiveness? Do people not prefer what Mbeki calls 'the transfer of resources'? And how should that happen? Do you want all the land back? What is it that people want?" I plead.

"The past is never repaid in one final grand gesture," says Walaza. "This is a country filled with poor people. Every white person can make a difference to the lives interacting with theirs."

Charity?

I thought, afterward: we are trapped. If there is no forum in which people can think what they want, and others worry about what they owe, then both are trapped in anger and guilt. By not determining precisely what is needed, the whites are exposed to constant reproach. If you give specifics they can be met. And should one not also be willing to be available as a punching bag? Can that be part of the deal? Just shut your big mouths when we blame you—for this, after all, is the only bloody thing we ask while rebuilding ourselves, by ourselves.

The two nations are both affected, one by injury, the other by guilt, and the first reaction is to withdraw from each other. People withdraw physically or mentally from each other after injury. A mother in front of the Truth Commission said that she did not want even to see a white person. People are leaving the country or pulling back into their own family or group spaces of language or history. Academics say that this withdrawal may last one second or for centuries, but that it is a necessary and healthy psychological response.

There were two Afrikaners on the Truth Commission: Wynand Malan, appointed to bring the moderate Afrikaners along with the process, and Chris de Jager, who belonged to the right wing. The latter resigned from the commission after it took former President P. W. Botha to court for refusing to appear before the TRC. Wynand Malan, who complained bitterly throughout the workings of the commission about the hostility of his colleagues, ultimately submitted a minority report in which he defends apartheid.

In a recent article in the English press a black academic asked: "We have Mandela pleading reconciliation, we have Tutu pleading reconciliation—where, oh where is the White Prince of Reconciliation?" Indeed: where is he? And, of course, it can be nothing else but a "he."

One of the stipulations in the act that established the TRC is that recommendations should be made to prevent future governments from re-

peating the mistakes of the past. But as time has passed, it has become
clear that old habits die hard. The most telling example relates to the
chemical and biological warfare secrets of the old regime. These are
locked away in a safe. And where are the keys? The new government holds
them. While the TRC was exposing the horror of the country's death row,
the population was baying for the reinstatement of the death penalty.
Switching on the radio in the middle of a bulletin, it is sometimes difficult
to make out whether the story of torture is relating a historical occurrence
or reporting current news. The accusations that Parliament was never told
about the apartheid regime's destabilizing incursion into Angola continue
to ring out. But the nonracial South African Defence Force of the first
democratically elected government of the majority moved into Lesotho,
and Parliament was only informed of this action two weeks after the
event. A BBC documentary about police brutality saw a country ambivalent in its rejection of such deeds on the one hand and its thirst to revenge
itself on the perpetrators of vicious crimes on the other.

When the first victim hearings started, no one thought it particularly
strange that blacks and whites were sharing the same stage—that a
mother whose child was killed by the apartheid state sat next to and
wept with a mother whose child was killed defending apartheid. It is
only since looking into the treatment of victims in Europe after the
Second World War that I have realized what a remarkable step South
Africa took in regarding both sets of victims the same way. By treating
pain and grief identically, the TRC exploded the myth that whites and
blacks experience grief in a lesser or greater manner. That grief and sorrow are ethnically exclusive.

> The defining parameter in our continuing struggle for
> national unity and reconciliation is the question of race.
> —Thabo Mbeki, during the second parliamentary debate
> on reconciliation.

Deputy President Thabo Mbeki led the South African Parliament in a
national debate on the final report of the Truth and Reconciliation
Commission. A debate was scheduled at the end of the final session of
the first democratically elected Parliament. The gallery was packed with
students, victims, academics, and representatives of NGOs. In the pres-

ident's lodge I recognized a small, mottled group—two truth commissioners and a few members of their staff. The powerful, flamboyant figures were gone. Those left behind were out of context, out of power, and out of favor. Somewhere on the gallery I recognized another familiar Truth Commission face or two. In the corridors of power the only voice which had challenged political power for two years had now grown unobtrusive. The TRC, once something to boast of or to go to court about, had become dispensable.

Mbeki was the first speaker. He referred to the 340-year-old almond and thornbush hedge planted by Dutch settler Jan van Riebeeck "to ensure the safety of the newly arrived white European settlers by keeping the menacing black African hordes of pagan primitives at bay."

It was deathly still in Parliament when Mbeki made these opening remarks on the Truth Commission's final report. The last time Mbeki had spoken about the TRC was when the ANC explained why it was taking the commission to court to prevent it from releasing its report in October 1998.

People were confused at the time. No one could quite understand what the problem of the ANC was with the TRC. After a media briefing the only accessible phrase was that the TRC's final report was "criminalizing the struggle." Yes, and that, everyone agreed, was bad.

Mbeki's opening speech put the TRC squarely within the context of race. "It is this reality of a state founded on conquest, that had to be retained by the same means with which it was conquered, which led, inevitably, to the gross violations of human rights which constitute the heart of the work of the Truth and Reconciliation Commission."

Egged on by expressions of shock and horror from the ANC parliamentary benches, Mbeki proceeded to build upon his argument with quotations by early European travelers in Africa about the blacks they had encountered. "In a word, a beastlike people"—Dutchman Cornelius van Purmderend in 1609. "They eat . . . as dogs do . . . they live . . . like animals"—Frenchman Pyrard de Laval in 1610. "It is a great pity that such creatures as they be should enjoy so sweet a country" —Englishman Ralph Standish in 1612. Mbeki then used this racial context to explain why the liberation struggle had been a just war and why it was, therefore, outrageous to accuse the ANC of gross violations of human rights.

Then it was time for the other parties. IFP leader Mangosuthu Buthelezi, of whom the TRC report said that it had erred by not proceeding to subpoena him to appear before it, was not in the house. The IFP member in his place implicated Commissioner Khoza Mgojo in gunrunning in KwaZulu-Natal and thus dismissed the report in its entirety. The PAC complained that the ANC's history had become the only liberation history.

Subsequent to the Truth Commission process, the debate among Afrikaner politicians has changed. They no longer bemoan the national budget's prioritizing of rural health and education for the poor. They no longer defend apartheid. Interestingly, the key words used by the white speakers on that day were fear, humiliation, and incomprehension.

Leader of the (New) National Party Marthinus van Schalkwyk began by defining the Afrikaner in a way that no Afrikaner politician had done before: "The biggest battle the Afrikaner fought was, however, not a physical one against somebody else," he said. "It was a psychological battle with itself. Apartheid was the Afrikaner's self-imposed concentration camp of the mind. The Afrikaner's biggest battle with itself was the referendum of 1992. That referendum showed that the vast majority of whites and Afrikaners chose a new dispensation and so freed themselves from the self-imposed psychological imprisonment."

The leader of the right wing party, Constand Viljoen, reiterated that no reconciliation could be expected if the Afrikaner was humiliated and portrayed as worse than he was. "We are a product of our own history; our aspirations have been real and legitimate. So also our obsession to be in control of our own destiny. I am not asking for sympathy. Nor am I suggesting that we don't have some liability for the past. We, all South Africans, must in honesty consider what went wrong, what went right. . . . We Afrikaners are indigenous. We are here to stay. We are not perfect, but we are genuine and honest."

The debate lasted for nearly seven hours and deep into the night. One of the last speakers was National Party member Jacko Maree. A member of the Justice Committee that drafted the TRC legislation, Maree has consistently attacked the TRC for being biased. His arguments over the years have become so familiar that few people were listening when he started to speak after the supper break.

But it was a different Maree who stood at the podium. Addressing himself to Mbeki, he said, "I have a prepared speech, Mr. Deputy President, but I want to speak to you about what is in my heart." Maree dropped all the formal phrasing he is usually so fond of—"point of order," "Madam Speaker," "the honorable member," and so on. "I first want to say I have the wrong credentials—I am middle-aged, I am white and I am Afrikaans and I am a man. . . . You made a speech that shocked me. . . . It gave me shivers down my spine . . . and I thought . . . for a terrible moment I saw in this chamber the ghost of Mugabe. . . ."

Finance Minister Trevor Manual: "Is the honorable member prepared to take a Breathalyzer test?"

Maree: "I feel perturbed, and I cannot understand why the Deputy President quotes what Jan van Riebeeck said about the Khoi and what white people said about blacks three hundred years ago—[it] is of no relevance today but to create tension. . . . Why, when we talk of reconciliation, do you pitch white against black? I think of my future. . . . I think of my children's future and I wonder about their future if the next president of the country makes these kinds of remarks, which I don't understand."

The noise in the chamber became overwhelming. Maree seemed to be swaying. Welfare Minister Geraldine Fraser Moleketi rose to ask the Speaker to stop him. He had a speech, she said, but he was seeing double and therefore could not read it. " This is no joke, honorable Speaker. You must help this man!"

Whether Maree was tipsy or not is beside the point. Mbeki's casting of the TRC in racial terms had obviously induced a feeling of helplessness in him. To Maree, Mbeki became a Mugabe, for white South Africans the epitome of black hatred toward whites, holding whites accountable for all that is wrong, yet himself accountable to no one. As always when South Africa's past is the theme, the debates in Parliament are highly charged with emotion, anger, bitterness, and accusations and low on positive reconciliatory comments.

Mbeki spelled out the problems the ANC had with the findings of the TRC report. The ANC felt that whatever went wrong happened within the context of a just war against a racist dispensation and should be treated as such. On the basis of the Geneva conventions and protocols, the ANC rejected the finding of the TRC that it was guilty of gross violations of human rights. But from reading Volume I, Chapter Four of the TRC report on its mandate, it is clear that the ANC has no proper understanding of the Geneva conventions and protocols. Or that it deliberately forwarded a very unnuanced formulation for reasons only known to itself.

Current human rights approaches are indeed arguing to enlarge the protected group and to decrease those who have a right to kill. This means that all decision-making should always favor the defenseless. In order to achieve this, the Geneva convention makes three classifications. Combatant against combatant, combatant against "protected persons" (meaning prisoners of war, ex-soldiers, soldiers off duty, defectors, wounded soldiers, etc.), and combatant against civilians (meaning all those who are not combatants).

A combatant killing another combatant does not constitute a gross human rights violation. A combatant killing a civilian is a gross human rights violation. It is therefore a grave mistake to call on the Geneva convention to justify the killing of civilians. Mbeki has reasoned that "One of the central matters at issue was and remains the erroneous determination of various actions of our liberation movement as gross human rights violations, including the general implication that any and all military activity which results in the loss of civilian lives constitutes a gross violation of human rights." This is precisely what the Geneva convention stipulates (convention 4, article 47; protocol 1, articles 48–50). But it goes further by stating that the "wounded, sick and shipwrecked members of armed forces and civilians, prisoners of war; civilians including those interred and those on the territory of the enemy . . . including those who have laid down arms and those placed outside combat by sickness, wounds or detention . . . should be treated humanely, may not be murdered, mutilated, tortured or receive cruel treatment, humiliated with degrading treatment or be executed without previous judgement."

These phrases, formulated in part by the ANC itself, thus condemn the ANC for the killing of civilians *and* for the torture in its camps, the killing of informers, and necklacing. "But who is talking about gross human rights violations in Kosovo where civilians are daily being bombed?" ask some ANC members in defense. But that is hardly the point. If the ANC disagrees with the Geneva protocols regarding protected persons and civilians, then it should say so.

The ANC's unnuanced response to the final report and the fact that most of the political parties rejected the TRC was a severe blow to the process. Consequently there is no debate—not on accountability, not on how to prevent future abuses, not on how much of the past is already reoccurring in the present, not on collective guilt. What is worse is the absence of a debate on compensation, on the participation of the guilty, on the relationship between the beneficiaries and the exploited.

Mbeki initially said that the white rich nation should make up to the black poor one, but during the TRC debate he stressed the contrary—people did not go into the liberation struggle for money, and they were not expecting compensation. A closer reading seems to show that Mbeki does not want those identified by the TRC as victims (and all victims were treated equally and came from all groups and were violated by all groups) to expect or receive compensation. He would prefer that all blacks, because they are the black, poor nation, should receive from the white, rich nation. The difference therefore does not lie in the ability to exercise moral choices in difficult circumstances, or to reward those who upheld human rights, or to sympathize with all of those whose rights were violated. The difference between the past and the present appears, rather, to lie solely in skin color.

With the main TRC infrastructure gone, the Amnesty Committee was struggling to stay afloat on a choppy political sea. In its own clumsy way it tried to manipulate the public effects of its rulings. First it released a statement saying that the killers of Steve Biko were refused amnesty. On its heels followed a statement to say that twenty-seven high profile ANC activists (among them Thabo Mbeki, Joe Modise, Mac Maharaj, and others) were also refused amnesty. In one of the later paragraphs the committee says it could not give amnesty because no violation had taken place. I phoned them—this media statement was wrong. They were not refusing amnesty; the official decision said the committee could not give it because according to the applications the ANC did nothing wrong. "So what's the difference?" I am asked. "The difference is that you make it sound as if the Amnesty Committee is consistent —it refuses amnesty to both ANC and former regime perpetrators." Then amnesty was given to those who killed the American exchange student, Amy Biehl.

Two weeks after this news the Amnesty Committee announced that it had refused amnesty to seventy-nine other ANC activists—among them the rest of the ministers, premiers, and ANC leadership. The next day saw publication of the statement that the committee had also refused amnesty to the killers of Chris Hani—Clive Derby Lewis and Janus Waluz.

I remember how the ANC brought in their boxes of amnesty applications on the deadline day. They were carried on shoulders along Adderley Street, accompanied by photographers and roving television cameras. It was hailed as an example of transparency and accountability. Now we learn there was nothing on those application forms. They had not been completed. We also know that the Amnesty Committee actually granted amnesty that was subsequently overturned in court.

"We have been cheated and made ridiculous," one of the foot soldiers hissed through his teeth at the hearing. "This is a farce—those with the political power and access to Bizos, they walk free. We sit because we are nothing. Those who killed Biko, those who killed Hani—they are not ordinary murderers, they killed within a political context. But it suits those in power to take away our political context to project us as ordinary murderous criminals."

"The TRC process was a deal between the Africans and the Afrikaners," someone in the president's office sighed, "but it was hijacked by too many white legal liberals and turned into an arrogantly moral, self-righteous spectacle."

In the meantime a National Prosecutor has been appointed, who in turn has put together a special task force to look into prosecuting those who either did not apply for amnesty or had their amnesty applications refused. Bulelani Ncuka has promised that he will sue perpetrators if there is sufficient evidence and if it was in the interest of national reconciliation to do so.

"How successful was the Truth and Reconciliation Commission?" is the question most often asked. The answer is both complex and simple.

If one regards the TRC as a mere vehicle to grant amnesty, it succeeded reasonably. A lot of amnesty applications were dealt with, albeit unfairly on occasion. It has also left the country with a large number of white generals and IFP warlords, as well as some ANC politicians, without amnesty. This means that the state and the ANC are vulnerable to claims from victims. A government that must deal with the enormous challenges of development simply does not have the resources to pay out endless claims or to fund costly legal battles launched by victims against former perpetrators. General amnesty is not an option, promised both Mandela and Mbeki. But what else? Mbeki and former Justice Minister Dullah Omar have both said that it is an oversight in the Truth and Reconciliation Act that individuals can obtain amnesty that indemnifies them from claims, while the state has to take responsibility for the apartheid perpetrators as well as for the liberation movements. Government is currently exploring ways to indemnify the state without undermining the TRC process, it is said. Whether or not this is possible, and whether amnesty to organizations is not general amnesty, South Africans will have to wait to see.

Most people, however, seem to be so thoroughly sick and tired of the TRC process that they simply would not care if a general amnesty were declared. "I don't care," a police brigadier confessed to me, "as long as we can get this over and done with."

If the TRC is regarded as an effort to create a forum for victims to bring some form of balance to the political ideal of amnesty, then the commission succeeded in a most remarkable way. The experiences of victims did indeed become part of the national psyche and part of our country's acknowledged history for the very first time. But, in terms of repairing and healing the trauma of the victims, the TRC itself was the first to declare that this was, singularly, its biggest failure.

If the TRC is seen as a body to establish the truth, it also succeeded fairly well in establishing factual truth, in determining "what happened." It was far less successful in convincing South Africans of the moral truth, in answering the question "Who was responsible?"

If the idea of the TRC process in South Africa was to prevent violations of human rights from ever happening again, the commission has failed. There is no debate or discussion on its recommendations whatsoever, and the nation is so besieged by crime that it is desperately seeking ways to punish the criminals.

The biggest question, however, is whether or not the TRC process achieved reconciliation. Few people believe that it has. Surveys have found that people are further apart than before. It has also become fashionable among some academics to trash the TRC—seldom pointing out that the first casualty of conflict is identity and that redefining identity is a fundamental step toward reconciliation. Blacks are redefining themselves with the African renaissance; Afrikaners are redefining themselves with the Anglo-Boer War. A group that neglects this essential stage is likely to become frozen in a permanent quest for identity that often expresses itself in rigid and aggressive forms of ethnicism or nationalism.

But what is indeed not visible in South Africa is reconciliation as a mysterious Judaeo-Christian process. What we do see daily is reconciliation as one of the most basic skills applied in order to survive conflict. Scientists have found that monkeys, apes, and humans all engage in reconciliation behavior, which tends to indicate that reconciliation did not originate in the minds of humans and it cannot, therefore, be appropriated by an ideology or a religion. The essence of reconciliation is survival. Its key is negotiation. Survival forms part of our genetic make-up and the ability to reconcile via negotiation is the reason why some of us are still around.

Peculiarly, the word "reconciliation" still resounds in the land. It carries within it the full variety of survival strategies—among them choice, flight, amnesia, rituals, clemency, debate, negotiation, brinkmanship, and national consensus. The goal is not to avoid pain or reality, but to deal with the never-ending quest of self-definition and negotiation required to transform differences into assets. Reconciliation is not only a process. It is a cycle that will be repeated many times.

A multitude of ordinary lives in our land continually find new pathways toward each other amid the fragility of South Africa's new realities. In many ways, we are remarkably well reconciled. All the political parties that participated in the June 1999 election have, at some stage, rejected the TRC or its final report. Politicians of every ilk have, nonetheless, been fundamentally challenged by these ordinary lives. The reconciled diversity of our land forced each politician in search of votes—particularly those who assumed a mantle of leadership—to traverse our roads, to eat our foods, embrace all our children, and suddenly, almost, to speak all our languages.

That, in this country, is surely a wondrous thing?

Antjie Krog
Cape Town
June 1999

Acknowledgments

A book like this has to start somewhere. It started when Professor André du Toit discussed overseas truth commissions with me in the offices of *Die Suid-Afrikaan* way back in 1993. And it started when Pippa Green asked me to become part of her political reporting team and later insisted that I head the SABC Radio team covering the Truth Commission. Thank you both for a loyalty and a friendship that I don't deserve. Thanks also to Franz Kruger and Barney Mthombothi, my SABC bosses.

I survived the coverage only thanks to my unique colleagues: Kenneth Makatees, Angie Kapelianis, Dumisane Shange, Zola Ntutu, Tapelo Mokushane, Andries Sathekge, and the unshakeable Darren Taylor. I am grateful to them, and to Ross Colvin (for checking the facts), John Yeld, Roger Friedman, Stephen Laufer (whose phrasing I have used in places), and Adri Kotze. Prabhakara fed us all with oatmeal cookies, and François du Toit of the SABC Archives patiently found the material I was looking for.

Thank you to Anton Harber, then of the *Mail & Guardian*, who was the first editor to ask me to write something in English, and to Shaun de Waal for editing my work for the paper.

I am deeply thankful to the staff of the Truth Commission for always being so helpful and accessible, and especially to John Allen. I would like to send a whole lot of government liaison officers to him for a crash course. Thank you also, Allan Colam and Merwede van der Merwe, who helped me mentally and physically through a breakdown.

Thanks to my children, Andries, Susan, Philip, and Willem, who installed me into Windows with infinite patience, never despaired when

I yelled, "Where is that piece I wrote last night?" lied relentlessly on the phone about my whereabouts, took endless messages, and cooked their own suppers. My special thanks to Andries, who spent hours on the translations.

How do I thank a publisher who refused to take no for an answer when I said, "No, I don't want to write a book about the Truth Commission"; stuck with me when I said, "No, I can't write a book," and also, "I dare not write a book"; and was still there when I came round to saying, "I have to write a book, otherwise I'll go crazy." Stephen Johnson of Random House had me signing my first contract as thick as a Bible, and not only fussed about the book like a man with a vision, but provided a cheerful thread through my bouts of depression and self-doubt.

Without Ivan Vladislavi, this would be half the book it is. His care and dedication, help with finding a poetic style, editing of text and testimonies, and quiet encouragement make him a crucial part of this product.

But the man behind this book is my husband, John. When I told him I simply had to do it, no matter the cost or the consequences, he gave a double gulp and rolled up his sleeves. Throughout the writing, he kept everything together with love, grace, and an angry brow. He is the man of my heart.

I have told many lies in this book about the truth. I have exploited many lives and many texts—not least those of my mother and my family on the farm. I hope you will all understand.

Antjie
Cape Town, February 1998

Glossary

African National Congress (ANC)—governing party; founded in 1912 as a liberation movement; banned in 1960 by the apartheid government

Afrikaanse Handelsinstituut—Afrikaans Institute of Commerce

Afrikaner Weerstandsbeweging (AWB)—Afrikaner Resistance Movement; far-right paramilitary organization working toward an Afrikaner state

Amandla—Power! (populist slogan)

ANC—see African National Congress

Antjie Somers—androgynous figure in Afrikaans folklore who catches naughty children

APLA—Azanian People's Liberation Army; former armed wing of the PAC

askari—former guerrilla recruited by the security forces

AWB—see Afrikaner Weerstandsbeweging

bakkie—pickup truck

bioscope—cinema

Black Consciousness—ideology of black self-reliance and liberation from white values, developed mainly in the 1970s

Black Sash—women's organization engaging in protests and vigils against apartheid

Blood River—battle between Voortrekkers and Zulus in 1838, later commemorated on the Day of the Vow (now Reconciliation Day)

boere, boers—Afrikaners; sometimes used disparagingly

boeremusiek—traditional, country-style dance music

boere-orkes—a band that plays *boeremusiek,* usually for dancing

boerewors—sausage

boesmans—bushmen

borselkop—brush cut

braai, braaivleis—barbecue

Broederbond—secret society promoting Afrikaner control of all areas of society

bush war—an undeclared war between members of state security structures and guerrilla opposition forces that took place in rural African areas, especially in Zimbabwe, Angola, and Mozambique

bywoner—tenant farmer; usually a poor white farmer

Casspir—police riot-control and combat vehicle

Codesa—Convention for a Democratic South Africa; convention that led to the first democratic elections in 1994

comrade—militant ANC supporter, usually young and male

Conservative Party (CP)—right-wing white political party; split from the NP in 1982

CP—see Conservative Party

Currin Commission—Government commission under human rights lawyer Brian Currin, set up after the elections but before the Truth Commission to grant indemnity to political prisoners

daggazolletjies—marijuana cigarettes

Democratic Party (DP)—liberal, predominantly white and English-speaking political party

dominee—religious minister

dongas—dry gullies

Dorkay House—center for music and drama in Johannesburg, active in the 1950s and 1960s

DP—see Democratic Party

Freedom Front (FF)—right-wing party campaigning for an Afrikaner homeland

gramadoelas—the back of beyond, the sticks

haelgeweer—shotgun

Harms Commission—judicial commission of inquiry presided over by Judge Louis Harms into the alleged existence of state-sanctioned death squads

Hippo—armored police personnel carrier
Hoër—high school

IFP—see Inkatha Freedom Party
impimpi—informer, spy
Inkatha Freedom Party (IFP)—party that grew out of the Zulu national movement founded by Buthelezi in the early 1970s; mainly black, based in Natal

jong—man
Julle Kapenaars—You people from the Cape

kaffer—a derogatory word for a black person
kanferfoelie—honeysuckle
keelvelle—dewlaps
Khotso House—Johannesburg headquarters of the South African Council of Churches, destroyed by a bomb in 1988
kitskonstabel—"instant constable," a police recruit given minimal training
Koevoet—notoriously brutal police unit active against SWAPO guerrillas in Namibia
Koki—felt-tip pen
kopdoek—headscarf
kuier—visit
kwela—style of pennywhistle music developed in the 1950s

Laerskool—primary school
Lekker—Nice

manne—men, "the guys"
marabaraba—board game, similar to checkers
maroela—marula tree
mispel—meddler
MK—abbreviation for Umkhonto we Sizwe, the former military wing of the ANC
moerse—"hell of a," almighty
mos—indeed; after all
muggies—gnats
muti—medicine, especially regarded as having magical properties

National Party (NP)—former governing party; predominantly Afrikaner party responsible for implementing apartheid

necklace—car tire filled with gasoline used to burn political opponents, especially those regarded as collaborators or informers

NG Kerk—Nederduits Gereformeerde Kerk; Dutch Reformed Church, the largest and most powerful Afrikaans church

Nkosi Sikelel' iAfrika—"God Bless Africa"; ANC anthem, now the national anthem

NP—see National Party

OK—OK Bazaars supermarket

Oom—Uncle; also used of any older man, not necessarily a relative

op-en-wakker—wide-awake, on the ball

Operation Vula—ANC operation to set up underground structures inside South Africa as a backup in case negotiations failed

ossewa—ox wagon

Ossewabrandwag—Afrikaner organization formed in 1939, opposed to the war against Germany

ouderlingsbank—pew in the Dutch Reformed Church for the elders of the congregation

oupa-grootjie—great-grandfather

Pan-Africanist Congress (PAC)—black political party that broke away from the ANC in 1959

pappot—porridge pot

patats—sweet potatoes

P.E.—Port Elizabeth

plotte—smallholdings

Poqo—underground black nationalist movement generally associated with the Pan-Africanist Congress; the first black political movement in South Africa to adopt a strategy that explicitly involved violence

potjie—little pot

Rapportryer—association of Afrikaner male business and cultural leaders

Ruiterwag—junior section of the Broederbond

SABC—South African Broadcasting Corporation

SACP—South African Communist Party

SADF—South African Defense Force

SASO—South African Students' Organization; Black Consciousness students' movement of the 1970s

SDUs—see self-defense units

self-defense units—armed units set up in the early 1990s by the ANC to protect neighborhoods; some of them turned against the ANC and their own communities

sisi—sister

sjambok—a whip made of cured rawhide or rubber, commonly issued to South African police during incidents of political unrest

skattige ogies—sweet little eyes

skoentjies—little shoes

skoonma—mother-in-law

snorretjies—little mustaches

Sowaar—Really; it's true!

spoggerig—boastful

State Security Council—body that advised the apartheid government on security policy

stront—a bad sort, a shit

sus en so—like this or that; one way or the other

SWAPO—South West African People's Organization

tackies—sneakers

tannies—aunties

tarentaal—guinea fowl

tjoepstil—completely quiet

toyi-toyi—dance performed during protest marches, etc.

ubuntu—philosophy of humanism, emphasizing the link between the individual and the collective

UDF—United Democratic Front, alliance of antiapartheid organizations founded in 1983

Umkhonto we Sizwe—"Spear of the Nation," military wing of the ANC

vastrap—a fast and lively country dance

Vat-hom-Dawie—"Tackle-him-Dawie," nickname of politician Dawie de Villiers, a former Springbok rugby player

Vlakplaas—farm near Pretoria used as a base for police hit squads

volk—the Afrikaner people, nation

Voortrekkers—first Boers to move into the interior of South Africa in

the 1830s; also the name of an Afrikaner youth movement similar to the
Boy Scouts

windpomp—windmill for pumping water

witdoeke—vigilante faction who wore white scarves as a mark of
identification

Wit Wolwe—"White Wolves," ultraterrorist group

World Trade Centre—Kempton Park venue of negotiations toward a
democratic order

Cast of Characters

Truth and Reconciliation Commission

Archbishop Desmond Tutu, Chair Anglican archbishop of Cape Town from 1986 to 1996, Tutu served as general secretary of the South African Council of Churches and became a major figure in the anti-apartheid movement inside and outside South Africa, especially from 1978 onward, receiving the Nobel Peace Prize in 1984.

Alex Boraine, Deputy Chair Former Methodist minister and elected member of Parliament for the opposition Progressive Federal Party in 1974, he remained in Parliament until 1986, when he resigned and formed the Institute for a Democratic Alternative for South Africa, together with Van Zyl Slabbert.

Mary Burton Active in the Black Sash from 1965, Burton was elected its national president in 1986.

Bongani Finca Previous president of the Eastern Cape Provincial Council of Churches.

Chris de Jager A senior advocate, De Jager is a former member of Parliament for the Conservative Party and as an independent.

Sisi Khampepe An attorney and member of the Black Lawyers Association.

Richard Lyster Human rights lawyer who served as director of the Legal Resources Centre in Durban.

Wynand Malan National Party member of Parliament from 1977 to 1987, when he became leader of the National Democratic Movement, meeting the ANC in exile on at least two occasions. He briefly served as coleader of the Democratic Party in 1989 and after his resignation, he became involved in business activities.

Khoza Mgojo An activist in the church, Mgojo served as president (presiding bishop) of the Methodist Church of Southern Africa for two terms—1982–83 and 1987–88.

Hlengiwe Mkhize Chairperson of the Reparation and Rehabilitation Committee of the TRC, Mkhize, a clinical psychologist, is a former director of mental health and substance abuse in the Department of Health.

Dumisa Ntsebeza A human rights lawyer, Ntsebeza was charged with furthering the aims of communism in 1976 and sentenced to four years in prison, followed by various banishment orders. Active in the Black Lawyers Association. He presently has a legal practice in Cape Town.

Wendy Orr District surgeon in 1985 who made an urgent appeal to the Supreme Court to stop police ill-treatment and torture of hundreds of detainees under her care at Port Elizabeth prisons. Deputy registrar, student affairs, at the University of Cape Town until her appointment to the TRC.

Denzil Potgieter An attorney who handled a number of defense cases for political defendants both in South Africa and Namibia, Potgieter became an advocate at the Cape bar in 1985 and was appointed senior counsel in 1996. Former vice president of the National Association of Democratic Lawyers, he has served as chair of the TRC's portfolio committee on media and communications.

Mapule Ramashala Now vice-chancellor of the University of Durban-Westville, Ramashala has a master's degree in clinical psychology. She served as chairperson of the TRC Research and Information Management Committee and as a member of the Reparation and Rehabilitation Committee.

Fazel Randera A medical practitioner in Johannesburg, Randera served as deputy chairperson of the Human Rights Violations Committee.

Yasmin Sooka An attorney and president of the World Conference on Religion and Peace.

Glenda Wildschut A psychiatric nurse, Wildschut was national coordinator of the trauma interest group of the South African Health and Social Services and chairperson of the Trauma Centre for Victims of Violence and Torture. She served as a member of the Reparation and Rehabilitation Committee of the TRC.

Amnesty Committee

Hassen Mall, Andrew Wilson, and Bernard Ngoepe are all judges of the Supreme Court.

Other Characters

Asmal, Kader While in exile, a founder of the British and Irish antiapartheid movement and for many years a law professor at Trinity College, Ireland. Asmal joined the ANC in 1965. Presently minister of water affairs.

Benzien, Jeffrey Notorious for his torture and interrogation techniques, Benzien was a police captain who was promoted from the Murder and Robbery section to the security police. During his amnesty application, he detailed the torture and interrogation techniques used, and demonstrated to the commission how the "wet bag" method was applied.

Biko, Steve Bantu Leader of the Black Consciousness movement and the South African Students' Organization in the late 1960s and 1970s, Biko died on September 12, 1977, while in police custody in Pretoria.

Botha, Pik A career diplomat from 1953 to 1970 and later National Party minister of foreign affairs from 1977 to 1994, Botha has retired from politics.

Botha, P. W. National Party member of Parliament from 1948 to 1989, Botha served as minister of defense from 1966 to 1980, as prime minister from 1978 to 1984, and as state president from 1984 to 1989, when he suffered a stroke and was nudged from power by F. W. de Klerk.

Buthelezi, Mangosuthu Gatsha Minister of home affairs in the Government of National Unity since 1994, Buthelezi served as chief minister of the KwaZulu Bantustan from 1976 to 1994. He founded the largely Zulu-based conservative Inkatha movement (now the Inkatha Freedom Party) in 1975, and is still its leader.

Cachalia, Azhar A lawyer by profession and presently secretary for safety and security, Cachalia served as a senior official in the United Democratic Front from 1983 to 1991. In the 1980s, he was detained and restricted under state-of-emergency regulations.

Coetzee, Dirk Following Almond Nofomela's affidavit detailing Coetzee's role in the murder of human rights lawyer Griffiths Mxenge, Coetzee left South Africa in 1989 to meet with the ANC in London, where he confessed to participating in police hit squad activities. He later joined the movement.

Cradock Four Consisted of Mathew Goniwe, rural organizer of the United Democratic Front; Sparrow Mkhonto, chairperson of the Cradock Residents Association; Fort Calata, UDF Eastern Cape executive member; and Secelo Mhlawuli, a UDF activist, who disappeared on June 27, 1985, while traveling from Port Elizabeth to Cradock. Their bodies were subsequently discovered in overgrown sand dunes near Port Elizabeth.

De Klerk, F. W. The last white state president, De Klerk joined Parliament in 1972 and served as minister in various portfolios until taking over the leadership of the National Party in 1989, following P. W. Botha's stroke. He became state president later that year and is known for his dramatic announcement on February 2, 1990, that the ANC and other parties were unbanned and that Nelson Mandela would be released from prison. He left active politics in 1997.

De Kock, Eugene Presently serving two life terms plus 212 years in prison on eighty-nine counts, including six of murder. Colonel Eugene de Kock served in the notorious Koevoet unit in Namibia before taking over as commander of the C-10 unit based at Vlakplaas near Pretoria, where many hit squad activities were planned and implemented.

De Lange, Johnny Presently chair of the parliamentary Justice Portfolio Committee, De Lange is a lawyer who was active in the National Association of Democratic Lawyers in the 1980s and served as treasurer of the Western Cape Region of the United Democratic Front in 1988. In the early 1990s, he participated in the ANC negotiating team at the constitutional talks for a new South Africa and became a member of Parliament in 1994.

De la Rey, Koos A general in the Anglo-Boer War of 1899–02, De la Rey opposed the 1914 campaign to invade German South West Africa. He was shot and killed by troops under orders to intercept a criminal gang, and his death led to an escalation of a Boer rebellion against the Union government.

Dingane Zulu king who succeeded Shaka, Dingane ruled from 1829 to 1840. In 1838, following the signing of a treaty granting land to the Boers, Boer leader Piet Retief and his party were murdered by Dingane's followers.

Fischer, Bram Afrikaner lawyer and communist who defended Nelson Mandela in the Rivonia Trial in 1963, Fischer was himself sentenced to life imprisonment in 1966 for contravening the Suppression of Communism Act. He died in 1975.

Goosen, Glen Director of the investigative unit of the Truth and

Reconciliation Commission, Goosen played a key role in investigating the Motherwell car bomb incident, in which security police killed one of their own members who they believed might reveal information regarding hit squads.

Guguletu Seven Seven young men, suspected of being members of Umkhontu we Sizwe (MK), who in 1976 were killed in the Cape Town township of Guguletu by apartheid security operatives linked to Vlakplaas.

Hani, Chris Hani served as political commissar and deputy commander of Umkhonto we Sizwe from 1982 to 1987, when he was appointed its chief of staff. He became secretary-general of the South African Communist Party in 1992, relinquishing all other posts. He was assassinated in 1993.

Harrington, William Refused amnesty, Harrington was a junior constable who became involved in destabilizing communities—and killing ANC members—in the Pietermaritzburg area.

Kasrils, Ronnie Presently deputy minister of defense, Kasrils joined MK in 1961 and later worked abroad for the ANC in various capacities, including as head of military intelligence. A member of the central committee of the South African Communist Party since 1979.

Lapsley, Michael Anglican priest and ANC member, Lapsley was the victim of a 1990 parcel bomb that resulted in the loss of his hands and an eye.

Madikizela-Mandela, Winnie Ex-wife of President Nelson Mandela and now president of the ANC Women's League and member of Parliament, Madikizela-Mandela was banned continuously from 1962 to 1975, following which she was banished to the town of Brandfort in the Orange Free State. A symbol of resistance to the apartheid state, she later became a controversial figure when her Mandela United Football Club bodyguard brutalized her neighborhood in Soweto and when she was linked to the kidnapping of fourteen-year-old Stompei Seipei, who was murdered in 1989. From 1994 to 1995, she served as deputy minister of arts, culture, science, and technology.

Maharaj, Mac Presently minister of transport, Maharaj served as a senior ANC official in Lusaka from 1977 to 1987, when he returned to work underground in South Africa. In 1990, he was arrested on charges of terrorism associated with his involvement with Operation Vula, an ANC covert operation. Charges were dropped in 1991.

Mamasela, Joe A member of the Vlakplaas unit, Mamasela was implicated in a number of killings associated with the hit squads.

Mandela, Nelson Rolihlahla State president of South Africa since 1994, Mandela was active in the leadership of the ANC Youth

League, in the ANC, and in the 1952 Defiance Campaign. He was commander in chief of Umkhonto we Sizwe in 1961. He was imprisoned in 1962 on charges of illegally leaving South Africa when he went to Algeria for military training. During his imprisonment, he was charged with sabotage and conspiracy and was sentenced to life imprisonment on Robben Island. Released in 1990, he was elected ANC president in July 1991.

Maree, Jacko National Party member of Parliament from KwaZulu-Natal, Maree has consistently voiced his opposition to many aspects of the Truth and Reconciliation Commission.

Mbeki, Thabo Presently deputy president of South Africa, Mbeki left the country in 1962 and completed a master's degree in economics at Sussex University. Active first in student circles and later in the ANC's London office, Mbeki moved to Lusaka in 1970, where he held various ANC posts, including that of ANC director of information. He took over as head of the ANC's Department of International Affairs in 1989. In 1993 he became national chairman of the ANC and was elected its president in 1997, following the retirement of Nelson Mandela.

Modise, Joe Minister of defense since 1994, Modise served as commander of Umkhonto we Sizwe from 1965 until it was disbanded in the 1990s.

Morobe, Murphy Morobe played a key political role in student politics in 1976, which led to his conviction for conspiracy and imprisonment on Robben Island from 1979 to 1982. An office-holder of the United Democratic Front in the 1980s, he was frequently detained.

Moshoeshoe Founder and first paramount chief of the Basothos from 1823 to 1870, Moshoeshoe managed to defend from white encroachment the region that would eventually become the independent state of Lesotho.

Mxenge, Griffiths Human rights lawyer and underground ANC activist who spent two years on Robben Island. Mxenge was assassinated on November 19, 1981, by Vlakplaas operatives.

Nofomela, Almond Former Vlakplaas security policeman under the command of Dirk Coetzee who admitted in an affidavit from death row in the Pretoria Central Prison his role in a police death squad that murdered Griffiths Mxenge; the first member of Vlakplaas to publicly reveal the existence of such a squad.

Omar, Dullah A human rights lawyer since 1960 who acted frequently for political prisoners, especially those on Robben Island. Omar served as chairman of the Western Cape United Democratic Front from 1987 to 1989. Presently minister of justice.

Pebco Three Qaqawuli Godolozi, president of the Port Elizabeth Black Civic Organization; Sipho Hashe, secretary-general of PEBCO; and Champion Galela, PEBCO's organizing secretary, who disappeared during the night of May 8, 1985, after they had traveled to Port Elizabeth airport to meet someone. Their bodies were never recovered.

Retief, Piet Voortrekker leader who, on the instigation of Dingane, the Zulu king, was murdered in 1838 together with his followers.

Savimbi, Jonas Founder and leader of the National Union for the Total Independence of Angola (UNITA).

Sekonyela A powerful Tlokwa chief who was defeated by Moshoeshoe in October 1853.

Sisulu, Albertina An ANC activist since 1948 and Transvaal president of the United Democratic Front from 1983, Sisulu was charged with high treason in 1985, but charges were later dropped. Wife of well-known ANC leader Walter Sisulu, she worked as a nurse for Dr. Abubaker Asvat, who was murdered in 1989 after witnessing the condition of Stompie Siepei. She is presently a member of Parliament.

Slabbert, Frederik Van Zyl A former sociology professor, Slabbert was leader of the opposition Progressive Federal Party from 1977 to 1986, when he resigned to form the Institute for a Democratic Alternative for South Africa. He is presently involved in business and academia.

Slovo, Joe An active South African Communist Party member from the 1940s, lawyer Joe Slovo joined Umkhonto we Sizwe in 1960, going into exile in 1963. He worked for the ANC and the SACP abroad in various capacities, and was general secretary of the SACP from 1986 to 1991. Following the 1994 elections, he was appointed minister of housing. He died in 1995 from bone cancer.

Smuts, Dene Previously editor of *Fairlady* magazine, Smuts became a Democratic Party member of Parliament in 1989.

Suzman, Helen Opposition member of Parliament for the Houghton constituency from 1952 to 1989, Suzman represented the Progressive Federal Party for thirty of those years, thirteen of them as its lone voice in Parliament.

Tambo, Oliver A lawyer and founding member of the ANC Youth League in 1944, Tambo served as deputy president general of the organization from 1959, leaving South Africa in 1960 to establish the ANC's mission abroad. He subsequently led the external mission until his return to South Africa in December 1990. He died in 1993.

Terre'Blanche, Eugene Leader of the far-right, nationalist Afrikaner Weerstandsbeweging (AWB), which he formed in 1973. Terre'Blanche's activism increased in the 1990s, culminating in the 1993 storming of the World Trade Centre in Kempton Park, venue of the national negotiations for a new Constitution. Since then his support has dwindled significantly.

Van der Merwe, H. W. Founder and director of the Centre for Intergroup Studies (now Centre for Conflict Resolution) in 1968 and one of the first to become involved in research and the practice of conflict resolution in South Africa. Now retired.

Van der Merwe, Johan Former head of the Security Branch and commissioner of the South African Police Service from 1990 to early 1995, when he retired.

Van der Merwe, Koos Member of Parliament from 1977 to 1992, representing the National Party and the Conservative Party and as an independent, Van der Merwe now represents the Inkatha Freedom Party in Parliament.

Verwoerd, Hendrik Frensch Prime minister of South Africa from 1958 until his assassination in 1966, Verwoerd was known as the "Architect of Apartheid."

Viljoen, Constand Joined the South African Defense Force in 1952 and served as its commander from 1980 to 1985. Viljoen became politically active in 1993 and subsequently became leader of the Freedom Front in 1994. He is presently a member of Parliament.

Vlakplaas Five Brigadier Jack Cronje, Captain Jacques Hechter, Captain Wouter Mentz, Colonel Roelf Venter, and Warrant Officer Paul Van Vuuren were members of Vlakplaas who sought amnesty for their hit squad activities, including more than forty murders.

Index

About the Author

Antjie Krog was born on October 23, 1952, in Kroostad, a town in the Free State province of South Africa. She grew up on the farm Middenspruit.

She has published eight volumes of poetry, several of which have been translated from Afrikaans into European languages and have won prizes both in South Africa and abroad. Krog's first prose work, *Relaas van 'n moord* (1995), was translated into English under the title *Account of a Murder.*

Reporting as Antjie Samuel, the author and her South African Broadcasting Corporation radio team received the Pringle Award for excellence in journalism for their coverage of the Truth and Reconciliation Commission. Krog also won the Foreign Correspondents' Award for outstanding journalism for articles on the Truth Commission. At present, she covers South Africa's parliament for SABC radio.

Antjie Krog is married to architect John Samuel, and is the mother of four children.